EXTRACT

We must have been introd
Bedales, but my memory is
clearest picture of the second
now unsensational, were then quite eccentric, such as a ....
open at the neck, sandals and knickerbockers. He showed us over the
whole school, ending with the earth closets, where he indicated roughly
the posture and principles associated with their use. (Page 38)

It was a fine afternoon and most of the Bedalians were out of doors.
Later they began to show themselves in the quadrangle. We noticed
large moustached men and were surprised to find that they were not
masters but boys. (Page 39)

At Bedales, we slept between blankets on wooden beds, chosen,
according to the Chief, for 'simplicity and comfort'. Instead of spring
mattresses there were wooden laths or slats, which were liable to break
in the hurly-burly of ragging. (Page 44)

Frank and I did not find the cold unpleasant until the winter when we
would ask each other 'What is the point of keeping us frozen?'
Windows were kept open and the central heating was not very
effective. Occasionally the ink froze in the ink-wells. (Page 39)

I suppose that spankings were no worse than at many other schools,
but there was, in fact, a veritable pyramid of flagellation. At the broad
bottom one found 'a plurality' of slippers and hair brushes wielded by
the dormitory bosses; on the upper slopes were the ash single-sticks of
the consortium of prefects … I have myself seen one of them literally
broken across the backside of a boy. (Page 41)

At this co-educational school a 'healthy' attitude towards sex was
encouraged, an attitude which today would often appear laughable or
priggish. But these standards were common to most schools and
institutions of the Victorian and Edwardian era. The prudery, no
doubt, resulted in some guilt-ridden and unhappy marriages. (Page 61)

The girls' costumes were not designed to make them particularly
attractive. Except for games and gymnastics, when the gym tunic was

much as it is in schools to-day, they wore a one piece sack-like garment, called a Jibbah, derived from Arabian peasant costume. Around the shoulders was an embroidered yoke. (Page 62)

It was from [Frank] that I heard first about the Wright Brothers. The Wright Brothers had made the first powered flight in history. Many people were then doubtful about the authenticity of their claims ... A contributor to the *Bedales Chronicle* in November of that year ... held that 'they have always kept their performances so secret that one cannot know whether to believe them or not.' (Page 56)

Once a year it was customary for the headmaster to produce a play to which parents and local people would be invited. At the end of our fourth term it was *A Midsummer Night's Dream*. Frank and I were allotted parts as fairies ... I was placed discreetly behind Titania's bower, on account of my long thin legs. (Page 53)

Frank and his friends designed a large instrument to play the first five notes of the C minor scale. They called it the 'KLANGENOHEILISSO-CYCLOSTRIGOTONITON'. It was accompanied by the school orchestra. Unfortunately when the foot-lights were switched on, the speed of the motor-driven disc was reduced and this affected the pitch. (Page 199)

Frank made no hard-and-fast distinction between serious or classical music and light music. For instance, he would discuss and analyse Pelissier's compositions with the same zest as he would the works of Wagner and Debussy. Throughout these last years at Bedales the influence of The Follies made itself continually felt. (Page 198)

We went to a pantomime where George Robey and Fred Emney produced some of the liveliest fooling I have ever seen, including what was probably the first performance of a sketch, now over-familiar and hackneyed, known as 'Papering a Room', in which the wallpaper paste went over everything and finally got emptied into an upright piano. (Page 30)

'Before setting off for Düsseldorf, a notice was put in the local newspaper to the effect that a young Englishman, who intended stopping in Germany for a year, required a home to live in. Applicants should please state terms.' (Page 206)

'With backsight on your verhonoured announcement, believe I that for a young Englander containment seeking, in proper form offer can. I bed well a Lordshiply residing (central heating, electric light and bath) of which one side on the Spree looks, and from where the middle of the town in few minutes to reach is.' (Page 208–9)

———

On Tuesday I went to see *Tristan und Isolde*. If there's any doubt over Goethe's statement that 'Art makes a good companion but a bad leader', one has only got to study *Tristan und Isolde* for a bit. It was the embodiment of Wagner's outlook on life. Most beautiful it certainly is … but as a Lebensanschauung you couldn't find a more rotten, pessimistic, morbid piece. (Page 227)

———

The 'Parseval' airship has been here this week. On Friday she left and the 'Schwaben' came. I saw the two in the air together. The Zeppelin looked gigantic, sauntered along at a terrific speed, majestic and wonderful. At midday, we heard that it had been broken in two places by the shed and blown up. I must try and get some photos. (Page 234–5)

———

I love the quiet businesslike way [Zumbroich] goes about everything— took off his coat, rolled up his sleeves, laid all his tools out on the bench, and started cleaning up the inside of my nose and cockaining it. As far as I could gather he first took away the little bone ridge near the front of the nostril. It's a peculiar sensation hearing the crunching of bone and seeing it pulled out and feeling practically nothing. (Page 236)

———

When war was declared, Frank and I were at a school reunion. Our friends in the Territorials were at the annual training camp. The camp was held that year at St Asaph in Wales but within two days of having put their tents up on Saturday, August 3, they were ordered to take them down again … Frank and I, accompanied by Father, were interviewed a week or so after our return and offered commissions. (Page 15)

———

A few days later Frank became involved in the first of those festive nights that are peculiar to army life … 'Grand feast given by newly-promoted officers. Although only about 15 of us, we polished off 12 large Ayala champagnes—foolery, with singing solos, etc., at first. As evening drew on, so innumerable brandies and sodas did their work. It finally consisted of wrestling duels all round.' (Page 18)

———

In France after 1914, when both sides had settled down to trench warfare, cavalry infrequently came into action, but horse transport, especially those agricultural-looking General Service wagons, were still the principal means of transport within five to ten miles of the front line ... Horsemanship was therefore of the greatest importance. Hacking (or joy-riding) was encouraged. (Page 18)

'Got up for stables before breakfast and took our vet round the lines. Horse No.3 had died in stable in early hours of morning. During breakfast time I went round still helping to adjust loads and wagons in cold snow and rain—pretty chilly. Horses looked much better for rest generally, but No. 1 turned much worse and eventually had to be shot. One other died in the Headquarters Company.' (Page 22)

As Lieut. Walter Meakin commented, 'privates had to learn to call even their own relations "Sir".' Frank summed up the situation: 'Bob must salute his little brother on parade but may give him a playful kick up the arse afterwards.' (Page 27)

In January Frank was writing a musical setting for some verses he had seen in *Punch* called 'The Bells of Berlin'. This proved to be a popular number in many concerts, and in France he went to some trouble in order to find a publisher for it. (Page 31)

Frank sent home over a hundred letters and postcards during his first term of service overseas. Many of them ran into six- or seven-hundred words ... Mingled with his detailed observations are frequent references to such things as football boots, cereals, jam and chocolate, which suggests schooldays and dormitory feasts. Military life in France at that time took place within an aura of eating possibilities. (Page 65)

The division's third move brought them to Sailly-sur-Lys, near Bailleul, which they reached on March 11. This was the second day of the battle of Neuve Chapelle, then raging some five miles to the south. 'Here they were,' Frank wrote, 'within a few yards of our big guns. They have been belching out hell all day at the rate of six to twelve to the minute (when not at lunch or supper). Also, at least two aeroplanes have been hovering over us all day, and sometimes four. It is very consoling to know we are being so well looked after.' (Page 69)

'We have got a very decent piano again,' Frank wrote home, 'so send any good old songs or light music such as "You're Here and I'm Here" and *Ragtime Selections* in cheap conglomerated editions, and any of our old songs, particularly Stanford's.' If they stayed there any time they would get to know them all by heart ... The music was sent. (Page 74)

———

'In his platoon they were all sportsmen and about twelve crack shots, so they fairly gave the Germans hell. They kept on advancing about two deep at intervals of 100 yards or so in long lines—close formation—the officers driving them with swords. A little to the left of the trench was a lane, along which the Germans were allowed to advance quite close before we opened a withering fire. The bodies were just piled up in long lines two or three deep, and whenever they saw a wounded German trying to crawl away they always shot him.' (Page 77)

———

The gas used by the Germans was chlorine but in August, Frank describes what is obviously 'Tear Gas'. They 'got a slight "whiff" of a Boche stink shell,' he wrote, and it reminded him of the amyl acetate, pear-drop aroma in our lacquering department (the Zapon Room) at our father's works. It made the eyes run like anything. (Page 78)

———

'The Boches caused terrible havoc to the men on the left of our division by spraying burning vitriol and tar into the trenches. I was talking to a typical Tommy last night ... who had seen the trenches on his left in flames leaping up like a factory fire. He remarked, "But if the Germans would only play the game fair and square, we should soon lick them." I think this absolutely hits off the British spirit. You don't wonder at our chaps being sick.' (Page 79)

———

During the afternoon Frank and his colleagues generally retired for a siesta, after which there would be some sporting event, such as a football or cricket match, or perhaps a little music, with philosophical discussions after dinner. As described in his letters, the atmosphere vaguely suggests a military version of the Bedalian 'good life', with its rural pursuits and hygiene, such as the construction of an oven or a carefully designed and highly efficient incinerator. (Page 79)

———

Frank was getting keyed up about taking leave to come home and wrote home that they should 'leave the door open', as he had a latch key. 'Expect me when you see me,' he said. He asked me to 'have the days more or less planned and to think if possible of tennis' … I was to invite the Aston girls over on spec. He intended 'to have a decent time and plenty on'. (Page 87)

The day before Frank's leave came through he 'rode on through Ypres—an indescribable, uncanny nightmare city'. It was 'very hot, muggy and dusty'. The 'country was buzzing with military traffic, otherwise the complete calm of evening was most impressive'. (Page 87)

At about this time, the Two-Step and what we now call the Old-Fashioned Waltz had given place to the Boston, Fox-Trot, One-Step and a step called The Twinkle. Frank and I badly needed basic instruction in these new dances. Beryl supplied it readily, twirling around in her pleated tango-skirt. (Page 132)

The scene seemed to us then a brilliant one. The predominant khaki colouring contrasted pleasantly with the blue and scarlet mess kit of the staff officers and generals and with the beautiful full-skirted frocks of the women. (Page 133)

'I more than once (and the others did too) met the Prince of Wales, walking or riding a push bike about the lanes, and would just say "How do!" He was a thorn in the side of the Staff.' (Page 100)

I was still at Kingstown [now Dun Laoghaire] when the 7th Batallion was attacked and it was not until the next day, Thursday 27, that we made our own trek to Ballsbridge, where I was put in charge of bombs and accordingly visited the bombing school. It was on that day that I witnessed a bombardment of a disused distillery. (Page 146)

Éamon de Valera, one of the leaders of the Rising, had himself hoisted the Irish green Sinn Fein flag with the yellow harp on a small square tower on the roof of a disused distillery overlooking Grand Canal Quay … The naval officer in charge of the gun had received orders to shoot the flag down. Some 75 shells were exploded on the distillery, but at the end of the bombardment, although only two outside walls of the small tower remained standing, the flag had not been dislodged. The naval officer shrugged his shoulders and moved on. I was alongside when this event took place. (Page 147)

It was not surprising that officers began to think about getting a transfer. Frank and I decided to act quickly. We exchanged letters and telegrams. What branch or unit would give us more scope, we wondered. The Cavalry Machine-Gun Squadron sounded as if it might have possibilities. But how about the Royal Flying Corps? (Page 167)

―――――

[Frank's] mind went back to our kites at Berrow, the news of the Wright Brothers and powered flight passed on to me in the dormitory, the paper darts, the model aeroplanes, and his affectionate admiration for 'the professional aviators'—the seagulls. His enthusiasm was infectious. Although not naturally drawn towards hazardous service, I felt stimulated by the prospects of actually flying. (Page 167)

―――――

'Dearest Father and Mother, since we have made up our minds about transferring, the world has assumed a very different aspect ... Bob and I talked the thing over at length and I am confident that it is quite the best decision I have arrived at since joining the A.S.C.' (Page 169)

―――――

Frank's training took two months. This was followed by five weeks of Elementary Flying at Thetford. We were then separated for four weeks while he trained at Dover on B.E.2cs and Martinsydes for Scouts, which were the Fighters of the First War. On May 7 we came together for an aerial gunnery course which lasted a fortnght. (Page 289)

―――――

'Barbara very beautiful', Frank noted, and summed up: 'Blissful evening—very high standard of youth and beauty and dancing.' After the dance he 'went back on the box of their cab' to our aunt's house where they re-lit the drawing-room fire and made cocoa. (Page 133)

―――――

In 1087 Archbishop Bollinger had the room next door to us and on returning one day bumped his nose against the bedstead—hence 'Brasenose College'. The room was known thereafter as 'Bubbly's Bedroom'. (Page 291)

―――――

Our theatregoing had hitherto tended to be serious—opera and the drama—but now we found ourselves more and more led into a world of glamorous frivolity by our brother officers, one of whom would even go round to the dressing room of a well-known star, after the show, and take her out to supper. (Page 131)

―――――

We invited [Douglas] Furber and his co-composer George Ellis to tea next day, which happened to coincide with our first flight. We received them at Brasenose, where we had found a piano. We tried over our song for them. Stimulated by the experience of flying, we felt that a brilliant theatrical future was somehow opening out. (Page 305)

Frank felt quite at home with the aerial cameras, but the machine guns and flying instruments constituted a completely new field of study. As we contemplated the bomb sights, release gear and bombs, we were reminded of H.G. Wells's *War in the Air* and the bombing of New York. (Page 293)

While in some machines Morse messages could be sent to the ground by wireless, there was no telephony between aircraft. Communication was made by certain signals, rocking the wings, and so forth. If your gun jammed, you were to catch up with the leader and rock the machine fore and aft. (Page 341)

Although luck played its part, success in the main went to the pilot with the keenest judgement, coolest head and split second advantage in speed of reaction. The more experience of stunting a pilot could acquire, the better. (Page 344)

ABOUT THE AUTHOR

Robert Dudley Best (1892–1984) was a British manufacturer deeply involved with the Modern design movement in and immediately after the interwar years. He took over Best & Lloyd, his father's light industrial engineering works in Birmingham, after training as a metal designer at art school in Düsseldorf. He went on to design the Bestlite, an iconic Bauhaus-styled desk lamp that remains in production and was used by Winston Churchill in Whitehall.

An early apostle of the posture therapist F.M. Alexander, of the Alexander technique, Best campaigned for better art school education for industrial apprentices and co-founded the Common Wealth political party in 1942. His social circle of Birmingham artists and intellectuals included Professor Philip Sargant Florence and others associated with Birmingham University. He hosted the first visit of Walter Gropius to the Midlands after Gropius's departure from Germany in 1934 and befriended Nikolaus Pevsner during Pevsner's year in Birmingham between 1934 and 1935.

Best wrote and diarised prolifically, though only one of his books was published in his lifetime: *Brass Chandelier* (which Pevsner reviewed in the *Architectural Review*), a history of his father's metal manufacturing experiments and promotion of progressive German pedagogic ideas.

ABOUT THE EDITOR

Stephen Games is a designer and writer specialising in architecture and cultural history. Formerly with the BBC, the *Guardian* and the *Independent*, he has written extensively about Nikolaus Pevsner and John Betjeman, runs the New Premises design studio in London, and edits the UK books magazine *Booklaunch*.

FROM BEDALES
TO THE BOCHE

THE IRONIES OF AN EDWARDIAN CHILDHOOD

Robert Best

Edited and adapted by
Stephen Games

Published 2020 in Great Britain by
EnvelopeBooks
with Booklaunch
A New Premises venture

EnvelopeBooks
12 Wellfield Avenue
London N10 2EA
England

editor@envelopebooks.co.uk

Adapted and edited by Stephen Games from the privately circulated two-
volume manuscript *A Short Life and a Gay One* by Robert Best, based on his
own contemporary diaries and letters and those of his younger brother Frank
Best.

Typeset in PostScript Baskerville 10.5/13
Designed by New Premises Publishing

British Library Cataloguing-in-Publication Data: a catalogue record for this
book is available from the British Library.

ISBN 9781838172022

An EnvelopeBook
www.envelopebooks.co.uk

NOTE.—

Correspondence in this envelope need not be censored Regimentally. The Contents are liable to examination at the Base.

Contents

Frank Best in 1917: 'Frank became air-borne for the first time. There may have been more thrilling episodes in his life but I doubt it. Here at last was the real thing ... Frank's mood was intensified: "The world has assumed a different aspect. We are both full of hope and confidence."'

Introduction

From Bedales to the Boche is a beautifully written First World War memoir, with evocative material about the life of two soldiers—brothers from Birmingham, born in the 1890s, sent by their Germanophile father to the experimental, humane and expensive coeducational Bedales boarding school in Hampshire, and then trained at art college in Düsseldorf.

Robert (Bob) and Frank Best had planned to become music-hall entertainers, in the mould of George and Weedon Grossmith of a generation earlier, and this account—based on their original diaries and letters, and written by the older of the two—is strong on period detail about the comedy culture of the George Robey years.

But instead of realising their dreams, the brothers ended up enlisting in the army on the outbreak of war, serving with the Army Service Corps first in northern France and then in Dublin (to help quell the 1916 Easter Rising) before, in a rush of schoolboyish enthusiasm, fulfilling a long-held dream and joining the Royal Flying Corps, learning flying and gunnery at Oxford, Thetford, Dover, Turnberry and Wyton before being posted to a squadron at the R.F.C. training school in Vendôme.

Both brothers could have become high achievers in the performing arts, or in any other field to which they might have turned their hand, but after the war Robert returned to Birmingham to work in the family metalworking business. Having learnt the craft of a metalwork designer before the war,

1

he became interested in how design was evolving in Germany and how new thinking could be incorporated into the work of his father's firm, Best & Lloyd. He went on to design the Bestlite, an iconic Bauhaus-styled desk lamp that was used by Winston Churchill in Whitehall, and that rivaled his father's best-selling light fitting a generation earlier, the ceiling-mounted, height-adjustable Surprise pendant. Through his efforts he also built up the firm into one of the largest lighting manufacturers in the world, traveling to the USA to win contracts, maintaining his father's showroom in Paris and supplying light fittings to hotels, ocean liners, cinemas and town halls internationally.

Best was actively involved with the Design and Industries Association and other artistic bodies set up to improve aesthetics, working practices and apprentice education, both nationally and in the Midlands. Tormented by a nervous speaking ailment, he became an early disciple of the Australian posture therapist and health guru F.M. Alexander, sponsoring an expansion of Alexander's activities into the Midlands but later criticising him for his artistic and personal insensitivities. He helped to co-found Common Wealth, an egalitarian co-operative political party that sat uncomfortably between the Labour and Liberal parties. He married twice.

After retiring in the 1960s Robert Best committed himself to writing a partly biographical, partly auto-biographical account

'As small children at home they had drawn cartoon strips about the Boer War.'

of the early 1900s, dedicated to and built around the life of Frank, his younger brother. Printed in two volumes and circulated in a limited edition of 200 comb-bound photocopies in 1969, the book was titled *A Short Life and a Gay One*.

Its scope is enormous. The two boys had been immensely energetic and talented, and the book documents in compelling and convincing detail their many interests and activities. As small children at home they had drawn cartoon strips about the Boer War, learnt the piano and performed in ingenious home entertainments of their own devising. Their talent for performance was developed further at Bedales, where they were part of a tight-knit group of school humorists, parodying school celebrities and the musical and political events of the day, on stage and in the *Bedales Chronicle*.

Though irreverent, Bob and Frank took seriously the spirit of open inquiry and self-education—'the will to fuller life'— fostered by Bedales's founding headmaster John Haden Badley. Much of what was studied in class was taken further after hours when the boys carried out experiments of their own into the physics of acoustics, aeronautics, acceleration, optics, photography and subsoil temperatures, amusing themselves but learning at the same time. To the credit of the school, there was little distinction between work and play. Frank and his friend Peter Eckersley toyed with improvised radio transmitters in a hut in the school grounds; a decade and a half later, Eckersley would become the BBC's first Chief Engineer.

Thus, whatever else Frank was engaged with, his school career was one of immense promise and abundant energy—a life richly lived, of sporting prowess, of performance skills, of self-confidence and self-possession, and of sociablity. Through him we learn about the novelty of new music, both popular and serious, about the relative merits of different music-hall entertainers of the day, and about what made his contemporaries laugh. His love of gadgets and new technology translated after school into a fascination with motorcycles and cars. A 'young buck' (in the language of the time), the world he aspired to was one of theatre-land, well-made clothes, flirtations and high spirits.

3

From the account of Frank's time in Düsseldorf in 1913 and of Robert's the previous year, we learn about the wide cultural differences that still existed between Germany and Britain. Of particular interest are the descriptions of attending local performances of operas by Wagner and Strauss (*Parsifal* could not be performed outside Bayreuth until the end of 1913, 30 years after Wagner's death), of the tedious repetition of 'Stille Nacht, heilige Nacht' ('Silent Night')—still unknown in England—at Christmas, of German medical procedures, of the excessive patriotism and militarism of the Germans, of the last flowering of pre-Bauhaus art-school teaching, and of the unhappiness of German schoolchildren and the incidence of Easter suicides among those not promoted to the next class.

The prevailing mood of the brothers' contemporary writings is one of engagement and excitement. Even in the adaptation of that material that he wrote after retiring in the 1960s and that *From Bedales to the Boche* is in turn an adaptation of, Robert maintained a spirit of positivism that is wholly at odds with today's distrust. His title—*A Short Life and a Gay One*—was taken from the comic song 'I've gotter motter—always merry and bright', from the popular 1909 musical comedy *The Arcadians*, which would have been familiar to everyone of his generation.[1] The 'motter', in the context of how the book ends, is indicative of

---

[1] I've always been, since quite a lad, cheery and gay when things were bad,
  That is a way I've always 'ad—I look on the bright side!
I've gotter motter—always merry and bright!
  Look around and you will find, every cloud is silver lined;
  The sun will shine, although the sky's a gray one.
  I've often said to meself, I've said, 'Cheer up, Cully, you'll soon be dead!
    A short life and a gay one!
Trouble may be upon the mat, I never care two straws for that,
  I simply whistle and cock my hat—I'm horribly reckless!
I've gotter motter—Always merry and bright!
  Look around and you will find, every cloud is silver lined;
  The sun will shine, although the sky's a gray one.
  I've often said to meself, I've said, 'Cheer up, Cully, you'll soon be dead!
    A short life and a gay one!' Tra, la la la la la, la la!

4

a refusal to be beaten that typifies its age.[2] Not only did Robert read this spirit into his brother's sensibility, he adopted it himself 50 years later. This was in spite of his immersion in radical liberal politics in the intervening years and in spite of the anger and accusation that had come to frame attitudes to war in general and the Great War in particular—attitudes that we now associate with works such as Joan Littlewood's *Oh, What a Lovely War!* which came out in 1963, four years before Robert completed *A Short Life and a Gay One*.

Of great interest to today's social historian is the compulsion of both brothers to take note of everything around them at the time—their documenting of trivia—and Robert's subsequent concern to take those notes seriously, making *From Bedales to the Boche* a perfect sociological study. Quotations from diaries and letters provide surprising insights into the language of the time. We learn, for example, that as early as 1915, the English were using the word 'dough' to mean money: it was not a later borrowing from Hollywood. We get chapter and verse on the new dances that were coming in, what was played on portable Deccaphones in the drawing room, and of the etiquette of social life. We get glimpses of the popular literature of the day and even, through Frank, of the emerging movie industry in Paris.

In respect of the war, what strikes today's reader at the start of the book is how indispensable the horse was and yet how casually horses were dispensed with. The A.S.C.'s ability to keep troops supplied depended on the horse and yet repeatedly in Frank's diary entries we read:

Passed dead horse at bottom of first hill from another company, shot by vet.

Got up for stables before breakfast and took our vet round the lines. Horse No. 3 had died in stable in early hours of morning. During breakfast time I went round still helping to adjust loads and wagons in cold snow and rain—pretty chilly. Horses looked much

---

[2] Such positivism was satirised in, for example, the song 'Always Look on the Bright Side of Life' in the 1979 film *Life of Brian*.

better for rest generally, but No. 1 turned much worse and eventually had to be shot. One other died in the Headquarters Company.

Another horse died during the night, probably through undue exhaustion, etc.

Spent most of the day arranging wagons and adjusting load. Three horses in very bad state: 1) Pure old aged, 2) Pneumonia, 3) Laminitis (foot fever). Went for the vet on company car but he thought they looked too far gone.

Got horses paraded for veterinary inspection. Still left with 10 wagons workable, and nine pairs not, through mange and other diseases ... Chanced on stabling-shed for 20 horses—great find! Arranged for next day's move, then sampled Picture House.

This contrasts markedly with the care and respect given to aeroplane engines and guns in the Royal Flying Corps, which Bob and Frank joined in December 1916 in the hope of a more flamboyant military existence. Pilots had to have a detailed understanding of their machines because their lives depended on it. Machine guns 'were inclined to jam, lock, and suddenly cease to function,' wrote Robert. 'Nothing could be more exasperating than to get the enemy machine nicely into the ring-sight, press the trigger—and then—after perhaps a short burst—silence ... We were shown, again and again, how to free these "stoppages".' They were also shown how to strip down and rebuild an engine, how to creep up on an enemy plane unseen, how to go into and get out of a spin, what to do if their engine failed while flying in formation, and how to communicate with other pilots while in the air:

While in some machines Morse messages could be sent to the ground by wireless there was no telephony between the machines. Communication was made by certain signals, rocking the wings, and so forth. If you gun jammed, you were to catch up with the leader and rock the machine fore and aft. Coloured 'Verey's Lights' (fireworks discharged from a pistol) were supposed to indicate that the pilot was going home, in cases of engine failure. A rendezvous was fixed to which the pilots should repair after a scrap.

As soldiers, Bob and Frank were deeply conscious of how the Bedales legacy sustained them. They believed in, acted on and debated with others Badley's belief that for states to be better run, leadership must arise from a citizenry trained to strive for the highest values. Alongside this high-minded mission, they were able to treat deployment to the Western Front as tantamount to a more than usually hazardous school camping trip—a combination of strict regimental duties, chance encounters with Bedalians friends, juvenile horseplay and comical efforts to acquire pianos for concert parties in the officers' mess.

Their relatively privileged wartime experience was possible because they at first enlisted in the Army Service Corps, which kept the fighting brigades provisioned. Although they were part of the North Midland (46th) Division Train, they enjoyed a greater degree of shelter than the infantry divisions, sloping off when they could to neighbouring *estaminets* [cafés] for leisurely afternoon lunches, in spite of occasional German sniping and the dropping of bombs from Zeppelins cruising overhead. In his narrative, Robert was at pains to say, however, that neither he nor Frank had enlisted in the A.S.C. in order to stay safe but because the A.S.C. was their nearest recruiting post and because their only army connection was their cousin Jack, whom they admired and who was already attached to the Train.

The brothers' experience of the First World War was therefore somewhat different from the horror stories of mud and massacre that have come to dominate the public's under-standing of war since then. In addition, Frank spent only nine months of the war abroad, compared with 17 months in England and eight in Ireland. This made his first three years of war fairly comfortable, compared with that of the hundreds of thousands of frontline troops who were sacrificed in the stalemate of trench warfare.

From Frank's diaries and letters home, we learn that the daily lives and attitudes of non-combatant officers had a quite different emphasis from those who spoke out against what they saw as the crime of war in general or, more specifically, of the way in which this particular war was conducted by the General Staff: the troops who mutinied at Étaples, the pacifists, the war poets, the unionists and the intellectuals of the 1920s who came to define what the First World War meant for the century that followed.

This does not make *From Bedales to the Boche* a revisionist piece of writing. It merely records that alongside the anger, bitterness and condemnation there were other responses. At one end of the scale there was an acceptance of hostilities that might now be seen as passivity or suggestibility. At the other end there was an enthusiasm not so much for war—though this certainly inspired the first recruits—as for the accessories of war: the soldier's life, the camaraderie, the routines, the language, the jokes, the sentiments, the horses, the machinery, the guns, the rough conditions, the sense of being at war, of serving one's country, of being put to what was regarded as a high purpose, of living on the edge.

For many, war was a thrilling alternative to peace. In *Stagnation* (November 1916), the first of his two unpublished plays, Robert Best wrote of the boredom of A.S.C. officers whose wish to see action was constantly being frustrated by the War Office:

> Godstruth, we've been in training since the war started! I tell you we're about fed up. Why, only just now, my man told me as the drivers daren't go 'ome on leave, they get codded on so. Month after month, it's always the same training—let alone the transport, which is as much as it 'ud be in France. We get all the work and none of the glory. We've been 'going' about fifty tines, but we never 'go'.

Written more than two years after the start of hostilities, Robert could have been in no doubt about the conditions of service and the likelihood of death. In spite of newspaper censorship, especially about the scale of slaughter and problems with supply, those who wished to grumble had every opportunity to do so: fighting men knew exactly what they were up against, as did Lord Northcliffe, who had used his *Daily Mail* to predict and encourage war with Germany before using the paper to challenge the way in which the war was being conducted.

In this context Robert records a letter of Frank's from October 1915, a few days after he had watched the bombardment of Vermelles, Noyelles and Béthune:

> When you hear folks say the Boches on this front are absolutely 'skint' and that they can't possibly hold on, you tell them they are talking piffle. It may be true that once we get uncomfortably near their frontier their morale may waver, but as far as ingenuity in fighting goes, they can't be touched.

Yet an A.S.C. character in Robert's play is able to complain that 'We're going to stagnate here (because) we never get any casualties to replace' whereas the *more fortunate* infantry officers are losing men and sending off drafts of newly trained recruits every six months, leaving 'the Tommies … fighting amongst themselves to be included in it'.

There is little indication of disenchantment either during the war or in its immediate aftermath in the contemporary material that Robert collated into *A Short Life*, at least among his friends. He observed Frank calling for 'punishment by military law' of civilians who were insufficiently supportive of the war effort, and even regarding the sinking of the Lusitania as having its 'bright side' because, like gas attacks, only something big would 'bring neutrals to their senses'.

It is clear that half a century later, Robert found such attitudes troubling but he withheld criticism, ascribing Frank's conservatism to the 'war-hysteria' of 'otherwise sensible people' who competed to be 'more-patriotic-than-thou'. Robert had been guilty of it too, he now saw, and suggested that it was 'symptomatic of the general witch-hunt for spies, slackers and *embusqués* … being whipped up by the gutter press' and that it 'intensified as the casualty lists lengthened'.

In short, the brothers belonged to the last generation to whom what we might regard as certain essentials of modern liberalism did not come naturally: scepticism, distrust of authority, independence of mind, even nihilism. They believed in King and country and in the war rhetoric of honour and glory—or they behaved as if they believed in it. Frank shared the impatience often felt by troops on active service in the face of criticism at home from cossetted newspaper readers, and even though he was able to distinguish between the bravery of the troops and the failures of the General Staff, he felt that criticism of operations needed to be respectful and restrained. In May 1915, when the *Daily Mail* attacked Lord Kitchener, the Secretary of State for War, for ordering shrapnel instead of high explosive shells, Frank recorded :

> here we nearly all agree that what [the *Daily Mail*] said was correct, but that its *manner* of doing it was dirty, to say the least of it, and uncalled for.

What the *Mail* had written was that Kitchener had 'persisted in sending shrapnel—a useless weapon in trench warfare' and one that 'has caused the deaths of thousands of ... our poor soldiers'. The claim was true but was widely regarded as an offence against etiquette. Readers changed papers, advertisers canceled bookings and copies of the paper were publicly set on fire outside the Bank of England. In the still deferential culture of the times, public exposure was considered a dishonorable practice, unbecoming of a gentleman, and certainly not the job of the press. Though Northcliffe thought Kitchener needed ousting, and was taking advantage of the government's 'foolish conspiracy to hide bad news' to hold onto his job, others thought the *Mail*'s disclosures presumptuous and shabby—the equivalent of 'ratting' on a friend—and, moreover, that they risked demoralising the country and its men while giving encouragement to the enemy.

All of this Robert struggled with. Half a century earlier, he too had been a young officer with a trenchcoat and a swagger stick; now, having spent many years as a pacifist, he wondered at his own and Frank's insensitivities. By way of answer, he concluded—quoting Saint-Exupéry—that wartime imposes its own logic and that we respond accordingly, whether we like it or not. Cultural aggression—the wish to separate a good 'us' from a bad 'them'—was masked by personal charm. To demonstrate this, Robert quoted the tributes of Frank's colleagues: 'He never lost his temper with anyone', 'he always thought of the well-being of his men before his own', 'he was always cool, calm and efficient'. In routine jobs, which he could have delegated to juniors, he always did his share, 'and no general, however much his chest was covered with medals and red tabs, could drive him round the bend … It was a happy ship, and no one "rocked the boat".' It would be difficult 'to describe his popularity in the Train, and indeed with the Transport Officers of the Infantry Batallions'.

Today, scepticism about war comes more easily to us. Western liberalism's detachment, its concern for the rights and welfare of individuals, and its validation of psychological complexity makes us wary of institutions, especially after what the First World War taught us of their rigidity and capacity for inhumanity. Frank belonged to an earlier culture that had no apparent moral position on war—this is what bothered Robert—and that could demand loyalty to a cause without being able to state more than vaguely what that cause was. It is this that makes *From Bedales to the Boche* different: as well as being an entertaining read, it is an important educational resource precisely for its authentic tone of lost political artlessness, something difficult for us to imagine and recapture today.

I first came across Robert Best in 1983 when I started carrying out research into the life and work of the art historian Sir Nikolaus Pevsner. Best contacted me in response to a request I had put out, telling me that he had invaluable first-hand information about Pevsner's life in Birmingham after leaving Germany in 1933. He then sent me a transcript of a draft history that he had written of the emerging design profession in Britain during and immediately after the interwar years. Three versions of that history exist and are still looking for a publisher.

Following the death of Robert, his son John continued to give me invaluable assistance and made available to me the entire archive that his father had assembled and that had been loaned to the Birmingham Central Library, where resource pressures meant that it had lain uncatalogued for many years. It was in that collection of papers that I discovered the two-volume history on which *From Bedales to the Boche* is based, as well as all the original letters, diaries and other memorabilia, including army logbooks, that he quoted from in *A Short Life and a Gay One*, with the exception of the numerous photographs used to illustrate the text (most of which do not appear in this adaptation).

Although it was Robert's design history that first attracted my interest, *A Short Life* also made compelling reading, and I became increasingly convinced that it ought to be edited and adapted into a book. A Kindle version appeared in 2013 and I am delighted to be able to bring out a print version now in 2014, appropriately, on the centenary of the outbreak of war. I wish to record my thanks to John and the other executors of the Robert Best estate for allowing me to do so.

In my adaptation, I have retained the text but reordered it, alternating earlier and later chapters to give more immediacy to references that otherwise got lost in Best's simpler chronology. Anyone wishing to refer to the original, which also contains useful explanatory supplements, illustrations and notes not included here, can make application to the editor, whose contact details can be easily discovered online. A copy is also housed in the Bedales School Memorial Library.

I wish to record my thanks to Sam Warshaw and Sheila Games for their editorial assistance, and to Bea for her patient endurance.

Stephen Games
Muswell Hill
November 2014

Chapter 1
Signing up

On 28 June, 1914, a Serbian student assassinated Archduke Franz Ferdinand, crown prince of the Austro-Hungarian empire. If at the breakfast-table the next day, an invisible loud speaker had announced that my young brother Frank would soon be serving in His Majesty's Forces, Father, scanning the headlines in the *Birmingham Daily Post*, would have listened incredulously and then exclaimed—whistling through his teeth in the manner of the music-hall entertainer George Robey— 'AND—VERY—NICE—TOO!' And yet only a few weeks later Frank accepted a commission in the North Midland (46th) Divisional Train (Army Service Corps), Territorial Force, and find himself in the company of a friendly group of young Birmingham men led by our favourite cousin Jack Best.

Hostilities in Europe had begun on 28 July when Austria declared war on Serbia in retaliation for the assassination. Russia responded by mobilising its forces in support of Serbia and called on France to do the same. Germany replied on 1 August by declaring war on Russia in support of Austria, and two days later on France. On 4 August, in reaction to the German army's trampling on Belgium as a land-bridge to France, Britain declared war on Germany.

Britain had been under the threat of war with Germany for years. While we were still boys, the Handsworth Volunteers, marching up and down Birmingham's Hamstead Road in their scarlet uniforms, had competed for our attention with the first motor cars. This body of men was the B Company of the 1st Volunteer Battalion of the Staffordshire Regiment, headquartered at the Drill Hall, off the Soho Road, Handsworth, not ten minutes walk from our house. Several of our neighbours and friends served in this unit until the Territorial Force was formed in 1908. The Drill Hall was then taken over by the Army Service Corps and many of the volunteers then transferred to it, as it happened to be nearer their homes.

Jack Best's interest in military matters had been aroused by Guy du Maurier's play *An Englishman's Home*, produced at the Theatre Royal, Birmingham, in March 1909. Jack was very impressed, and talked of the play so keenly that Eric Milner, his future brother-in-law, his friend Don Holmes, and others made up a theatre party to see it for themselves.

The scene is set in the living room of a suburban family, irresponsible and insular folk, chiefly interested in sport and amusement. At the end of the first Act, invaders from 'Nearland' enter unannounced. Although obviously intended to be Germans these soldiers were tactfully clad in fantastic uniforms. (Recalling the scene many years later, Eric Milner said they looked as if they had come from Mars.) Later, the local volunteers give a farcical yet appalling exhibition of inefficiency. The house is shelled, set on fire, and in the last act the indignant house-owner is shot for being a civilian in possession of arms. Jack and his friends came away shocked but resolute. Convinced of Lord Roberts's wisdom in appealing for universal service, he himself enlisted at the Drill Hall as an A.S.C. driver—a private soldier—and persuaded Eric Milner and Don Holmes to do the same. Jack continued to serve after they had all completed four years' service and later took a commission; the others rejoined when war broke out.

Jack Best and Don Holmes later went into the jewellery trade. Eric Milner's firm, Benton and Stone, was in a similar line of business to that of my father, manufacturing metal goods.

Of the other company officers and friends of Jack whom Frank soon met, Allan Court was in the timber trade, though his father was an engraver. He had finished his education in Brussels and his knowledge of French proved useful while they were overseas. He took a commission at the Handsworth Drill Hall in 1913. His cousin, Gordon Whittall, was the son of a building contractor. Like me he had been in Germany at the time of the Agadir crisis of 1911 during his long vacation from Birmingham University where he was studying for the Bachelor of Commerce degree, and his German was excellent.

When war was declared, my brother Frank and I were at a school reunion. Our friends in the Territorials were at the annual training camp. The camp was held that year at St. Asaph in Wales but within two days of having put their tents up on Saturday, August 3, they were ordered to take them down again. They returned home on Monday 5, a Bank Holiday, and then moved to Luton via Burton. A skeleton staff remained at the Drill Hall and it was there that Frank and I, accompanied by Father, were interviewed a week or so after our return and offered commissions. Frank accepted but my parents discouraged me and at first, I dutifully refused.

A big question was whether I was physically suited for a soldier's life. To settle the matter I went over to another drill hall at Walsall where I knew someone, and offered myself as an infantryman. There I was told that I could get a commission in the Staffordshire Regiment. This was all set to go ahead until my father discussed the matter again with a business friend. Together they convinced me that as the older son, my first obligation was to the family firm.

Throughout his war service Frank kept a diary, giving about three square inches per day. With his microscopic writing he managed to cram quite a lot of vivid detail into this space, but sometimes when events inspired him he would spread out onto supplementary sheets.[3] Three weeks after accepting his

[3] His diary was a Walker's Loose Leaf, size 64 and there is reason to believe that he would often make a rough draft of the day's events at the

commission he was still hanging around at home. It was not until Tuesday, 8 September that he wrote his first war diary entry:

Received letter from Jack permitting me to go down to Luton in civilian clothes without waiting to be gazetted.

Frank arrived in Luton the next day and was met by Jack, who conducted him to the Headquarters and Officers' Mess at the Luton Steam Laundry.

Outside the Headquarters and Officers' Mess at the Steam Laundry, Luton, Beds. Left to right: Allan Court, Frank Best, Don Holmes and Gordon Whittall.

After lunch Frank was immediately introduced to A.S.C. work, assisting at the inspection of horses and harnesses. He was later inoculated against typhoid and on Saturday took an early train back to Birmingham where he ordered up his uniform and kit. Here he recorded the 'surprise visit of [our aunt] Alice Ward from Paris during the first German retreat. Great stories of Tommies in Paris' (14 September). At this time, according to the

---

time and expand it later. 'Wrote up diary for period including almost a month' (3 August 1916). He enjoyed recording.

historian A.F. Pollard, 'the fighting extended in a curved line from Meaux, which is almost a suburb of Paris, to Lunéville, which is almost on the German frontier.'

Frank was back at Luton the following day and throwing himself into the life of an A.S.C. subaltern. He learnt that a company of A.S.C. supplied each of the three infantry brigades which go to make a division, while a fourth (The Headquarters Company) supplied the 'Divisional Troops' (i.e. Artillery, Engineers, Medical Corps, etc). Jack Best commanded No. 3, or the Staffordshire Brigade Company. The essence of the job was to draw food, fodder and other supplies from various points and deliver them in horse-drawn wagons to each of the units in the division. The accounting and requisitioning activities were called 'Supply'—as opposed to 'transport work'.

From now on Frank was eager to gain experience. He was not alone. To quote Lieut. Walter Meakin, historian of the 5th North Staffords Brigade, 'The training for territorials had hitherto been short, and it was always recognised that at least six months' further training would be required for active service. The officers, too, had much to learn.' Frank was not a slow learner, however, and the touch of sport in the work could not fail to please him. The day started with 'stables', i.e. grooming and feeding the horses, which at first were in the open, tethered in rows to a long rope.

> Saturday, 19 September 1914. Stables 6.0—drill—read name gazetted in Times. Private sword instruction with R.S.M. Redman. Instruction with M.T., division on the rifle—typical Bargentine discourse. Tea—letters till supper. Ride to Dunstable. Evening with vet at pictures. Rotten show. Found sing-song in billets and played and sang for them.

This was the first mention in his diary of music and entertaining, which was to play such an important part in his military career.

As part of his equipment Frank bought a pipe. This symbol of maturity put the finishing touch to his emancipation. He later developed strong preferences in pipe tobaccos, which he greatly enjoyed, but at first, like many another Mr Verdant Green (another music-hall entertainer of the time), found that this taste should be gratified in moderation. 'After supper smoked a bit too much pipe and participated in a little stroll for antidote—baccy rotten sort.' (15 September)

A few days later Frank became involved in the first of those festive nights that are peculiar to army life, having as a pretext the celebration of promotion. He had been forewarned and took a 'walk over downs till 7 to augment appetite for supper'. Then,

> Grand feast given by newly-promoted officers. Although only about 15 of us, we polished off 12 large Ayala champagnes—foolery, with singing solos, etc., at first. As evening drew on, so innumerable brandies and sodas did their work. It finally consisted of wrestling duels all round.

In France after 1914, when both sides had settled down to trench warfare, cavalry infrequently came into action, but horse transport, especially those agricultural-looking General Service wagons, were still the principal means of transport within five to ten miles of the front line. Care of horses and sound, though not spectacular, horsemanship were therefore of the greatest importance. Hacking (or joy-riding) was encouraged. Frank enjoyed the exhilarating gallops over the downs.

> Afternoon ride with R.S.M. was singularly exciting as I had a horse which started off as though trained in Russian ballet. It quietened down later. (1 October)

> Went for joy-ride with Jack. Very enjoyable but nag quite unruly as usual on such occasions. (20 October)

On 9 October, after an hour or so of musical composition, Frank took the train to Harpenden, where he was to spend a week, messing with the 8th Notts and Derby battallion and billetted in a 'spacious house—just built'. He was struck by the 'delightful country and picturesque village'. He 'took notice of issue of supplies and accompanied convoys driving part of the way'. He noted that 'chaps can read and make themselves comfy when in the country.'

'Supply-work' involved the selection and slaughter of a beast:

14 October: Visited slaughter house and saw heifer 'teed off' at 6.45. Rather gruesome but felt a great deal wiser afterwards.

During the next few days Frank continued to take part in convoys and attend lectures. At the end of the week he again found himself at home on leave, following a programme which was to become customary—visits to the works, dentist and relatives, Sunday morning at Nelson Street Adult School, shopping and golf.

Back at Luton he found that martial preparations were taking another interesting turn. Orders had been received to sharpen weapons and he was instructed to see what could be done. With memories of our father's tool-room at the Best and Lloyd workshops he 'Took sword down to Davis Works to see about sharpening. Good appliances but too much ground off blade. After lunch took seven swords and 12 bayonets in 'Float' and had Jack's ground beautifully.' (2 November)

Frank had bought himself a second-hand Webley and Scott automatic pistol and practised shooting at tin cans in a disused quarry. The horses (they were referred to by the romantic name of Officers' Chargers) were to be trained in steadiness under fire. 'After trying Don's horse, which is singularly sleepy, during afternoon, took it to range and fired six shots from Webley and Scott. It did not appear very perturbed.' (4 November)

The Territorials had originally been formed for home defence but all over the country various units volunteered almost unanimously for foreign service. Throughout October and early November they frequently heard rumours of moving into action. But where? France? India? Egypt? Training continued in routine fashion until 15th November when an order came through: 'The whole division will march at 7 a.m. tomorrow. The Germans are now embarking.' That day Jack Best recorded in his diary: 'Germans said to be half-way across the North Sea.'

This was to be the men's first experience of those false alarms initiated in order to test efficiency. The division was actually about to move to Bishop's Stortford as an exercise. In this manoeuvre Frank was to have the first glimpse of that Blimpish generalship which was to result in such devastating losses and frustrated efforts.

Sunday, 15 November. At 11.30 p.m. heard artillery trumpet sound for 'fall in' and then Headquarters A.S.C., after a good deal of commotion outside, decided that some manoeuvre was on which did not concern us. We were eventually put out of doubt by Don Holmes and Whittall coming up with news that the Division had been ordered to move at daybreak. At midnight I dressed and went on to the field, finding Jack Best whom I helped to despatch wagons to the various units to load up. Was much assisted by three acetylene flares which we got up from builders to shine out over the thick mud. Chalked each wagon and got them all off. Strong wind and occasional shower did not accelerate proceedings.

At 2.30 a.m., Monday, 16 November, directed Dickinson[4] in packing kit at billet, finished about 4.15. Went downstairs and wrote will, in form of letter in case of shifting abroad. Was told that the Germans were embarking and reinforcements were needed on coast. Finished correspondence and arrangements at 6, 6.30— breakfast—did not eat much—thoughts occupied with kit, etc. Got through on the phone to 146 [the Best family home] and after great mouthings, told Father of departure. Orders to move at 8, then 7.30. Got all accessories packed onto saddle and self and took leave of hostess. Quite exciting to try full kit for the first time.

Weather still cold—mounted with some little difficulty and rode to assembling street for our company. At 9 a.m., after much adjusting of wagons:

GOT STARTED.

Passed dead horse at bottom of first hill from another company, shot by vet. It was my job to ride up and down trying to keep the

---

[4] His batman, for whom he had a high regard.

wagons at proper distance. Stopped several times for watering. Part of the afternoon very beautiful; most picturesque woods and private parks to wind through. It all seemed more like a dream to be actually 'tracking it', after so much talking and speculation.

Passed through Harpenden and arrived at Hertford about 6.30 with lamps lit. Had supper with all the other A.S.C., officers at 'The Green Dragon', but not before seeing the wagons lagered in the proper fields. I was woken up once during supper (which was jolly good) so naturally dropped off like a log when I got to bed. Jack, Don, Whittall, Court and self in three rooms.

Tuesday, 17 November—Hertford. Lovely morning after sharp frost. Got mounted and off by 10 o'clock with wagons at the tail of a long divisional column. Had a little difficulty in collecting officers' kit on wagons. Halted at Ware for something blocking us in front— wasted much time, but got going again and was sent on at foot of long hill to take up water cart to suitable position on top for watering horses. After about 20 wagons had halted, I had the idea of taking the water-cart to the rear, to save men carrying buckets up so far. The road, however, was very narrow, and to make matters worse, who should turn up at the critical moment but the General—Stuart Wortley—with much Rolls Royce, staff and temper.

After behaving like a —— he turned from swearing at me to Jack (who by this time had ridden up) and carried on a terrific harangue against the principle of feeding and watering horses at all. Consequently the first rest the horses had was at 4.30 and most of them looked a bit off.[5]

Darkness closed in after a perfect sunset. Typical Autumn cloudless evening, gorgeous red and blue effect with sky and trees. The wagon lights then glow out and the 'serpent' creeps along as before but in a series of twinkles.

At one place, just after a ford, Don had to dismount and sit on one wagon box himself, to encourage a pair [of horses] to tackle a

---

[5] In his diary, Jack Best wrote: 'Steep hill E of Ware—sent wagons up separately with success, but unfortunately G.O.C. arrived and sent them close up interval with result they were stopped as horses unduly fagged. G.O.C. told me off very hard for watering and feeding at top, although horses had had nothing since morning stables (7.30 a.m.). Went on but had to stay at Widford as horses were fit to drop.'

hill. Eventually we got a farmer with a spare horse to assist. With just our little electric flash-lamps and the dim glow from the candles it was no easy job.

When we got to the field [the horses] were mostly dead done-up. I stopped there long enough to see wagons and guard fixed up for the night. Found myself billeted at house next door to the birthplace of Cecil Rhodes, with old lady and spinster daughter of elderly type and spectacle (Thorleybourne, Bishop's Stortford). Very comfortable bed.

Wednesday, 18 November. Bishop's Stortford. Delightful dry morning, sun after heavy hoare frost. Horse lines just in front of our house. Spent most of the day arranging wagons and adjusting load. Three horses in very bad state: 1) Pure old aged, 2) Pneumonia, 3) Laminitis (foot fever). Went for the vet on company car but he thought they looked too far gone. Very enjoyable day— did us all good and also the animals.

Thursday 19 November. Got up for stables before breakfast and took our vet round the lines. Horse No. 3 had died in stable in early hours of morning. During breakfast time I went round still helping to adjust loads and wagons in cold snow and rain—pretty chilly. Horses looked much better for rest generally, but No. 1 turned much worse and eventually had to be shot. One other died in the Headquarters Company. We don't put two and two together after directions from the 'G'. Horses exercised in the evening but rain still continued.

Sunday, 22 November. Another horse died during the night, probably through undue exhaustion, etc.

It was at Bishop's Stortford that Eric Milner joined the Train and was posted to No. 4 Company. He went with the Division to France but in November 1915 transferred as a workshop officer to the Mechanical Transport where he found scope for his considerable abilities as a practical engineer. Frank remained at Bishop's Stortford until Christmas Eve, billetted with the Blyths, taking 'the very proper Miss Blyth to the cinema' and accompanying her to church; indeed he seems to have attended some place of worship every Sunday, commenting on the proceedings in his diary: ('Accompanied the vet to chapel. Grotesque preacher—pure comedian—but "Terriers" singing ["March of the Terriers", composed by Frank] wonderful.')

There was a great outcry for men but no vacancies for officers at Handsworth Drill Hall. Getting more and more impatient, I enlisted as an A.S.C. driver on November 24, 1914 and it must have been then that I applied for a commission. I was successful, was sworn in and revelled at being 'in the clothes' at last.

I enjoyed the life. Horses arrived. I took part in the riding school and in the guard duty which was mounted at some stables near. We had route marches and drilling in Handsworth Park and I started to get very fit. I was billeted at home and, of course, well fed. My diary records that I found life worth living and I forgot about getting a commission. My father lent his little car for me to take the N.C.O.s on enjoyable pub-crawls (bless him). We also enjoyed theatre parties. Sometimes Frank came home on leave from Luton and there was amusement when I saluted him.

Meanwhile at Bishop's Stortford, the results of the General's ignorance of horse management continued to tell and a few days' later at a General Inspection, the vet gave Stuart Wortley a piece of his mind or, as Frank expressed it, 'had his little say undaunted'. November 28 new horses arrived from Luton and things began to settle down. Frank spent his time on convoy work, 'making out new lists of wagon arrangements', 'paying billets—no easy job as so many houses', training horses: 'mare behaved badly during convoy, jibbing frightfully and standing in front of moving wagons, took her all round again as soon as we got back.' There were accidents: '...Headquarters Company let two bolt into our lines causing driver a broken arm, and lucky at that...' or 'took out horses ride and led without wagons. Bit of chaos, such heavy beasts without proper bits or head collars. Cotterill got kicked, but not seriously.'

On Wednesday, December 9, the Staffordshire Brigade moved to Saffron Walden, No. 3 Company providing the transport. Frank records:

Moved off at 9.40 with about 28 wagons, four carts (and cooker). Had lunch at invitation of vicar at Quendin in vicarage. Arrived Saffron Walden about 3.30 and slept night at White Horse with Jack and Don. Left Court and Whittall there to look after Staffs Inf Supplies … comfortable bed.

He returned to Bishop's Stortford next day and on the Friday 10 December got permission for a day trip to Bedales, our old school, in Petersfield. He sent a wire to his school friend Vyv Trubshawe inviting him to come along but it later turned out that Trubshawe had already been posted abroad. The next day,

Left 7.37 and though late at Liverpool Street just managed to catch the London and South Western Railway [L&SWR] connection. Walked up to Bedales about 11.15. There met Murray[6] (the only Old Bedalian) and other friends. Had dinner at top table soon after Bellot,[7] Nicholson, Winser,[8] and Hill[9] turned up, so we had a good footer match. School won 4–2, but delightfully typical sloshy field. Got very muddy but had a good bath and tea about 5 o'clock.

After chatting in Library, got Murray's motorbike ready, then listened to Messiah rehearsal till 8 p.m. Said goodbye to Chief and departed on Murray's carrier, belt broke but hastily repaired— caught train. Over half-hour late at Waterloo—no chance of connection, slept night at Great Eastern Hotel. Got up 7.30, had cup of tea and caught the 8.05 arriving at Bishop's Stortford 9.15.

With the Staffordshire Brigade at Saffron Walden it was later found more convenient to locate the transport near the infantry. Accordingly, on 24 December Jack Best received orders to send

---

[6] George Anthony Murray took part in the 'Changing the Guard' act. He was in the same group of friends as Vyv Trubshawe, Oswald Horsley and Frank, who visited him at Cambridge the following February. He served in the Gunners and died of wounds received in action 5th April, 1918.

[7] All the Old Bedalians mentioned, except Henry Hill, had captained the Bedales football XI. Bryson Bellot was studying farming. He served in the Inns of Court O.T.C. and the North Somerset Yeomanry. He died of appendicitis at the Abbeville Hospital, 27th March, 1918.

[8] Both Daniel Nicholson and Eric Winser appear again in the story.

[9] Henry Hill served in the Gunners 1915–19.

'eight more wagons and 10 men [there] with Frank Best in charge'. Frank wrote:

> ... moved off by 3.0. Heavy frost on damp road made roads like ice, also heavy fog prevented us getting in before 8.30. Comfortable billet with Mr Midgley.
>
> Xmas Day! Brekker at Midgley's after inspecting horses, etc. Refereed for footer match. Took car to B. Stortford again and had Xmas Dinner with Mrs Blythe. Still very cold. Heavy hoar frost, partially melted, only to freeze again at night. Second Xmas dinner at Saffron Walden.
>
> Boxing Day. Took it pretty quietly, as Xmas dinners turned out rather hostile Wrote letters home. Got to know the Midgley family a bit. The father a bit like Pastor Funke, but with angina pectoris. Very fond of painting on china, etc. Lived some time in Australia and had therefore many relics in house. The mother and three daughters very sympathetic and arduous workers at [Friends] Meeting House where Tommies can get good drinks etc, for moderate prices. All staunch Quakers, plain spoken, etc, strong TTs,[10] but very kind and decent to me.

Just how kind and decent they were comes out in a letter home written soon after Frank had left them. 'Mrs M is absolutely charming for kindness, sympathy, etc.' he wrote, at the same time making suggestions for inviting them to stay at 146; I am sure it would do them both good and you would enjoy their company.' He goes on to describe two of the daughters. 'Irene is an adult-school worker and over 30 tho' she still looks quite young and Bessie is three years senior. She is also a hard worker but not so brilliant.'

A good mixer himself, Frank liked to put people in touch with each other. The Midgleys readily agreed to invite for a meal his two brother officers, Gordon Whittall and Allan Court who, having learnt that their hosts were abstainers, prepared themselves beforehand. During the meal the talk turned to the Midgley family background and the Society of Friends. Their host explained that the emphasis on teetotalism had been a

---

[10] T [for 'temperance'] total: committed to abstaining from alcohol.

relatively recent development and that his forbears had in fact been maltsters—which, he stressed, had been considered a worthy trade in those days. Though Frank's two friends may have wished that the Society's policy had been a bit more conservative in this respect the meal progressed pleasantly enough. Afterwards someone suggested a little music. For this they had also come prepared, for Frank, banking that the conversation might possibly flag, had persuaded his friends to bring their songs (left politely in the hall) and had even rehearsed them. With him at the piano the others went into action with confidence and bravura:

> 'Grapes and girls were made to press,
> And lips and cups to kiss,'[11]

sang Alan Court. Gordon Whittall followed it up with 'The Bandolero':

> 'My army is my gallant band,
> 'My law enforced by carbine shot!'[12]

This was Frank's first command. He was responsible for supplying the Staffordshire Brigade, two of his wagons being allocated to each battalion. Their main task was to draw supplies from the railway-deck at Bishop's Stortford and from other places, delivering them to the appropriate battalion headquarters. It is clear from his diary that at first he encountered difficulties:

2 January 1915. Got horses paraded for veterinary inspection. Still left with 10 wagons workable, and nine pairs not, through mange and other diseases. Got disinfectant started and after lunch told them off on punctuality and made five, late on stables that morning, start to scrub out the empty house which they had used previously and left in a filthy condition. Chanced on stabling-shed

---

[11] The Inkeeper's song from *Gypsy Love*.

[12] Having met Miss Bessie Midgley in 1959 I have reason to believe that this Quaker family secretly enjoyed the situation as much as the young men.

for 20 horses—great find! Arranged for next day's move, then sampled Picture House.

A few days later Colonel Mears, who had replaced Colonel Wright, 'came round and gave N.C.O.s a scathing telling off, though very friendly to me, considering,' Frank wrote. Frank strengthened up discipline:

> 9 January. Got a move on with grooming and cleaning up generally; being able to send the 'itchy' horses to Mange Hospital gradually relieved situation, although many chaps were on leave at the time of Colonel's inspection.

> 11 January. Got the men on cleaning harness, etc. Spent long time making out returns—started giving C.B. [Confined to Barracks] to defaulters, but horses and equipment generally improving.

There were the usual accidents:

> 5 January. Dugmore got fractured skull with kick and was taken to Newport Hospital.'

A Board of Enquiry was held to discuss the nature and cause of the accident. Dugmore's by this time was progressing wonderfully well.

> 13 January. Defaulters again—visited Dugmore at Newport Hospital—he is going on splendidly. Veterinary inspection during afternoon—visited Mange Hospital.

On November 28th of the previous year I had enlisted as a driver at the Handsworth Drill Hall after having applied for a commission. A few weeks later I was promoted to the rank of lance-corporal and on January 16th Frank came home on leave. 'Paid a visit to the Drill Hall,' he wrote, 'to look up the Reserve Company and "Corporal Best."' The troops were amused. As Lieut. Walter Meakin commented, 'privates had to learn to call even their own relations "Sir".' Frank summed up the situation: 'Bob must salute his little brother on parade but may give him a playful kick up the arse afterwards.'

In Birmingham, at the end of 1914, we spent weeks expecting to be moved down to our war stations. But we finally got the order when we were least ready for it in late January 1915. I was then doing night-guard duty at Stafford House. Everyone had to turn out and help load up the two wagons. Next day I had an hour for a bath, change and packing my kit bag. The G.S. wagons consisted of a long open box with an elevated seat in front of the driver, where I was seated on the one loaded with the men's kit bags. We only arrived at the station in time, as we dropped a kit bag every few yards, the wagon being grossly over-loaded.

We arrived at Luton and proceeded to 42 Highfield Road. With me in the billet were Jack Holmes of Handsworth, Joe Tuckley, and Bodie (a nephew of Dr Walford Bodie, the music-hall artist). Mr and Mrs Parsons presided and treated us wonderfully well.

We lay on mattresses on the floor, four in a room. Jack was the first victim of Luton throat, with a high temperature. I came next, the attack brought on during my guard duty in a lean-to during high wind in a snowstorm. Then Bodie and Joe Tuckley succumbed. It was very unpleasant lying on the floor and sweating, and my hip bones got bruised, but we preferred it to the hospital, of which we had heard dreadful tales.

The move to Luton took place in January 1915; I wasn't gazetted until March 13th. Between those two dates my thoughts turned more and more towards getting my commission, as Frank had done. I began to get restless at the idea of remaining in the ranks indefinitely but when I learnt that my father was doing what he could to hasten matters by talking to influential friends, I felt more resigned to waiting.

Our duties at Luton consisted mostly of grooming, feeding and watering horses. We exercised them on convoy work, delivering supplies to surrounding detachments. Many of the horses were only half-broken-in and bolted when we took them out. We moved about in mud much of the time.

For weeks none of us actually rode a horse, but one day I was given a saddle and allotted a horse to exercise.

Unfortunately, when I tried to mount, the animal shied, someone let go of the bridle and I went over too far, falling head-first on the road. I was knocked out and suffered an abrasion, emerging later from the hospital with a picturesque bandage round my head. In this accident Joe Tuckley proved a good friend and sucked the abrasion while I was unconscious.

When my head was better I had one or two days on convoy work. All the rest of the time at Luton I felt very fit. We paraded at 6 a.m. and finished the day at about 6 p.m., returning to the billet ravenous from the effects of the cold wind. After tea and cleaning boots, buttons and spurs, we went into town, often to hops, and for the first time in my life I began to meet girls, socially, who worked in factories (mostly hat production).

Some time in February we moved billet to the house of Mr and Mrs Hunt. They were as kind to us as Mr and Mrs Parsons had been. I was getting experience of living with lower-middle-class and working-class people—I enjoyed it.

From the Drill Hall, Frank went on to Cambray Works, which had been our grandfather's factory. 'All said they were pleased to see me, etc,' he wrote, 'as on previous occasions when on holiday from school, but not this time "what a big boy you're growing!" Had a delightful cross-country ride with Bob. Exquisite colliery scenery.'

Next day Frank rose early and went to Nelson Street Adult School, where he gave a short talk on Ciphers. After some visits and a round of golf in the afternoon, the day ended hilariously, for after supper our Aunt Lucy played one of her own compositions, a new and original National Anthem, the first six bars of which are quoted here:

Having heard it through several times, Frank considered carefully whether or not to stand to attention while Aunt Lucy's National Anthem was being played; finally he decided to stand on his head, a procedure he later sketched in his diary.

The following evening we went to a pantomime where George Robey and Fred Emney produced some of the liveliest fooling I have ever seen, including what was probably the first performance of a sketch, now over-familiar and hackneyed, known as 'Papering a Room', in which the wallpaper paste went over everything and finally got emptied into an upright piano. Frank recorded: 'We laughed ourselves weak!'

Entertainment always roused in Frank the interest of a practitioner. He wrote to George Robey to express his admiration of the great comedian's art, and received an auto-graphed photograph together with the pantomime libretto, which he then sent on to me with these observations:

Dear Old Bob,

I like the way that brilliant masterpiece of humour 'the paper-hanging scene' is referred to as 'business with supper and redecorating ...' or something similar. In fact the whole libretto consists of:

– Enter funny man disguised as: Tramp, Policeman, Rajah, Ape, M.P., Villain, Tragedian, Poet, Artist, Sea Serpent, etc.

– Business with: Tea-pot, Cabbage, Sausage, Pie, Centipede, Poker (not cold), Cat, Breeches, etc. etc.

I hope you will endorse my survey of the situations. I really think we shall later have to get into touch with a man like that—of such infinite genius and resource.

I also like the way they refer you to the publishers of the various humorous songs:

'E Warnt 'arf Kidded.

Joseph Feldman,

5 & 6 New Bond Street, etc.

I found it all very entertaining and instructive, and should like your views as well. It struck me that it's not so much what is laid down, but what the author 'suggests' that is really the humorous part.

Frank often affected an inflection and elaborate turn of phrase that did not pass unnoticed by his brother officers. Robey undoubtedly influenced him, and no one could ever forget the scandalised eyebrows and exhortations to his riotous audience: 'Temper your hilarity with a modicum of reserve.' Following in the master's footsteps, Frank was one day overheard giving instructions to his batman, 'the noble Dickinson', then engaged on some fairly straightforward job such as cleaning a Sam Browne belt: 'Dickinson, I should be very glad if you would exercise a little ingenuity.'

Returning to Saffron Walden, Frank 'felt a cold coming on, so after arranging affairs in the morning, spent most of the afternoon and all evening in bed—and very nice too! Surrounded with hot cold-antidotes. Colonel inspected us during morning and was very pleased.' (20 January). Next day he bought numerous remedies from three different chemists' shops, after which he 'took it slack in the afternoon and evening on sofa—kept warm'. The treatment failed, however, and after two days of outdoor duty in wet, cold and heavy snow he was ordered to bed. There he remained for five days, well looked after by the Midgleys.

On reading his diaries and letters I am struck by Frank's promptness and persistence in carrying Bedalianism—the spirit of our old school, Bedales—into his war service, and yet he never allowed what our headmaster John Badley called 'The Will to Fuller Life' to interfere with his regimental duties, which he discharged with keenness and imagination. He wasted no time in getting to work with his music, for on October 7 he had already 'started writing manuscript of War Song composed partly at Bedales', and throughout these first few months of training he was active fairly continuously in composing, practising or performing. In January he was writing a musical setting for some verses he had seen in *Punch* called 'The Bells of Berlin'. This proved to be a popular number in many concerts, and in France, as we shall see, he went to some trouble in order to find a publisher for it.

Work, sport and music were intermingled:

31

4 February. Got most of the new cards for systematising wagons, horses and men arranged. Had a beautiful long ride with Capt. Court, about 13 miles, interviewed old farmer re hay. Found myself rather stiff and with a headache during evening (first time on horse for ages) but at the piano a new march shaped itself, nevertheless.

This was the first reference to Frank's 'March of the Terriers', which was played at my wedding.

Frank was delighted with the magnificent Jacobean mansion, Audley End, and the immense lawn where Reg Morley-Pegge had captained the estate cricket team. Adjoining the estate is the village of Wendens Ambo where lived Reg's distant relatives the Ackland family, local solicitors. From time to time Frank was invited to their house, where music would be combined with a 'select little bridge evening'. There he would try out some of his compositions.

5 February. Walked to Wendens to show 'Bells of Berlin' before sending MS home.

'I miss you very much on these social occasions,' he wrote to me on 16 February. 'Miss Ackland was hugely amused at the Till Ready indications. She knew at once what I referred to, though I could not give her the whole gala performance.'

Frank had a flair for finding nice pianos and instruments. In November he 'had fun with gramophone and beautiful grand piano' and later we found the first of those deals, recurring wherever he went, which involved buying or hiring pianos for the mess.

21 December 1914. Fixed up about piano to be hired and to be sent the following day. It turned up that night—nice tone. Spent good part of the evening playing.

He would also turn an appraising ear to musical events, such as an organ recital at Saffron Walden old church, or

Sunday 10 January 1915. Evening concert given by civilians not as good as previous evening, but best turn, out and out, was that of

Miss Joan Lloyd (aged 7) who played the piano and then danced to perfection. Got invited to tea the following day. At 3.45 once more took car to Wendens and had enjoyable afternoon with Mrs Ackland where kiddy Joan played like Paderewski.

Frank described one memorable Saturday afternoon in a letter home:

I got away by car to Cambridge and having looked up Sergeant [Crane] in hospital, spent the evening with Murray,[13] who is at Trinity. I had no idea what a wonderful place it is and I am anxious to go again when the darkness and wet are less eminent.

The place is black at night; they all carry little electric torches in the streets—and quite rightly, for if bombs were dropped, they would be sure to hit something beautiful, as the buildings are so close.

The hospital is a marvellous concern—all bungalows connected by raised gangways and will accommodate about 500.

I thoroughly enjoyed the evening, as it is my first peep at 'Varsity life. Murray's little room was quite sumptuous, and after chatting hard about Bedales we went to the Music Hall.

They had all been of a bustle with the King's visit. M took photos quite close.

I am really beginning to have a fine time now.

The music arrived and I had my usual ripping Sunday evening over there at Wendens. They were very pleased. (15 February)

Frank was, as he wrote, 'beginning to have a fine time now'. Discipline and the horses' health both improved. His chestnut, General Joffre, proved to be 'very comfy on the trot' when he 'rode to Littlebury to see wagons loaded up with straw' and 'Audley End was exquisite'. But his two months at Saffron Walden were coming to an end all too quickly. There were constant preparations for moving abroad. He was vaccinated and took part in entraining practice.

On 26 February Jack Best and the rest of the company arrived in Saffron Walden, preparatory to leaving for France. To Frank fell the task of fixing up stabling for the 52 additional

[13] Murray rode over from Cambridge to return the visit on several occasions.

horses. This he arranged at Engelman's Carnation Sheds, at the same time sending home to Mother the first in the series of packets of flowers. Further assignments were to provide billets for 50 men, issuing breeches and jackets, and so forth.

Saturday 27 February. Buzzed around on bike, paying billets, settled up with Engelman. Got finished pretty well by dinner, ready for leaving early Sunday, when news came through that departure was delayed 24 hours—accordingly had to make out all billeting forms again for 28th only, plus those men who had been here all the time; did not finish before evening. Wrote home, paid a/c's in town, bought chocolate, etc.

Sunday 28 February. Had to make out all the billeting forms again just for one day. Paid them off, or rather distributed them in afternoon. Spent evening packing up kit, etc, with help of the noble Dickinson, and arranging other matters. Got to bed about 11.30 with bedroom a mess of assorted equipment, principally on floor.

On Monday 1 March, they left Saffron Walden and the following day Frank wrote home from The Royal Pier Hotel, Southampton:

I jumped up at 5.45 and somehow got dressed and finished packing for 6.15 brekker which Miss Midgley had arranged for us all—hot and sumptuous. It was a pity we did not feel inclined for more. Took leave of them at 7.0 a.m and thanked them to the best of our ability for all they had done for us. I have been thinking what we could do for them" [e.g. invite them to stay at our house].

Well, to get back to the journey, we got the horses in and wagons on without more than the ordinary trouble, tho' a horse, as you know, is the limit for passive resistance at best.

We saw that our luncheon box (which the Midgleys had prepared in their usual lavish way) got into the carriage with us and settled down (Jack, Don and self) in a 1st-class compartment for a six-hour journey. There was great speculation as to the route, as the English lines are about as unsuitable for cross country as you could want. It turned out, however, Stortford, Tottenham, Hampstead Heath (!), Kew Gardens, Kingston, Basingstoke, Winchester and Southampton.

We did not embark, however. Although a bright day it was frightfully windy. The proprietor here told us the usual whopper about the worst ... for x years. Even the naval man admitted it was not fit.

We hear, however, a rumour that we got hold of a submarine mother vessel and without destroying her, met these Deutsche Pirates at the rendezvous (for the ship's papers) as though to supply petrol, etc, and then sunk each one as their heads appeared above water. Perhaps six or eight in number. No substantiation yet.

We fixed the men up in a prodigious rest camp. Fortunately the weather has been absolutely ideal for March. It was just like being at Bournemouth. Our sitting room looks out over the sea and after brekker we take the tram up to the common. The horses are thoroughly enjoying the sunshine. The men no less.

Wednesday 3 March. Drizzly morning. Moved to station and dock about 2.15 having polished off remains of luncheon basket in tent. Got horses on board with some difficulty and remained overnight alongside quay. Four very comfy in cabin.

Thursday 4 March. Still alongside the quay. Men drilled off ship. Staff came on board about 4.0 p.m. and the boat, S.S. MAIDAN, was pulled out of dock by three tugs about 10.0 p.m. Wonderful search-lights all down the Solent; picked up two destroyers for escort off Isle of Wight.

At some point my own duties were cut short by being detailed as Orderly N.C.O. for a week. The work consisted of sitting in the Orderly Room from 6.15 a.m. to 10.15 p.m. and doing odd jobs, such as organising the Company Sergeant Major's transport book. This N.C.O. was 'a triumph of ineptitude and inefficiency, so he loved me for getting his books straight'.

Towards the long hours of the week I began to get fed up with the rather long hours, but on Saturday, March 13, I paraded the sick as usual and took them round to the R.A.M.C. in Mansfield Road. While I was waiting in the examining room, R.S.M. Redman, a fine soldier, knocked, entered and saluted me, saying 'Congratulations, sir! You're a second lieutenant, gazetted this morning in the *Times*.' I had great difficulty in stopping myself dancing round the room. We shook hands and parted. I continued my duties, assisting over the examination of the lame and lazy. I was told to go back to Birmingham, get my kit and report to the Drill Hall in Handsworth. By a coincidence, I met the C.O., Colonel Wright, in Leicester. He told me to return to Luton as soon as I had bought my kit.

During the next few days in Birmingham, I walked on air. I soon bought all my kit and looked forward to returning to Luton; but one evening, returning from the theatre, I found a phone message telling me to report to the Drill Hall the next day instead. So here I was with every prospect of being at home for months and little chance of joining my brother Frank in France.

Chapter 2
Schoolboy spirit

I have mentioned that Frank and I, and many of the people who meant most to us in life and whom we would come across again and again during the war, had been to Bedales, the pioneering English boarding school. Bedales had been founded in 1893 by John Haden Badley, whom we called 'The Chief', and was intended as a radical improvement on existing educational and social institutions. It was informed by a vision of offering 'The Good Life' to young people—a life, as Badley understood it, rich in texture, varied, and one in which the Arts, Drama and Music, as well as the Sciences, played an important part.

John Badley certainly accomplished what he set out to do, but for the first twenty years—certainly during many of Frank's school days—he was obviously groping, sometimes rather wildly. He had not the knowledge available today and could only go forward by trial and error from what he had himself experienced in the course of a classical education at Rugby and Cambridge, followed by a spell of two-and-a-half years as a master at Abbotsholme. It was to Cecil Reddie, the head of this British prototype of the German Landerziehungsheime [boarding schools in the country], that he owed many of his ideas. These, and a quantity of his own, have since been taken up by other schools and are now commonly accepted practice. In the first decade of this century, however, he was many years in advance of his time.

As we shall see, Frank became steeped in the Bedalian conception of The Good Life. After leaving school he continued to give practical expression to what he had learnt of John Badley's doctrine and his war service, if anything, seems to have given him the opportunity to take this even further. His warm feelings towards the headmaster were mingled with respect, if not awe. Headmasters of that period seem to have had awefulness thrust upon them as part of their professional equipment. Perhaps John Badley would have preferred it otherwise. That he was often not quite at ease was evidenced by the quick nervous movements which he made as he sat or talked. But the Chief mellowed with time and for most of us fear was later replaced by affectionate understanding.

Many of Badley's forebears were rooted in the country surrounding Birmingham. His father, grandfather and great grandfather, had been doctors practising at Dudley. His mother was a Miss Best and we have reason to believe that there is a distant kinship between her family and ours. On going away to school he had a slight Black Country accent and, as in the case of Frank and myself during our first term at Bedales, this did not go unnoticed. At one point in his life he suffered from an inferiority complex, being, as he tells us, 'the youngest of the family and having, up to the age of thirteen, no boy companions except, now and then, my two older cousins. This at times led to compensatory outbreaks, giving an impression of conceit and self-assurance that I was far from possessing.'

We must have been introduced to the headmaster by our parents on arriving at the school, but my memory of the encounter is vague. On the other hand I have the clearest picture of the second master, Oswald B. Powell, to whom we were handed over when our parents took their leave. Like the Head he was bearded and wore clothes which, though now unsensational, were then quite eccentric, such as a flannel shirt, open at the neck, sandals and knickerbockers. He showed us over the whole school, ending with the earth closets, where he indicated roughly the posture and principles associated with their use—a most necessary and understanding demonstration.

It was a fine afternoon and most of the Bedalians were out of doors. Later they began to show themselves in the quadrangle. We noticed large moustached men and were surprised to find that they were not masters but boys. A few girls were also to be seen. Music was in the air. Whistling and singing were fairly continuous. The graceful lilt of Ethelbert Nevin's 'Narcissus' mingled with tunes from Mendelssohn's *Elijah*. After high tea, we hung about until bedtime. This was in two relays. We, as early bedders, retired at 7.30.

Bedales was the name of a house in the Tudor Style near Haywards Heath in Sussex, where the school had been founded; but some 18 months before our arrival it had been moved to new buildings near Petersfield. The estate lay on the southern slope of the North Downs. It comprised about 100 acres of farm and woodlands. The surrounding country is some of the most beautiful I know.

Up to 1911, when Frank left, there was almost continuous building of additions to the School. During the first few terms the quadrangle, round which the main block was planned, had not been fully glazed, so that on leaving a classroom one found oneself, immediately, almost in extreme climatic conditions. Of those first three months we read, 'The Summer Term has been the least summer-like that we can remember. Rain, wind and arctic cold seem to have filled most of it.' Frank and I did not find the cold unpleasant until the following winter when we would ask each other 'What is the point of keeping us frozen?' Windows were kept open and the central heating was not very effective. Occasionally the ink froze in the ink-wells. At night we washed in cold water and on getting up we had to sponge cold water over ourselves while squatting in a flat metal bath. It happened that at times it was necessary to break the ice before the water could be poured from the 'goose-cans'.

To send us to this school from the hot-house climate of our home constituted an act of faith for which our parents deserved our gratitude; but I sometimes wonder whether they realised just what it was going to be like. Bullying, though not as savage as formerly, had by no means disappeared. There were still practices which, though not directed against Frank and myself, can only be described as shameful. For instance we saw some violent treatment of certain so-called 'dirty Jews'. The social-psychologist of today might note that there appears to have been a number of 'non-dirty Jews' who were, indeed, never looked upon as Jews at all, and it was a surprise, years later, to learn of their racial origins.

There was, too, a sort of legalised bullying, though, to be sure, we had not much cause for complaint. In wet weather we were organised in runs of about four miles. Stragglers were urged on by means of a switch. But longer runs were occasionally imposed as a punishment when there had been an epidemic of untidiness and disorder affecting a large proportion of the school. The prefects then decreed that retribution should be wholesale. In February 1904 we were sent off for a run over the downs—a distance in all, of about ten miles. This was for the Juniors. The Seniors had a longer assignment. The prefect in charge of our run was armed with a switch to whip up the laggards. The distance was then beyond the powers of Frank and myself and after a few half-hearted cuts and exhortations, the prefect left us alone. The whole run passed us on their return when we were only about half way towards the turning point. We regained the school some hours afterwards, just as dusk was falling, having been still further delayed by an ill-judged short cut. Frank wrote home: 'There was a run yesterday for fines [i.e. bad marks] (which I very much dreaded) so at the beginning I tumbled down (by mistake on purpose) and scunked a great deal of it which was jolly fine.'

Some years later a more intensive form of the same punishment was revived, called 'The Toil'. Frank and I escaped this punishment, but even though the distance had been reduced from two miles to half-a-mile it broke the pluck of one boy who ran away, thus drawing the Head Master's attention to this abuse of power. It was then stopped.

As they gained experience, Frank and his friend Vyvyan (Vyv) Trubshawe found that they were quite able to look after themselves. A boy who was somewhat older than them, a member of a gang, tried to exact some sort of personal service by mild persecution. Threats from a water pistol and frequent squirting became so tiresome that Frank and his friend decided that something must be done about it. They arranged together that when next threatened they would show great alarm and, as they ran away, shout to each other that they were escaping to a certain outbuilding. This they did and, outstripping their victim, they actually concealed themselves outside the building before he arrived at the door. The older boy unsuspectingly went inside and began looking around for them, whereupon they quickly slammed the only door and locked it. After this they negotiated forfeiture of the water-pistol in return for liberation.

Officially, there was no system of personal fagging. The school motto was 'Work of Each for Weal of All' and accordingly we took our turn at such chores as bed-making, preparing the Hall for meals or meetings, cleaning boots, clothes, the earth closets and so forth.

I suppose that spankings at Bedales were no worse than at many other schools, but there was, in fact, a veritable pyramid of flagellation. At the broad bottom one found, what the patent agents called, 'a plurality' of slippers and hair brushes wielded by the dormitory bosses; on the upper slopes were the ash single-sticks of the consortium of prefects, but handled by the head-boy of the school, and I have myself seen one of them literally broken across the backside of a boy;[14] while at the summit was to be found the shaft of a golf club, applied by the Head Master to the bare flesh of the worst offenders. The purple results of these administrations, visible at the swimming baths, may have served as a warning to others.

Bedalians were able to see how near they were to punishment by a system of bad marks for untidiness or disorderliness. We were allowed six in each week, a liberal allowance one would have thought, but each garment found out of place in the changing-rooms counted as one bad mark and it was not unknown for clothes to be deliberately pulled down out

---

[14] According to Peter Eckersley, this was because they were dry and rotten.

of malice. The more apprehensive boys would tie things onto the pegs.

Thus it might come about that on a Sunday one suddenly found that the allowance had been exceeded. There would then be six days to wait for the thrashing which was reserved for Saturday evenings. This was roughly the predicament in which Frank found himself once during his first year. I have reason to believe that the prefects showed mercy in the way they dealt with him. His character was such that the incident would certainly not have depressed him for long.

During those pre-war years there was a gradual lessening of the physical violence, though corporal punishment was not abolished until during the 1914 War. In furthering this growth of kindliness I believe that Frank and his two friends, Vyv Trubshawe and Oswald Horsley, played their part.

It was not until the term following our arrival that a junior school was started, which took over the work of a Third Class where Frank and I were taught during our first term. The form master, Russell Scott, a young man of advanced views, had great faith in Esperanto as a promoter of international peace. He loved music and played the flute in the school orchestra, but was not very successful as an executant. The quality of his tone was so piercing that often, during rehearsal, one could hear it, above all the other instruments, on the playing fields nearly a hundred yards away. He was often slightly off-pitch. He taught us French, using a phonetic system which I personally found extremely difficult to understand. We were also encouraged to sing traditional French songs and amongst them was one called 'Les Noçes du Papillon'. The tune was so charming that one day, unsuspectingly, we sang it at home. For years afterwards, to our great embarrassment, whenever there was company, we were pressed by our aunts to sing 'that dear little French song'.

Russell Scott also took us in Nature Study—a subject hitherto completely unknown to us. Frank and a boy called Raisley Moorsom made, under Scott's guidance, a nest for ants out of plaster of Paris covered with glass. They kept copious notes, starting with 'We took a cigar box and some ants.' At that time the attitude towards Nature, though humane, was not fully in accordance with the doctrine of 'Reverence for Life'; for instance, eggs were collected and butterflies and moths were pinned on to boards, a practice once criticised by Bernard Shaw while on a visit to the school.

Nine years later Russell Scott, in an article, stated that this Third Class, among all the classes he had ever taught, held one of the best places in his affection, no less surely than Frank held one of the two Best positions in that class. After which Russell Scott gives the following two examples of 'infantile composition':

> Exam.—Best 11.
> Subject—With a joyful spirit I.
> Noun—Spirit
> Predicate—Sir Richard Grenville die.
> Verb—Sir Richard Grenville.

Horatious (cockles) and the Romans were fighting against the kings whome they had turned out of Rome. The cause of the war was that Horatious and the Romans had turned these out of Rome, you see, and these kings wanted to get Rome back again so they came one day with a lot of other men.

For Best 1, grammar had already lost its mysteries in 1903, but convention had not yet crushed the originality of his composition:

'The Romans had been, for a long time, very tyraneclecly ruled by their king (texas and the proude). So the Romans made up their minds to exile their rulers, which they did. Texas and Co. immediately went to Larze Porsna. P. gathered his army and marched to fight the Romans.'

In spite of a certain vagueness Russell Scott had a real gift for teaching young children.

The dormitories, on the second floor, were of different sizes ranging to accommodate anything between four and nine boys. We slept between blankets on wooden beds, chosen, according to the Chief, for 'simplicity and comfort'. Instead of spring mattresses there were wooden laths or slats, which were liable to break in the hurly-burly of ragging.

The day started at 6.55 with the ringing of a hand-bell outside each door. After our cold sponge we dressed and at 7.20 assembled outside in the drive for a morning run of about half a mile. Breakfast was at 7.30. Bed-making at 8.00 and work started at 8.30. Games and outdoor work occupied the afternoon, followed by a hot tub and high tea. Between tea and bedtime there was generally singing or free-time work, which was much encouraged, as will be explained later.

Writing in the *Bedales Record* (1905–6) Frank describes a typical day, 'not literally true but only founded on fact'. He was then about twelve. It gives a clear picture of his carefree mood. He admits that he did not take his class-work very seriously. He evidently enjoyed his food, which was quite good and plentiful. There was no tuck-shop and sweets were forbidden. Most Bedalians, however, yielded to temptation and at times an epidemic of flagrant breaching of the rules would break out.

One such occurred in the Spring term of 1908. The Chief called upon all guilty parties to own up and a number did so. The punishment was quite mild (missing part of a fancy-dress dance) but the situation fired the lively imagination of O.B.W. 'Mooner' Wills who produced a wholly fictitious drawing. Members of the staff are recognisable. They are drawn larger than the children. From left to right: E.G. Casey, T.J. Garstang, O.B. Powell, Miss Townshend and Dr Fred Hodgson. Mr Killick, the head male domestic, is looking out of the window. A tall boy in the queue is Laurence Collier. The girls have been sentenced to punishment drill on Bargentine lines under the gym mistress Miss Catherine Simeon (later Mrs R.A. Marshall). According to J.S. Lawrence, who gave me these drawings, she is reputed to have remarked indignantly: 'I've never worn such a brief gym tunic.'

Frank records that, in the afternoon game, he 'made 17 runs, not out, and took one catch'. He appears to have been either late or only just in time for each of the day's events. At tea:

made extremely personal joke and get 'stood out' in front of Head Master. After tea start French detention—very dry; each minute seems to be an hour. Write out something about French chap who makes an ass of himself. Go on until I tell myself that if I do any more work it will be wicked. Put work under desk. Then slack. Start making 'Water bombs' [made out of paper and filled with water and used for throwing at people]. Finish making the fifth one and put them in pocket. Bring up work. Master thinks I have written rather slowly.

From that time until bed-time Frank appears to have changed for singing, had a hot bath, which he enjoyed thoroughly, and arrived late for singing, which he enjoyed also. The diary ends as follows:

7.40—Fill water-bomb and hurl it out of the window—'Splosh!' Yells of 'Good shot!' from the rest of the dormitory. Look out and see workshop Master looking up in amazement. He stares at me then retires.

7.45—Whole dormitory shams sleep.

7.50—Boss comes up and tells me to get out of bed; he then spanks me. I get back into bed feeling rather warm and sleep well till next morning.

During our first term Frank was playing hockey, a game that was new to him, when he came into contact with a boy much heavier than himself, fell down and was obviously in great pain. He explained that he had broken his arm, but at first nobody would believe him. After his diagnosis had been confirmed by a medical examination, he was well looked after by the Matron, Miss Withers, and by her assistant, Miss Thorp.

Describing the Matron, our headmaster wrote: 'Of those who saw the school through its adolescent years the most memorable figure was Gertrude Withers. Hospital trained, her manner may have seemed to some as starchy as her uniform; but it covered a warm heart and a devotion to the school which made her one of its staunchest pillars.'

As for Miss Thorp, who succeeded her, how to describe her amiable disposition and slightly tremulous voice, her solicitous manner when, on cold days, she enquired whether we had 'both' on (i.e. vest and underpants) or her tendency to gullibility? Some years later that *farceur* of genius, Mooner Wills, entered her room one day, apparently in agony, and explained that he had accidentally immersed his hand in sulphuric acid during some chemistry experiment. Miss Thorp asked to see it; whereupon, drawing back his cuff, he showed the hand of a skeleton, borrowed from an anatomy class. Miss Thorp took some time to recover from this shock.

Both Miss Withers and Miss Thorp came under the spell of Frank's disarming smile. They christened him 'The Cheshire Puss'.

During most of our outdoor life we were supervised and instructed by Sergeant-Major Cordery ('The Bargent'), late of the Royal Dragoon Guards. Moustached and dressed in khaki riding breeches and leggings he was a soldierly figure. His eyes, like Kitchener's, had a far away look as if from scanning horizons. He had seen service in India and had some interesting tales to tell of his experiences there.

Arriving during our second year (1903), he seemed, at first, somewhat out of place in that liberal and, on the whole, non-militaristic climate; and yet, looking back, the Chief's instincts in making this appointment were, I believe, sound enough. It must be considered in the context of a war on the horizon and another, then recent history, which had been conducted with almost unbelievable inefficiency and lack of professional standards.

Through the Bargent we gained experience of the typical N.C.O. instructor, so that when, eleven years later, Frank and many others were caught up in recruits-drill or machine-gun instructions, they knew where they were and what to expect. On such occasions they re-heard the Bargentine vernacular. Frank carefully studied the original and made notes in his pocket-book under the heading 'Vocabulary'.

Frank was not the only one to become fascinated by this soldier. Laurence Collier published in the *Bedales Chronicle* many witty Gilbertian verses signed 'Og'. One of his verses starts:

> Oh, everyone knows of the B-rg-nt,
> His tales are the talk of the town.
> So I think it high time
> To say something in rhyme,
> Explaining his mighty renown.
>
> In letters of or and of argent
> Let the tale of his prowess be told—
> His narrative powers
> Enthral us for hours,
> His counsel is better than gold.

Thereafter, in five more stanzas, we read of the Bargent's adventures and sayings—how he had 'been blown from guns [and] swallowed rajahs' poisoned buns'; and how, when some small boy asked him 'what Alexander did on Punjaub's sunny plains', the reply was 'Alexander 'oo?'

The Bargent initiated barrack-square defaulters' drill. Offenders were issued with broom sticks loaded with lead and made to run round the quadrangle carrying them at arm's length above the head. He also took other forms of drill, shooting, riding, boxing and served as groundsman. He was the clerk-of-works in many an ambitious project, such as levelling and extending the cricket field and tennis courts. To expedite this work he bought, second hand, a set of rails and some small metal tip-trucks. In operating them the possibilities of ragging were immense. Trucks were derailed. The noise of metal to metal became deafening. He would shout, ''Oo's that a'banging and a'tinking of? Hevery time I turns my back I sees you doing something!' He would become speechless. Things had gone too far. Walking up to the offender he would sentence him to an impossible number of hours 'extry drill'. The sentence was usually reduced later for, at heart, he was a kindly soul and, although somewhat blustering and heavy-handed, a likeable character.

Besides teaching us certain skills and disciplines, which were useful to us after 1914, he provided Frank and other comedians with unforgettable material for parody and burlesque.

In 1907 Frank and I came under the spell of Leslie Kent, then a ruddy complexioned, bespectacled youth of about 17. He was the son of an army officer, a born leader, good natured and never bossy but capable of arousing enthusiasm in others. His initiative had first shown itself when, in the winter term of 1905, he had reorganised the Fire Brigade. He reported: 'The brigade is rapidly becoming efficient; our hoses and other apparatus are excellent and our hydrants are numerous, but there is just one little detail which seems to have been omitted: we have no water! The last time a hydrant was turned on quite a gallon came out; the water supply and pressure is not at all adequate.'

In the Winter of 1907 Frank accepted an invitation to join the brigade. That term there were three alarms, 'the first due to a tar bucket having caught fire in the quad; but by the time the brigade arrived on the scene the fire was put out.' The other two were 'arranged', one being in the middle of tea: 'All the brigade turned up in very good time, but more damage was done to cups and plates etc., in our hasty exit, than by the fire.'

It was characteristic of Leslie Kent that he introduced a custom whereby a fresh captain was appointed every term and, on completion of his period of office, dropped back into the ranks, taking a position immediately below the squad commanders and ex-captain.

In the same year Leslie Kent was able to launch two other important projects. One, a school magazine, has continued to this day; the other played an important part for some years but eventually faded out. This was 'The Corps', a combination of Boy Scouting, not yet started, and military field manoeuvres. The Chief approved: 'We have always encouraged hobbies. Some need little encouragement, as, for instance, [the] one this Term which took the form of covering all the hills on a Sunday afternoon, and fields and even corridors at all times, with little flags, dipping out messages to watchers at any distance from yards to miles. So far this is the only way in which the new "Corps" (the latest idea to spring, Athene-like, fully armed from the teeming brain of Captain Kent) has been much in evidence.'

The full strength of the Corps was 42 but acted as a company of infantry, divided into half companies and sections, a lieutenant and sergeant commanding each half-company. A member of each section was detailed as a scout and two others as signallers.

The Corps occupied itself with the principles of outposts, skirmishing and the formations preliminary to it, attack and defence, range-finding, map-reading, road-reporting, sketching and plan-making. Kent took as his model a Boer Commando. There was to be a minimum of drill and, as he wrote, no 'machine-like discipline which is sometimes cultivated at the expense of individuality, initiative and self-reliance. In this way we hope that any person after being in the Corps for a year or more will be able to shoot at least reasonably well, will have a knowledge of semaphore, and probably Morse, signalling codes, and a fair knowledge of the elements of national defence; in addition to which he will increase his mental and physical faculties.'

It was the signalling which proved the most popular. In the *Bedales Record*, I find an article, by myself, entitled 'The New Epidemic'. It opens:

Bedales has been suffering for the last two months from strange and insidious diseases. Whooping-cough came first, then measles, and last, but by no means least, a lamentable epidemic of signalling. This disease is easily distinguished by the dotty nature of the victim. The symptoms are to be looked for not on the body of the unfortunate but in his Maths, Latin and English books, whose pages are covered with inscriptions of this kind:

Y O U   A R E A N   A S S
-.--/---/..-/ /.-/.-./ ./ /.-/-./ /.-/.../.../ /

The signalling went on for several years. In July 1909, the results of a cricket match against the village of Horndean, about seven-and-a-half miles away, were transmitted by flag-wagging across the South Downs in two relays. At the fall of each wicket the score was picked up, with the aid of a telescope, by Frank and another and then posted on a blackboard in the Quad.

The Corps continued for two years, taking on more and more from Baden-Powell's *Scouting for Boys* (published in 1908).

In the spring of 1909 the leadership passed out of Leslie Kent's hands and a patrol of Baden-Powell Boy Scouts was started under the able scoutmastership of Mr Powell.

The different attitudes towards arms and war to be found at this school were, to some extent, reflected in the country as a whole. There were, for instance, the pacifists and international socialists. Many others were liberal-minded, politically aware, and watching events. Bedales in 1907 had its Fabian Society. As for Frank and myself, at that time, we never believed in the possibility of a European War. We had heard 'Wolf! Wolf!' so often at home that we rejected all warnings. They were associated in our minds with authority. Some of us thought that the whole idea of defence was slightly ridiculous. Laurence Collier marked the dissolution of the Corps by a 25-line composition beginning:

> The end of the Corps is a fact we deplorps.
> That great institution was much to the forps.
> Its members were "brorps" and every one worps
> The most bellicose aspect that ever you sorps.
> Of signalling lorps they'd a wonderful storps;
> They'd send you a message in smart semaphorps
> Or Morpsse. And they swore all invaders to florps,
> And, perhaps with the aid of the new Territorps-
> lal Army, to scorps a success in the worps
> That is said to be coming (see *Daily Mail* orps
> An Englishman's Home, not by Gorpsge Bernard Shorps
> Whose plays I adorps, but by Major Du Morps-
> -Ier—son, I believe, of the man who could drorps).

Captain Du Maurier's play about a German invasion (referred to in the previous chapter) must have encouraged recruiting for the then newly-formed Territorial Army. As I have said, it certainly influenced our cousin Jack Best. He enlisted in 1909 and it was through him that Frank took a commission in 1914. But the humorists could not leave the piece alone. It was to have been one of the 'Potted Plays' produced by The Follies—an inspired concert party of individualists under the leadership of the burlesque producer, H.G. Pelissier. The parody was never performed, however, for it was banned by the censor.

Oswald Powell, the second master, saw the approaching danger. An article by him in the *Bedales Record* (1908/9, page 11) has now a certain historical interest. In it, he describes the Scout Movement for the benefit of those 'whose curiosity or amusement may have been aroused by P.G. Wodehouse's *The Swoop! or How Clarence Saved England ...*' He adds: '*Scouting for Boys* owes its origin to the shock produced on thinking men by the spectacle, at the time of the South African War, of our unpreparedness as a nation, and of the greenness and general incapacity of our officers and men, compared with the common-sense and resourcefulness of the colonial troops. Some people hold that no system of education is complete that does not provide periods in which the learners are sent to a desert island to fend for themselves.'

Leslie Kent's third achievement was the foundation of the *Bedales Chronicle* in 1907. The school's official publication was the *Bedales Record*, which appeared annually. In 1901 an attempt was made to produce an alternative monthly magazine that was duplicated on a 'jelly graph'. It only ran for two numbers. Other half-hearted hand-written or duplicated news sheets appeared thereafter from time to time but quickly failed. Leslie Kent's publication was different. It required great determination and organising ability for it was reasonably well printed and, at first, came out every three weeks. He also contrived to make it pay. The second number included 'A Word of Welcome' in which the Headmaster suggested that these 'self-sown and "unofficial" activities' were signs of 'a healthy life within'. 'Some have feared,' he wrote, 'that they must absorb energies better given to examination subjects. For my part, I do not share the fear, for I believe that it is almost always true that the more one does, the more one is able to do, and the more one follows up one's self-chosen pursuits, the more one learns the need and the value of the other kinds of knowledge and of effort.'

Frank later became closely connected with the *Chronicle*, first as a frequent contributor and eventually as sub-editor. In 1911 he introduced illustrations.

The programme cover of Bedales' end-of-term school play, Christmas 1903.

When Bedales was founded, people entertained themselves in their own homes much more than today. One early recollection is of a recitation by Frank and me (disguised in false beards) of a topical poem written by Mother. Thereafter followed, year by year, a series of sketches, drawing-room comedies, humorous songs and so forth. Most were written by members of the family.

Drama and entertainment also played an important part in the life of the school. Acting is reputed to be 'of immense educational value' and once a year it was customary for the headmaster to produce a play to which parents and local people would be invited. At the end of our fourth term it was *A Midsummer Night's Dream*. Frank and I were allotted parts as fairies, Frank and the smaller boys dancing round in a circle, whereas I was placed discreetly behind Titania's bower, on account of my long thin legs. It so happened that this was also the play chosen at the end of Frank's last term, when he doubled the parts of Peter Quince and Egeus. Between these two productions the following plays appeared: *Alcestis*, *Antigone*, *Coriolanus*, *Twelfth Night*, *The Merchant of Venice* and *Henry IV*. It seems obvious to us now that more can be learned about classical drama by taking part in a production than by swotting up passages for an exam. It did not appear thus, however, to many teachers at that time.

But the medium that seemed made for Frank's particular gifts was the school variety show; it went by the rather forbidding name of Merry Evening. Like the Greeks, according to John Badley, we loved to parody everything in heaven and earth, including the tragedies. Merry Evening was also a vehicle for criticising authority. Intense and varied were the pungent comments, presented to an uproarious and delighted audience, not only on plays, but on those who were accustomed to give orders. During our first few years Frank and I were the enthusiastic spectators of one brilliant burlesque after another.

A Wellsian fantasy stands out in my memory. A certain Mr Poltebright is taken back in time and, during his absence, his house is sold and the laboratory turned into a dining room. Shortly before Mr Poltebright is due to return, the purchaser sits down to a meal but on lifting the dish cover, 'lo! instead of cutlets, Mr Poltebright's head is discovered in the dish'. After exactly so many weeks, hours and minutes he has returned to his point of departure. The scientist and the table then have to be carried out into the yard; there are sounds of sawing and he re-appears with a 'sort of stratum of wood and china round his neck'.

It was an age of outstanding Bedalian eccentrics. Pauley Montague, joint author, with Laurence Collier, of *Mr Poltebright's Discovery* and other farces, was attracted by the portrayal of inanity in its various forms. His acting as Sir Andrew Aguecheek was irresistible. He wrote a play called *The Grand Lunar* largely in order to give himself scope to act as an escaped lunatic. Laurence Collier wrote the words for some songs, one of which started:

> When I became a lunatic it didn't occur to me
> How frolicsome a personage a lunatic might be,
> But recently I've come to think entirely differentlee –
> Oh a jovial sort of lunatic am I.[15]

Our acting at that time tended to be what would now be called hammy. Pauley Montague certainly never under-acted. His eyes and eyebrows suggested Holbein's portraits of Henry VIII. He would roll them, gesticulate, making his voice crack and perform tricks, piling one absurdity on another. For this he had much scope in a play written by W. Bridges Adams, a farcical version of A.W. Hornung's gentleman cracksman, Raffles, who, according to the report, 'finally run to earth ... distracts the attention of his pursuers by springing a mine, and makes good his escape ... in a donkey-cart, driving his accomplice, the Hon. Jasper Tranmere, between the shafts disguised as a donkey. To the study of this character P.D. Montague brought just the necessary touch of imbecility.'

The plays written and produced by W. Bridges Adams, later a director of the Shakespeare Memorial Theatre, were marked by a professional finish, or so it seemed to us at the time. In his burlesque of Arthur Conan Doyle's *The Speckled Band* he himself took the part of the great detective Sherlock Holmes, acquiring

---

[15] The idea of lunacy was central to British comedy in the twentieth century. The London Palladium ran a comedy show called *Crazy Week* in 1931, and its leading performers called themselves the *Crazy Gang* from 1937. The first series of the BBC's comedy radio show *The Goon Show* in 1951 was titled *Crazy People*.

an aquiline profile, very simply, by sticking a cone of paper on to his own, not very pointed, nose. There was much bogus melodrama, incidental music, limelight (the school magic lantern), and blood-curdling noises off. If I remember aright, instead of the hissing snake in the original, the villain threatened his victim with a soda-water syphon.

In a school fancy-dress ball (Spring 1909) the reporter notes: 'As to what one may term the grotesque characters Best II deserves first mention, with his legs as thermometers, his head registering the wind velocity and his chest resplendent with a barometer of an original type. With him we must not forget the inevitable Wills, this time as a pet monkey, and the fancy dances were enlightened greatly by his acrobatic feats.'

Of all the eccentrics of Frank's time, Mooner Wills stands out in my memory as the most engaging. He always seemed to be mooning around in a trance-like condition. His voice was so soft as to be at times almost inaudible. His manner, too, was gentle. His imitation of a monkey, based on close and accurate observation, was a mild-mannered monkey. He would also imitate a new boy, told by his parents to 'stand up for himself', meeting some aggressive challenger. Taking up what the poor boy imagined to be a pugilistic posture he would half close his eyes, turn his head away and whisper 'I'm not afraid of you, so there!', all the time contorting his face to show extreme apprehension. Mooner's drawings and caricatures had a Max Beerbohm quality. He could make excellent shadow-graphs and accompany them with a sound-track greatly helped by a near-ventriloquial gift.

Some of his most imaginative turns took place in the dormitory after the lights had been turned out. One of them started with an imaginary conversation supposedly taking place on Mrs Badley's birthday, as her husband handed over his birthday present—a powerful motor-bicycle—and insisted on an immediate trial run. It was all very real and convincing. The voices were unmistakable—the gentle expressions of alarm, mingled with gratitude, answered by the well-known staccato phrases and slightly *voilé* voice of the Chief. Presently, protesting slightly, Mrs Badley was placed firmly on the machine, the engine started up and the whole set in motion by a firm push. After rapid acceleration one heard the receding noise of the motor as Mrs Badley disappeared down the drive. In those days it was possible to make a circuit of about a mile, returning by another drive, and after an incredibly short time one heard the crescendo of the approaching engine, obviously rotating at great speed, Mrs Badley's cries for help mingled with the Chief's exhortations and advice. This sequence, lap after lap, would then be repeated until the noise generally brought down the firm hand of authority.

During the period covered by this chapter I can find no published report of Frank's taking part in any Merry Evenings, except in a piano duet with myself which served as an overture, or incidental music, to one of the burlesque plays.

In 1907 Frank and I found ourselves in the same dormitory, I being then the dormitory boss, and it was from him that I heard first about the Wright Brothers. The Wright Brothers had made the first powered flight in history about three-and-a-half years previously. Many people were then doubtful about the authenticity of their claims and this was the attitude of a contributor to the *Bedales Chronicle* in November of that year. He held that 'they have always kept their performances so secret that one cannot know whether to believe them or not.' The facts, however, were exactly the opposite. How the American press, with the world's greatest news story on its doorstep, failed to realise what had happened on December 1903 can only be mentioned here.

During the period prior to and covered by the model aeroplane competitions at Bedales (1907-09) an equally surprising blindness seems to have been prevalent throughout Europe. The physicists had all the clues necessary for the achievement of practical powered flight but, according to the aviation historian C.H. Gibbs-Smith, 'Despite the presence of able engineers among them, not a single man—let alone a team—got down calmly to the problems involved, and conducted systematic research and development, as the Wrights had done. And so, for five tedious years, the Europeans blundered gropingly across the field of aviation ... It was not until November 1907 that any European aeroplane could stay in the air for a single minute.'

The same groping and lack of sound principles were, of course, implicit in the models entered for the first Bedales competition in December 1907. The conditions were as follows: The flights were to be made from the upper corridor of the quadrangle (i.e. from a height of about 18 feet); the distances were to be 'measured by means of a line taken from the place of alighting, at right angles to the lower corridor.' This, it was claimed, gave an advantage to properly controlled machines. 'Instead of a limit to size, no "shove off" of any kind was allowed, so that large and small aeroplanes would have the same chances.' Among the ten entrants was Frank, partnered by Vyv Trubshawe.

Some weeks later the *Chronicle* recorded that aeroplanes were beginning to appear, as the time for the competition drew near: 'The designs ... are many and varied. Some of the machines may be seen giving excellent gymnastical performances in the quad. Why are there not any prizes for the most skilled gymnastoplanes? One aeroplane was seen to do an excellent back somersault the other day. Some constructors seem to be somewhat surprised to find that their machines go better backwards or even upside down.'

The competition took place on December 8th. The largest model was a bi-plane tractor, wing-span 4 ft, the propeller being a foot in diameter. There was no rudder. Two machines were entered by a lad called Jack Gotch, whose squadron was stationed on an aerodrome that Frank would later be stationed on.

The winning machine 'consisted of two triangular wings set at a slight angle, with a horizontal plane between, the front half moving on a pivot so as to form a horizontal steering plane. Underneath there was a curved keel in the front and a rudder at the back.' It was a 'pusher' driven by twisted elastic. The distance flown (twice) was 23 yards.

Frank's machine flew eight yards. It was 'constructed on the box-kite principle', span: 3 ft 9 ins, length 1 ft. 'As the length was so short, twisted elastic could not be used, but instead the propeller was rotated by eight feet of elastic, which passed over pulleys, and was fixed at the back. The elastic stretched itself round a drum connected to the propeller shaft. There was a horizontal steering plane in the front, but no vertical rudder.'

From a later article we learn that 'The idea of Best's aeroplane didn't get a fair trial, because the bearings, etc, were not quite finished.' The writer criticised the design of most models for not paying enough attention to the angle of glide (which he called 'drift'). Instead, competitors apparently wished to make their machines soar, with the result that they fell backwards.

This criticism of the model aeroplanes has an important bearing on Frank's subsequent flying adventures and indeed on powered flight generally; for, whereas the model makers of that period were neglecting to design their aeroplanes so that they would hold a steady course, like a well-folded paper dart, the European pioneers were paying too much attention to this quality (which is known as inherent stability), instead of incorporating devices, such as ailerons or wing warping, to give lateral control. To quote Gibbs-Smith once again: 'From the start, the Wrights firmly eschewed all ideas of inherent stability, and their aeroplanes could only be kept flying by the pilot's skill. This was in direct contradistinction to previous experimenters: "We resolved", wrote Wilbur, "to try a fundamentally different principle. We would arrange the machine so that it would not tend to right itself."'

It was easy to see why, during the first years of the war, the Royal Flying Corps Command should have assumed that unstable machines would be the most suitable for instructional purposes. It was only towards the end of the war that elementary flying started using machines which tended to right themselves in whatever position they were put.

On August 8, 1908, the year following the model aeroplane competition, 'The revelation was vouchsafed to us Europeans after our five years in the wilderness,' added Gibbs-Smith 'for on that day Wilbur Wright first flew in public. One thing and one thing only reduced the excited spectators to tears. It was simply the spectacle of a man flying as God clearly intended that he should: banking, turning and circling, all with such ease and grace that it seemed to the spectators more like a horse and rider in the sky than a man in a mechanical flying machine.'

In November 1909 there was an article in the *Chronicle* by an old Bedalian, then a Sandhurst cadet, describing a flight of Cody's aeroplane, after he, the O.B.C., had ridden over to Farnborough eight or nine times. 'His usual height for a spin [spin in the sense of an outing, not a twirl, as the word later came to be used] is about twenty feet, but for longer flights he rises to sixty feet or more.' The writer gives a full account of the construction of the machine.

In December of that year a second model aeroplane competition took place. A comparison between reports of the first and second shows the same rapid progress as in aviation generally. Between them there had been a good deal of scrappy experimentation in gliding. This took the form of 'making paper model aeroplanes, dropping them from the upper corridor, letting them glide to the ground, and then leaving them there to litter the quad'. A competition was therefore organised with the primary object of giving the inventors something more to think about. The rules were such as to exclude gliders, the plane surface was to be limited to four square feet and, instead of from a height of 18 ft, models were to be launched from ground floor level, but a 'flying start [was to] be allowed'.

It was reported that the models showed 'an immense advance in Bedales aviation to have taken place since our last aeroplane meeting. Though the machines are only to be started from 7 ft above the ground the quad will obviously be too short; several machines have flown the length of the quad and one has risen nearly to the height of the top of the fives court walls in that length. This, of course, is not to be wondered at when we consider the vast amount of good practical and theoretical information that can now be obtained on the subject, which rather robs aeroplanes of originality, and does not tend to bring out inventive genius. The predominant type of machine [is] a monoplane, consisting of a long shaft, which is supported by two planes, a small one in front and a large one behind. The propeller is turned by a length of strong elastic stretched along the shaft.'

Some of the wings appear to have been made from thin laminae of wood, bent over a block to the required camber, whereas Frank and Vyv Trubshawe used tracing linen stretched over a wooden frame. This would later become flabby, so that, before flying, they had to place their model on the hot water pipes. Their plane was considered by the reporter (myself) to be 'original in the "V" shape set of the planes, which gave it great lateral stability'. Once again Frank had bad luck. 'They broke their propeller at the last minute, and the substitute did not give sufficient forward thrust.'

A striking-looking model was made by Mooner Wills. It had 'two large tissue-paper wings of somewhat bird-like appearance; in front [was] a small elevating plane. The machine,' I reported, 'is a very good glider, but it does not rise to very great heights.' The winner 'flew the length of the quad., hitting the back wall about 4 ft high'.

In its sixth year the school had become co-educational. A start was made by admitting four girls. Four years later, during our first term, the number was increased to 12, out of a total of 94. When Frank left in 1911 the school had grown to 168 and the girls numbered 60.

During our first four or five years at Bedales, Frank and I were quite ignorant of the reproductory processes or indeed that the sexual act existed at all, Mother and Father having made their exposition obscure by references to plants, pollen, bees and what not. When I was about fourteen-and-a-half a boy who was a year older than me explained to me, in simple but colloquial language, exactly what happened. Soon afterwards, puberty and elder-brotherhood created a barrier between Frank and me, so how and when did Frank acquire this important biological information? A clue has been suggested by a friend. There was an episode during an epidemic of influenza. Frank and I were both in the sick-bay, or sanatorium, when my talk became candid and highly coloured. I can vaguely remember the occasion: a high temperature, like alcohol, may have lowered my inhibitions. Frank appears to have been shocked, but possibly enlightened.

At this co-educational school a 'healthy' attitude towards sex was encouraged, an attitude which today would often appear laughable or priggish. But these standards were common to most schools and institutions of the Victorian and Edwardian era. The prudery, no doubt, resulted in some guilt-ridden and unhappy marriages. It is difficult for those who have not lived through these times to understand the beneficent effect of Marie Stopes, whose teaching was summed up in the words of a German Music Hall song of 1911, 'Sie haben es gern wie die Männer' (They like it as much as men).

During our time, a marked change took place in the relationship between the girls and boys, the boys having, at first, kept to themselves and talked about 'beastly she-males'. But around 1906–7 things seemed to loosen up, though sublimation and suppression was still the official policy of the Establishment. Flirtatious conduct was discouraged but nevertheless couples began to be seen continually in each other's company. Many of these sentimental attachments were on a rarefied and romantic plane. Others, however, came down closer to earth. More and more, sexy talk, among the boys at any rate, became accepted as human and in no wise as a falling away from ethical standards. And yet the *pudeur Bedalienne* [Bedalian decency] gave even the smut an innocent style of its own.

Years later, replying to my suggestion that there was a humorous or gay aspect of sex and love, John Badley wrote that he was 'no upholder of any ideal of "purity" [a word he detested] which would refuse a place for natural impulses and withdraw one side of life from the play of humour ... You have been more fortunate than I was if you have never been sickened by the kind of talk that was rampant at Rugby in my time, which took for granted there was no possible kind of love that was not mere sensual gratification and that girls existed only to provide such gratification, no other common meeting-ground being thinkable. It's the attitude of mind behind the talk that matters, not the words used.'

The girls' costumes were not designed to make them particularly attractive. Except for games and gymnastics, when the gym tunic was much as it is in schools to-day, they wore a one piece sack-like garment, called a Jibbah, derived from Arabian peasant costume. Around the shoulders was an embroidered yoke.

Like the boys, they were promoted to prefectdom. They sat with us at meals (except for breakfast) and shared our class and free-time work. They had their own games of hockey, lacrosse and cricket. Two of them, however, were so good at cricket that they sometimes played for the boys' 1st XI, to the astonishment of the visiting side.

The girls slept and took breakfast in a separate house, but I know of at least one adventurous maiden being encouraged to leave it, during the night, by means of a ladder. I am convinced that the erotic encounter that followed never went beyond kissing and cuddling, mingled, no doubt, with the typical Bedalian philosophical and intellectual exchanges.

Frank was never shy in the presence of girls or women. He had an easy way with him. Towards the end of his school years he became particularly friendly with an attractive girl called Sylvia Mundy. He and another boy spent a holiday with the Mundys at Criccieth. She was invited to my 21st birthday dance and was Frank's partner at supper. This friendship persisted during the War.

In the broadest sense Father was deeply religious. His connection with Nelson Street Adult School, of which he was president, led him to give much thought to 'values in which religion, philosophy, science, with manufacturing and commercial practice, were all curiously mixed. The results are recorded in the collection of notes for his Bible classes. Never in all these writings or, for that matter, in the practice of his life, did he try to separate religious or other values from those which went with his work. For him they were inextricably associated.' During holidays we would often accompany him to Nelson Street on Sunday mornings and, on leaving Bedales, Frank took an active part in the work as a class teacher or leader. Home from war service, he never failed to attend.

Mother was equally sincere in her religion. In spite of her gift for caricature, she was never cynical about Christian teaching, which she sought to impart to us as children. In this, as in many other fundamental matters, our parents understood each other perfectly. Speaking the same language, they tried to pass on to us their values and beliefs without a trace of dogma, though Mother, perhaps more than Father, believed in regular attendance at some place of organised worship. At first both had attended the Hamstead Road Baptist Church. One day, however, Father, tired by his Adult School work, which had started at 7.30, found that he had slept through the sermon. Henceforward he concentrated on the Early Morning School, though Mother continued as a member of the Baptist Church congregation.

For some reason Mother insisted on Frank and me participating in the Anglican Service at Petersfield Church, in addition to the broad service at the school in the evening. Our parents agreed with the Chief that the essence of religion lay in an attitude of mind towards life and its problems. It was implicit in the school life and explicit in John Badley's many writings. There was no chaplain or chapel and the service was held in the Hall that was used for all occasions of assembly. The service started with music, then came prayers—'not in the form of requests for favours or petitions to a higher power but rather expressions of aims that we desire to keep before ourselves and means of gaining clearer vision and strengthening resolution'. This was followed by a reading, hymns, and an address given by a member of the staff or by someone from outside the school. Another hymn and prayer ended the service, after which the staff lined up and shook hands with every member of the school as he or she filed out. The proceedings lasted about an hour.

Every weekday evening finished with 'Prayers'—a much shorter service—consisting of a reading from the Bible, a hymn or psalm and a prayer. 'We have to see to it, then,' wrote John Badley, 'that our weekday teaching, and still more our weekday practice, does not run counter to the ideals that are associated with religion.' Father and Mother agreed.

Chapter 3
From behind the front line

Starting at the rate of five a week but becoming less frequent later, Frank sent home over a hundred letters and postcards during his first term of service overseas. Many of them ran into six- or seven-hundred words. They are humorous and warm in tone, giving the impression of an explosive urge to record the astonishing and rich impressions that he was receiving, together with what for him was yet another manifestation of the Good Life—for in spite of the grim events taking place within a few miles of where they were stationed, he was obviously keenly interested in his job and enjoying himself. Mingled with his observations are frequent references to such things as football boots, cereals, jam and chocolate, which suggests schooldays and dormitory feasts. Military life in France at that time took place within an aura of eating possibilities. There was indeed a hierarchy of catering in which the A.S.C. occupied a fairly high position—probably next below the R.F.C. Frank describes fully his efforts at good housekeeping and the devices for keeping the flies, drains and ventilation under control. To interest Father he made detailed sketches—often of incinerators and ovens, carefully designed to make maximum use of natural draughts.

All communications were supposed to be censored. In carrying out this duty Frank was very soon introduced to strange figures of speech, peculiar to the class-structure of that period. These he described to our parents with some surprise:

> 15 March. Altho' you have both a good experience of working chaps' letters, I have never before noticed to such an extent their standardised forms of incongruity. Perhaps some of them are a bit shy of the censor; anyway, they rarely put 'with love' at the end, even to wives or parents: it's usually 'I am, etc.' or just 'Yrs'.

He goes on to contrast this formal address with the sweethearts' practice of prefacing each sentence with 'and dear —', so that it was difficult to know which was the first page. Much space, he found, was taken up with explaining what they were not allowed to say, the same phrase being repeated about six times, with slight alterations, finishing with 'that's about all.' He also noticed certain standard phrases, such as 'hope it finds you in the pink as it leaves me at present' and 'I take pleasure in replying to your kind letter.'

(Jack Best was very amused by Frank's letters and always wondered what he had got to say. He said he was glad he did not have to read them through, although sometimes his signature as Frank's censor was seen on the outside of the envelope.)

Frank's first letter home, dated March 7, was from Nordpeene, a small village near Cassell where they had detrained after a twenty-two hour journey. It was some 150 miles from Le Havre, their port of entry. Frank starts by describing their crossing from Southampton:

> The sea was absolutely calm, no boat could even get past where we came. I counted 14 searchlights feeling aimlessly for aircraft. These never swept the water, which was raked by as many horizontal ones. A more gorgeous sight you could not imagine. The special codes of coloured lights and signals, the still water and the misty land disappearing gradually into the haze, all helped to form a curious compendium of artificial and natural beauty while we were gliding down the Solent. The water looked a dazzling blue-green in the zone of light. Further south a couple of destroyers escorted us—

priceless little black streaks ploughing along in the dull light—which made us feel very secure All sorts of signals made it quite stagy. I picked out an out lights Morse message from one.

I never felt so thoroughly at home and casual on landing this side—quite different from the usual *Wanderjahr* sensation—I suppose principally on account of all my English friends on board, who had never been to France before. A sudden inspiration occurred to Don and me, namely that we were performing what we had seen for years and years at Hamilton's Panorama, viz Troopship leaving Southampton (plus little lighthouse, etc).

Talk about horses scragging—they had to go up a gangway at 45 degrees then along, then down one even steeper, and having got the beasts started, the chaps bunked on ahead with the rope, while hoofs and a snorting mass of heavy-draught tonnage scrambled and leapt in the wake. I am very glad for the sake of man and beast that it was such a calm crossing.

We anchored among several other vessels of the same capacity and destination outside the harbour—French and English destroyers flitting around all the time. The Pilot then led us in.

We took a short time to land and proceeded to a large shed at the side of the line (one and a half miles from the dock). We were joined later by other masses; I slept on a pile of horse rugs (and kept warmer than most thereby) in the midst of these horses. I found sleeping cap and cushions very useful. Every time the horses below kicked—and this appears to be the army horse's chief aim in life—my tower would quake.

Early morning (6th March) we were all traipsed off in convoy to the loading deck. During the wait for departure I went behind the counter of one of the numerous English coffee stalls provided on station and helped the good woman to get a bustle on for the men who had formed a queue to the coastline waiting for a spot o' summat warm to drink.

Saturday 6th March needs little description. The four corners of a first-class compartment were occupied by Jack, Don, the vet and F.B.B. (me), who ate and slept principally between the halts. The trucks in the rear stretched for 200 yards at least and betrayed dangling khaki legs from each. At one place we shunted off a truck with its back half kicked away by a playful gee-gee.

Here in Nordpeene, we are quite up country—none of your staying at base for months business—at a very decent farmhouse. I am jolly thankful for my stay at Paris. Madame and Monsieur very kind to us. We are within sound of the guns.

All very fit indeed. It is wonderful what one can stand. I am surprised they haven't all got pneumonia or something.

Frank's division remained two days at Nordpeene. The wind was 'bitterly cold, though sunny rifts between occasional snow showers'. They 'rode to the village to hear Major-General lecture all officers.' An army aeroplane descended close by and Frank 'found the pilot by chance in a mill and had coffee with him' (8 March).

On Tuesday 9, they got away by 9 a.m. and 'trekked all day with many annoying little traffic blocks'. At 4.30 they arrived at a small village called Borre, near Hazebrouck, 'which the Germans had evacuated in October'.

Frank was beginning to feel the strain:

10 March. I am very glad they have given us a day's rest. I did not feel a bit like pushing on last night. In fact I was a bit feverish after the cold ride, but I have got an A1 comfy bed and plenty of wherewithal for warmth. Today I feel much better. I could hardly walk upstairs yesterday morning, as I was so sore from a fall.

They sent me on to look up a wagon and my old gee-gee was not at all keen on leaving his pals behind. When I got on a little way it jibbed a bit. I tried the game of backing it, as I lost a spur the previous day and had no crop either; but I pulled a little too vigorously and we both toppled over backwards. I was not hurt, though the horse's weight numbed my muscles a bit.

The local people are all frightfully hospitable and if we consented we could drink coffee from morning to eve at every house.

On closer inspection of our village by daylight, we find ourselves in the hum of military life. All day long the motor service up the main road is terrific—armed cars, buses, A.S.C. lorries, swanky landaulettes for generals, and certain scratch English delivery vans.

There are plenty of houses which are riddled with bullet holes and the men have found pieces of shell in the walls of their bedroom. The Germans never got possession of the Town Hall, but were driven off when the English appeared in October. Any open place which is not metalled is ankle deep in mud; it is rather disheartening for the men when the horses, which are picketed out, roll in the mud after they have been groomed with great attention.

They have supplied us with 12 different maps of the country, made to War Office specification. It would fairly make your mouth water if you saw them, knowing your affinity for same.

Have you heard anything from *Punch* about 'The Bells of Berlin'? They ought to have come to some decision by now.

For the next seven-and-a-half months, Jack's company was moving about at a distance of between four and ten miles behind the line, the northernmost post being opposite Ypres, near Poperinghe, and the most southerly about twenty-five miles away, opposite La Bassée and near Béthune. Five of their moves brought them to near the River Lys. The longest sojourns were at Le Seau (twelve weeks) and at Busseboom (ten weeks). Their moves during the period under review (fourteen in all) may be traced on the accompanying map (*see next page*).

The division's third move (i.e. from Borre) brought them to Sailly-sur-Lys, near Bailleul, which they reached on March 11. This was the second day of the battle of Neuve Chapelle, then raging some five miles to the south. Here they were, Frank wrote,

within a few yards of our big guns. They have been belching out hell all day at the rate of six to twelve to the minute (when not at lunch or supper). Also, at least two aeroplanes have been hovering over us all day, and sometimes four. It is very consoling to know we are being so well looked after. (12 March)

The next day he wrote:

There has just been a terrific cannonade going on. Usually we can distinguish each gun, but this afternoon after tea they evidently let fly with such ferocity that it blended into one gigantic thundering rumble. The Germans don't appear to have replied to our heavy artillery at all. (14 March)

Although from time to time Frank refers to shells being dropped in neighbouring villages (25 April and 4 May), they never themselves actually came under shell fire, even though they were amongst the heavy artillery. Aerial reconnaissance was then in its infancy. Frank noted that, on the German side, it

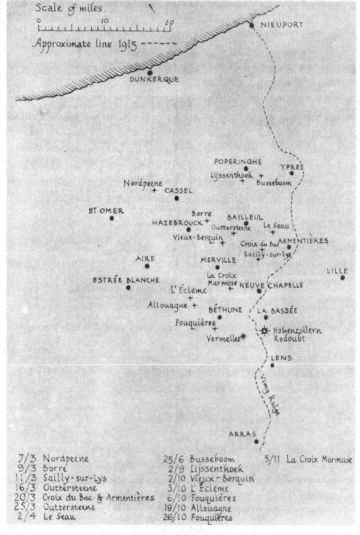

seemed to be limited to one 'sausage' balloon while on ours, provocation was later much limited by shortage of ammunition.

During this, Frank's first term of service in France, at least four major battles took place. These included the assault of Hill 60 (April 17), the first gas attack (April 22), and the Festubert offensive, opposite Lens and Lille, on May 9. In the last two of these engagements, our cousin Douglas Lloyd was involved. The heroic assault on the Hohenzollern Redoubt by the Staffordshire Brigade took place on October 17.

At Sailly-sur-Lys they were making themselves 'thoroughly comfortable and at home'. Frank's cold had left him, the weather was turning much warmer, and they had 'converted an uninhabited part of the cottage attached to the barn into their office and living room'. The routine did not seem over-strenuous. Frank found it hard to remember the date and the day as they 'are all the same to us ... even Sundays and Bank Holidays'. During their six days at this village he wrote home at some length, describing the daily programme of work. Allan Court and Gordon Whittall presided at Refilling Point, usually an estaminet or roadside café; to this spot, 'the motor lorries usually take the stuff from rail-head,' he explained, 'where they dump each brigade's stuff at the side of the road in heaps of hay, meat, groceries, petrol, etc.' Jack's wagons 'come along each morning and the Supply issuers check it off while on-loading.'

This sounds all right on paper, but when you get to the real thing and have to manoeuvre your dozen or so wagons in a narrow lane among, literally, ten or twelve times as many others, it says a lot for the A.S.C. that we do ever get things right at all. As a matter of fact, we got much too little oats for a bit and a sack of salt instead of sugar; otherwise nothing to grumble at.

Generally speaking every small road is a facsimile of its pal half a mile away, and has branches very numerous in every direction except the particular one that one desired. I set out after the convoy yesterday afternoon, found my way on horseback ... with the help of a map. I did not see the others at the rendezvous, so I retraced my hoof prints and rode up other possible branches, finally arriving at my starting point before anyone was found who had seen the others. They had arrived by immensely circuitous roots, being told that the way was blocked. By this time it was quite dark. (14 March)

'Never mind, I thoroughly enjoyed it,' he declared, and in an article for the *Bedales Chronicle* explained that, although they had had no casualties, 'every night our drivers run a certain risk in taking up the requisites for the trenches to the various 'dumps' mostly within a quarter of a mile of the firing line.' He continued:

> Although the Germans cannot actually see our road at night (and all the transport is done at night to avoid shelling) they know exactly where it is, and during the day fix their rifles sighted on special open points such as cross roads, etc. [and then fire] chance shots ... periodically at night. There is far more rifle fire at night as it is safer for them to put their heads above the firing parapet. When these star shells go up (about every two minutes or so) everyone drops flat if exposed, while a volley of lead is poured overhead.

On March 21, after four days at Outterstene, the company was stationed partly at Croix du Bac and partly at Armentières, to which town Frank was sent ahead as billeting officer. He was taken there on top of a 'common-or-garden city bus painted the military grey green all over'. 'It was just like a Cook's Country Drive,' he wrote; they 'went slow enough to see the country all round, which looked gorgeous after a sharp night's frost'. Armentières had been shelled fairly regularly.

> The inhabitants all sleep in the cellars with sand sacks over the cellar windows, so the pavements are lined with sacks of all sorts, in long lines either side of the street.
> The day was simply gorgeous. Bright blue sky and no wind.
> The chief interest of the day is watching aeroplanes, both friendly and alien, being shelled by their opponents. One sees a lot of little white-brown clouds which usually increase in number rapidly to the tune of eight or ten; each looks like a brilliant snowball in the sunshine:

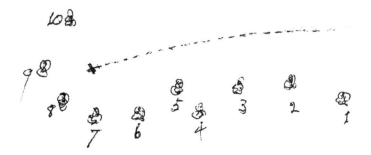

A German Taube flew over as Don and self were taking a couple of wagons into the town. As a rule it is not possible to see the machine that is being aimed at (except with field glasses) but in this case we could see the little 'puff balls' chasing it right overhead. It got away, however; it is frightfully hard to guess the range. (21 March)

Tell the Aunts that the glasses they gave me play an essential role on all these occasions for distinguishing aeroplanes. (9 March)

On 25 March they moved back to Outtersteene, two-and-a-half miles south-west of Bailleul. They were there quartered in the house vacated by Bruce Bairnsfather, the creator of 'Old Bill'. On April 2 they found themselves at Le Seau.

At first, as Frank explained in the article quoted above, the 'division was split up and attached to various units of the regulars for instruction and "polish".' He 'was treated extremely kindly and there was no suggestion of snobbery. The division took up its official position in the line as a complete unit on Good Friday.' The Staffordshire Brigade took over a line of trenches between Ypres and Armentières and on that day Frank 'rode on in front to topping new billet just over Belgian frontier'.

This was Les Deux Nations, an *éstaminet* surrounded by a collection of houses—hardly a village—called Le Seau. Frank enjoyed the ride. He 'could hardly believe it was Good Friday'. It reminded him of 'the last act of *Parsifal*—the misty and soft sunny appearance of the landscape'. For the first time the division had its own company billet and 'own batmen cooking the food'. He was 'pushed into the job of Mess President' and had to see that they got 'about twenty eggs per day and provide a certain amount of variation in the way of vegs ... You bet they'll kick their Mess President if anything goes wrong. (2 April)

The position of Mess President could indeed be precarious. Frank explained later how faddy his brother officers were at times. 'Each one fancies or dislikes whatever the others don't ... and they don't hesitate to shout about it to the President' (30 October). Sometimes, however, they were united in complaining. One unfortunate Mess President, on being asked what was for dinner, replied through clenched teeth and retreating to the wall, 'Sorry you chaps, it's rissoles again.' There were cries of 'We'll give you rissoles, you b....r', while he found himself driven into a corner, with arms raised, to ward off a threatened shower of these spherical objects. Even Jack, who was most restrained, was one day heard to say, 'I'm not complaining, but I'm bloody disappointed.'

'We have got a very decent piano again,' Frank wrote home, 'so send any good old songs or light music such as "You're Here and I'm Here"[16] and *Ragtime Selections* in cheap conglomerated editions, and any of our old songs, particularly Stanford's.' If they stayed there any time they would get to know them all by heart; they were all fairly musical, he explained, and only lacked male voice music. The music was sent. He was requested 'to bang the piano of an evening when we all get together'. Gordon Whittall had a wonderful memory for words and music; he knew most of the musical comedy songs by heart. They stayed at Le Seau nearly three months and, as we shall see, music occupied a great deal of Frank's attention.

Ten days after their arrival they experienced an incident of a sort that has since become, alas, well known to many, for during the night a Zeppelin cruised over their heads and dropped bombs on Bailleul, about three miles away, killing four women and wounding one soldier. Frank 'rode round to have a look'.

---

[16] Composed in 1914 by Jerome Kern (1885–1945).

18 April. They make colossal rabbit holes,' he wrote, 'large enough literally to hide a lorry in. In one place a cottage was completely removed from a long row. It might have been cut away with a razor on either side. One could see into the rooms. Just the outer wall—a minus quantity; but furniture and everything intact inside (glass unbroken).

The days were 'getting very much the same type' as their 'routine settled itself down'. The spring weather was perfect. Each day, as they rode along what was 'really an immense avenue joining up Bailleul and Armentières about eight miles apart', they already noticed a change. 'All the trees are beginning to take on that beautiful yellow effect, when massed on each side, but each separate tree is hardly advanced enough to notice any young leaves on it.' (29 April)

On April 19 'the noble Dickinson' was thrown off Frank's new ride Broncho, a chestnut that would probably be a first-class steeple-chaser if only it were not a roarer, he suggested. Dickinson was bringing the horse round without having first altered Frank's outsize stirrup-lengths and was seen to pass 'the mess window like a flash of lightening'. They 'raced 200 yards or so down the pavée road when its feet slipped from under him in trying to round the corner. The horse rolled on top of him [and] the poor chap was laid up for three days with a badly bruised shoulder.' (4 May)

Frank himself came off the same horse the following day, having lost his stirrups at a little ditch after clearing a jump. 'I could not stop the beggar,' he wrote, 'so I pulled myself onto its neck from the saddle. I can understand Dickinson having no bloody earthly chance sans stirrups. We are both wiser. I still like Broncho (which the General used to ride, by the way) and have ridden several times since. This afternoon it jumped a treat. So that's that.'

The night of April 26 was eventful and marked by a tragi-comic occurrence that was not only reported at length by Frank but formed the subject of a short article in *Punch*—one of a series called 'The Watch Dogs' written by 'Henry', the nom-de-plume of an officer in one of the Staffordshire Batallions. On coming out in the morning Frank was surprised to find 'one of the HD horses[17] lying dead on the ground'. The sergeant informed him that one of their guards had 'fired a couple of rounds during the night, for some unknown reasons. An enquiry followed. It seemed that 'one chap had had a bit more than his share of liquor and had been marched off to the guard-tent for custody.' The guard gave witness as follows:

> I was just a' comin' along and passed the waggins when I sees three suspicious chaps, so I gets behind a tree and says ' 'Alt, who are you?' But they only sloped off. I then loaded and fired to wake the guard, but when I closed the breech the second time it went off by mistake.

He was then asked 'Did you fire into the air or into the ground to give the alarm?' 'Mostly downwards,' he replied. ('We nearly collapsed!' Frank commented.) 'And what did you do then?' he was asked. 'I gave my rifle to the prisoner, who had run up to see what the trouble was. "'Ere Bill," I ses, "for 'Eaven's sake take this gun off me; it keeps going off of its own."' According to Frank, 'It turned out that the chap was in a perfect funk and might easily have hit the three other men on guard, for the prisoner was only being escorted to find his coat on a wagon.'[18]

A few days before the shooting of the horse, the Germans had 'treated the defenders of Ypres to their first experiments in poison-gas. They had indicated their intentions by accusing their enemies of the practice they themselves had in mind; but it came as a ghastly surprise to the French Territorials and British and Canadian Troops along the Yser on 22 April.' On April 25th Frank wrote home: 'I am glad we are holding Hill 60 still.

---

[17] 'Heavy Draft'. Horses were classified according to the thickness of their legs and the density of 'feathers' round their ankles.

[18] This account was pieced together by the author from versions by Frank and Jack Best and from the article by 'Henry' in *Punch* (May 26th 1915, p.405).

While they were shelling up there, the wind happened to be North East and even down here everybody's eyes were sore with poisonous gases.'

Our cousin Douglas Lloyd was serving with the Canadian Division and was involved in meeting the gas attack. 'Wasn't it peculiar,' Frank wrote home, 'when, after a long ride, trying to find Douglas's billets, I should have found him waiting for me in our mess, on returning on 7 May.' He went through the whole thing.

The first thing of note happened suddenly when their Sergeant-Major discovered the Germans advancing on them about 200 yards off. Douglas said that in his platoon they were all sportsmen and about twelve crack shots, so they fairly gave the Germans hell. They kept on advancing about two deep at intervals of 100 yards or so in long lines—close formation—the officers driving them with swords. A little to the left of the trench was a lane, along which the Germans were allowed to advance quite close before we opened a withering fire.

He said the bodies were just piled up in long lines two or three deep, and whenever they saw a wounded German trying to crawl away they always shot him. The Canadians had had their pals so badly handled that they gave no quarter—and one doesn't blame them. He and his pals had strong glasses and could pick them off singly at a distance. He, Douglas, accounted for thirty-eight which he counted singly—this was apart from 200 rounds or so which he blazed into their masses.

About three quarters of his platoon returned and half of them wounded to a varying degree, but they did not leave a single wounded chap behind, for they knew they would never see him again. Our losses were heavy, but Douglas swears that theirs were six to one of ours. He had four days of it—and when the gas came on at first they began to cough and no one could make it out. The second time they could see it rolling on to them in a thick yellow-green low-lying mist, while they were lying behind the hedge. Some stayed there—any who suffered at all from bronchitis died outright—but Douglas gauged his distance, raced forward and dropped exhausted into his own trench. He then tore at the ground, buried his face and with his hands heaped up the earth all round. After half an hour or so, he began to get his strength back and helped to resuscitate the others but he says they all felt so limp that the Boches could have just advanced without the least resistance, if they hadn't been hopelessly unnerved by our rife fire previously.

The Germans eventually got a machine gun mounted behind a hedge close by, but not without enormous loss. After that the Canadians had to keep their heads down.

The dressing stations were crammed to bursting point and under fire as well. One driver succeeded in rushing his motor ambulance through machine-gun fire without either himself or the wounded inside being hurt. Coming back empty the Germans never fired a shot.

Douglas Lloyd's trenches eventually had to be evacuated as they projected beyond our others and were subject to enfilade; but Douglas said they would have still gone on if they had not had orders to retreat.

By mid-May Frank reported that 'Now all our men carry respirators. We see all our Tommies now wearing them on their caps— above the peak, so they can easily be lowered over the nose.'

The gas used by the Germans in this first attack was chlorine but in August, Frank describes what is obviously 'Tear Gas'. They 'got a slight "whiff" of a Boche stink shell,' he wrote, and it reminded him of the amyl acetate, pear-drop aroma in our lacquering department (the Zapon Room) at our father's works. It made the eyes run like anything. Frank asked for 'a pair of motor goggles, of the rubber type with glass' and suggested they could be tested 'by holding your breath for a few seconds in Zaponny atmosphere and see whether it makes the eyes run' (19 August). He did not realise, of course, that tear gas only smelt like amyl acetate, the solvent in Zapon lacquer, and did not have the same irritant properties.

He seemed satisfied with the effectiveness of the goggles:

8 September. I am quite alright with goggles now ... the idea is that they would be of most use when the gas is sufficiently diluted to make the eyes run, but not when it smelt badly, which is often the case. Of course if it were strong the smoke helmet would be put on immediately.

He was also to hear at first hand of an early form of Flammenwerfer (flamethrower):

> 2 August. The other night the Boches caused terrible havoc to the men on the left of our division by spraying burning vitriol and tar into the trenches. Although there were very few left to get back safely we retook the trenches they gained, on the following day …
>
> I was talking to a typical Tommy last night … who had seen the trenches on his left in flames leaping up like a factory fire. He remarked, 'But if the Germans would only play the game fair and square, we should soon lick them.'
>
> I think this absolutely hits off the British spirit. You don't wonder at our chaps being sick if we don't use all the means that they do.

Although within only a few miles of the front line, life at Le Seau went smoothly enough and, for Frank at any rate, it was not without a certain charm. 'The country is transformed during the last fortnight into summer scenery,' he wrote. '… The frogs make a terrific row. I did not realise, in the role of mock Hercules at Bedales (in the *Aristophanes* farce) that I should find them making such a brekky-ki-keks coax in reality' (13 June). He was alive to the beautiful sky-scrapes above the flat Flemish countryside and described them in his letters home: 'Wonderful sunset—sky a perfect blue green, just a few pink-splashed clouds westward and an extraordinary purply-brown smoke cloud effect blowing south-east from Ypres way' (10 May).

The nightly convoy to the line was carried out without casualties. During the afternoon Frank and his colleagues generally retired for a siesta, after which there would be some sporting event, such as a football or cricket match, or perhaps a little music, with philosophical discussions after dinner. As described in his letters, the atmosphere vaguely suggests a military version of the Bedalian 'good life', with its rural pursuits and hygiene, such as the construction of an oven or a carefully designed and highly efficient incinerator. It was here that his elevations, plans and sections became most detailed and informative. Father received them with the greatest interest.

They reminded him of the equipment he had designed for the foundry furnaces and ventilation.

In accordance with Frank's requests, sheet music was sent out from home and every evening they had their bit of fun. 'My education in rag-time has been neglected,' he wrote, 'but already I am improving, they tell me.' (9 April)

He continued to keep in touch with *Punch* and to make suggestions in his letters home for getting his song, 'The Bells of Berlin', published. 'It's not hard to play and a child can sing it,' he wrote. 'Whether it's what's wanted remains to be seen. They may be inundated with similar efforts.' (14 May)

The sheet music was, he said, 'a great source of pleasure' and 'the piano is very good, considering. I have plenty of practice at sight-reading. You could not have found a happier selection to start with. The other chaps here are very good, but I do not practise much while they are in the room. I generally practise in the morning after early stables.'

He enjoyed the concerts by the Staffs Brass Band on their ground. '[They] gave us two very enjoyable evenings. In each case the beautiful summer evenings in the green hay made us almost forget the war. One becomes almost numb to the irregular boom of the guns, the rattle of musketry and machine guns, together with the "blue-bottle-through-a-megaphone-purr" of the machines overhead.' (29 May)

Almost every post brought news to our parents of his enthusiasm for the music. It was 'a veritable blessing'. He was 'really practising a bit seriously'. It was 'such a relief to have something really beautiful to go at from time to time'. It was 'fortunate that the mess are all so tolerant'. 'The music was top-hole,' and he was 'so glad that they all appreciate Chopin's A-flat Ballad in the mess', 'although it was 'too hard to play *à la* concert platform'. (3 June, 5 June)

On June 10 we find the first mention of Thelwall's correspondence course in piano sight-reading, which Frank was to study regularly for the next three months. He was 'awfully pleased' that it was 'possible to pick up a few wrinkles' even out there. The principle was to 'fix one note in the mind's eye by one figure only, no matter what the expression for it on paper'. He thought it was 'a brain wheeze of abnormal proportions'. Although there were at least twelve to fifteen hours' work in the week's exercise, Frank found it 'very interesting and quite a relief'. (15 June)

His musical reputation spread and he was brought into touch with people of like taste. One was Lieutenant Whitehead of the 38th Battery Ammunition Column. On May 12 they 'had a marvellous evening', Whitehead giving them 'a heavenly programme of songs, etc.' He was extremely affable and could play, whistle, sing and compose. Frank was delighted to hear some old favourites which the Towles had sung at Pwhelli, including 'The Night That The Old Cow Died' and 'Hush-a-Bye Baby'. He also gave 'all sorts of marvellous selections from operas, like *Faust*, etc.' Frank was 'so thrilled' that he 'felt different since'.

He had been introduced to Whitehead by their interpreter, Jean Dupont (known as 'Pont') who, since they were serving in Belgium, was a Belgian. He had been studying for the priesthood but his affaires with girls, as he explained, were all part of his clerical training, for he submitted himself to these adventures in order to acquire experience of sin.

Pont's English was sometimes original and laced with adaptations of French colloquialisms, mixed with what he imagined was popular English slang. For instance, on tasting some delicacy which pleased him, he was heard to murmur, ' 'Eet is like an angel —ing in ze mouth.' On another occasion his brother officers suggested that after the war, Belgium would probably be 'absorbed' into the British Empire: they had read all about it in the *Daily Mail* and besides, they explained, 'You don't suppose we should expend all these men and munitions if we weren't going to get something out of it at the end, do you?' 'Do not sp-e-e-ak of it,' protested poor Pont. 'You hurt me. I s—t your *Daily Mail*.'

Frank and Pont became friendly and would sometimes share the same billet or bivouac. Pont was not only accepted at the time as a member of this closely knit group but was remembered years afterwards with friendly feeling.[19]

Sporting activities were frequent and varied, not only football and cricket but 'regimental sports'. 'The greasy pole over the corner of a muddy pond afforded great mirth', the competitors being dressed in 'the regulation A.S.C. swimming costume of honest pants. The entire population of the village formed up round the water to spectate.' Continuing his report, he wrote home:

> The most shouting event of all, however, was the band race. Here all the players were formed up at the starting point with their instruments, and handicapped accordingly; thus, triangle and cymbals started at scratch, tuba well forward, etc. The Conductor started them all playing 'Come Lassies and Lads'—the Staffs 'March Past'—and instructed them to continue until I dropped my stick. I let them play on for at least fifteen bars or so, and on dropping the stick at an unexpected moment, the whole mass moved forward while the harmony groaned and slid all over the scale. I was doubled up with laughing at this point, but learnt that the tenor trombone overhauled the big drum in the last five yards! Everyone thoroughly enjoyed it. (29 April)

Football continued into June. 'After practising piano, rode over the Headquarters Company for footer match. We won 3–2. Very fast game.' (6 June)

By the end of the month the football season was over and they had moved their quarters to Busseboom. 'It is ripping in the evening—we play cricket nearly always and then, as we sit at supper, we look over the water and listen to the gramophone.' (30 June). 'Wrote music exercises during morning. Played cricket against No.2 Company. Draw in our favour and by some fluke made immense score of 28!' (20 July)

Frank's practical interest in aviation, which went back to the

---

[19] Later, when the Company moved across the border into France, Dupont was replaced by a French interpreter, Armand Marlier.

Bedales model aeroplane competitions, must have been powerfully stimulated by what he saw going on around him. He felt that his present job was 'better than being in a beastly trench'. The way his mind was working, however, is clear from the following extract from a letter written home shortly after landing in France. 'If there was any other alternative, I should choose the Royal Flying Corps. I had a long talk with a pilot, at our last place, whose machine descended quite close. He had been over the German lines every day for six months regularly. He let me get up into the machine while a new tyre was being put on. It fairly made my mouth water—but that's another tale. I am A.S.C. now.' (14 March)

His eager, optimistic, and observant approach to flying comes through in many of his letters. 'The aero section is very much on its game every day, and the machines sail over our lines for their evening promenade over the Germans. After having had about twenty shells fired at them, they return as fit as ever.' (17 April)

In the mess, lengthy discussions on the theory of flight took place. Gordon ('Dad') Whittall loved an argument and would go to some lengths in order to establish his point. (In a phrase that has often been repeated, one of his brother officers, speaking through clenched teeth, his lower jaw projecting, commented, 'You're a bugger to argue, Dad, you never give in!') Frank could be persistent too, and in this case wrote home for references (such as Sir Hiram Maxim's book on artificial flight) to support his thesis that a bird or glider can mount in a rising wind without self-propelling. 'What I should really like,' he wrote, 'would be an account of the Wright Brothers, if they say they ever glided upwards—and I feel sure I remember it. You remember the seagulls at Llandudno, don't you?' (2 May)

During early June he was obviously working towards the decision he took some fifteen months later. 'One cannot possibly carry on the daily routine with aeroplanes perpetually flying overhead by the score, droning away, mounting in great circles, being shelled sometimes, then swooping down again without giving a thought to the R.F.C.'

In the same letter he tells how he 'had a chat with one of the flight officers on the subject of what a chap might expect' who applied for a transfer. He learnt something of the life, preliminaries and instruction, which he reported at length. It would be 'a wonderful training, educationally and technically useful later' in 'the duty of carrying on the business and all the expenses would be paid by the War Office'.

> They are fairly strict in passing you and will not take chaps over a certain weight. There are risks, of course but the chances of getting through safely are far greater than in the case of an infantry subaltern who happens to be in a proper scrap.
>
> I should not like to commit myself at all, but should very much like you all to talk it over at home and to hear the result, supposing I became very keen. There is no hurry for an answer. I shouldn't rush into anything blindly. I should not like to act without your full consents. (5 June)

On June 25th the company moved from Le Seau to Busseboom, another small collection of farm houses, about two and a half miles South East of Poperinghe and still in Belgium. Here, for the first time, they were to be under canvas. In spite of a thunderstorm ('the first wet day for weeks') which flooded the ground 'the supply section stuck manfully to the work, putting up posts and canvas, and got the sheet[20] over before nightfall.' The next day they 'all set to on their private bivvy construction at the side of the big ditch pond' that separated their field from that of No. 2 company. Dickinson proved 'a first-rate chap for helping'. Frank added an apse later to the bivouac, the sheet projecting all round 'rather like our light-weight tent'.

Frank was expecting soon to go home on leave, and a week after pitching the bivouacs he 'borrowed No. 2 Company's car and went back to Neuve Eglise and got souvenirs for home'. He then 'tidied up mess before siesta'. Eric Milner came in to tea and entertained them with humorous anecdotes. He also told them something of his plans to transfer to the Mechanical Transport.

---

[20] Wagon covers.

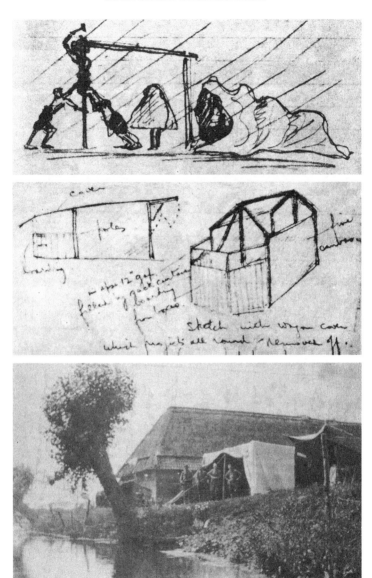

Top and middle: Bivvy construction at Busseboom, from letters dated 27 June and 30 August. 'In spite of a thunderstorm which flooded the ground, "the supply section stuck manfully to the work".' Above: The Busseboom mess tent.

85

Above: 'We have got a piano in the mess room at last ... Pont and I set out on horses ... The wagon turned up about half an hour after we got there, so we just had "one or two" at Tina's before going round to the house.' (see Page 93–94)

Below: Frank's photograph of the Cloth Hall in Ypres: 'an indescribable, uncanny nightmare city ... very hot, muggy and dusty.'

Frank was getting keyed up about taking leave to come home and wrote home that they should 'leave the door open', as he had a latch key. 'Expect me when you see me,' he said. He asked me to 'have the days more or less planned and to think if possible of tennis'. He wanted 'to get a lot in and a fair amount of shopping'. I was to invite the Aston girls over on spec. He intended 'to have a decent time and plenty on'. (2 July)

The day before Frank's leave came through he 'rode on through Ypres—an indescribable, uncanny nightmare city'. It was 'very hot, muggy and dusty'. The 'country was buzzing with military traffic, otherwise the complete calm of evening was most impressive'.

On Monday July 5, Frank 'left by car with Whittall and two Staffs. officers' and 'drove part of the way'. It was, he recorded in his diary, a 'lovely road after Arques going to the coast'. They were 'messed about from 11.15 till 2 a.m., but got a good, though hurried supper at the Folkstone Hotel'.

To come home on leave from a European war was an experience hitherto unknown to Britishers since Napoleonic times. For Frank, the return to Blighty evidently provided an astonishing contrast to the crossings of his student years. They embarked on a 'small steamer, very full'. The atmosphere on board tended to be carefree and alcoholic. The night was 'misty and cool, daylight beginning even at 2 a.m.' On the train he was made aware of the return to civilisation by such phenomena as the silver and napiery on the table of the London and North Western Railway (L&NW) breakfast car. Arriving at New Street at 11 a.m., Frank was met by Father, Mother and me (by then commissioned and serving at the Handsworth Drill Hall). Mother thanked him again for the weekly bouquet of carnations sent from Engelman's at Saffron Walden.

It was a touching re-union. Once home at 146, Frank 'had a good hot bath before lunch and produced souvenirs'. He 'went to sleep afterwards, and then got measured in town and joined Uncle Sydney [Dr Short, by 1915 a major in the Royal Army Medical Corps] at the Grand Music Hall for the evening—very amusing. Came back for supper.'

Frank's leave followed a customary pattern. He had to visit the dentist and Allport's, the tailors. He made sundry purchases, including an air pistol, which was to afford him much amusement. He had a jolly evening with the Aston girls … great fun with 'March',[21] and sundry instruments afterwards.' He visited the works and mentions in his diary 'short speechifying at 5 p.m. Then tennis with Bob.' On the last night of his leave there were 'rows of people in after supper'. (9 July)

Frank had only three nights at home and as the time to depart approached, his emotions must have been ambivalent. He was probably reminded of the sad leave-takings before going back to school and yet, let us face the fact that he had been enjoying himself so much in France that he was to feel quite at home when back at Busseboom once more.

Saturday came. Frank paid a final visit to the works, left New Street station by the 3.40 p.m. and Victoria at 7.15. He notes that he witnessed some 'pathetic sights', had a 'fair crossing' and that there were 'no incidents'.

That Frank's return to duty constituted no hardship is brought out in the following letter. 'Well, I am beginning to feel quite "at home" and getting on my game again now and shall soon be tuned up to concert pitch. Tho' I felt pretty well while at home, all the rush of [those] five days on top of the journey just makes the difference between A1 and A2 for fitness.' (13 July)

July 15th was Frank's twenty-second birthday. 'It has been a rummy birthday,' he wrote:

The horses and everything were all polished up to the ears, and harness too, for an inspection. Some big bug turned up with the Colonel in his car and, as usual, the actual inspection was a wash-out. It is a pity for the men so often having to make such terrific preparations unnecessarily.

In the afternoon I did a bit of music exercise for Old Man Thelwall. I am awfully pleased it is possible to pick up a few wrinkles 'without a piano'.

---

[21] Probably his 'March of the Terriers' song.

After tea we had a top-hole little cricket match in which our Company won, the two sides being composed of Officers and N.C.O.s v. Men …

The air pistol provides for quite a long-felt want, as we are not allowed to fire our revolvers behind the lines for practice. I had some very good sport both with paper and rat targets.

Unfortunately Jack, Don and Court could not be in for dinner this evening so we shall 'fizz it' tomorrow night. (15 July)

A 'young storm' took place. 'The pond in front has filled up and got very muddy. Whittall and I both had the same thought this morning when the sun appeared for a short time. "What a lovely day for the fish." He has done a lot in Wales also' (17 July).

Eel fishing in the ditch-pond aroused great enthusiasm. 'We have had very good fun with the tackle,' he wrote, 'and caught some eels every day, particularly with the night line. PS: Don't forget the Fishing Holiday we are all going to have in Wales as soon as things have cleared up a bit, n'est-ce-pas?' (28 August)

Frank located a piano and spent the evening with the gifted Whitehead for a bit of singing and fun. He described the ride back that night. 'Bright moon and not a breath. My little pony Jinny shot along like an arrow all the way. It is a tiny beautiful little animal—such a relief after the old galumphing great horse I had. Everything was so beautiful it makes you forget about being at war altogether, until the bright glisten of a sentry's bayonet flickers on ahead and later a voice challenges you from out of the black shadows. Passing through the town, a clatter of the iron shoes seems to echo for miles (like cinematograph noises through a megaphone), for everything else is dead quiet to all intents. I turn in at the little by-road to our farm, hand over the gee-gee to the guard with the lantern and pass on. The dying embers of the batman's fire, the reflection of the moon in front of our choice little bivvies and lastly my own comfortable home-made bed waiting for me—with all these, our surroundings are far from ugly.' (26 July)

Frank with Jinny: 'My little pony Jinny shot along like an arrow all the way. It is a tiny beautiful little animal—such a relief after the old galumphing great horse I had. Everything was so beautiful it makes you forget about being at war.'

Throughout June and July these young men seem to have spent many hours in philosophical discussions. As with the talks on aerodynamics, Frank wrote home for 'a little literature' but this time 'concerning Transmigration of Souls or, broadly speaking,

Spiritual Afterlife. The debates on this subject are numerous and furious,' he explained (2 June). He read Sir Oliver Lodge's *Reason and Belief*, which he thought splendid. He suggested that their life in France at that time might be compared with 'a pleasant sort of illness in that it knocks normal everyday routine on the head and forces one to look up and gaze around' (27 June). He thought that 'By living for some time with pals, away from home and business, one discusses subjects which in the ordinary run of things would almost be a waste of time. We think, discuss and read, then discuss, read and think. The situation is only made more interesting by the fact that of the six of us, one is Roman Catholic, one Swedenborgian, one Wesleyan, one Church of England, one (myself) a nominal Congregationalist, I think, and one Highly Modern and of doubtful category. Anyway, whichever one of us happens to be nearest the truth, it is remarkable that, having such varied ideas, we should just be brought together out here, and also of an age when each can speak out in the bluntest of language if he chooses, without shocking any "elders".' (17 June)

> During times like these one would have just cause for despondency, without some fairly sound and reassuring principle to work on and be guided by. It is a bloody proceeding and no mistake. I should think the poor chaps in the trenches will brace themselves to anything in civilian life afterwards. We get a comparatively luxurious time of it, don't forget. (1 August)

During Frank's leave in July I learnt for the first time of his interest in the teaching of Dr H. Emilie Cady, a homeopathic physician as well as a metaphysician, practising in New York during the 1890s. I gathered that her doctrine was related to faith healing, for I entered a room at home in the middle of an exposition by Frank and overheard Father comment, 'But do you mean to say that if you were to sit on a red-hot stove you would not get burnt?' I cannot remember Frank's reply but writing home, some months later, he explained that he 'came across *Lessons in Truth* [by Cady] through one of the

91

quartermasters, Wilner (6th S. Staffs) who was a bit of a Wesleyan preacher till he became convinced of this new way of thinking and shocked some of them. Of course it absolutely embraces Christian Science.'[22] (3 November)

Wilner must have been a sincere seeker after truth. He was a thick-set man and sometimes had difficulty in mounting his horse. One day his colleagues noticed that he was perceptibly slimmer and more active. They learnt that he had given up all alcohol and fattening foods, only taking an apple for breakfast. He informed his friends that he felt he had been strengthened by certain doctrine which he sought to pass on to them when they all met at the dump. 'Its general line of argument,' Frank explained, 'appears to be this: Good and Evil cannot exist in exactly the same place. If God-good is recognised as omnipresent, then there is no room for evil. And the only explanation for what is apparently evil to us is that it is not REAL, for anything real, in the true sense, must be eternal. The world is governed by our thoughts which are creative, and by thinking anything is as we would like it to be, we literally influence it.' (3 November)

> Before the world will make any rapid spiritual progress, everybody must be convinced in themselves that they are really divine, having at their disposal powers as great as any of the Biblical Disciples. The idea of 'miserable sinners and offenders', as laid down by the Church, is knocked on the head. (1 August)

Lessons in Truth was first published in 1894 and was written for what became The Unity School of Christianity. To some extent it reflects the over-optimism of that period and of the New World. Much of it, however, is only indirectly related to faith healing which, as the author said, 'is truly "a branch of the vine" but not the only branch' (p.105). In my opinion Cady's book

---

[22] 'In 1890, the name of Christian Science was used not only by Mary Baker Eddy but also by many others who were teaching what we today call Truth, or Christian metaphysics.' *The Story of Unity* by James Freeman, Unity School of Christianity, 1954, Lee's Summit, Missouri, p. 59.

constitutes a simple and enlightened introduction to Aldous Huxley's *The Perennial Philosophy* of a generation later. Life affirming, it contains much that concerns man's inner psychological and spiritual development, Frank finished reading it in July, but re-read it repeatedly.

The Company's eighth move, on 2 September, was to Lijssenthoek, another small collection of farm houses about three miles south of Poperinghe. The field they had vacated was immediately taken over by artillery. They were still under canvas. 'The weather, tho' showery, just held during the shift,' Frank wrote, 'but Pont and I had scarcely got our bivvy posts placed when it broke with a rush. We just got the wagon cover on temporarily without getting all our kit drenched.' (3 September)

As there was an adjacent house that they used as a mess, Frank once more took up the search for a piano, a search that had been fruitless while they were at Busseboom, where he had been forced to work on *Thelwall's Sight-Reading Course* by mind's-ear. Although this was excellent training for the musical imagination it was no substitute for practical work at the keyboard; and furthermore his colleagues missed their singsongs and his solos.

At the end of August Frank was still frustrated, even though he had 'practically clinched a deal for hiring a decentish piano' at a bargain rate, putting his 'French to perhaps the keenest possible tactical use'. Unfortunately many pianos had already been hired out to other messes while a few others had been 'completely done in by an occasional rowdy lot', so that 'private folks' were 'very loath to let their instruments out to farm houses'.

Then came the move to Lijssenthoek. After a few days of renewed effort he was able to report: 'We have got a piano in the new mess room at last. It just makes the difference and is a gigantic success ... The quality is excellent at the price. We sent a wagon and fetched it from Bailleul. Pont and I set out on horses. It was a perfect September morning—hot and misty—and the ride over the hills (Mont Noir, Mont Vidaigne and

Mont Rouge) was delightful. The wagon turned up about half-an-hour after we got there, so we just had one or two at Tina's before going round to the house. The ride back was just as lively. We got the instrument safely into the mess and found no damage had been done. It has rather a decent tone, slightly metallic like an old harpsichord, I should imagine. We have just taken the instrument into an adjacent barn and had a jolly decent singsong. It is very dull for the chaps without something of this sort.' (11 September)

Two days later, helped by Dickinson, Frank 'took every note out of the piano and cleaned it, together with the action,[23] then put it back.' From then on his diary and letters make repeated references to music and piano. For instance:

Band came at 3.30, so we had our footer match after dinner. They played selections during afternoon and evening. After dinner, piano moved into barn for joint concert. (15 September)

Practised Bach and songs before dinner, and went round to HQ Company with Don, where we had supper after sing-song. (18 September)

We are getting a huge amount of pleasure from the piano. (20 September)

Played the hymns for church parade on our piano. (22 September)

All this time Frank was gaining experience as an entertainer, and, wishing to pass on something of what he had learnt to myself, he wrote to give me some advice, reminding me 'of the importance, in our repertoire, of having the words of loads of songs off pat' in my head. I was to write them out and learn them 'during stable hours when time lags. Don't be afraid to send in any new words for a song,' he continued; he would prefer them short—two or three verses at most (29 September). He looked forward to a renewal of our partnership.

---

[23] The hammers of the piano.

On the same day he wrote home: 'Last night we had a very successful smoke and singsong. It is hard to say which contributed most to the success of the evening—the piano, general talent, or rum and hot water. I sang 'Haar Dyal'[24] and I think it went down all right. It is easy to execute for one thing. Those songs of Stanford's[25] are tricky to play and sing oneself. I also gave them Uncle Tom Cobley the other night and took for my chorus Staff Edwards (Farrier), Staff Cheetham (Wheeler), Staff Dixon and Staff Dann (Supply Section), Major Rogers (Company Sgt. Major), Mr Keey (Warrant Officer), and Uncle Alf Parker and all (Company Quartermaster Sgt.) They were very amused.'

They left Lijssenthoek on October 2 and for the next five weeks were moving about in the neighbourhood of Béthune.[26] The 46th Division had been holding part of the Ypres Salient but on October 3, taking part in a move of the whole division, the Staffordshire Brigade entrained at Abele and detrained twenty miles further south at Fouquereuil, a suburb of Béthune. This manoeuvre was preparatory to an assault on the Hohenzollern Redoubt—part of a large-scale but unsuccessful offensive designed to relieve pressure on the Russians, who had been driven back beyond Warsaw.

Jack's company moved with the Brigade and started with a trek of some twenty miles to l'Éclème via Merville and Rebec. They arrived at their destination the day after their departure, having spent one night on the way at Vieux Berquin, a few miles south-west of Bailleul. 'Before we moved I sold the piano,' Frank wrote home, 'and did not lose by it. I haven't touched the

---

[24] 'The Love Song of Haar Dyal', poem by Kipling, music by Mrs George Batten.

[25] *Songs of the Sea*: Poems by Henry Newbolt set to music for solo voices (and Male Chorus ad lib) Op. 91, 1904). *Three Cavalier Songs*: Poems included in the *Dramatic Lyrics* (1842) by Robert Browning. We heard these songs first at Bedales.

[26] Of the town of Béthune, Frank wrote: 'For quality and size it exceeds the rest up to now.' They went to the theatre, a 'beautiful modern erection, and saw the Divisional Pierrot Troup'. (9 October)

dough yet but have got the receipt.' (6 October.) In fact, as Jack commented later, 'X did the dirty on us and never paid.'

The scene changed. No longer were they amongst the rural landscapes of Northern France and Flanders, with their green fields, farmhouses and straight roads lined with tall trees, as in old Dutch paintings, for the merciless battles of Loos were fought out amongst the sombre industrial and mining towns of Lens, Noeux les Mines and Grenay. And yet there were also pleasant places, which Frank was quick to observe. L'Éclème, near Fouquières, was one such. They were billetted in a farmhouse near some ruins of an old château, surrounded by a moat, into which Gordon Whittall fell on the first night.

Three days later they moved on to Fouquières (6 October). There they were billeted in a 'grand old château, the Prieuré St. Pry, supposed to be the scene of *The Three Musketeers!*' The grounds were 'in typical French style, the trees carefully laid out in a *négligé* way, leaving a long stretch of grass with the house at one end. Although the grounds were not enormous,' Frank wrote, 'there is almost every variety of tree there.' He 'managed to cotton on to a little summer arbour—perfectly placed on a rising bit of ground at one side of the open lawn'. It made 'an admirable mess' for the five of them and a new interpreter (they were now in France), Armand Marlier. But there was a snag. Also billeted in the château were the Staffordshires' Brigadier and his staff, and although Jack and his Company officers were sleeping five in a bedroom, they hardly liked to intrude on these exalted red-hats; in fact, according to Frank, 'they made themselves scarce.'

The Staffordshire Brigade attacked on October 13. Frank recorded in his diary:

> Called at 2.00 a.m. Got off at 3.00 a.m. 6 o'clock dump at Vermelles[27]—very successful, thanks to the Boches' silent artillery. Saw the bombardment [which started at 12 Noon] from Noyelles. Big shells put into Béthune that evening.

---

[27] A particularly sticky place, where Gordon Whittall was stuck in a cellar for some days with reserve supplies.

A few days later Frank wrote home that they would read about the attack in the papers, and continued, 'The state of mind of everyone actually participating is so abnormal during the actual scrap that it is very hard to piece together everybody's impressions. When you hear folks say the Boches on this front are absolutely "skint" and that they can't possibly hold on, you tell them they are talking piffle. It may be true that once we get uncomfortably near their frontier their morale may waver, but as far as ingenuity in fighting goes, they can't be touched. Our losses are still uncertain. I expect you will surmise, on perusing the casualty lists, that which I must not write about. We had some jolly good evenings in here with our old pals before the affair. They showed few outward signs of concern up to the end.' (16 October)

Their relations with the officers and men of the Staffordshire Brigade were of the friendliest, and so Frank and his colleagues were saddened, if not appalled, by this engagement, especially in view of its negative results. There had been, to quote Lieutenant Meakin, 'considerable enemy sniping during the whole bombardment, and also bursts of machine gun fire … At 2.50 p.m. the Company Commanders jumped up and waved their canes, and the whole line rose and commenced a steady advance. They were met by a hail of bullets, and men fell fast, but they kept on. There has been much criticism of this attack. It is known now that the bombardment had been ineffective, and that the Germans were ready with their machine guns to sweep the line of advance. The gas attack, too, had failed, and no troops could have succeeded in the task. But there has never been a word of criticism of the behaviour of the officers and men. That was simply sublime.'

There remained three more moves before Frank could return to England. The first, to Allouagne, took place six days after the attack on the Hohenzollern Redoubt. The Brigade, which had been relieved by the Scots Guards, had also been moved to the same neighbourhood, about five miles north-west of Béthune.

From Allouagne they returned to Fouquières on October 26 and ten days later (November 5) Frank took part in his last trek while in France. This was to Croix Marmuse, another small group of houses, west of the main road between Béthune and Armentières. It was here that he was to receive news that he had been transferred to the Reserve Train.

While at Allouagne, Frank managed once again to meet Vyv Trubshawe, then serving as a 2nd Lieut. in the Kings (Liverpool) Regiment, having enlisted in the Artists Rifles. At first they encountered difficulties. Frank had arranged a nice little dinner in Béthune and Vyv was to meet the other company officers. 'Unfortunately the whole evening went futt' as the move to Fouquières was shunted a day earlier. 'This sort of thing happens so frequently,' he wrote, 'that it is not encouraging to make appointments at all' (27 October). However, they managed to have tea together and a champagne cocktail each, which Vyv had never tasted before.

Two days later the two friends met again, this time at Estaires, twelve miles north-east on the River Lys. Frank covered the distance on Jinny in three hours. 'I thoroughly enjoyed it,' he wrote, 'and got back about 9.30. We went through the last copy of the *Bedales Chronicle* together and discussed everything. It is great that my long jump record has been beaten by six inches (19 ft 4 ins) but what is more marvellous by far is the 5 ft 7¼ ins high jump for a lad at school. It is a regular varsity jump.' (30 October)

Frank commented on the frequency of chance meetings with people one had not seen for ages. This was a common phenomenon 'for everyone tells stories of running across friends in the most extraordinary situations'. He mentions four Bedalians, including Vyv Trubshawe, whom he had seen. (Marshall, Morgan and Margetson were the others.) Another Bedalian encounter was described in a letter home dated August 19.

The day before yesterday (17 August) it was my turn to take the convoy up to the usual R.E. stores. I had about 20 wagons or so and was meandering along at the head when suddenly a Tommy called out 'Hallo, it's Bug!' He jumped off the wagon, having almost ridden past me. I slowed up and he gave me the 'extra heavy' four-fingers-in-line-with-the-thumb-1¼-inch-above-the-right-eyebrow-etc., during which time I found to my surprise that it was none other than little Nicholson,[28] a most delightful and thorough sport who was in my dormitory at school. I gave him my address and position and told him to look me up on the morrow. His lines are really quite close to ours.

Yesterday Dan Nicholson came as expected. I had an awfully jolly afternoon and evening with him ... We did nothing all the time except sit in the mess-tent eating, or on the water's edge, sleuthing rats. He has had some experiences like Douglas and was all in the thick of it two months ago. It does seem a damned shame for such a topping kid to be involved in a mess of this sort. He is very jovial through it all—like all the others ... The lad is only eighteen and has got one of those natural 'sporting eyes' which enables him to hit or kick a ball travelling at full speed. [He can therefore] play any game perfectly without practising. He revelled in the air pistol and shot one, much to his delight. It is really a fascinating toy.

One day Frank found Ernest Lee of Dublin sitting at the next table. Frank had ridden over from Busseboom for a meal, probably at Poperinghe, when they found themselves talking together about his visit to Stillorgan in September 1912 and of holidays with the Lees at Rhyl. A few weeks later Frank learnt that the Lee family had suffered its first loss. 'Wrote letter to Mrs Lee sympathising on hearing from Ernest Lee of Joe's death and Tennyson's wounds in the Dardanelles.' (22 August) Ernest was a doctor in the R.A.M.C. and he in turn lost his life on the Leinster when it sank off the Irish coast in 1918.

On October 28 at Fouquières, Frank took part in an inspection by King George V. He saw the King thrown off his horse on the aviation ground. Here is Jack Best's account of the incident:

The King was reviewing three [army] corps, including ours, the 11th, today, and as only representative detachments of each unit had to parade, some of us went to look on and waited on the

---

[28] Then serving with the Hon. Artillery Company. He was commissioned in 1917 and died of pneumonia in 1927.

roadside at the aerodrome at Hesdigneul. As the King was riding along the line of R.F.C. men, they suddenly took off their caps and gave three cheers. This caused the King's horse to rear up and it fell over backwards on top of him.

Our M.O., Major Hewlings, happened to be right on the spot and started to render first aid, assisted by his medical orderly, Corporal Waterhouse (of West Bromwich).

At this moment the Prince of Wales arrived on the scene and, pushing through the crowd, asked curiously what had happened. Corporal Waterhouse, to whom he happened to speak and who could hardly speak for excitement, was heard to reply in [his] rich Black Country accent, 'Oh, please Sir, it's your Dad what's fell off his Ooss.'

Incidentally, the King looked terribly ill as he and the P. of W. were driven away.

In fact, the King returned to London on November 1 by hospital train, ship and special train ambulance. He was confined to bed at Buckingham Palace until 6 November and on December 13 was stated to be 'So far recovered as to be able to resume work with certain limitations.'

Jack Best wrote: 'I more than once (and the others did too) met the Prince of Wales, walking or riding a push bike about the lanes, and would just say "How do!" He was a thorn in the side of the Staff, from all accounts, as he wanted to get up into the line and they wouldn't let him have a car!'

Frank's last week with the company started with another trek, for on November 5 the company got up very early for its move to Croix Marmuse, a distance of about nine miles. 'All went without a hitch except for the supply lorries, which arrived late.' Frank 'went off early in the car to sit on billets. Everything except the field was very acceptable.'

On Wednesday, November 10, Frank went off with Allan Court to make purchases and later rode on to St. Floris, hoping to receive the cash payment for the piano. He was not successful, but sensational tidings awaited his return when he 'learnt news of going back to Reserve Train at home' and that he was one of the lucky ones in the change of officers.

The entry in his diary for the following day, Thursday, November 11, his last with the company, was as follows: 'While I was packing kit, Colonel[29] tried prisoner (attacked man drunk, under arrest) and gave him twelve days. Had tea with Colonel, who wished me good luck. Wrote multitude of letters.'

Next day was very wet. Frank 'got everything finished and said goodbye all round to Jack and Co,' catching the train from Merville which brought him to Boulogne at 8.00 p.m. There was no boat that evening and he 'got a room at Hotel Dervaux, traipsing around' and having a bit of fun with the lift, much to the lift boy's disgust.'

The next three days were spent at Boulogne. The weather was rough, 'blowing heavens hard and very big seas on'. Frank learnt of mines 'breaking loose and sinking two A.S.C. transport boats, but was this just a rumour?' he wondered. He passed the time writing a letter to Madame de la Fontinelle and getting his hair cut and then, after a good lunch, took the tram to Wimereux, and 'passed remains of casino, hotels, huts, etc. The tram could not go all the way and the sea was washing right over the promenade.'

After getting 'a good blowing' he returned to a café near Boulogne where the 'place was thronged with tarts and glad eyes'. He 'went to the picture theatre' where he experienced 'much the same atmosphere'.

Next day, Sunday, November 14, he was still unable to embark. He 'walked on the beach and saw a dirigible over the sea and a sand-yacht with a punctured tyre'. He 'rushed off to the station to catch a train for Calais, but after an absurd scramble and arriving with great baggages at station' he was 'told that the train was cancelled'. He 'got back to the hotel and had dinner at leisure'.

Proceedings on the Monday were just as frustrating. He paid his bill and got to the quay at about 1.30 p.m., only to find that 'news of the boat's probable timetable was hopelessly vague'. Firstly, they were told that there was no room on the Duty and

---

[29] Lieutenant Colonel E.L. Mears.

Staff mail boat nor on the leave boat. He waited till 4.45, left his luggage in the cloakroom, and went to the pictures for three-quarters of an hour, returning at 7 p.m. to hear the news: 'no boat tonight'. There was nothing for it but to get rooms, this time at the Hotel Louvre where, he dined. Afterwards he went round to a captain's billet and with two Canadian officers enjoyed a singsong till 1.30 a.m.

It snowed during the night, but on the next day, after lunch at the hotel, he went aboard at last. They cast off at about 4.30 p.m.

Frank's postcard from Boulogne, where he was delayed by bad weather en route back to England to join the Reserve: 'After getting "a good blowing" he returned to a café near Boulogne where the "place was thronged with tarts and glad eyes".'

Chapter 4
How we had fun

Frank's nine years at Bedales were punctuated by our holidays. My earliest memories of these now appear rather like a series of short film sequences or stills: Rhyl sands, the Hydropathic Hotel, the London and North Western Irish Mail Train and Travelling Post Office, the net gear by means of which the mail bags were exchanged as the train swept past, the model yacht pond at Llandudno and the beautifully constructed little cutter called Tiny (which Father bought from a local craftsman and then gave to us boys), the hull of which, carved from planks glued together, had sides so thin that they could be pressed in with the fingers.

Later, at Berrow in Somerset, where we spent seven consecutive summers, the sequences lengthen out and become an almost continuous film. It was at Berrow that, in spite of our parents' efforts to interest us, we became more and more bored with the flat country and lack of companions of our own age. (Obligingly, our parents then took furnished rooms in North Wales.) Then, during the Spring, we would sometimes accompany them for short stays in Paris and Germany where we both received a foretaste of the life we would lead during our Wanderjahre of 1911 and '12. There was also the very full life we led during our holidays at home.

My earliest holiday memory is of 1896 or '97. While Father

was studying the science and art of golf in Rhyl, Frank and I would be on the sands with our spades—wooden, for we were not allowed metal ones lest we hurt ourselves—and, because we lost them frequently, they were eventually tied to our smocks. We were prohibited from paddling owing to the danger of catching cold, which might lead to pneumonia. All this led to interesting relationships with other children who were not under the same régime. Our aunt Alice Ward closely observed us at play and wrote a perceptive study in child- and, for that matter, maternal-psychology. She took as her sub-title 'Thou shalt not covet thy neighbour's goods', her main theme being our various ruses for borrowing from a good-natured small friend (and from each other) his small metal spade. She also developed several subsidiary themes, such as: a) sour grapes, b) engaging fantasy games, and c) certain 'managerial' traits which we were already exhibiting.

It was at Rhyl that we first met the Lees of Dublin. They reappear later, for the two families became very friendly. Visits were exchanged. In 1912 Frank was invited to their house at Blackrock and once I attended the Dublin Horse Show at Ballsbridge, which suburb was to be the scene of tragic happenings in 1916; and, indeed, Frank and I were very hospitably treated by them during and after these events. The Lees also stayed with us during one of the Birmingham Triennial Musical Festivals, for both families were fond of music.

Mr Lee owned an important draper's shop in Dublin and another at Kingstown [now Dun Laoghaire]. They had four sons, but Frank and I got on best with Tennyson who was about our own age. At Rhyl, I can remember him as a small boy who appeared one Sunday in a beautiful velvet suit with a lace collar of the Little Lord Fauntleroy type. We were abashed by this sartorial brilliance. He had an attractive Irish accent and a manner which Mother said reminded her of a dormouse.

In 1901 for the first of eight years in succession, we took our summer holiday at Berrow, a small village about one-and-a-half miles north of Burnham-on-Sea in Somerset. From the coast to the Mendips, ten miles inland, the country is quite flat. There are few hedges, the fields being divided by a net-work of ditches. There, we noticed men with sacks and pronged spears which they would thrust into the mud at the bottom of the ditches and generally bring them out with an eel wriggling between the prongs.

In the middle of the plain stands a curious shaped hill called Brent Knoll. Nearly 550 feet high, it is in two layers and from the sea looks like an immense monitor or surfacing submarine. According to legend, it had been a shovel-full of earth dug from Cheddar Gorge by the Devil. It was Brent Knoll that we later used as a signalling station carrying on what we had learnt in Leslie Kent's corps. Out would come the flags, a telescope and field glasses. One of us would be on the rampart of what had once been an Iron-Age fortification and the other on the lawn of the house where we were staying.

Between Berrow and the sea came, first, the golf links and then a belt of sand-dunes. Sea bathing was limited to certain tides, because the mud flats came well inshore, leaving only a relatively narrow strip of sand. There were no 'dangerous' rocks.

Ivy House, where we stayed, might have been eighty years old. It was of red brick toned by weather and partly overgrown with ivy. Bay windows were placed each side of the front door, above which was a neat pedimented canopy and a small window with a semi-circular arch and wooden tracery. It had an unpretentious charm.

Behind it were farm buildings and an orchard. Opposite was a large field bordered with elms. It was studded with yellow ragwort which in August was covered with the orange and black caterpillars of the Cinnabar moth, names we had learnt during natural history walks at school. In this field we played golf or rode on Gipsy, a piebald pony. At our home in Birmingham there were no pets and, indeed, Mother was entirely out of sympathy with cats. But at Berrow we became acquainted with several animals and greatly attached to an amiable little fox-terrier called Spottie. The small chickens in the farmyard gradually came to trust us; they would eat out of our hands and even allow us to take them up and stroke them.

Mr Smith, our landlord, provided us with appetising

vegetables, poultry, fruit and farm produce. He had a red beard and waistcoat. His manner was quiet and somehow suggested conversation with his fellow farmers over a pint of rough Somerset cider. His wife cooked for us and scalded excellent Somerset cream. She wore her hair brushed back from her forehead. Her mouth and jaw showed firm character and a kindly disposition, and, indeed, the Smiths were always tolerant and good natured towards us boys. Their daughter, Queenie, was generally to be seen in a straw boater and a pinafore. She was about our own age and often accompanied us on our expeditions. In her, we found a gentle and unassuming audience for many of the games we invented.

In 1904 the Smiths built Osborne House. It adjoined a pleasant small old farmhouse which was washed over in a pale pink colour. The market-garden and greenhouses were on a much bigger scale, but the house itself, though more commodious, was, in some ways, a grotesque distortion of Ivy House. It was to Osborne House, however, that we returned year after year.

Our parents provided a tutor for us during our first holiday from Bedales, the second at Berrow. Father found it necessary to return frequently to Birmingham. He was afraid that we might become too much of a handful for Maud and that her apprehensive nature might lead to even more molly-coddling. How to keep us fully occupied was not going to be easy, considering the extreme length of the holiday. Obviously some form of instruction would be desirable. The boys mustn't be allowed to get rusty with their studies. He knew just the right sort of person to invite down as tutor and at the end of our first week Mr Ellerton arrived. He had just left a public school and his appearance and manner suggested the genus prefect, which one term at Bedales had taught us quickly to recognise.

Each morning we had rudimentary lessons—sums, of course, and, as our handwriting left much to be desired, copy-books, bought in Burnham, appeared on the table after breakfast. Under Mr Ellerton's supervision we also kept diaries of our activities, which I still have. Words wrongly spelt were corrected by our tutor and re-appeared in his sloping hand below the day's entry for us to copy out several times.

Mr Ellerton's own orthography, however, was sometimes unconventional: for instance, Frank, in his diary, referred to a 'resturnt'; our tutor re-wrote the word as 'restaraunt', which I find repeated below by Frank to impress it on his memory.

Under this supervision it was not surprising that our diaries seldom came to life. Of the two, Frank's is the more lively and informative, but even his became more and more laconic as the holiday progressed. Here is the first entry, written before the arrival of Mr Ellerton:

> August 1st, 1902—in the morning we set out to Burnham at 10.20; and saw the ships, men were scraping all the sticky mud from the Banks. in the afternoon we went a sail 3.30 and I did a bit of steering. We went a little way up the Bru[e]. we came home and had tea, shrimps, jam, and coco. after tea we went off on the sandhills and scouted, we played at making shoots [chutes] down the sand when we heard a muwing and we saw a cat. We played till 7.40. then we came home and scouted.

And here is the last:

> September 7, 1902. We went to church.
> Afternoon: We played catchball. We went on the sandhills.
> Evening: We went on the sandhills.

Mr Ellerton must have been with us for at least three summers for he re-appears in my diary of 1904. In spite of his prefectorial appearance and manner, he seems to have been a friendly and 'companiable' young man doing his best to keep us happy, reading aloud to us when we were made to 'rest' after lunch, cycling round the neighbourhood, playing games and putting up with what must have been at times our somewhat irritating behaviour.

The sailing boat referred to in the first entry was cutter rigged, with jib and mizzen. The skipper was Alfred Hunt. He was coxswain of the local lifeboat and had to his credit several courageous rescues. Like Father, he was an Adult School man and the two of them would compare notes as he sat at the tiller, which he would sometimes allow us to take over from him. We would cruise about in the estuary of the River Parrett and in Bridgewater Bay, watching the porpoises, a tug (Bonita), the Trinity House ship and other ships. On one occasion Frank recorded that 'we went on board a pretty big boat called the Good Templar and we went down into the cabin' and on another day that 'the sea was very rough and we had our mainsail down. We went down the river nearly as far as the bell buoy; we went along at a good rate at about four miles an hour.'

That pleasure boat proved a popular form of entertainment for the groups of guests who appeared at Berrow from time to time. Among them I can remember our cousins, the Andertons, and two graceful little girls of our own age, whom we met in 1902. Helen and Mary Aston were staying in Burnham with their mother, brother Wilfred, and sister Kay. Helen played the piano with, what seemed to us then, dazzling proficiency and confidence. A cricket match was arranged between us on the sands. We made 38 runs, the Astons made 18. Then we had tea.

During subsequent holidays and after leaving school we would often go over to the Astons' house at Harborne for tennis and music. Father had been Mr Aston's best man. Before the wedding, which took place at Malvern, there had been a mix-up which might have led to a disappointing situation, for bridegroom and best man arrived at the railway station (Dudley Port) just as their train was steaming out. Undaunted, they took a hansom cab and picked up the train at the next station.

At Burnham, Wilfred made a considerable impression as an ebullient young man with a tendency to show off. Indeed, Mother used to refer to him as 'Wilfred the Terrible'. Later, while on the staff of *Autocar*, he was successful as a writer and illustrator. He is said to have originated the 'exploded' drawing. He also had a weekly article in *The Sketch* under the pseudonym 'Petrol Vapour'. Another brother, Frank Aston, became a friend of Pauley Montague while at Cambridge, and in 1922 was awarded a Nobel Prize for his work on isotopes.

Father bought us small golf clubs and gave up a good deal of his time trying to teach us to swing correctly. He had made a special study of the mashie shot and, referring to copious notes and snapshots of Harry Vardon, instructed us in the wrist action. As at Handsworth, there was a sort of golfing backwater formed by a disused green and a fairway in reasonable condition. Here we practised, and came into contact with a number of caddies, several of them sons of Mr Ford, the professional. These caddies received our respectful admiration. We were impressed by their style—the slight forward movement of the hands for playing a chip shot and the free confident swing with the wooden clubs. It was often our clubs with which they played, for here we found ourselves in much the same predicament as our little friends on the sands of Rhyl. 'We had a foursome with two of the caddies,' Frank wrote, and on another occasion, 'I played golf with Auntie and I was two up at the end. I made rather a good brassie shot.'

On Sundays we all set out on foot along a sandy lane bordered by wind-swept poplar and buckthorn hedges for the little 13th-century church, tucked away amongst the sand hills beyond the golf links about a mile away. In the churchyard we noticed two recumbent stone figures. Someone explained to us that they were above the tombs of Crusaders, and the particular crusade in which these warriors had served could be readily ascertained from the positions of their legs, i.e. whether and how they were crossed.[30]

The vicar, the Rev. Edward Austin, preached an interesting sermon and, furthermore, held our attention by blinking rapidly as he continually removed and replaced his pince-nez. From our diaries it seems that we went twice to church on one Sunday. Father also directed our attention to serious and elevating

---

[30] And yet Nikolaus Pevsner, in the *Buildings of England*, states that the two figures in question are 'badly defaced late 13th Century effigies of a Knight and Lady'. In a letter he informs me that the story of the Crusaders and that about the crossed legs are both myths. It would be unfair, without further evidence, to attribute the interesting but inaccurate Crusader story to our Aunt Lucy; it has, nevertheless, a certain Coco-esque quality.

subjects by reading passages from Ruskin. Yet there were no Sabbatarian rigours, for our diaries record that games of hide-and-seek, also putting on the lawn, took place on Sundays. Our parents held that this day should be one of pleasant recreation, as well as religious observance.

Each summer, one day was set aside for a visit to Wells and Glastonbury. For this excursion we generally hired a horse-drawn break in which we sat facing each other. During the ride, about 10 miles each way, we passed the time by singing or playing Up Jenkins on a rug stretched between us. Once inside Wells cathedral, Frank and I were frequently to be found scuttling round the pillars to get back to the North Transept in time to see the famous Wells clock in action. Outside are two knights in armour, who strike a bell with their halberds. Above, in a scroll, appear the words 'Nequid Pereat' (Let Nothing Perish), which, to amuse us, Father translated as, 'My father hasn't got a quid.' After sight-seeing in Wells, we generally proceeded to Glastonbury, where 'We saw the Abbey and had tea.' Frank noted other expeditions:

> September 1 1902. We played golf up by the cottage. We had a four-some. Afternoon and Evening. We went to Cheddar. It is 17 miles. We went to Cox's Cave first. We had tea and then we went to Cough's Cavern. Then we went rock climbing. We sung rounds coming home.

This is followed by a note in Mr Ellerton's handwriting:

> I sing to-day
> I sang yesterday
> I have sung often.

The stalactites and stalagmites, delicately coloured, moist and glistening in the artificial light, seemed to us extremely beautiful. They suggested exquisite toffees or ices on a generous scale and made our mouths water.

Father taught us to ride a bicycle. The art of balancing was simple, he explained: always steer into the side towards which you are falling—excellent advice, which I have since used in teaching others. Even before we had reached an age when we were allowed bicycles at school, we would set off solemnly with him and one of our aunts, to do a little circuit of nine miles around Brent Knoll. We would visit the Church, with its series of carved Norman bench-ends. To us boys, these seemed like an early form of comic-strip, with a sadistic touch, reminiscent of Wilhelm Busch's drawings. Reynard the Fox, disguised as a mitred abbot, after first receiving respect from monks with the heads of pigs, is eventually put into the stocks and then hanged by some geese—obviously political cartoons of that period.

After a few years we were allowed to bicycle to the headland Breane Down, now a National Trust property. At the end of the promontory stood a disused fort. The powder magazine had been accidentally blown up by a drunken soldier and we were told that all his remains, except the head, had been collected and buried in Berrow churchyard. After exploring the sunken passage-ways, noting the defaced notices and depressing air of desertion, we were glad to come up again, to wander about amongst the heather and then climb down to the beach. Tired and contented we would bicycle across the sands by moonlight to Osborne House, where we would be welcomed by the warm glow of oil-lamps and candles.

Frank enjoyed flying his box kite and in August 1902 wrote: 'I flew my kite and got it up 700 feet and the string was 900 feet.' We were both eager for bigger and better kites. Around 1908 we tried to make a box kite measuring about 5 feet by 2 feet 6 inches but the result was disappointing. It fell to pieces on its first flight. Father then took the construction in hand and, while we were on one of those whole-day bicycling excursions to Wells and Glastonbury, he set about systematically rebuilding the kite on sound principles, measuring the struts (made of bamboo pea-sticks), cutting them to a uniform length, and, after waxing the twine so that it would not slip, binding the framework securely together. He also provided a windlass and a considerable length of cord. The kite was most spectacular and successful in action. Small parachutes were sent sailing up the cord, to be released, near the kite itself, by means of a special device. By chance, one of them landed in the garden of a house a mile or so away, where our aunts were then living.

Our minds were in a continuous turmoil of ideas and designs for things to make; these were often connected with wind, planes and sails. Our skill and craftmanship, however, were unequal to our ambitious concepts. Father was always ready to help us by providing component parts, which he would get made at the works; but he stipulated that we should first provide him with a dimensioned drawing. Even with his help, however, a sand-yacht proved wholly unpractical. The sail was far too small and there was no room to duck when tacking, a point that had not occurred to us. Actually it never came to tacking, or, for that matter, to anything at all. The pram wheels on which it was supposed to roll were quite unsuited to take the side strain, and consequently buckled. Furthermore, the rims and tyres were so narrow that they sank into the sand or grass.

On that first summer holiday from Bedales in 1902, Father took us from Petersfield to Burnham direct. It had been a long and tiring cross-country train journey and we finished it at nightfall with a drive of some miles in a cab. One of us started making up a tune and then the others took it up in what I now realise was a contrapuntal improvisation for three voices. There were no words. It was more in the nature of a sketch for an instrumental work. In after years, Frank and I would often sing together in this way, indicating, by suggestion, or even parenthetical explanation, which department of the orchestra was in action.

At Berrow, scarcely a day went by without singing and playing the piano. Each member of the house party had his, or her, selection of pieces and songs which we soon got to know by ear. One day, when Frank was about 12 or 13, to my great surprise he suddenly sat down at the piano and started to improvise, recognisably and convincingly, a few bars from each. For instance, we heard the portentous first theme of Rachmaninoff's popular *Prelude* in C sharp Minor (played by our cousin, Kathleen Wooton) or the opening bars of an 'Indian Love Lyric' (sung by Mother) or of a piano piece, slightly reminiscent of Chopin, composed by Aunt Lucy, or Handel's *Harmonious Blacksmith* variations as played by the Vicar's sister. This was the first indication of Frank's gift for musical composition, which invariably started at the keyboard. He had the material at his fingers' ends before trying to write it down. Later, as he acquired more facility, he would sometimes develop his ideas partly on paper alongside of his explorations at the piano.

He and Aunt Lucy played piano duets by the hour. One of them would state a theme, generally in the 18th-century idiom, the other would take it up and together they would continue in a fugal style. Our Aunt called such an extemporary composition (being, so they claimed, in the manner of Bach) a Bachlein, or a little Bach.

Until we were about 14 or 15 Frank and I worked together on what we called our 'Composures'—piano duets, some of them original and some settings of popular tunes such as waltzes and Sousa's marches. He would take the bass, while I drummed out the tune in octaves with one finger of each hand. We generally worked entirely by ear. Only twice did we attempt to write out any of these works. One was a waltz and the other a curious composition in three movements of 18 to 24 bars each. I suppose we had some misconception of the sonata form in mind.

Entertainment, as an art, had always attracted us and we would often bicycle into Burnham to watch the Pearows, ('very vulgar in some places' Frank noted), hoping against hope that these poor creatures would put on some new dramatic interlude or song. Alas, their repertoire was unimpressive and limited. They produced a few sketches, which even to our unsophisticated judgement seemed lame, especially when seen over and over again. Their songs were well known music-hall and pantomime numbers, such as 'Our Flo from Pimlico-co-co', or 'We'll all be merry, drinking whisky, wine and sherry; we'll all be merry, on Coronation Day' (King Edward VII was crowned on August 9, 1902). Another song seemed typical of that commercial age:

Oh, the business—it's fairly beginning to hum.
See the schoolboys—watch them as they come,
For every pound of twopenny twist, we give 'em a sheet of tin,
To put in the seat of their trousers and they all come trooping in.

But although we did not realise it, we were not only part of a
rather bored audience but, as future would-be amateur
entertainers, collecting material. We closely observed the
pianist, upon whom much depended. He was seated on a soap
box higher than the key-board, so that his arms and fingers,
quite straight, were somehow extended downward. Frank even
sketched him in his diary. We noted, too, certain features, which
we classified as typicalities, such as the opening chorus, meant to
be bustling and *mouvemente*, laced with topical and homely
allusions. Frank was absorbing it all, and some years later, when
he had got into his stride, produced an opening chorus meant to
end all opening choruses:

> We're all on the go,
> And we very much want to know,
> How long is the Man in the Moon going to last,
> And whether Keir Hardie is going too fast,
> Or whether good beer is a thing of the past,
> For I—and I—and I—and I
> We very much want to know—o-o-on the go.

The sea-side concert party led to some of the gayest and most
high-spirited entertainment that our generation was ever to
enjoy; for while, as we grew older, we became more and more
critical of what was presented to us on the front at Burnham, a
Bedalian friend, Peter Eckersley, then on holiday at Tenby, first
saw Pelissier's Follies; this was before their West End success. So
hearty was his appreciation of their genius that, after the show,
people asked him if he had been paid to laugh.

It was at Berrow that Father's enthusiasm for imparting skills
and knowledge took on a new and somewhat surprising turn.
He suddenly decided that our handwriting, and, for that matter

his own, should be remodelled. He himself had always been interested in shapely, legible calligraphy. His letters from Bonn, written in 1862 at the age of 19, are in a well-formed sloping Victorian hand. But he liked to experiment, and later acquired a Gothic style of Rundschrift, for which he used special broad nibs, made in Germany. He tried, unsuccessfully, to pass this style of writing on to us boys.

In August 1908, Frank being then 15 and I 16, he resolved to make yet another change. The disjointed strokes of the Rundschrift, he now concluded, held up the flow and reduced speed—a serious drawback for businessmen. After some search he found a style of writing in which the pen never left the paper at all. It was a rather niggly and self-satisfied fist. The strokes were upright and the loops well-rounded.

And so, once more, back we had to go to copy-books, for an hour each morning of our holiday. His instruction started with the correct way to hold the pen, flexing the thumb and fingers on the down-strokes. Frank took kindly to the new skill and from then on all his letters and diaries carried the stamp of August 1908, the time of our last holiday at Berrow. Even when serving in the War his letters home contain references to his progress in penmanship, as well as examples of it.

In reconsidering those Berrow years, I am impressed by the time and trouble taken by our parents to make our holidays full and happy. And yet, after eight summers, life in those parts seemed as flat as the plain and mud-banks. I think that we missed the company of young people of our own age, such as we mixed with at Bedales.

But another cause of discontent was the periodic change from the rough-and-ready school discipline, with its great freedom, to that very hot-house climate which had led our parents to send us away from home; try as she might, Mother could not prevent her over-anxious nature from re-asserting itself. This inevitably set up certain strains. As we grew older we opposed her attempts to restrict our activities and re-introduce the old molly-coddling. All would go well for the first week or two of our holidays; later there would be incidents and scenes, which became more and more serious as my powers of invective developed. Frank joined me in protesting, but never became angry or resentful.

On these occasions, Father, too, was often in a difficult position. He did not always agree with Mother and, I think, was secretly amused by her capricious behaviour. It must have seemed to him charmingly feminine. The difference in age between them was such that he probably looked upon her as only a small step removed from us in maturity. Still, it was necessary to uphold authority.

These stresses were negligible during the Christmas and Spring holidays, which were shorter and generally spent at home where, as we shall see, there was plenty to occupy us. By contrast the lengthy intervals at Berrow must at times have greatly tried our parents' patience. Would that Alice Ward, who sometimes stayed with us there, had continued her scenes and dialogues on the same lines as 'On Rhyl Sands'.

In 1909 our parents yielded to our requests for a change and took rooms at Criccieth. Here we were completely happy. The rocks and highlands were exciting and beautiful. We enjoyed the gay and alluring company of our girl-cousins, the Shorts and the Brittains, with their elegant figures and soft glances. Their brothers were good company too. Frank began to improve his tennis, for their form was superior to ours. As often as we liked we could bathe in a sea which was free from mud. Sometimes, we would paddle across the bay to Blackrock in a flotilla of canoes. We were introduced to trout and sewin (sea trout) fishing on the River Dwyfawr at Llanystumdwy by Mr Roberts, a one-handed local fisherman, who was paid to take us out. Supporting his rod with the stump of his left arm, he showed great dexterity in tying knots with his right hand. Father, himself a keen fisherman, gave us some of his own tackle. In the evenings, as we strolled about with our cousins, a trio, consisting of harp, violin and baritone, gave us selections from Edward German's works, waltzes, such as 'Nights of Gladness', and other light music. What more could one want?

The following year at Pwllheli, despite the dreary row of houses facing the sea, life was even more exhilarating. We continued to bathe, play tennis and cruise in our canoes. Our cousins joined us and again delighted us with their company. But a new character, Mr Albert Wood, a gypsy and an expert fisherman, one morning appeared beneath our window with a quantity of brook trout for sale. Father held him in conversation and concluded that he was a fisherman of parts; he therefore paid Mr Wood to take us off for the day and give us some more instruction. So much did we enjoy it that the next day and the days following he felt encouraged to announce that it would be a good day for trout. We would then fish the Afon Erch or take the train to Afon Wen or some of the many beautiful streams and brooks in the surrounding country. Mr Wood taught us to tie our own flies and fish them wet. Although he never actually introduced us to any illegal practices, we suspected that he had not been innocent of poaching. He showed us various tricks, such as going upstream and kicking mud into the water to make it 'coloured', for he had perfected the art of worming upstream with a 4x cast and 2 or 3 split shot about 18 inches from the hook. We were to keep well out of sight and give plenty of time before striking. With rain, and water the colour of stout, we knew that we should come home with a basket of brook trout. We were never disappointed.

Mr Wood had seen service in India and had acquired an amusing idiom which Frank recorded in his Note Book under 'Vocabulary':

'If you'd only take my device and use them casties, there'd be some proper little fish'd size your hook—champion good!'

'I fetched him a larrup—real proper.'

'When we was serving in the Elimayors.' (Himalayas)

'Tell the old gentleman (Father) he's left his scissums.' (scissors)

When our two kind old aunts felt uneasy, in case we might be causing the fishes to suffer, Father reassured them by saying: 'They've got as good a chance as we have.'

117

Sometimes our parents took us abroad during the Spring holidays. On two or three occasions we went with them to Paris, where we stayed in or near Alice Ward's charming little flat in the Rue Vaugirard. We were too young and insensitive to take in the agreeable effect of the waxed floors, dark interiors and rather ramshackle furnishings. Once, we were given a room in a flat above, belonging to an artist who was absent. Here we saw, at close quarters, a style of painting with which we were unfamiliar. The paint was put on in a multiplicity of dabs, oblongs or points and we noticed the same style at the Salon des Indépendants, where there was plenty to startle us.

A young Frenchman, introduced by Alice Ward, accompanied us on sight-seeing tours while Father was at our Paris Showroom in the Rue d'Hauteville. Our interests were juvenile. We were only half aware of the lovely lines and masses, to say nothing of the delicate colouring of Paris in April. Our attention was diverted towards what then seemed to us singular public transport—trams working by compressed air or smelly accumulators—or towards the size of electric sparks between the trolleys and overhead wires, or the engines in the Seine steamboats. Sometimes we would try to negotiate the escalators at the Bon Marché against the ascending flow, to the annoyance of shoppers carrying armfuls of parcels.

Mother did not like travelling, but once in Paris her spirits rose. She delighted in Alice Ward's company and loved the little flat, where they would laugh and giggle together. They used it as a centre for hilarious shopping expeditions. They would lunch at some petite bôite, and sometimes drink what they called 'little wickeds' (liqueurs, etc).

Certain French phrases became family catchwords. For instance, 'même chose', suggested by an occasion when, in some public place, they had asked the way to 'The Ladies' and had then enquired why men appeared to be moving freely in and out of the same door. Another was 'Champagne tout le temps', which was Mother's reply when a waiter enquired whether they would like to take a glass of champagne with the fish to be followed by some red wine as the meal progressed.

An important theme running through this book is the effect of Anglo-German relations on our family in these years. Parallel with the drama being enacted in our own home was another at The Lodge, a few doors away, where lived two close friends of the family, Walter and Alice Schürhoff. We met them in Berlin during the Spring of 1907. They were then accompanied by their son Fritz, who was going on to a school at Hildesheim, and a younger child, Lena. The young people were about our own age and the parents, on each side, enjoyed the courtesy titles of 'Uncle' and 'Aunt'. Walter was large and bearded and on this occasion wore a peaked, nautical type of cap. German born, but for long naturalised English, he was a partner in a Birmingham export business.

He and Father greatly liked, respected and probably influenced each other. Walter Schürhoff was generous and benevolent towards many friends and relatives, but his treatment of children inclined to be dictatorial. Frank and I felt intuitively and with distaste something domineering in his relationship with his family and this emphasised our prejudices against Germany and the Germans.

Alice Schürhoff, a distant relative on Father's side, was gentle and humorous and often acted as a mediator between this somewhat frightening figure and their offspring. In this situation Lena showed more resilience than anxiety to placate authority, an attitude which had our sympathy and support.

Circumstances were therefore such that Berlin, unlike Paris, seemed to generate friction between us and our parents, in spite of the Schürhoffs' unselfishness and eagerness to give us a good time. This kindness showed itself right at the start of our travels when, crossing by the night boat from Harwich to the Hook, Father generally organised a visit to the engine room, whence we were only driven away by incipient sea-sickness as we left the River Cherwell and gained the North Sea. (Only Frank and I suffered from sea-sickness: Father was a good sailor.)

The Easter of 1907 was exceptionally hot and sunny and our sight-seeing expeditions in Berlin included visits to several open-air beer gardens. I remember one day sitting in a large terraced amphitheatre, drenched in sun-light, among several thousand people, listening to a brass band playing Offenbach's 'Barcarole', the *Carmen* Overture and the March from *Aida*. The beer gardens were closely linked with Father's programme of Temperance Reform, which I have described in my book *Brass Chandelier*. Our sordid pubs, with their swing doors and sawdust, were to be converted into places to which men could bring their women-folk and drink, in moderation, the right sort of beer, amongst pleasant surroundings. German beer halls and gardens were his models. As for the beverage, he himself preferred lager beer to Bass or Worthington. It was, of course, a matter of personal taste, but he seemed to attribute mystical health-giving qualities to Dortmunder or Löwenbräu and he expanded as he lifted his Mass and surveyed these crowds, so replete with Gemütlichkeit. While we young people sipped our Himbeersaft (i.e. raspberry syrup—we were not yet considered old enough for beer), he would draw our attention to the conscript soldiers in their smart uniforms, extolling the advantages of discipline for the young.

We were taken to see the changing of the guard at the Königswache—no more ludicrous, I suppose, than the same ceremony at Buckingham Palace. Frank, however, took a mental note of the scene, the goose-stepping guardsmen, in their white slacks and spiked helmets, and, during 1911 and '14, he reproduced it in a sketch at Bedales before delighted audiences.

One day we accompanied the Schürhoffs to the Berlin Zoo, where there occurred an unforgettable incident. We had inspected the gardens as a party and after tea we young people were given leave to go where they would, but to meet later at a given time and place. Somehow we lost our way and found the rendezvous only after a frenzied search. We were somewhat panicky and undoubtedly late. Our arrival was followed by a painful scene. I doubt whether the delay was the real cause of Mother's displeasure. Her all too active imagination may have conjured up scenes of mutilating encounters with wild animals. She may also have become exhausted by Father's uncritical insistence on the excellence of all things German or by the authoritarian and somewhat heavy atmosphere of Prussia in

120

1907, contrasting, as it did, with that of her beloved Paris. Almost certainly I would have met any reprimand from her with resentful protest, instead of with tactful expressions of regret. But, whatever the cause, Mother was too angry to consider carefully what she said, and in addition to fantastic threats of castigation and enforced retirement to bed without supper (our ages were then 13 and 15) made some ill-considered remarks about Germany. The Schürhoffs were silent and embarrassed. Shocked and sad, we all left for our hotels, where the matter was patched up, sufficiently, at any rate, for the two families to meet for their evening meal in an atmosphere which was not too strained. What were Frank's feelings on this occasion? Although he joined me in protest, his loyalties were obviously divided.

Some days later, we left Berlin for the wonderful old town of Hildesheim. Fritz Schürhoff was being educated at an orthodox German Realschule. He was living at the house of one of the masters. Compared with Bedales this school seemed to us repellent, and served to strengthen our nationalistic antagonism.

During our holidays at home we had few contacts with young people of our own age. We went to no dances or parties. Perhaps we were unpopular. Be that as it may, as soon as we left school our social life began and invitations were not scarce. Before our first dance there was considerable excitement as we struggled with bow-ties and tail coats. While we were waiting in the hall for the four-wheeler Father said 'Now, don't guzzle.' We asked him what he meant and he replied 'Don't try and fill up your dance programmes with all the attractive girls—think of the others as well.' He believed that we would become *blasé* if we started this sort of thing too soon and, I think, deliberately discouraged his many friends from asking us to join in the social life of the young.

But in spite of this insulated life we were seldom bored. At home there were so many interesting and exciting things to do. For instance, each week we needed little encouragement to go to the works for a day or two, for the brass-worker's trade seemed extremely attractive to us. Frank spent much time with the Steventon family in the pattern-making shop where he was

121

much liked. He learnt to take a plaster mould from a wax model and work through the various stages until the article appeared in brass. He also acquired some skill in turning simple articles on a hand-lathe. Between them, they made an unusual looking model steam-boat, with a vertical slide-valve engine. The hull was of sheet brass beaten to shape, repoussé fashion.

On certain Saturdays one of the girls in the works would grill us chops on the lacquering stove; later, Father, who had given up his afternoon golf, helped to lay down our model railway in the despatch department. We had been given locomotives and extensive rolling stock (2-inch gauge) of the very best quality, manufactured by the firm of Bassett-Lowke.

Shortly before writing the following paragraph I was invited, with my old friend Peter Eckersley as co-dramatic critic, to form part of an audience for a little play in which my grandchildren were acting. I was then reminded of our performances at 146 Hamstead Road. Age for age, their standard was higher than ours, for, as boys, Frank and I generally started with overmuch attention to the tickets and the programmes, and this sometimes led to insufficient rehearsing, On one occasion, we were inspired by a Bedales burlesque to do a Sherlock Holmes sketch. During a very ragged performance we became over-excited and broke Father's best meerschaum pipe. He accepted this loss with good-natured self-control. At Christmas we took more time and care over preparation and were sometimes helped by our uncle, Dr Sydney Short. One year he wrote a sketch, with musical numbers called 'The Gay Deceivers' which, as I now realise, must have caused eye-brows to lift when, during the following term, I innocently suggested that it should be produced as a form-play at Bedales. Uncle Sydney could not prevent his amorous disposition from revealing itself in the text. Although there were no direct references to marital infidelity, the name of the piece suggested it. There were certainly frequent allusions to light-hearted love affairs with theatrical folk, including a young woman called Tootsie who, however, never actually appeared, Later, these Christmas sketches became more and more ambitious and often included songs and pieces which Frank had composed.

We had our own work-room and sank ourselves in all sorts of creative activity. Among our many hobbies of the years 1906 and 1907 was our model theatre, an ancient one, given to us by some relative. With it were some of the old sheets, 'Penny Plain' and 'Twopence Coloured', to be cut out and pasted on card. We tried to mount and assemble Douglas Jerrold's comic three-act play *Black-Eyed Susan; or All in the Downs*, but the characters and scenery seemed out of scale. We therefore decided to design them ourselves. The first presentation was of our own one-act adaptation of *Matteo Falcone*, a short story by Prosper Mérimée, which we had 'done' in our French class. The Corsican father shoots his son for having betrayed some friend who was being sheltered from the police. This piece, though dull and depressing, provided useful experience for next year's production, a dramatic version, which we had written, of Anthony Hope's novel, *The Prisoner of Zenda*. The scenery included some striking features; for instance, the library at the Château of Tarlenheim was lit by a high-class Best & Lloyd adjustable gas pendant.

While performing, Frank and I would sit on opposite sides of a small table, suitably screened, with the model theatre between us. Mother was alongside, at the grand piano, where she played the overture, *entr'actes* and incidental music. She also provided the appropriate sound-effects by such means as a chain rattling on a tea tray for the dungeon scene, or by rubbing kitchen knives together for the duelling.

We each had to play several parts and among the characters allotted to Frank was that of Princess Flavia; by this I mean that he manipulated the wire and clip to which her silhouette was attached, allowing his voice to take on a falsetto and supposedly feminine timbre. It was necessary to exercise care or the characters would fall flat and disappear or, alternatively, go flying upwards. During rehearsals such mishaps sometimes led to unseemly altercations which were quite out of character with this most romantic tale:

PRINCESS FLAVIA: Is love the only thing? If love were the only thing, I would follow you—in rags, if need be—to the world's end;

for you hold my heart in the hollow of your hand! But is love the only thing?

RUDOLPH RASSENDYL: Do what you will or what you must, I think God shows his purpose to such as you. My queen and beauty!

PRINCESS FLAVIA: 'My lover and true knight! Perhaps we shall never see one another again. Kiss me, my dear, and go!

At this point levitation takes place and the Princess sails up towards the ceiling.

RUDOLPH RASSENDYL: There you go again, you silly ass—can't you be more careful?

MOTHER: Now Bob, I am sure he didn't do it on purpose. It isn't very pretty to talk to Frankie-boy like that, etc.

We rehearsed this play many times and the actual performance, before the family, our two Aunts, Fanny Edwards, our nurse Emma Hopley and others, was marked by no mishaps. Indeed, Uncle Sydney was enthusiastic and immediately made plans to prepare a much more ambitious piece for the following year. There was to be a scene in St. Petersburg and another on board an air-ship. He even got as far as writing the scenario and some of the dialogue. Nothing came of it, however. *The Prisoner of Zenda* was the last performance on our model theatre.

During the Summer term of 1908, Frank underwent an operation. A photograph shows Uncle Sydney, who attended professionally at that time, keeping Frank in practice, as he lay in bed, with a Morse signalling device. There is also a photograph of a scene at Christchurch near Bournemouth during June of that year. Mother took Frank there for a period of convalescence. From many subsequent allusions and conversations they greatly enjoyed themselves during this holiday and were certainly happy to be alone together.

Chapter 5
Army training at Boxmoor

In November 1915 the 59th or second line of the North Midland Division (TF) 'lay in its billets in and around Watford, Hemel Hempstead and other towns and hamlets in Hertfordshire.' It was to this division that I had been transferred after a period of training with the third line at Helton Park, Grantham. I had been posted to No. 2 Company, then stationed at St. Albans.

On Monday, November 22 I met the 12.15 from St. Pancras and was waiting on the St. Albans platform as Frank alighted from the train. He was wearing his gaberdine tunic and cavalry twill riding breeches, newly fashioned by Allport's. (Nine days later on a 'very wet sloshy day, fortunately, trench coat arrived by post, via France and Birmingham. Huge success,' Frank wrote. The belted trench coat with detachable fleece lining, supplied by Thresher & Glenny, had then only recently come onto the market.)

Frank looked well and seemed in a particularly buoyant mood. We went off to lunch together and were soon exchanging reports of our more recent experiences and eagerly discussing future projects, such as the purchase of motor cycles, the composition of songs, how to make full use of local golf courses, and other matters. As for military duties, he thought it would be inadvisable for him to apply to serve in the same company as myself, as his seniority might cause difficulties. (Already six months my senior, he was in fact gazetted 1st Lieutenant two days later, his promotion dating back to August 15.) He talked about our parents and home, where he had spent the week-end; Father was enthusiastic about his experiments in grafting and the growth of his young apple trees in the garden. On Sunday morning he had accompanied Father to Nelson Street Adult School where he had found 'small numbers but good spirit'.

After lunch, I took him on the carrier of my motor-cycle and started for Felden Heath, Boxmoor, where he was to be stationed. We were soon overtaken by a car containing our C.O., Colonel L.G. Reading. Frank and he continued the journey together. They arrived just in time for a smoking concert in the large mess room. Frank recorded that he 'was very cordially received'.

His Company Commander was Major R.J. Greene who, unlike Frank, had seen no service overseas. Promoted from the ranks, he spoke with a marked Leicester accent. He was a plump man, in his mid-30s, given to repeating phrases and catchwords with mock solemnity, until their witty character overcame his studied self-control. His rounded features would then suddenly disintegrate as he exploded in falsetto chuckles. He could be moody and quarrelsome at times, but had a most likeable side to his nature.

This may have been Frank's first contact with a superior officer whose origins were not of the same bourgeois middle-class as our own. Our home and school-life had been anything but snobbish in the conventional sense, but we were becoming vaguely aware of the 'officer and gentleman' stereotype, and what we should now call 'U or Non-U' speech and behaviour. Frank wrote that Green was 'generally considered not quite— well—'. He had, however, been, all that was 'affable, confidential, polite and generally considerate' to Frank, who wondered 'whether his coming from France had anything to do with it'. Fascinated by Green's idiom he reported the following telephonic explanations in a letter home: '"We are at

126

Shot'anger, Felden-'eath—some people calls it Mor—Felden Mor or Roughdown—yer can call it whichever ya likes— though mind yer it's really Box Mor." By this time the poor person at the other end is asking for a little brandy!' (28 February 1916)

I was later to become well acquainted with 'Father' Green, for the transfer of officers from France caused a general re-shuffle of commands. As a result he was demoted to the rank of captain and on January 28 put in command of No. 2 Company with which I was serving.

As Requisitioning Officer, Frank was also to work closely with Captain I.A. Sutton ('Captain Sparker'), the Supply Officer. Wax-moustached, he was 'one of the dear old sort', Frank wrote, 'gazetted from Staff Sergeant. The sort that doesn't mind you taking anything in hand and pushing him, or it, through before his eyes in a quiet persuasive manner' (7 December 1915). As for these eyes, in the right one he had a slight cast, and 'when he had had a "session" at the Railway Hotel his "orbit" became rather more of a "swivel".' The last sentence is from a letter written nearly forty-five years later from another of Frank's colleagues, Harold Wardill, a young Luton dentist. Frank wrote that Harold was:

> a thoroughly decent chap ... musical, sensible, and with a sense of humour. He must have had a huge amount of work thrust on his shoulders before we came, by being so under-officered, but he is not the sort of chap to grouse about the second wart [or pip, i.e. promotion to 1st Lieut.]. He will probably get it soon. I like him the best of the lot and we pull each other's legs quite a good deal. I am at present taking on his job, including old Mess President again, as he is in for a course at Aldershot now. (7 December)

Harold's name keeps appearing in Frank's diary and letters. They played billiards and snooker together at the Railway Hotel, as well as golf and football. In a long letter he describes their adaptations of, first, swing boats from the pleasure ground, and then park seats for tobogganing in the snow. (28 February 1916)

In 1958 Harold Wardill wrote to me: 'I have so often thought of Frank and the very happy times we had with the 59th Divisional Train. [When he] came to us we were the only subalterns [but] in very close contact for the whole of our time in Bosmoor [sic]. We organised many concerts—Frank, as you know, had a charming voice—and I remember so well 'Oh Mistress Mine!' by Roger Quilter and 'Boot, Saddle to Horse' by Stanford and many other musical evenings we got up for the men. I cherish the memories of Frank—more than any of my contacts during my 59th days. His charming disposition, kindly manner stood out and still do in my memories after all these years.'

The house where Frank was to live for the next five months was a spacious Edwardian residence, empty except for their own camp beds, and a chair or two in the bedrooms. In the mess was a piano and pianola. Otherwise the furniture comprised camp chairs and a table covered with a saddle blanket on which a few tea cups and Bass bottles were generally to be seen. Against the walls were coats, service hats and riding whips on hooks. Boots of all kinds stood around the walls. Frank wrote:

> Although we call ourselves Felden, Boxmoor station is only just at the foot of the hill. Our empty house, which is the officers' mess, billets, offices and all, is only two or three hundred yards from the field and men's mess room. We are about 500 feet above sea level and get a lovely view; the disadvantage is only [the steep climb] for the horses when they come home. When the company first got here I understand they found roundabouts and Aunt Sallys, etc, for the Common was evidently a great place for outings from London ... The field became so thoroughly sloshy that finally the floor of what evidently was a large tea-shed was pulled up and our horses now have their meals there instead. (7 December)

As for the work, Frank at first felt rather overwhelmed by the size of the company (twice that of the Brigade Companies) which practically meant 'learning a fresh composition. The men are so understrength,' he wrote, 'the sick and unfit horses so absurd and the wagons so derelict, that really it rather takes

128

one's breath away. Even the old Warrant Officer, Mr Biddies (of all wonderful names) in spite of being a hardened old veteran, comes up blinking when I suggest one or two blatant cases of inattention, and with mouth turned down at the corners remarks, "Yer know I've told 'em, Mr Best, that them fowels, well they're not fit to —— —— ——" (the rest is better imagined).' (7 December)

Convoy work for the transport of hay and other supplies amongst the Hertfordshire villages and small towns provided a pleasant occupation. 'Most perfect ride to Markyate,' he wrote. 'Country estates lovely with hoar frost, particularly after France.' (25 November)

On February 9, for the first time, we happened to come together while on duty. The whole Divisional Train had turned out for a route march. It was 'another perfect day, after sharp hoar frost.' Frank wrote home: 'The chaps cooked their dinner at the side of the road during the lunch interval. The whole scene was very picturesque. I met Bob en route, in fact he was riding at the head of his little lot, and I was at the tail of ours, so for part of the way we came exactly together.'

Three days after arriving at St. Albans Frank informed our parents that he had seen a good deal of myself and expected to do so even more when he could 'get about more easily on his motor bike'. And so he did—indeed, we continued to meet three or four times a week, whether at St. Albans, Watford, or Felden, for Company smoking concerts, for collaboration in song writing, for dancing and social evenings, and for games of golf. From this time the motor-cycle (for Frank a new form of transport) played an important part in our lives. In the letter quoted above he went on to say that he had called at Clark's of St. Albans, a shop which had 'a good name for valuing machines and taking good class 2nd hand ones as well'. Before the week was over he had bought a 1913 3½ HP Triumph for £30 and rode it back to Boxmoor. The machine was belt-driven and fitted with a Phillipson pulley (many of the pre-war single cylinder Triumphs were 'direct drive', i.e. without gears), which made it possible to vary the gear ratio by putting one's foot against the boss of the pulley, making the belt slip somewhat and wearing out boot leather. In spite of this variable gear, his mount failed three times to climb the steep hill to the house,[31] making necessary a further visit to Clark's for a reduction of the gear ratio. Later, however, he was able to report: 'The Triumph is going marvellously. I am getting used to overhauling any defects by moonlight or no light at all ... I find an electric torch held in the teeth does very well.' (17 January 1916)

Motorcycles were then somewhat unreliable, and it always seemed as if mechanical defects, such as a broken chain or slipping belt, occurred late on a dark night, far from our quarters, when the acetylene lamp was giving out. The roads were often deeply pitted.

Frank rode his Triumph for three months and then, after preliminary trials and negotiations, made a deal which was to bring him complete satisfaction. He recorded in his diary: 'Bought the famous Indian, 1915, 5–6 HP, 3-speed; let Triumph go in part exchange. Indian £52 10s 0d. Triumph £26 0s 0d. Cheque £26 10s 0d. Rode Indian over to Watford in the evening, with Wardill on the Company Douglas, for Bob's concert. Butterfield could not turn up so played the piano a good deal myself. Bob sang "A.B.C." and "Oh Mistress Mine", I gave them my A.S.C. "Uncle Tom Cobley" and "The Story of Daniel"' (2 March). Unfortunately, on the return journey, it snowed. Frank also experienced a 'nasty skid in Watford with Indian going quite slowly at side of tarmac' and hurt his knee.

The theme of the Indian's sterling characteristics is repeated with variations again and again in this story, It was 'a lovely machine', a 'marvel—wonderfully sprung, with thick tyres', it would 'run up the side of a house,' on bottom speed. On

---

[31] According to Harold Wardill, 'The road leading up above Boxmoor station was not supposed to be used for cycles or motor bikes—There was a hairpin bend and one was indeed lucky to get round.' (24 November 1958)

middle, 8 to 22 mph. 'And on top, from 20 mph upwards, according to the road. At 35 mph she just purrs without the least suggestion of racing the engine. The roads are very pitted for the most party but on smooth tarmac she will bound up to 40 in no time. Being chain driven you don't worry about the belt slipping or breaking all the time. Weighing up the pros and cons I think it is about the best speculation I have made since the war. I could get a side-car any time and take one of the Aunties out.' (23 April)

A new and exciting feature of this Hertfordshire period was our introduction to a gay and what seemed to us then a sophisticated mundane social life. The proximity to London opened up alluring possibilities of evening jaunts. Our theatre-going had hitherto tended to be serious—opera and the drama—but now we found ourselves more and more led into a world of glamorous frivolity by our brother officers, one of whom would even go round to the dressing room of a well-known star, after the show, and take her out to supper! How the names of those war-time shows release trains of tragi-comic memories: *The Bing Boys are Here*, *Tonight's the Night*, *Shell Out*, *Follow the Crowd*, and others. Here are some characteristic entries in his diary:

Got off to Euston by the 5.10 and met Bob at Elysée Restaurant where we had dinner. Proceeded to Vaudeville Theatre after, where *Samples* (1915, one of the best revues out) was performed— Topping company. (3 February)

Aunt Marcella, Joy [Short] and Beryl Smith arrived ... and after showing them round the station ... we all caught the 5.10 train and were fortunate enough to get tickets for Tina ... Jolly decent little snack at the Euston New Hall just opened, then enjoyed Phyllis Dare and W.H. Berry immensely. Got the 11.35 back to Felden. Most perfect weather the whole day—quite extraordinary. (5 February)

Left by 5.00 with Wardill and went to see Doris Keane in *Romance*, a wonderful bit of heavy acting. Dined at Troc. (15 February)

Our Uncle Percy Short and our Aunt Marcella had moved to Wimbledon from St. Albans, where they had rented a furnished house in order to be near their son William; he was serving in an infantry battalion of the 59th Division. Their house was not far from my billet. With them lived their daughter Joy, dark, round faced, and then about 17. She was always cheerful and quick to grasp Frank's allusive jokes. Staying with them as a guest was a tall and lithe young woman, Beryl Smith, with whom I soon fell in love. Her hair was chestnut coloured, her eyes full, heavily lidded and with long lashes. A slightly receding chin gave her profile an innocent expression. We were attracted by her lighter-hearted and humorous conversation. She had arrived at short notice from Wimbledon in order to escape from an importunate suitor.

The two girls, Frank and myself went to theatres together, danced and made music. Our aunt was a competent pianist and delighted us all with her playing of Debussy's 'Jardin sous la pluie' and 'La cathédral engloutie'. Beryl Smith played and sang somewhat reluctantly but Frank and I needed no persuading to perform.

At about this time, the Two-Step and what we now call the Old-Fashioned Waltz had given place to the Boston, Fox-Trot, One-Step and a step called The Twinkle. Frank and I badly needed basic instruction in these new dances. Beryl supplied it readily, twirling around in her pleated tango-skirt. 'Miss Smith's dancing, hot stuff,' Frank observed in his diary (26 December 1915).

Joy, too, was a delightful dancing partner. We would practise by the hour, the portable Deccaphone playing away cheerfully, in nasal tones, 'The Rag Picker', 'The Fox-Trot Ball', 'Hors d'Oeuvre', 'Ragging the Dog' and extracts from the musical shows we were seeing one after another. Our Aunt encouraged us, put down drugget on the drawing room floor, and invited our friends in for informal dances, claret cup and trifle being provided.

At my billet, also, dancing became popular. My hostess, Mrs Linsell, had a larger drawing room and organised a more ambitious dance at their house. 'Ripping dance at Linsell's. Beautiful conservatory decorations and girls' Frank wrote (7 December). Then followed a still more ambitious project—a dance to be sponsored by the A.S.C. for the Division as a whole. After anxious weeks of selling tickets, balancing up men and women, booking a band, and dealing with dance-programmes and catering firms, it actually took place at the Town Hall on January 7 1916. On our arrival the scene seemed to us then a brilliant one. The predominant khaki colouring contrasted pleasantly with the blue and scarlet mess kit of the staff officers and generals and with the beautiful full-skirted frocks of the women.

Our quartet had been enlarged to six by including Peach and our cousin Barbara Anderton, who had been invited by the Shorts to stay with them—'Barbara very beautiful', Frank noted, and summed up as follows: 'Blissful evening—very high standard of youth and beauty and dancing.' After the dance he 'went back on the box of their cab' to our aunt's house where they re-lit the drawing-room fire and made cocoa. He then tuned up his Triumph, somewhat noisily, in the road outside and returned to Felden.

Next day he 'cut off after tea' and rode over to our Aunt's house. The girls were drooping somewhat. We did our best to liven things up. 'Had absurd foolery with Bob—Barbara, Beryl and Joy rather tired, like myself, but very appreciative. Did not stop long after supper.' (8 January)

A fortnight later we were invited by Beryl's parents for a weekend visit to their house on Wimbledon Common, and this entailed the first of those adventurous motor-cycle rides across London that always left us fearful of having a breakdown that might make us return late from leave. Our host, Mr Robert Smith, grey-bearded, lovable and unpretentious, was a retired manufacturer from Glasgow. Mrs Smith, in powerful pince-nez, radiated kindness and affability. Their house, and its interior appointments, gave us an overwhelming impression of fashionable good taste. Frank described the day's happenings in his diary:

Had machine cleaned and got off at 3 p.m. having filled up with petrol. Rode to the Smiths at Ardmore, Wimbledon Common, via Watford, Harrow, Willesden, Hammersmith and Putney, without mishap. Arrived 5 p.m. for tea. Bob, Shorts and others there for the evening. Music, dancing and ragtime selections, etc. Beautiful house—everything arranged just so so. Bob and myself put up for the night in beautiful rooms.

(Sunday, 23 January) I had early brekker at 7.15 a.m. and got off with machine (Triumph) at 7.45. Belt broke four times on way back. Beautiful morning, part foggy, after sharp frost. Came back up Edgware Road. Arrived 11.20 instead of 10 for inspection of ADVS (Assistant Director of Veterinary Services). Played golf with Wardill.

We were to make two more visits to Ardmore. One, as we shall see, took place on March 11 during a course at Aldershot, and one on April 16: 'Met Bob at Watford Cross Roads, at 2 p.m.,' Frank wrote. 'Got to Ardmore' at 3.30. Jolly afternoon, music, etc. Bob broke chain and belt returning.' (A link came adrift and dropped on the road ten or twenty yards before I was able to draw up. I had no spare link. The roads were muddy and the acetylene lamp dim. To my surprise we managed to find the link and fix it in position. Holding my breath I continued at a snail's pace.) 'I lost number plate. Roads fearful. Bed 2 a.m.'

A week later, and a few days before this enchanting Hertfordshire interlude was to terminate abruptly, Frank's optimistic and enterprising nature took us further afield—this time to Ewell, near Epsom. He wrote home: 'On Good Friday we both went down to the Shorts' latest little cottage at Ewell. It is a charming little place with garden and Bechstein grand. Although Bob had a job with his tyres just as we were due to start, delaying us 1½ hours, we had pleasant weather to travel by, and arrived about 2 p.m. Aunt Marcella and Joy in good form, likewise Beryl. Afternoon walk. Roads very congested, did not return via Harrow and Twickenham, but through Wimbledon. Bob ran into road repairs!' (21 April)

Fresh songs arrived from home and in his diary there are numerous references to song-writing in collaboration with

Harold Wardill and myself. As we have seen, there was a piano in the house, but the atmosphere was not always favourable to practising. Sometimes Major Green and Captain Button would come in and 'bang pianola violently'. There were too many people around. Frank often wanted to be able to sit and write at the piano himself but even then there were occasions when his inspiration would flag: 'Left alone for the evening. Studied route to Wimbledon. Later on unsuccessful at composing.'

Frank met musical people, not only at our aunt's house but elsewhere. At the Ushers he enjoyed 'a never-to-be-forgotten musical evening' listening to 'varied talent on cello, violin, piano and vocal chords' (17 December 1915). At other houses we were invited to play, sing and practice, and I remember his being present during a visit from a Miss Jessie Hall, who taught music at Bedales. Of striking appearance, she not only entertained us with dramatic recitations but played the piano, introducing us to César Franck's music. (12 January 1916)

The theme of looking for a piano is taken up again: 'Rode down to Apsley Rooms Club—borrowed piano for Company dance.' Frank returned a few days later to Apsley's where, 'left alone with piano', he 'got through beginning of a new song'. Two days later he records: 'left alone after supper, second verse of Bob's song was finished'. (5 January)

At some point the piano must have been removed from the mess at Felden, for towards the end of March Frank wrote: 'We have still got no piano in the house. On the days when duty takes me over to St. Albans I usually call at Elliot's ... and spend an hour or so upstairs practising. However, to my great joy I have had an invitation to come in and practise whenever I like on a most beautiful 'grand' in a house quite close up here, where the people are awfully nice. I am very keen on keeping my fingers unstuck as far as possible; just a little daily makes all the difference.' (23 April)

Training included a Refresher Course at Aldershot. Our turn came on Tuesday, March 7 and coincided with a spell of snow and ice. We shared a room with another officer at Thornhill

Lodge and messed in the Buller Barracks,[32] where the atmosphere was Kiplingesque. Silver candelabra were displayed on the tablecloths and oil paintings of distinguished soldiers, darkened with age, looked down from the walls to remind us of the glorious traditions of our Corps.

The programme comprised foot-drill, musketry, lectures, and indoor riding schools where we trained over fences under Captain Sadler, a wise and capable veteran instructor. Later there were exercises in driving wagons with a long rein on the roads and over the Aldershot sands. Although put in charge of drivers and wagons, I had never actually ridden one so Frank and I sat side by side on the box behind a very tough pair of draft horses, by turns trying to keep them under control. (This was long-rein driving.) From this we passed onto what was known as Ride and Drive, where a soldier rides on one horse— the nearside horse—and controls the other with a short rein and a short whip. To protect the right leg from the pole one wore a sort of iron legging. This method was admirably suited to driving over rough ground, but it did not help Frank's knee, damaged by his skid at Watford on March 7. As it was still painful and had to be dressed daily, he got permission from the Adjutant to change into slacks after riding.

The course lasted a fortnight. At the week-ends we were given leave when we would dash up to town, meet Joy Short and Beryl Smith, take them to a matinee followed by tea at Piccadilly Hotel, and thence to Wimbledon. By that time the Shorts had returned to Wimbledon and put us up for the night. On Sunday we would walk on the Common, inspecting the aeroplane hangars and playing golf on the Wimbledon Park Links. This would be followed by tea and music and a hurried return to Aldershot.

---

[32] General Sir Redvers Buller, VC, was appointed to the Aldershot Command in 1898. He was associated with the A.S.C. through being Quartermaster General at the War Office in 1898. As boys, we heard of his alleged shortcomings as G.O.C. in South Africa during the Boer War. It was then that, for the first time, we became vaguely aware of 'Blimpishness', though, of course, the term was not yet known.

The course ended with what was for us a severe test in horsemanship, namely, going over a series of fences on the Aldershot sands with our stirrups crossed. Somewhat to our surprise we survived without being thrown. As for myself, I have never been able to understand just how this came about. The horses were certainly well trained, but I recollect being, as it were, suspended a foot or so above the saddle, as I went over each fence, and I realised that it was a toss-up whether I would effect a landing on the horse or the sands. It gave me a foretaste of what to expect later in the Royal Flying Corps.

From Frank's diary we gather that the exciting atmosphere of the Aldershot sands was heightened by other military activities. 'Awful pandemonium of bombs, steam tractors, railway, machine guns, etc. Horses "some prance".' (21 March)

On Wednesday 22 March, the course finished with examinations (in which we appear to have done quite well), after which we were able to catch an afternoon train to London. For the second time during this Hertfordshire period we met Sylvia Mundy, to whom we had both proposed marriage, this time taking her out to see *More* at the Ambassador's Theatre.

Next day Frank called at the Hawkes & Son and discussed with them the possibility of publishing some of his music; then, after a meal at the Euston Hotel, we parted company, he returning to Felden, and I to Watford.

It was about this time that, strolling with my mother in Handsworth Park, I started some train of thought with the words, 'I'm awfully keen on …', then paused, wondering whether to continue with 'golf' or 'fishing'. My mother completed the sentence for me with the name 'Beryl Smith'. I was at first surprised but after a few seconds I said to myself 'I believe I am', and resolved to explore to matter further. I applied for leave to go to London for the afternoon and evening. I was very frustrated. In my diary it records 'remarkable journey from New Street to Watford. Five hours late—blizzard—all wires blown down.

However, on Thursday, March 30th, I was detailed for transport duty. After this duty I phoned Wimbledon, and met Beryl in London for tea, shopping and dinner at the Troc. We then went to see *My Lady Frayle*, a rather good musical on the theme of Faust where a lady sells her soul to the devil to get her youth back. I returned to Watford dancing on air. In the taxi returning from the theatre I had proposed to Beryl and her reply was not unfavourable. She was not committed anywhere, she said, but would like time to think it all over. In the meantime she suggested that we might become 'unofficially engaged'.

A day later (31 March) during lunch, Frank began to be aware that the skin of his face was sore and later discovered a fine rash on his body. He felt quite fit but decided to consult the M.O. at Gadebridge Park where he learnt that it might be a case of German Measles, as indeed it later proved to be. This did not prevent him, however, from carrying out a full and busy day, doing 'a bit of shopping', buying manuscript paper for his music, examining an English concertina 'for future reference' and other activities. His chin became worse as evening drew on, but he had been entrusted with the job of paying the men. For some reason or other the silver had been left behind, so he 'took Indian across to St. Albans to make enquiries, only to find the bank closed'. Unperturbed he 'returned a bit late to Boxmoor for evening revels at the Railway Hotel', where the genial landlord, John Marsh, a typical John Bull with side whiskers and red waistcoat and full of racing information, had provided a small barrel of oysters. The night ended with a game of poker in the mess. Next morning (April Fool's Day) he was covered with rash and ordered to stay in bed. He read, wrote and played the gramophone. The whole thing was 'a bit of a farce' as far as he was concerned, he said.

The same day I was entertaining the Shorts and Beryl Smith. We all had lunch together and started to play golf at the West Herts Club, Cassiobridge. That morning I had heard of Frank's 'childish complaint", which seemed to amuse my brother officers. I was vaguely aware of a slight itchiness of the face which I assumed was barber's rash. But as the afternoon wore on, it became impossible to ignore the fact that I was sickening for some malady. Bouts of shivers alternated with hot spells. The bunkers swam before my eyes. Putting became impracticable.

Reluctantly I had to send my fiancée and other guests home and report sick. (My diary records this as 'a ghastly anti-climax'.) I was isolated in a ground floor room, with an unfortunate hospital orderly detailed to look after me and sleep in the same room. The door was locked, the only access to the room being through the garden, around which I strolled 'a million times'. I read *A Knight on Wheels* by Ian Hay, *Love and Mr Lewisham* by H.G. Wells, and *Daddy Long Legs* by Jean Webster. I also occupied myself with tuning up my Douglas motor bike (two cylinders, horizontally opposed). At some point a junior medical officer put his diagnosis of me before the high-ranking divisional M.O. at a medical board. He said that I was suffering from V.D. He was corrected.

There was no telephone in my room, and somehow Frank only heard of my indisposition through a letter from home. After six days I was allowed to ride over on my Douglas and see him. He wrote home: 'We compared symptoms and found them almost identical, particularly *sore chins*! Quarantine applied equally to both so we were able to associate, tho' he was still isolated at Watford Hospital. Played golf on links. Lunch and tea with me.' (6 April)

From then on our convalescent period gave us a welcome opportunity for inter-visitation. We worked together on some new songs, such as an 'absurd Peat Moss ditty' and a fantastic musical disquisition on King's Regulations. We 'prepared gags', 'wangled gramophone ad lib' and exchanged records.

Near the house was a 'little course, all up and down—only nine holes but very sporty' and it was here that we spent the afternoons. I was suffering from a bad slice and asked his advice. Like Father, he approached the game in a scientific and analytical spirit, marking the ball with a chalk spot (as we had been taught to do) in order to see whether I was hitting it with the centre of the club. His coaching was fairly effective.

Soon after Frank's arrival at Boxmoor we had played a little golf together, but the climate had been wintry, with weeks of snow, sleet and rain. As late as March 28, returning from leave, we had sat for eight-and-a-half hours in the two hours

Birmingham–Euston express, high winds and snow having brought down trees and telegraph wires. Now, however, the weather was 'beautiful, like summer'. On his first day out of bed he had decided to apply himself to the game and described his experiences to Father:

> Yesterday, I took my putter and mashie out and had some good fun with six balls. I wish you had been there to give me a little instruction ... The greens aren't at all good, but it was like old times on such a beautiful evening doing "parroaches" (a Handsworth cabbie's expression) from the top of the hill and watching the little white specks drop plunk on to the green or wide of the mark.' (4 April)

My visits were held up for a day by a seized gear-box, but on Sunday (9 April) Frank rode over for a round with me on the West Herts course and from then on missed no opportunity of practising. Recovering from one infection, he succumbed to golf fever:

> 11 April. There are certain symptoms which I find always accompany a revival of enthusiasm for the game ... a sure sign is picking up a club from any corner and practising one's "stance" along the symmetrical flooring—also an acute passion for performing trick shots—not only in the house with niblick from bed to bed etc, but also outside, where I long to hit the ball from a comparative oasis among the hazards to a similar spot within range. If it can be worked that a crossroads, a sea of mud, a young gorse wood, a vegetable garden, or something interesting must be negotiated, 'tant mieux'.

Opposite the house was a 10-acre field of shortish grass. Frank's batman, Driver R Johnstone, made him 'half-a-dozen white flags, with staircase rods'. These were placed 'so that a good shot brings you right up to the pin (180–200 yards). By varying the order one could 'get any amount of choice of length'. He invented a triangular system of marking where the balls fell. It was 'far easier to carry a double triangle in one's head, than just leave it to chance'. 'I have never had a better opportunity of improving my game,' he wrote, 'than during this quarantine,' from which we were declared free on April 12.

During the next fourteen days Frank continued to enjoy himself in the fine summer weather, motor cycling to Wimbledon and Ewell, as we have seen, practising the piano at Elliot's or Winterbotham's, and taking one more evening in town for dinner and a show, including Marie Lloyd in a local music hall singing 'A little of what you fancy does you good!' Though from time to time there were rumours of going overseas, on April 6 he wrote 'we have heard nothing definite lately about moving.' There seemed every prospect of remaining in Hertfordshire for some months.

And so it continued until Easter Monday, April 24, when, returning to Boxmoor by train after spending the day with Beryl in Wimbledon, I was met at Watford station around midnight by Ewart Eames, looking grave. Everything was in darkness, because of a Zeppelin raid. Eames told me that the division had been ordered to move but the destination was unknown. We were to be on the first train due to leave, he said, in about an hour's time.

My wonderful batman hurriedly packed my kit and the trek to the station began. The train actually left at 3 a.m. and we travelled all day. From the names of the stations it soon became apparent that we were going north. Our destination was clear when we arrived at Holyhead and embarked.

It was all very sudden. To quote General Sandbach: 'On the afternoon of Easter Monday strange things were happening in Dublin. The Fairy House Races of the Meath Hunt took place as usual [but] on their return, motor cars were held up and shots were fired into the air, and there was an angry appearance of disturbance. In fact, the Irish Rebellion of 1916 had begun. As soon as the news reached London, the G.O.C. 59th Division was warned by telephone to send first one Infantry Brigade with some details, and afterwards the whole Division, to serve under the orders of General Sir John Maxwell in quelling the rising.' (The Zeppelin raid was part of the German support for the rising.)

We arrived at Kingstown (Dun Laoghaire) at 10.30 on Tuesday evening, the first troop ship to do so. Frank did not arrive until three days later. On Easter Monday he had been Orderly Officer for Bank Holiday. After morning stables he slept soundly and then went off from the depôt to see about a hay convoy for the following day. On his Indian ('running wonderfully') he rode to Winterbotham's and 'practised on their beautiful little grand'. It seems that at 6 p.m. there was 'WIND UP'. 'Wagons were sent off under any old driver. Being Bank Holiday, many of the drivers were on leave and had to be located in pubs, cinemas and so forth. The 'Supply Section was rounded up (some sober) to dish out all the iron rations for transport to Watford'. Frank retired to bed, but was 'routed out at midnight after 10 minutes' dozing' and then 'went down to depôt', took 'hot tea in signal box,' and 'traced supply express goods train from Nottingham [the main depot], which arrived at platform 3.45 a.m. Lovely dawn.' he observed.

From dawn until late at night Frank worked all through Tuesday 'inspecting loading ramps', 'issuing from a mobile depot, and with transport'. At 6 p.m. he began issuing to cyclists under old Winser (Eric Winser, an old Bedalian who served with the Sherwood Forresters) and continued with S. Staffs & R.A.M.C., sending off five trains in all.

Next day (Wednesday 26 April) found Frank still issuing rations from Boxmoor Hall; he did not finish until midnight. 'Everything very dusty and fragrant after hot day,' he wrote. He was able to get a little sleep from 1.00 till 4.00 a.m. on Thursday, after which he 'got kit put on limbered wagon at 6.00 a.m. and was taken to station. Lovely morning, though cool at first,' he observed. 'Jolly decent breakfast at John Marsh's.'

Frank had made final arrangements with Harold Wardill, who was to stay behind to clear up and, amongst other things, take charge of the cherished Indian. Frank, however, had 'smuggled Government Douglas bike on to troop train last thing'. But at Liverpool he met with a disappointment, for he 'unfortunately had to unload it and send it back to St. Albans'. They boarded the Wicklow at 7.30 p.m. 'along with 500–600 others', the ship being 'registered to take 120 passengers', and arrived at Kingstown early next morning.

Chapter 6
Quelling the Irish Rebellion

As the Wicklow steamed into Kingstown Harbour, Frank examined the long curved granite walls of the East and West piers leading to the landing quay and loading sheds. It was 6.30 a.m. of Friday, April 28 and I had landed on the previous Tuesday. Leaning over the handrail Frank could not help making comparisons with his last visit in 1912. The buildings were the same but the atmosphere had greatly changed. 'The good old quay was quite deserted,' he noted and was told that strict martial law obtained everywhere. A curfew was being enforced and inhabitants had to turn in by 7.30 p.m. The ship came alongside. Disembarkation proceeded slowly. He soon realised that for military purposes the arrangements were quite inadequate. As I recall, the cranes were fixed and it was sometimes necessary to move the whole ship in order to get the wagons out of the hold.

During that first period of hanging about after the troop ship tied up, Frank expected to be fairly free to look around and, accordingly, decided to examine an elegant white building that he had noticed as they had approached the quay. The building was the Royal St. George Yacht Club. It was an exclusive club, but it turned out that all officers had been made honorary members. Frank went in and 'enjoyed a first-class breakfast'.

143

Then he went round the rooms, found them very comfortable and resolved to spend some time in the billiard room at the first opportunity. The architecture, he noted, was classical and it occurred to Frank that Best & Lloyd's 'Georgian' lighting fittings might suit the interior.

Eventually he had to turn away from the inviting deep arm chairs, return to the quay and issue loose hay. He fixed himself up wth a room for the night with a Mr McNeal, owner of the offices of the Board of Public Works, which was promptly annexed for the A.S.C.. He then worked the whole day and after supper went off on a petrol dinghy to tow out a petrol ship into the middle of the harbour. He was, he wrote home, 'actually officiating in the capacity of Requisitioning Officer for Divisional Troops' (i.e. Artillery, R.A.M.C., etc,) but, he explained, it was not like going abroad where practically everything was provided before you ask. Here no one knew anything about the sort of stuff we wanted' (30 April).

During the whole of the next day (Saturday, 29 April) Frank was fully occupied transferring a cargo of six 60-gallon petrol drums from the ship 'into a suitable place for storage' and, when in position, tapping and issuing. Over the next four days he issued some 400 gallons and, in general, found himself extremely busy—with 'rows of bills to settle up'. 'It is very decent being on my own,' he thought, 'with a responsible job to work out to my own satisfaction, and no one to interfere.' On Friday a week later (5 May) he handed over his petrol stock and audited the detail issues.

The events of that Easter week had moved with tragic speed. On Monday, 24 April, the Irish Volunteers had paraded in various parts of Dublin, and in the first surprise had occupied the General Post Office in Sackville (now O'Connell) Street, which gave them command of the whole telegraph system. They were also able to install themselves in a number of buildings both sides of the River Liffey.[33] All these posts were engaged, but

---

[33] From east to west they occupied: a) the group of buildings adjacent to

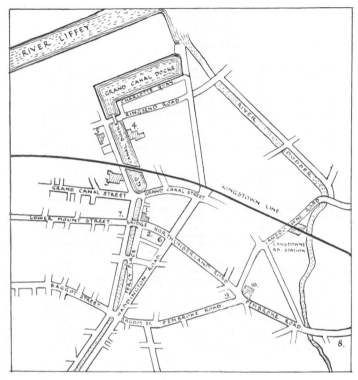

1. SCHOOL
2. PAROCHIAL HALL
3. BOLAND'S BAKERY
4. BOLAND'S MILL
5. DISTILLERY & TOWER
6. 25, NORTHUMBERLAND ROAD.
7. CLANWILLIAM HOUSE
8. 178th. BRIGADE HEADQUARTERS
9. CARRISBROOK HOUSE.
10. INTERCONTINENTAL HOTEL.

some were more fiercely involved in the fighting than others. On that first day the Irish also suffered reverses. The attack on Trinity College was beaten off, and the Castle, too, remained in

the Canal Docks, i.e. Boland's Mill, Boland's Bakery and the Distillery (S); b) Clanwilliam House, the Parochial Hall and other buildings near Lower Mount Street bridge (S); c) the G.P.O. (N); d) Jacob's Biscuit Factory (S); e) the Four Courts (N); f) the Nendicity Institution (S); g) the South Dublin Union (S). The distance of the line from east to west was about two miles. Note: (N) and (S) indicate whether North or South of the Liffey.

the hands of the British, who by mid-day Tuesday had set up a series of counter-posts separating the insurgents north of the Liffey from those on the south. In the evening, as we have seen, the first troopship docked at Kingstown. On board was the 178th Brigade (The Sherwood Foresters) to which No. 2 Company of the A.S.C. was temporarily attached. Unloading continued during the night, and on the next day (Wednesday, 26 April) the brigade marched up to Ballsbridge, a mile-and-a-half south-east of the city centre, in columns of fours. From there it continued in two columns. One took the Stillorgan Road and reached the Royal Hospital at Kilmainham, on the other side of the City, without opposition. Of the second column, one detachment proceeded via Pembroke Road and Baggot Street Bridge. Unmolested it reached Trinity College by way of Kildare St. The other detachment—the ill-fated 7th Battalion—continued along Northumberland Road and was mown down at comparatively short range as it approached and tried to cross Lower Mount Street Bridge. Four officers were killed and 14 wounded, while of other ranks 216 were killed and wounded. These losses were inflicted by an incredibly small number of Irish Volunteers,[34] and the engagement seems to have been the most sensational struggle of the whole insurrection. Lower Mount Street Bridge was not crossed by the main body of troops until the following morning (Thursday 27 April).

I was still at Kingstown when the 7th Batallion was attacked and it was not until the next day, Thursday 27, that we made our own trek to Ballsbridge, where I was put in charge of bombs and accordingly visited the bombing school. It was on that day that I witnessed a bombardment of a disused distillery. A gunboat, Helga, had shelled Liberty Hall and Boland's Mill from

---

[34] Accounts of the battle differ but according to Desmond Ryan: 'the entire strength of the garrisons at 25 Northumberland Road, Clanwilliam House and the Parochial Hall numbered 13 men … Clanwilliam House had seven Volunteers to defend it.' (The Rising, Golden Eagle Books Ltd., Dublin 1949, pp 195–6).

the Liffey on Wednesday, and on Thursday a small cannon was taken from it, mounted on one of our A.S.C. wagons and driven around. The gunner would look down the bore at the window of an occupied or suspected house and then put a shell or two into the room. On this day Éamon de Valera, one of the leaders of the Rising, had himself hoisted the Irish green Sinn Fein flag with the yellow harp on a small square tower on the roof of a disused distillery overlooking Grand Canal Quay. He had at his disposal insufficient forces to occupy it. The naval officer in charge of the gun had received orders to shoot the flag down. From Percy Place, at a range of about three-eighths of a mile, some 75 shells were exploded on the distillery, but at the end of the bombardment, although only two outside walls of the small tower remained standing, the flag had not been dislodged. The naval officer shrugged his shoulders and moved on. I was alongside when this event took place.

On this Thursday (27 April) James Connolly, the Trade Union leader, was twice wounded, and it was on the next day that the Wicklow docked at Kingstown. General Sir John Maxwell also arrived on that day (possibly on the same ship), having been put in command of the forces in Ireland by Lord Kitchener. Before one o'clock a shell had set fire to the roof of the G.P.O. and late in the evening De Valera was forced to evacuate Boland's bakery. In the meantime the British troops, reinforced by a battery of field artillery, had formed a complete cordon round Dublin. That night the sky was an angry red from the burning buildings. The situation of the Volunteers and the Citizen Army had become desperate.

On Friday, I motored over to Kilmainham to make contact with the 155th Brigade. I strolled up to Trinity College but ran over the bridges in the hope of avoiding the attention of snipers. Next day, we trekked over to the Royal Hospital and it was here that we took up our quarters. The place, built in 1684 and based on Les Invalides in Paris, was the equivalent of the Chelsea Hospital in London, just two years its junior. On that Saturday, (29 April), while Frank was busily occupied with storing and tapping his 60-gallon petrol drums, Patrick Pearse, Gaelic

147

educationalist, idealist and joint leader with James Connolly of the rising, surrendered unconditionally to General Maxwell.

The Rising was now suppressed, but on Sunday (30 April) occasional rifle fire could still be heard, although Jacob's Biscuit Factory had not surrendered. Frank obtained a small two-seater, driving and journeying about through Kingstown after local purchase estimates. 'It is still very warm,' he wrote. 'There are swarms of people in town, though all officers are carrying revolvers still. Life seems to be once more normal, and yet, it is in fact,

> All changed, changed utterly:
> A terrible beauty is born. (W.B. Yeats)

In retrospect I am appalled by our blindness to that terrible beauty. What we called cinema warfare, with troops clambering about on the roofs of Pembroke and Northumberland Road, had been spectacular. But now, as I noted in my diary, 'boredom sets in after exciting events' (30 April). During those critical days Frank and I had been cheerfully going about our duties, only vaguely aware of the crisis in Anglo-Irish relations, leading inevitably to the Black and Tans, Bloody Monday and, contrary to anything which we then expected, the independence of Ireland. Like most of the troops then engaged we were almost completely ignorant of, if not indifferent to, the historical background of the events which were then taking place—the hungry years, and the tragic blunders committed by the governments of our own country.

On Monday (1 May) Frank took tea with the captain 'on board the Arnfried, re-christened Hunsdon on being captured off German East Africa'. He then 'laid the foundation of an immense baled hay dump and got another 12 drums of petrol going'. Up to Tuesday (2 May) we had seen nothing of each other since our expedition to Ewell 10 days previously, but on that afternoon we met by chance for a moment at the roadside near Ballsbridge. Frank was with Captain Button in a borrowed car. 'Well, that's over,' we said, as we parted company.

Irish Rebellion – May 1916.
Liberty Hall, Dublin, the Rebel Headquarters,
after the storming.

Irish Rebellion – May 1916.
Holding a Dublin street against the Rebels.

This page: Frank (left) and Robert Best. 'Rode over to Kingstown where Mr Cooke risked his lens on our physiognomies.' (Letter, 24 April 1916)

Previous page: three postcards in Robert Best's collection. Top: Liberty Hall, the head office of James Connolly's union, the Transport and General Workers, and the headquarters of the Rising, though empty at the time of its bombardment. Middle: A street barricade set up against 'the Rebels'. Lower: Overhead view showing the destruction—a 'flea-bite compared with Ypres', in Frank's opinion.

150

On the way back Frank happened to encounter Mr Edward Lee, an old friend of the family, with whom he had stayed in 1912. Frank readily accepted an invitation to go to their home for tea. He found that they had moved from the Palladian House at Stillorgan to Bellevue, Blackrock, which was later to become the residence of De Valera. Mrs Lee, high complexioned, with a fine head and beautiful strong features, was of an exceptionally maternal and kindly disposition. She was the mother of four sons: Ted, the eldest, was helping his father in the business. Joe, the barrister, as we have seen, had been killed at Gallipoli. And Ernest, the R.A.M.C. doctor whom Frank had found sitting at the next table during August of the previous year, was still serving in France (he was to be drowned on the Leinster when it was torpedoed in the Irish Channel on the way back to Dublin on October 10, 1918). As for Tennyson, the youngest and the friend of our childhood, who had been wounded in the Dardanelles, Frank was delighted to find that, having been on leave from Cork at the time of the Rising, he had been detained and detailed to serve in the office of the A.P.M. (Assistant Provost Marshall or chief of Divisional Police) at Kingstown and was busy writing out passes. During this first week Frank would visit him frequently and together they would go off to lunch at the Royal Yacht Club to gossip, amongst other things, about their holidays as little boys at Rhyl. Edward Lee, tall and grey-bearded, was a passionate admirer of the poet Tennyson and would recite long passages from 'In Memoriam' and other works. He had built up a chain of department stores from modest beginnings, one of them being in the main street of Kingstown. During his stay in Ireland, Frank was often a guest at Bellevue. The warm welcome and hospitality he received, the beautiful house, and the garden and greenhouse chrysanthemums are described appreciatively in his diary and in fact we both made frequent visits to their house during our stay in Ireland.

On Wednesday (3 May) Patrick Pearse was executed, together with two other Irish leaders. Accounts of these sickening scenes filtered through to us at Kilmainham Hospital.

There were rumours that it had been necessary to finish off one of the condemned men with a revolver, and that the APM, or officer in charge of the firing squad, had not been able to stand the ordeal and had felt faint.

On that same day I went in search of relics and found a Sinn Fein haversack. I also collected a Sinn Fein bayonet and cartridges with the end of the bullet fired off, dum-dum fashion. (These I gave up when the Second War broke out, in accordance with official orders at the time.) Frank meanwhile went into Dublin for the second time, having once more borrowed a car, 'raised by the G.R. Volunteer Reserve. They are quite the most efficient body of men here, from my point of view, for knowing the surroundings and people intimately,' he wrote home. 'They tell me the best person to go to for anything and save me hours thereby.' He came on to Kilmainham Hospital for tea. Eagerly we went over our experiences together, speculating on the possibilities of future musical and sporting cooperation. After tea he 'had to go to the Command Paymaster, Irish Command, and get a draft to open an imprest account at a bank here (£100).'

Frank 'did the town and saw all the sights'. He was not impressed and thought the people were making a fuss about the damage, which was a 'flea-bite compared with Ypres. The rifle bullet marks from the snipers are the most interesting part,' he wrote; 'snipers have shut up completely, at any rate for a time. The banks are open again.' (4 May)

The next few days passed agreeably enough. At Kingstown 'the first demonstration of any feeling towards the troops was a friendly one, and cheers and even bouquets of flowers greeted the soldiers'. 'The Irish hospitality was liberal everywhere,' Frank found. For instance, no sooner had he set foot inside Edward Lee's Kingstown store ('to buy a small despatch case') than he found himself taken off to the manager's office and given an immense whisky and soda. The Yacht Club had 'saved the situation, thanks to the generosity of the members'. He used the club daily for private correspondence. The prices of the meals were moderate and he was 'in and out a good deal'. It was 'worth pounds to be an Honorary Member', he wrote, and was 'quite close to the depôt'. He would sometimes meditate on the seascape from an easy chair and closely observe the flying techniques of the bird. Father called them 'professionals'.

> The sea is rough to-day and the spray splashes onto the big bay windows of the lounge. It is very fascinating to watch the sea-gulls doing 'gliding cantrips' over the mail boat which draws up within a stone's throw. (7 May)

In the evening Frank would dine at the club with Captain Sutton and then spend an hour or two playing billiards. In due course he could not help noticing certain symptoms in his companion. The Captain's right eye began to swivel, causing him to miscue and as the evening wore on he tended to look to his cue for support (6 May). After billiards the two would return to their billet. Frank felt 'exceedingly comfortable' with Mr and Mrs McNeal. They were 'awfully decent' but had no facilities for providing meals.

Frank's arrival had coincided with a spell of fine weather, and for some days he had been sleeping on the balcony of the Public Works Offices. But on Tuesday night (2 May) it 'started to rain at 11 p.m. and attained its zenith at 2.45 a.m., when it became 'quite unbearable even under a water-proof sheet'. He hurriedly moved into the office for the night. The 'howling rain' continued and on the following Monday (8 May) he decided to find a billet where meals were served. In his search he was accompanied by a plain-clothes detective.

Edward Lee's store was at the corner of Northumberland Avenue and a few doors from the back was a building called 'Dungar House' at 8 George's St, which Edward Lee also owned. As he approached the front door Frank could hear a girl singing. He was struck by the voice—a mezzo—and by the song. He rang the bell and announced himself. Entering the living room he noticed that it was lit by a 'Surprise Pendant' manufactured by our company and invented by Father. He was attracted by the feel of the place. The household consisted of a

Mr and Mrs Simmendinger and their two daughters, Nellie and
Ivy, aged 16 and eight. Mr Simmendinger, dark, with hair
brushed straight back from his forehead, was the son of a South
German. He represented a firm dealing in paper and stationery,
in which trade he was building up a reputation for expert
knowledge.[35] Mrs Simmendinger said she was a 'Cockney
Sparrow'—born within earshot of Bow Bells. The
Simmendingers, Frank told our parents, 'are very English, as
opposed to Irish. They are of a thoroughly homey sort, so
Captain Sutton and myself have quite entered into the family
life.' (14 May)

He moved in on Tuesday, May 9, on which day James
Connolly was court martialled at Dublin Castle. In his speech to
the Court Martial, James Connolly said: 'We succeeded in
proving that Irishmen are ready to die endeavouring to win for
Ireland those national rights which the British Government has
been asking them to die to win for Belgium. As long as that
remains the case, the cause of Irish freedom is safe.'[36] He faced
the firing squad two days later.

While entering into the family life Frank found himself paying
more and more attention to Nellie. She was a graceful girl of
medium height. Her eyes were of an unusual green hazel colour,
her hair was a dark brown which in certain lights glowed with a
copper sheen. She wore it in a pigtail and was known, at first, as
'The Flapper', but later he referred to her in his diary as 'NS'.

Two days after moving in Frank was introduced to Olive
Holmes, whom he was to meet from time to time during his stay
in Ireland. The daughter of the proprietor of a local hotel she
was a friend of NS, although much older and more experienced.
Later Harold Wardill was invited to make up a four. Together,
they enjoyed each other's company and the life at Dungar
House, especially in the evenings, 'playing and singing into the

---

[35] His firm was later absorbed into Wiggins, Teape & Co. During the
second World War he went back to England, having been asked to take
over an important job for the firm at Bristol.
[36] *The Rising* by Desmond Ryan.

small hours, ragging with music sheets and putters' (17 May). Tennyson Lee knew the family. One evening he 'turned up after supper, and after terrific threats was induced to sit at piano, where he soon settled down and played beautifully'. (18 May)

According to Frank's diary I must have met NS and Miss Holmes for the first time 'by accident' on Monday 15 May. He took them to Dublin in the Lees' Napier and after settling up at Castle Stationery Depot, made up a party of four at the pictures, Grafton Street. Later we motored out to Wicklow where we had cold supper at a small hotel. A few days later I drove over from Ballsbridge, No. 2 Company having been moved there from Kilmainham. Olive Holmes came and after supper we played and sang in uninhibited fashion—The Big Bamboo, Moon, Moon, Serenely Shining, and other songs from the Follies programme. Nellie introduced us to a haunting little song called Heatherland. We were impressed by her singing. She was taking lessons from a former singing master of John McCormack. Frank noted, too, that 'The Flapper plays rather nicely.'

To the east of Kingstown Harbour lies a rocky inlet called Scotsman's Bay, which L.A.G. Strong has written about in his two novels The Garden and Sea Wall. He describes the latter as 'a narrow promenade, little more than a ledge, a few feet above the rocks ... The gardens sloped to the edge above the Wall, giving access to it through a gate and a short flight of steps.' Some three-quarters of a mile eastward is Sandycove Harbour, the Forty Foot Bathing Place (for men only), and the Martello Tower which is the scene of the opening section of Ulysses and is now the James Joyce Museum. Along the sea wall, N.S. and Frank would go for walks together in the evenings, the first of them a week after he had moved in.

'Walk to Sandycove and 40 ft Bathing Place with NS. A VN evening too 2. Beautiful sky.' (16 May)

Three days later Frank 'took NS for another walk up the coast and came back inland'.

Frank's stay at Dungar House lasted only ten days, during which time he was able to see something of the country round

155

Dublin. On Saturday 13th May he made his 'first day's run to Blessington, in Mr McCormick's Talbot car, en route for Glenmalure, where the artillery were to fire their course up in the Wicklow mountains. Frank passed through the village of Knockanarrigan, where Father had once fished, and then on to Dunlavin. He thought the beautiful waterfall at Pollaphuca (now dammed up) was 'the last word'. 'The country is marvellous,' he wrote. And so it is.

I, meanwhile, spent the weekend making 'arrangements for Middleton's move' (14 May). Since leaving England, my excellent batman had been looking extremely preoccupied and worried. At some point he confided in me that the move had clashed with his plans for a very 'necessary' marriage. By pulling strings, leave was obtained and we 'accompanied him to the boat'. Four days later I found a billet at Mrs Ringwood's, at Ballsbridge. We moved in that night. Our hostess[37] was extremely friendly.

On Saturday May 20 the Headquarters of the Divisional Train was moved to Phoenix Park, where Frank was to remain until August 28. He left Dungar House with regret but fully resolved to keep in touch with the family, especially with the eldest daughter. The day was beautiful, and before leaving Kingstown, he 'engineered a bathe from the petrol store boat-house. Every facility was provided, including a bridge,' from which he dived. 'The water was a beautiful blue and breezy.' In the afternoon the R.N.A.S. drove him with his kit up to Phoenix Park in one of their cars.

The following day, Daylight Saving came into operation for the first time. The clocks were put forward half-an-hour. 'It is a great scheme,' Frank thought. For a day or two, some of us noticed a different 'feeling', especially on early morning stables—but this soon wore off.

Frank's visits to my billet at Ballsbridge stand out in my memory. Our hostess, Mrs Ringwood, had introduced us to a

---

[37] I was to meet her daughter, a Mrs Martin (petite and auburn), again at Fermoy staying with her friends, the Dicksons.

Mrs Gore-Browne. They were army people and extremely good company. At Ballsbridge Frank, as we shall see, was also to meet them there on what was to be a decisive weekend in his existence. He was invited to play tennis, Peach and Eames making up the four. We played the gramophone and danced. Our hostess had a 'beautiful Challen upright auto-piano', and he was delighted when we were once more able to play and hear Chopin's Ballad in A Flat.

My twin-cylinder Douglas motor-bike helped me to get around and visit Frank, and on May 22 Harold Wardill arrived with the Indian. Frank had missed their 'joint-buffoonery very much'. Now he 'felt very different', and a few days later wrote that he was 'getting along nicely,' having equipped his private tent with table, camp-bed and deck chairs. He 'enjoyed being under canvas again'. It reminded him of his old bivouacs in France.

Opposite his tent Frank found the Divisional Cyclists under the Old Bedalian, Captain Eric Winser, whom he had met at Boxmoor. Together they would stroll about under the chestnut trees exchanging Bedalian gossip. The A.S.C. played in a cricket match against the cyclists, when 'Winser distinguished himself'. The marquee and park suggested the leisured pageantry of country house cricket.

'It is really so beautiful here,' he wrote, and yet, for the first time, we sense a slight clouding of his sunny outlook. There is a change of tone in his letters home. We miss the compulsive recording of vivid detail. He excused himself. 'There is so little of interest going on that I don't feel at all like writing from day to day' (28 May). The zest and sense of purpose which he had experienced in France—were they fading? To be sure it was all very pleasant. The atmosphere reminded him of holidays at Burnham-on-Sea. Work finished late in the evening, when he liked to lounge outside the marquee in a deck chair, chatting with the other officers or listening to the gramophone. Sometimes he would 'saunter round the park on the Indian in middle gear doing 17 or 18 mph.'

'I suppose the park is at about its best just now,' he

continued. 'What with the great chestnuts in bloom, eaten by the cattle up to a certain level like an inverted billiard table, and with all the May and young beech-green, with these little deer strolling all over the place, this place would be hard to equal. It is a sublime camping ground.' (28 May)

Frank took his friend Wardill 'for a slow amble on the back of the Indian at 10.30 p.m. The cobbles are very bad in the city,' he explained, 'but the main drive through the park is straight and smooth as a billiard table.' There had been 'Heavy rain all day, but at sunset it turned out a beautiful evening. With the new summertime the afterglow was still perfect—we did not need a headlight. The whole landscape was steaming and all the low ground bathed in mist. As we passed along, the different perfumes, carried in the cool evening breeze, were delicious. I have ridden over to see Bob a good deal. He expects to leave tomorrow. Apart from his new field boots there is little news' (28 May). (Those boots, tailor-made by Abbots, fitted my long legs and indeed gave me great satisfaction.)

On May 29 I left for Fermoy on the River Blackwater, about twenty miles north of Cork. [Frank] met me at the station in Dublin to say goodbye. Together we made provisional arrangements to keep in touch. Then he went on to the Simmendingers at Kingstown, where he was forming a close relationship with Nellie Simmendinger. We saw nothing more of each other until September 8.

As those showery summer months at Phoenix Park dragged on, Frank experienced little to re-kindle his enthusiasm. His emergency requisitioning duties were over. He had closed his imprest account and the military 'had got back to peace-time conditions'. He 'no longer felt that there were many things on hand which could not 'bide awhile'. His duties became more and more of a routine nature, with his turn for Orderly Officer coming round every few days. He was far from being fully extended.

Any spiritual or intellectual life seems to have been dormant. 'I haven't been doing any more philosophy reading,' Frank told our parents. 'The Sundays have either been spent in clearing up papers or visiting friends,' (7 June). No longer, as during his overseas service, do we find him recording his appraisals of large-scale political events. The war seemed very distant, though on June 6 he noted in his diary, 'News of Kitchener lost with staff on board the Hampshire.'

As things were slackening off a bit Frank began making arrangements for a piano. These arrangements followed a familiar pattern. The dealers were not keen. The man in the shop heard it would be under canvas and refused at first. However, he eventually allowed himself to be wangled, 'and by mid-June the instrument was installed in the marquee'. He got a fair amount of playing, but since the marquee served as Mess and Anteroom and was rather public, he was reluctant to practise steadily. Indeed, he missed the intimate and sympathetic atmosphere of Le Seau.

Frank's services were, nevertheless, still much in demand for smoking concerts. He was invited to play at one organised by the Divisional Cyclists and from time to time at guest nights or 'celebrations' in the A.S.C. Mess. These often led to rough houses and displays of alcoholic exuberance. One such evening took place at the end of June when Colonel Hazelrigg, a regular soldier of experience, replaced Colonel Reading who, with a number of other senior officers, was to leave for home. 'There was little or no speechifying but after dinner an immense rag including 1) a sort of chair bunting, and 2) an undiluted rugger-scrum.

While this was going on Frank continued 'to play suitable melodies instead of participating in the shoulder work'. He 'summoned a body guard' to protect himself while he played. 'When I come home,' he wrote, 'and am asked to play the piano, if you see me plant both feet forcibly against the wall, assuming a defensive attitude, you will know it is from force of habit. As long as I could keep the instrument on its legs I reckoned I was doing fairly well' (1 July). His diary and letters contain several references to these 'binges', but, although he enjoyed a drink and company, one gets the impression that he was beginning to find them a little tedious.

The prolonged postponement of Frank's leave constituted a certain source of disappointment. Captain Sutton and the other supply officer had first right to make application. He was, nevertheless, due to get away on June 30 but when the date arrived he found that his leave looked like being 'blued' as deep as it had ever been. Some brass-hat had decided that the troops might become slack unless special measures were taken. These consisted of 'a new extensive training programme'. Colonel Hazelrigg, however, fully recognised 'the farce of trying to train men like our drivers to do everything under the sun while they were doing regular work daily' in supplying the troops, 'which was the best possible training in itself'. He knew what the men would have to do later and would therefore 'eliminate rubbishy time-wasting' where he could. In this he seems to have been only moderately successful.

During the first week in July, the men were given two days on the rifle range at Dollymount, situated 'on a golf links along the sea-shore—very much like Burnham-on-Sea. In the heat of the day the concentrated grass smell brought back happy recollections of golf and tennis.' Frank enjoyed the experience and did 'pretty well on the first day'. At 100 yards his score was a 'possible' 25 out of 25. At 200 yards, 19 out of 20 (5 bulls and an inner). At 300 yards 17 out of 20. Total 61 out of 65 possible.

The training course proper started the following week, and in spite of the Colonel's good intentions, seems to have been tiresome. On the first day (10 July) 'it was fearfully wet before breakfast and on-and-off all day'. For the whole week the 'rubbishy time-wasting' took the form of foot-drill in great-coats, harness instruction, and classes in knots and lashing, followed by riding school. Stables—early morning stables (5.30) and again in the evening—took place as usual.

> So many men are taken away from their regular duties that everybody is having to do someone else's job at the same time. I have been 'snaffled' for Orderly Officer for two days running and seen nothing of the supply work during the time. (7 July)

On July 26th the Headquarters Company moved to the

Curragh Camp some 27 miles from Dublin. Frank and Harold Wardill were left behind to clear up accounts, dispose of the marquees and tents and take charge of Kingsbridge Depot, supplying detachments of troops remaining in Dublin. On August 15th, after 'great preparations' the previous day, 'General French inspected the troops—soaker most of day, fair intervals.'

If Frank's natural zest for his work was being checked, his interest in Nellie Simmendinger increased each time he met her. He found her company altogether charming. He rarely spoke to me about her, but I remember he once said that she was 'pet'— an adjective suggesting the endearing quality of the young. There were times when she was quiet and reserved. I retain a mental picture of her sitting composedly at table in the hotel at Wicklow, not saying much but closely observing the company. Yet when she was in the mood no one could be more lively and articulate. More and more he found that they understood each other, not only in their love of music but in their attitude to human beings. They were both gentle.

Frank's diary shows that as long as he remained at Phoenix Park he and Nellie met at least once a week. He would take her to the cinema or theatre, or invite her and her parents to the camp, where they would 'sit outside the marquee with gramophone and "sips" till 10.30' and then walk through the park together as far as the gate. (21 July)

On occasion, although it was quite impossible to get leave, Frank managed to get away to Dungar House for the week-end. He would then take 'a rowing-tub and let down the anchor weight opposite the band'. He appraised the programme. One day they 'gave us a particularly good selection. The water is like a mill pond as you know,' he wrote home 'and the daily departure and arrival of the mail boat is always very picturesque when viewed from surface.' Once Mr Simmendinger rowed and Frank, in the stern, 'had to inspire the ladies with confidence'. He did his best 'and thought of the days when we took our aunts out at Pwhelli—a great adventure … Mrs Simmendinger, who averred she always hated the water, apparently enjoyed it very much' (29 July and 14 August). Frank sketched a plan of the harbour:

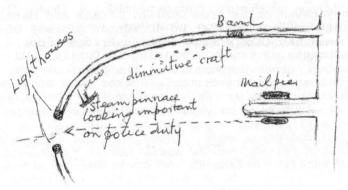

The Simmendingers welcomed Frank at the weekends. He felt himself one of the family. Writing home, he describes how he had given them a full account of our parents, 'with special supplement about the aunties of course'. He enjoyed Nellie's parents' company and the cosy evenings at Dungar House, where they would play the piano and sing under the light of the Surprise Pendant.

These weekly meetings continued until Frank moved to the Curragh at the end of August. He was then too far away to slip over to Kingstown for an hour or two in the evening. Petrol rationing had been introduced. It was necessary to justify the use of the Indian through some service commission, so that during the last three months of the Irish period they were only able to meet four times. (During October, as we shall see, he was confined to barracks for eleven days.)

In many ways Frank was able to convey to NS that his intentions, though 'strictly honourable', were not platonic. How do we know this? His diary and letters tell us little beyond the frequency of their meetings, and until I began to study them I had only vaguely suspected how matters stood. In 1960, however, I discovered one precious source of information, namely the lady herself, now Mrs Vaughan McFerran, of The

Peak, Killiney. (Her husband, Bobby McFerran, became a well-known Dublin Solicitor, and they had one son.) Early during that year Tennyson Lee came across her married name and address, and in June that year she and her sister met me at Dublin Airport. We all dined together. The talk flowed. 'He was a wonderful person,' she said.

Two days later we drove in her car along the route Frank had taken in the Talbot during May 1916 to Blessington, through Knockannarrigan and then on to Dunlavin. The country is indeed beautiful. It reminded me sometimes of the South Downs and sometimes of North Wales, near Capel Curig. Before I left I dined at their pleasant house overlooking Killiney Bay. After dinner she showed me a letter that Mother had written to her, together with a ring made from his tie-pin, and the photograph in a leather case of herself that he had carried around with him after he left Ireland.

Although Frank had expected a last minute cancellation of his leave, he was able to get away from the Curragh during the afternoon of August 18. He had tea at Kingstown, probably with Nellie, and on a grey drizzly afternoon went on board. Next morning (Saturday) he arrived home early and was 'welcomed by the redoubtable Fanny Edwards'. After breakfast he 'went straight to the works' which he visited each day of his leave except one. Important matters were being discussed, such as those relating to 'the big question of the Gardner 3 grenade'. During 1915 there had been a continuous shortage of grenades on the Western Front. As a result a number of patents were taken out that year. The 'big question' may well have been whether or not the grenade would be approved by the War Office and the Ministry of Munitions, and also whether the company should undertake the production of it. By August 1916 the Mills Bomb had been generally accepted. Production had overtaken expenditure so that large stocks had accumulated.[38] The

---

[38] I am indebted to the Imperial War Museum for this information. In May, 1916, Messrs. Danills and Gardner patented a Projectile Fuse relating to

163

company may indeed have been faced with a difficult decision.

Frank was glad to get back amongst his fruit trees in the garden. He 'obtained cuttings from a Cox's orange Pippin tree in our Uncle Arthur Short's garden and budded them onto a tree near the water tap'. (25 August)

On Sunday morning Frank attended Nelson Street Adult School with our parents. He made visits to relatives and to the dentist, shopped, 'was tried on at Allports', went to the cinema and the Grand Music Hall, and took a 'fleeting glance round the Art Gallery' where Raemaekers' bitter war cartoons were being exhibited. In the evenings he would make music—'much foolery with duets, etc'.

On the Thursday Frank and Father caught an early train to Bakewell in Derbyshire and went straight to the Rutland Arms. 'After substantial early lunch,' he wrote, 'we withdrew to the river and had quite the best bit of dry-fly fishing of my life. Very hot, and simply ideal positions. Caught 6.12 train back. Rather crowded. Home at 10 p.m.' (24 August)

The return crossing was marked by a 'Marvellous display of Northern Lights phenomenon over the sea on leaving Holyhead.' On the other side Frank noted an 'exquisite dawn in Kingstown Harbour'. The seagulls, with which he always felt sympathetic, particularly on account of their gliding skill, were 'very tame'.

Frank had arranged to meet NS on board for breakfast. She was late, but he went ahead with his meal thinking that there had been a misunderstanding or that she had been delayed. Her friend. Olive Holmes, who claimed to be experienced in such matters, had suggested to her that Frank would be impressed, and probably more attracted, if she showed, by arriving late, that she was not too eager for his company. The manoeuvre passed unnoticed. He greeted her affectionately when she came aboard at 8 o'clock. She was wearing a white embroidered muslin frock, a gift from her aunt, with which she was very pleased. He 'handed over to her Mother's songs and music',

grenades, and another in October of that year.

talked to her of his leave, and made tentative arrangements for their next meeting.

They were to be disappointed, however, for at Phoenix Park he found 'orders awaiting to proceed to the Curragh'. In his diary he noted, 'Heavy afternoon, rain cleared a little and turned out beautiful evening. Got to A.S.C. Mess, Curragh Camp, in time for supper. Johnstone, his batman, arrived in Maltese Cart, 11.15 p.m.' (27 August)

During August Frank had been in continuous touch with his company officer by telephone. Reports of the conditions at the camp had not been encouraging: 'Opinion of the Curragh forcibly expressed through trunk line' (16 August). But later, on looking around, his eager artist's eye met much to attract it: 'A simple horse-drawn cart consisting of a box about 5 ft square by 2 ft deep, resting on an axle between two large wheels. At the back was a short tail-board. There were two shafts. The driver sat inside on a board placed cross-ways near the front.'

> The Curragh is rather an extraordinary place; just an undulating expanse of perhaps five to eight square miles of turf—quite short and beautiful grass like the fairway of Berrow golf links. In some lights you get a brown sheen effect from the thin seeding grasses which grow sparsely several inches higher than the green turf. (31 August)

Frank found quite a lot to do, though supply work was almost nil. Much of his time was occupied in attending Boards (i.e. formal committees investigating and reporting on discrepancies in stock, accounts, and untoward events, such as accidents). He found them 'rather interesting, but in places tedious—wading through entire company equipment, etc.' (21 August)

They were now somewhat isolated, and for the first time Frank was to experience the typical male world of barracks life. Later he met several local people who invited him, with other officers, for tennis or bridge. But at first the evenings were taken up with interminable games of poker, 'guest nights', and occasional visits to the 'one Picture House of the brown-painted-

iron-girder- and Stockholm-tar-matchboarding-type'. So much
for the interior; outside, 'for a wonder there was little pretence
at plaster modelling'.

He missed Harold Wardill, who was still at Phoenix Park.
From time to time, however, Wardill would appear at the
Curragh, when they would enjoy each other's company.
'Drizzly wet. Met Wardill at station and gave him lift up. Went
through supply papers, etc. and circular letters for sacks. Long
chat with Wardill in room. Evening turned out wet again. Rode
back to Newbridge station and saw him safely on train for
Phoenix Park, although half-hour late.' (31 August)

The wet weather continued. A few days after his arrival Frank
had intended to take Peach to Newbridge station on his carrier,
but that day, for the first occasion in years, the train was punctual
and they arrived just in time to 'watch it saunter out of the
station'. They then 'proceeded to Dublin by road. Peach's legs
not long enough to reach foot-boards, but put up marvellous
performance sticking on carrier, through equestrian training.'

They passed through Phoenix Park, 'very depressing in
Autumn evening mist, turf wringing wet—very different from
previous month'. His spirits revived, however, after oysters and
savoury omelette at Jammett's. Afterwards he 'Phoned
Kingstown and met Mrs and Miss Simmendinger at the station
(Westland Row). Took them to Joyland at the Hippodrome—
quite a good show. Met Peach on train going back—negotiated
Indian into guards van. Pitch dark ride back to barracks from
Newbridge.' (2 September).

Soon after Frank's return from leave, a change of policy at the
War Office was to involve us both in a momentous decision. He
explained our dilemma in a letter home.

> In one way the prospects are not too bad, yet very black in another.
> You see they are on the point of sending out a few drafts of Infant-
> ry right away to France—which amounts to removing the cogs of a
> machine at home. This Division, being the machine, has consequen-
> tly either to be dismantled or else fresh 'cogs' trained. I don't relish
> the idea of remaining on this side over the winter. (31 August)

In my own diary I find the following entry: '(Fermoy, Monday 28 August): Orderly Officer—News of the DRAFT causes acute depression of all ranks.'

This depression spread throughout the whole Division. I listened to the discussions going on around me and wrote up what I heard in the form of a one-act play called *Stagnation*. For over two years we had had the carrot of Foreign Service dangled in front of our noses and now it seemed that we were to be kept in Ireland on garrison duty. There had been so many promises. Dates had appeared in orders and had then been cancelled. When the drivers went home on leave they were teased. They felt that the Division was getting talked about. They heard references to 'The Rag-time Army'. A paragraph had appeared in John Bull asking why the 59th Division had not gone abroad. Promotion was blocked. There was a feeling that if you hadn't been in France you were nobody.

It was not surprising that officers began to think about getting a transfer. Frank and I decided to act quickly. We exchanged letters and telegrams. What branch or unit would give us more scope, we wondered. The Cavalry Machine-Gun Squadron sounded as if it might have possibilities. But how about the Royal Flying Corps?

Frank found the words exciting. We have seen how closely he observed the aerial activities in Northern France during the previous year, his long talk with the pilot on March 14th, his inspection of the cock-pit, and his 'feelers' about joining the R.F.C. in the long letter which he wrote in June that year. And now his mind went back to our kites at Berrow, the news of the Wright Brothers and powered flight passed on to me in the dormitory, the paper darts, the model aeroplanes, and his affectionate admiration for 'the professional aviators'—the seagulls. His enthusiasm was infectious. Although not naturally drawn towards hazardous service, I felt stimulated by the prospects of actually flying.

It was now important that we should meet, and in this we were fortunate, for within a week of the depressing news I arrived at Kildare about to go home on leave. He came over to the station on his Indian, met the train, and immediately we began our talks over tea at the Railway Hotel, continuing them on the train to Dublin. We had still not quite made up our minds as to choice of unit or the tactics needed to get out of Ireland. At Kingsbridge we changed onto the boat train for Kingstown. We were still deep in conversation as we reached the mail-boat. With a number of points still to be cleared up he left me and then 'called at Dungar House—flying visit. Returned 10.45 from Kingstown—Kildare at about 12.45'.

On September 17 I was back at Fermoy. There must still have been some slight doubt as to our plans for, according to his diary, on the 22 he 'saw Capt. commanding Cavalry Machine-Gun Squadron re. possible transfer'. But on the same day he 'received wire from R.D.B., saying that application for R.F.C. had gone in'. There remained two questions: a) how to unravel the red-tape at Irish Command, and b) how best to inform our parents.

On Saturday (23 September) Frank 'left for Fermoy on Indian machine at 8.45'. The ride, and indeed the events of that memorable week-end are described in greater detail than usual in his diary:

> after 40 miles got a puncture with a large nail and had to mend at roadside. Fortunately a beautiful day and the patching place obvious. Rain came on when approaching Michelstown, and was also delayed through petrol-tin and baggage in sugar sack on carrier constantly jolting loose. After covering 102 miles by 1.45, with 'innards' almost jolted out by road surface, had scratch lunch at 3rd. class hotel in Michelstown, consisting of tomatoes, cheese, biscuits and a bottle of stout. Set off at 2.15 for the last 10 miles and got to Bob's barracks at 2.45. (23 September)

With broad grins and jokes we greeted each other. We were eager to compose the letter to our parents which would set the seal on our decision; but that could wait a little. It was his first visit to the delightful little town of Fermoy, where I had spent four happy months.

I took him down the hill to the River Blackwater, hired one of Jack Duan's boats and drifted slowly down-stream through lovely wooded country, idly casting a fly below the over-hanging branches and at the tail of the most likely runs—as we had been taught to do by Albert Wood. We gossiped, but could not prevent ourselves from coming back again and again to the question of our transfer.

Having returned the boat, we strolled round to the Dicksons' house. Mr Dickson was the Resident Magistrate. I introduced Frank to the two good-looking and lively daughters, with whom I had become friendly. Mrs Dickson—deaf and kindly—invited us both for tea, which was followed by a little music and dancing. We then walked up the hill to the Old Barracks for Mess, and an evening of poker, billiards, and more music.

The following day, Sunday, we drafted the letter:

Dearest Father and Mother,

Since we have made up our minds about transferring, the world has assumed a very different aspect. Ever since I wrote that original letter from France ages ago touching on the R.F.C.. I have always felt a bit uneasy morally about staying in the A.S.C. Recently, with the casualties increasing daily and becoming more and more intimate, the feeling has become more and more oppressive, till recently I have gone about the daily routine with little interest and almost mechanically. You may or may not have noticed the difference when I was last on leave.

Bob and I talked the thing over at length and I am confident that it is quite the best decision I have arrived at since joining the A.S.C. in '14.

I shall always have an admiration for the A.S.C. as well, and it would appear the height of luxury to belong to that corps all the time, and serve in another.[39]

Leave will be more enjoyable than ever before and the insinuated aspersions will be knocked on the head once and for all.

Altho' the 'What did you do in the Great War, Daddy?' has become such a joke now,[40] and is usually met with 'Minded the

---

[39] In those days, officers were seconded from their regiment to the R.F.C. They retained their rank and might continue to wear their G.S. Tunic and regimental badges or the R.F.C. 'maternity jacket' as they wished.

[40] The reference is to the famous recruiting poster.

water cart', or the like, there is really a lot in it … With this big
load off our chests we are both full of hope and confidence.

I am already doing the map reading part of the tests which is
only made interesting with such a goal in sight.

I am sure you will all see it later if not already.

Fond love to you all,

Frank

With this off our minds Frank, 'Father' Green and myself took
the horses out and galloped several times round the Fermoy
race course. Then, 'bit of music after lunch. Fished from boat
on river. Rather windy. Supper at Dickson's. Gramophone and
stepping after. Returned to Mess at Barracks for winding up
game of poker.'

Next day, Monday (25 September) Frank 'got back without a
hitch at 12.15 p.m. (112 miles) and within 24 hours he had
copied out the draft letter and posted it to our parents. He then
lost no time in following up our decision. There were several
simple tests to be taken, such as making a 'sketch map,
consisting of enlarging a square inch of an ordnance map to
four inches square'. This he accomplished the day following his
return, and on the next day an examination by a medical
board[41] established that he was physically fit for a pilot's career.
He read in an article that pilots were 'tested with the most hair-
standing-on-end tricks—provided one survived, even as pulp,
there was not much wrong,' he wrote (17 October). We had to
listen to alarming tales of such tests of nerve and endurance.
They all proved to be mythical. We were, in fact, made to take a
fairly simple examination in technical matters, but nothing even
faintly corresponding to these rumoured ordeals ever took place
except, perhaps, in the course of actually learning to fly, and we
neither of us found stunting particularly disconcerting. By the
time we had finished our period of instruction the need for pilots
was such that standards were not too exacting.

Mindful of Father's insistence on tüchtig theoretical study in

---

[41] 'McAllister Hewlings (of 46th Div. & Luton fame) presided; Col. Dent (of
Saffron Walden fame) called in.' (27 September)

connection with any practical activity such as skating or golf, we wrote home for some suitable text books. These were sent out and we both of us applied ourselves to mastering the principles of engine design, rigging, and theory of flight, a preparation which stood us in good stead when we moved to the Ground School at Oxford the following year.

Ten days after returning from Fermoy Frank learnt that our application had gone forward. Much depended now on an official interview. He 'expected the interviewing officer would be round in three weeks' time' (5 October). He looked round for some opportunity to speed up the bureaucratic wheels of Irish Command, which seemed to turn exceptionally slowly.

Writing home on November 2 Frank told how luck had been with him.

> Things are already beginning to hum. When two officers from Hdqtrs Irish Command lunched at our mess. I sounded the major about the R.F.C. interviewer. He said 'Well, here's just your man,' introducing me to a Capt. King, who offered to give me a note of introduction to Col. Trench, a personal friend at [R.F.C. H.Q.]. I wrote to King next day and now I have a letter of introduction from King to Trench, who has replied with a request to fill in two forms. I have passed them on to Bob, who is getting very fed up with dormant proceedings. I think we are on the right track at last ... I have just spent the day with my old friend Wardill, who passed through here on his way to Dublin. He also is on the point of joining us in a transfer as soon as he hears that his [previous] application for a dental appointment has been annulled. He is a dear chap.

By Mid-November there was still no news of our interview and, impatient, I asked for week-end leave to visit Frank at the Curragh. He met me at Kildare station with an 'outside car'. We immediately started going over the relative merits of alternative plans and tactics for speeding up the procedure. After hot baths, mess, and an inevitable game of poker, we invoked the advice of Colonel Hazelrigg, who came into Frank's room. The ensuing council of war went on till a late hour.

While at St. Albans we had been half aware of a young woman moving in what for us seemed exalted military circles. This was Jenny Bradbridge, a school friend of Beryl Smith's sister Muriel. Since she was also to become a life-long friend of the family she deserves a place in this story, even though she only appears once. Auburn-haired and handsome, she reminded us of a Gibson girl (the heavy-eyed, swan-waisted American beauty idealised by the illustrator Charles Dana Gibson). She had recently married Col. E.U. Bradbridge, a divisional staff officer, and was having to adjust herself to being the wife of a professional soldier, with all its Kiplingesque protocol. She found herself being 'helped' with hints from the wives of those above her husband in the hierarchy, on such things as when to wear white kid gloves, who should not be invited to the house on account of inferior rank however close the relationship or friendship, and other questions of military etiquette, such hints amounting almost to army orders. But in achieving our ends Frank and I were undaunted by red tape, red tabs, or brass hats. The Bradbridges might well fit in with our little combinazione, and accordingly we readily accepted an invitation to take tea with Jenny on the day following my arrival at the Curragh.

She gave us a warm and friendly welcome; she had a quiet sense of fun and made us feel at home. As the conversation drifted round to our transfer, her husband happened to enter the room. We stood to attention, but later the talk continued in a more relaxed and informal climate. We learnt that our application was already receiving attention at Divisional Headquarters. He promised to do what he could to help us, and I believe that he was as good as his word.

Next day, Monday (13 November), Frank noted in his diary: 'Ran Bob to station on Indian carrier, saw him off, then visited units. Received instruction during evening that I should be taking draft across on following day.'

Two days later Frank presented himself, with his draft (50 men and a sergeant) at the Park Royal Depot, after travelling all night. His presence in London provided another opportunity to be fully exploited. After lunch he 'proceeded to Adastral House'

(R.F.C. Headquarters at No. 1 Kinsgway) to follow up Capt. King's introduction. He waited about for Col. Trench for some time, and then decided to come back later. In the meantime he went off to meet Father who, as he had learnt, was to be in London on a visit to Woolwich—probably in connection with the Gardner 3 Grenade. He then returned to Adastral House and at last succeeded in bringing off that decisive interview with Col. Trench for which he had worked so hard. This completed, he 'saw Father off at Paddington 6.00 p.m.' and from there went on to Wimbledon to spend the night with the Smiths at Ardmore. He was back at the Curragh on November 17.

During October Frank was asked to organise a concert for wounded soldiers at a neighbouring hospital. He threw himself into the preparations and looked around for talent to make up his programme. 'I rather enjoy being back again in my old jacket,' he informed our parents. As a result of enquiries he invited two soldiers round for tea and an audition. One was 'a wounded corporal who had been a professional pianist before the war'. From a letter home it is clear that he was greatly impressed.

> Tho' shot through the left fore-arm he is rapidly regaining full use of it. He is a pupil of Matté's (the new school—loose wrists, *à la* Irene Scharrer[42]) and can play almost anything even now after no practice. I asked him up to tea the other day with a Sergeant friend (Greenhalgh, possessing a good voice). It was just perfect to listen to. Altho' he looked such a quaint little humble object in a blue togout, much too large and swamping his wrists completely, his touch was perfect from pianissimo to fortissimo. (21 October)

The day before the concert, during a special visit to Dublin 'on a lorry conveying ordnance stores', Frank became involved in some rather typical complicated arrangements for the transport of two pianos. 'After sundry telephoning, etc.' the lorry arrived at the piano shop but only shortly before it was due to close. It

---

[42] English concert pianist.

then had to complete 'another W.O. job' delivering goods to Ballsbridge 'with the instruments on board. It was blowing a young gale and raining coming home, but landed at hospital at 11.00 p.m.

'The concert (25 October) was a huge success,' Frank thought, 'judging by applause and after-criticisms.' The Tommies were very appreciative, in spite of being somewhat blasé. He warned Mother that they 'will not tolerate any dud turn', and added, 'so be careful what you do if you are asked, my love! The concert proceeding mine was a pitiful performance, I was told.'

The programme was enclosed. As his opening number Frank played his own composition 'The March of the Terriers', with its rather sad theme of eight reiterated Fs, its chromatic modulations and rousing Trio section. Lance Corporal Robinson, the professional, played Grieg's 'To The Spring Time' and 'Wedding Day' together with Rachmaninoff's *Prelude in C Sharp*. Sergt. Greenhalgh sang 'The Deathless Army' and 'Glorious Devon'—'serious'. Frank classified the songs on his programme into three categories: serious, light-serious and comic—a procedure which he was to develop later. There were 20 items and the concert ended with two chorus numbers, 'Ragtime Cowboy Joe' and 'Tipperary'.

During his term of service in Ireland he did not feel greatly moved to compose. He produced a waltz which he called Smoke Rings. Unfortunately he left no manuscript and I cannot remember the work. He seems to have been occupied for some time on The Island in the Year, which he finished roughly writing out on October 17th. Shortly before the concert Frank wrote to our parents: 'I have been released from certain restrictions about leaving camp which were imposed on me as a result of rather a long story. I am rather bucked tonight' (21 October). Thus ended the first and only punishment he received during his military service. His turn for Orderly Officer had come on October 10th. Unfortunately his alarm watch failed at 5.00 a.m. It so happened that this was a 'heavy morning with coal, etc.' He 'got back to lunch at 3 p.m. through a drencher'.

Next day he was summoned to the Orderly Room and 'congratulated' by the C.O. on the previous day's doings, which would occur twice weekly now' (11 October). In addition to taking Orderly Officer every three days he was confined to camp. The punishment seems to have been a mild one. The 'restrictions' did not prevent him from visiting friends' houses in the neighbourhood, playing golf and going to the local cinema. His final discharge, four days later, was timely. It left him four days to collect his pianos and make final arrangements for the concert.

Perhaps this episode was symptomatic of the prevailing mood of those last four months in Ireland—waning interest on the one hand, and pressure to maintain discipline on the other.

In spite of the dreary camp conditions his life seems to have been tolerably care-free. As usual, sport claimed a good deal of his attention. His rod and tackle were sent out to him from home and he would ride out on a pedal cycle to Athgarvan Bridge over the Liffey where he had some sport with what Frank Aston called the 'red buzzer' or worm. For three days in succession he attended the Curragh races. He 'followed the pack of Beagles—saw one hare sprint but did not stay'. He played half-back for No. 1 against No. 4 Company and beat them badly. Once more he came under the spell of golf. He 'borrowed an iron and cleek, then played quickly round Curragh Golf Course to see what the holes were like' (20 October). Two days later he 'wrote home for golf clubs'. His 'redoubtable' batman Johnstone cleaned and oiled them and 'got them into fighting trim, soaking the caddy bag in dubbin in front of an open fire. He 'played Emu (Ewart Eames) in the first round of the Mess Sweep golf competition with own clubs'. From his letter home (29 October) it is clear that he was not averse to winning. 'I was about 3 up at the fifth and for the next nine holes never gave away a hole without a hard fight (often a long putt at the end). This upset him so much psychologically ... that he finished 5 and 4 to play.'

Then, early in November, he managed to work a Sunday off

at his old billet, Dungar House, and to meet Nellie Simmendinger again, for she was never long out of his mind. It was 'a great relief to get out of the Curragh atmosphere for a little while'. He had not been able to use his Indian for a long time, but he had recently received a petrol allowance, and 'although only two gallons a month,' he could 'work short trips without having to trouble about a duty excuse'. On the way to Kingstown he called at Bellevue and found the Lees at home. Tennyson had been having 'a rotten time of it. Beginning with typhoid fever, bronchitis, etc', he had been taken to hospital where he had 'contracted every imaginable malady under the sun'. He still had a bad cold. 'Their chrysanthemums in the greenhouse are wonderful,' he noted appreciatively. 'They are to be sold for the Red Cross later.'

After an 'immense lunch' Frank rode on to Dungar House in time for tea and to stay the night. 'It is a very homey place,' he felt, 'which one appreciates especially after mess rooms and barracks.' Mother's songs, which had been lent to them, he found were 'all in order'. Olive Holmes had been invited for the evening. They 'played solo and had a bit of music. The family were in good form and they retired to bed at 1.30.'

From time to time Frank would mislay his Sam Browne belt and he did so this Saturday. Next morning (Sunday, 5 November) he searched the house for it in vain. After a late breakfast, however, he remembered where he had mislaid it and took Nellie up to Bellevue on the carrier of his Indian in order to collect it, a scarf tied round his thick unruly hair. It was 'still very windy and drizzly.' That these two days constituted a land mark during the Curragh period is borne out by the fact that he uses capital letters underlined to head the entries in his diary: 'KINGSTOWN WEEK END'. They conclude: 'General Slackit for remainder of day. Walk to Forty Foot Bathing Place in evening, Tide very high and wind dropped. 'Lovely moon'.

In early December Frank was expecting to come home on leave but, alas, as he explained in a letter home, he was to be disappointed. 'The Division is ordered to get ready for a move to England, probably Salisbury Plain, in the course of the next few days. Those on leave are being recalled and of course our leave is knocked right on the head for the moment but should be easier [to get once we are] in England. So that's that.' (3 December)

A week later the way home seemed to be clear, but once again he found himself involved in a typical military situation, which, as usual, he accepted philosophically. 'I can't say I was frightfully surprised or disappointed when, after saying goodbye to all my friends at Kingstown, I walked on to the pier to find a telegram handed me by the R.T.O. instructing me to return to the Curragh. I spent the rest of the evening at Kingstown.[43] I understand that Bob has got his leave granted.' (9 December)

From my diary[44] I find that on that evening I was, indeed, on my way to Wimbledon, via Rosslare, and that Frank's leave could not have been long postponed, for on 13 December, as I noted, he had gone to the War Office, probably to make further enquiries about our transfer. Next day, he and I went back to Wimbledon and stayed at Ardmore for a few days. There, for the first time, we met Doris Tankard (later Doris MacLaren), who was one of the bridesmaids at my wedding and was also to become a life-long friend of the family. She and Beryl had been together at a finishing school in Paris. On Saturday, after Frank and I had taken the girls to a theatre, we sat round a blazing fire at Ardmore, with the lights out, telling ghost stories.

Our release came earlier than we had expected. We both of us returned from leave during the week before Christmas. On Boxing Day I received orders to report to the Royal Flying Corps School of Instruction at Oxford in two days' time. That

---

[43] No doubt at Dungar House. This may well have been the last time he and Nellie were together, although it is possible they met before he went on board the night mail boat a few days later and on December 27. He wrote a number of letters to her from England and France.

[44] There is no record in Frank's diary for the month of December. We have seen how he would sometimes wait several weeks before writing it up, presumably from rough notes. His war record is fairly complete except for two gaps. This is one, and the other is for a period in France.

same day he posted two letters to our parents. In one he informed them about the instructions I had received, but continued, 'my papers have not come through to Train Hed [sic] Qtrs yet, being two days behind.' In this he was mistaken, for in the other he writes, 'I expect to meet Bob on the night boat tomorrow evening. I can't say what arrangements we shall make about proceeding straight to Oxford or not.'

We did meet, on the ship at Kingstown, and probably went together straight to the bar. We were both of us in high spirits. With us was Colonel Hazelrigg who happened to be going home on leave. We reported to Christ Church College the following day and were allotted rooms at Brasenose College.

Chapter 7
Back to school

After recovering from his operation in the summer term of 1908 Frank had returned to a school life of extraordinary fullness and variety. Something of this richness of texture has already been described, but in addition to the signalling, the construction of model aeroplanes, and the entertainments were a number of other exhilarating activities, as may be seen from the pages of the school magazines of those years. To mention a few, the Societies, in 1908, had 'come very much to the fore as a factor of school life during the winter terms'. There were five of them: the Scientific; the Classical, Literary and Artistic; the Musical; the Fabian; and the Junior Science Society. Frank was a member of the Scientific and Musical Societies, and some reports of his lectures to these learned bodies are given below. Mention must also be made of his lecture to the Scientific Society on 'Aviation' (October 1909), a subject which continually interested him. He covered 'The study of birds—Soaring and the behaviour of kites—Balance in the aeroplane—Forces acting on a glider when in action—Rigidity and systems of steel wire stays—Theory of curved wings.' In his last term he himself actually piloted a man-carrying glider in a flight of a few yards.

During the Spring and Summer terms competitions and

exhibitions of free-time creative work and study took place. In the currency of those times the prizes of five shillings were quite attractive, but more so the fun and excitement of organising one's exhibits. The Spring Exhibitions ('Prize Work') were chiefly for indoor occupations, arts and crafts, written-work, musical compositions, singing and so forth. The Summer Exhibitions ('Show Work') were of outdoor work, such as natural history observation, or architectural and topographical studies, illustrated with sketches and photographs. Experience of 'the market' (i.e. what sort of qualities the judges favoured) sometimes led to a certain amount of 'window dressing'; this could be overdone and on one occasion the official critic warned participants '... against wasting work by putting it where it is not most valuable, either by trying to cover much ground and never going below the surface anywhere or by allowing a beautiful and neat execution to take their interest off the idea of their work. "The matter matters most."'

In all this ferment of activity, groups of Bedalians were also busy excavating Roman villas—first at Bramdean (1903-04), a second at West Meon (from 1904) and a third at Stroud (1906-08).

In *A Schoolmaster's Testament* Badley wrote: 'I am glad to remember that the BBC owes something to the hut, called by the temporary owners Wavy Lodge, where 30 years ago two or three of our boys carried on their voluntary experiments in what was then a new line of discovery.'

Wavy Lodge was initiated by Peter Eckersley who later became Chief Engineer for the BBC. He was some 18 months older than Frank; they nevertheless came into contact in free-time work and sport. The 'Bedales Wireless Telegraphy Syndicate' was formed in 1908 and contributed to the general climate of initiative and creation. (I was its other partner and my life-long friendship with Peter Eckersley started in that year.)

Esmond Romilly was at Bedales one term in 1934. According to his book Out of Bounds he found that 'the whole atmosphere was nearer, in a way, to a prep school. Compared with Wellington [where he had spent about four years], it was

Oswald Horsley (centre), son of the distinguished brain surgeon Sir Victor Horsely, 'was one of the Three Graces who in 1910 had grouped themselves round the Atwood machine in the Physics Lab'. He went on to become a captain in the Gordon Highlanders, where he was wounded three times, mentioned in despatches, and awarded the Military Cross. Also seen here: Frank (right) and Vyv Trubshawe (left). In this photograph, taken in about 1907, the three friends are seen exploring the laws of acceleration.

181

the difference between a country-house and a prison.' Perhaps it would be truer to say that the whole atmosphere then was like that of some lively cultural or political summer school to-day.

With his roots re-settled in this fertile soil, it is not surprising that Frank's last three years at school brought about a marked development and maturing of his character. His early reports suggested that he seemed 'rather inclined to fancy himself sometimes' (Autumn 1905). There were also references to 'cheap humour at unseasonable times' (Autumn 1907). As usual, the Headmaster was generous in his comments: 'Like his brother he is a keen and capable fellow in all ways and with just a little too much sense of his own importance, too! At most schools this would soon be knocked out of him—here he must set to work to knock it out of himself' (Spring 1907).

Although Frank had 'a thoroughly nice character', he was 'too much of a child still. It was time he took things rather more seriously' (Autumn 1907), and even on his return in Autumn 1908 he was 'still not out of the childish stage' but was 'coming out of it'. By Autumn 1909 the Headmaster wrote that he was 'much less childish than he used to be' and from then on his 'boisterousness' and ' casualness of manner' gave way to a 'marked growth of steadiness of manner'. (Autumn 1910)

In his last report (Autumn 1911) Frank's housemaster wrote of him: 'A very keen and public-spirited prefect. In Merry Evenings, and at other times, he has shown great skill in organising, and will be much missed. He has taken a very full and active part in all the life of the school. His most characteristic trait has been his ability to make people laugh without ever being vulgar.' The Headmaster summed up as follows: 'A thoroughly good term for his last. He has always been cheerful and keen, and though full of humour has not let it go too far or failed to be serious when seriousness was required. We shall all miss him greatly, but I feel sure it is now good for him to be at work.'

Frank's care-free attitude towards class work comes out clearly in his account of a 'typical day'. He was intelligent, inventive and 'quite a capable mathematician, although too fond of trying to amuse the class' (Autumn 1909). Yet, his was no steel-trap logical mind, as is borne out by his reports, written work and the recollections of those who knew him. In this respect I believe that he took after our grandfather and father.

Before leaving, he took the Higher Certificate, passing in Mathematics, English and Mechanics, but failing in German. He enjoyed the practical side of scientific work—designing and constructing the apparatus, taking the readings and recording results. His first project on returning in 1908 was an investigation into the temperature of the earth at different depths. For this work he was awarded a prize. In describing these experiments he chose notes—somewhat copious ones— rather than a bare table of figures. The opening section describes his difficulties in purchasing the apparatus and is entitled:

EARTH THERMOMETERS
The procuring of them

He 'had a good deal of trouble', he said, 'in getting something suitable' during the holidays, and 'went with the intention of getting them carried out to his instructions, probably at the works'. Then, he writes: 'I let the Xmas week slip by without doing much and only thought how it could best be done, at odd times. Towards the end of the holidays, however, I managed to give more attention to it and succeeded in getting a little advice from different people. I then procured a catalogue, but when I had examined it I found nothing very suitable.' Further enquiries and shopping expeditions proved unprofitable. He returned to school and consulted the science master who 'seemed to think that an ordinary thermometer, well insulated, would serve the purpose'. Whereupon he wrote 'straight home asking Father to get forwarded three tubes as soon as possible and like the drawing which [he] enclosed'.

As a result of his observations he concluded that the thermometer at '2 feet (depth) is generally warmest in the evening after the mid-day heat and the [one at] 1 foot is generally hottest at noon,' whereas 'a nocturnal effect is rarely answered to by the one at 3 foot.' The delay before marked changes in air temperature were felt seems to have been about one day per foot.

From February 1 until June 29 of that year Frank's daily earth-temperature readings were published with the Meteorological Report in each number of the *Chronicle*. This feature also showed barometric readings, humidity, wind velocity, sunshine, rainfall and other data. Started in 1903, the school Meteorological Station seems to have been quite well equipped and keenly exploited. It came under Frank's charge in 1910.

During the same year he and Vyv were also busy with a series of experiments to test the thrust of a model aeroplane propeller. These were not altogether successful and later in the same year he went into partnership with Peter Eckersley. The experiments went better, but Frank thought there was still room for improvement. Once again he asked for Father's help, referring to Sir Hiram Maxim's book, which he had been studying at home. 'He manages his [apparatus] in a much sounder way,' Frank thought, and enclosed a sketch of an alternative arrangement, requesting that it should be made up at the works.

His scientific co-operation with Peter Eckersley took other forms. A photograph of 1910 shows them both seated in the Bedales quadrangle experimenting with Foucault's pendulum designed to show the rotation of the earth.

Drawing and craft work not only formed part of the school curriculum, but were encouraged as free time occupations. Frank and Vyv were awarded a prize for their pottery exhibit in February 1907. (They can be seen in a school photograph of the time, with Ivon Hitchens, who went on to become a leading English artist.) Frank's drawing and water colour painting often tended to be impressionistic and slap dash; but when he liked he could also bring his work to a high degree of finish. His drawing master, GH Hooper wrote: 'Has done some work this term as good as anything I have ever had done in my classes' (March

1909). A year later, 'There is a thoroughness about his work which means everything' (March 1910). 'He has given every minute he could reasonably spare of his time, on which demands are very great on account of his many sided interests' (January 1911).

In his last term Frank qualified for the Bedales higher drawing certificate. In his final report GH Hooper wrote, 'Has finished up with some excellent work. It is almost a pity he cannot follow an art career, but he has other talents.'

One of Frank's many-sided interests was photography, in which field Father was also busily engaged, and amongst the gifts that he showered upon us were cameras. During my first term I received an impressive Thornton Pickard—no ordinary box affair but a real camera with bellows and tripod. Frank's turn came later with a Goerz Anschutz, complete with telephoto lens. From 1907 on he used it extensively.

Frank and another boy were put in charge of the school dark-room (Spring 1910) and began to interest themselves in elementary planning and organisation. He explained their policy in a short article in the *Record*. It seems that they had set about re-arranging the sinks, lighting and 'rubbish arrangements', 'with a purpose of preventing people handling, borrowing without leave, and generally spoiling other people's work though lack of care—a point that has been a source of infinite trouble during the last few years.' The changes, he wrote, were proving satisfactory.

Frank's photographic services began to be much in demand. He made no charges but good-naturedly tried to oblige as many as possible. This sometimes led to technical disasters as he recounted in one of his many published articles. For instance, on his way to photograph the school orchestra he would be side-tracked by the 'Bargent' and asked to take one of the levelling operations. Then, re-starting off in that direction, he would once again be deflected to have a shot at the carpentry work-shop. After further mishaps, diversions, and mixing up darkslides, he tells how he arrived at the Hall, where tea was being laid and the orchestra about to go into action. His camera, set up on a table, collapsed, just as he had turned his back. His report goes on to describe the development of the negatives and concludes: '... four were blank, one was black all over. But one, this was the treasure—I held it up eagerly to the light. It was good. But what was it of? The more I gazed the more it bewildered me. It looked as if trucks of earth were being emptied on to the heads of several boys busying themselves in sawing the hands off violinists.'

Later, Frank was invited to give a lecture to the Scientific Society and took as his subject 'The Telephoto Lens'. His discourse was illustrated with diagrammatic slides of the construction. As usual he sent home a full report of the proceedings. He showed a series of slides showing the fallacy of the popular idea that a T lens gives a false perspective; in reality, he wrote, it is just the opposite:

> After pointing out its advantages from an architectural point of view I showed several subjects that I had taken myself, including the 'Nequid Pereat'. I then showed the actual workings of my camera with the Tele attached. I concluded by showing the instantaneous ones I had taken. I had 33 slides altogether. They asked to have them through once again before going. (Autumn 1910)

Frank took care in preparation and had an easy and effective manner when lecturing, making his points quite clear.

During the Summer terms Bedalians were encouraged to explore the beautiful surrounding country either on foot, bicycles or in a horse-drawn break. Some of these expeditions and walks were undertaken for their own sake and had no purpose other than open air enjoyment, with perhaps a little sight-seeing thrown in; certain of them might stand out as bringing to a head some trend in human relations, or as leading to a memorable adventure, such as a flight in a heavier-than-air machine; others led to study and exhibits for 'Show Work', in which case we were advised to give the sketching and photography a purposeful turn.

Accordingly Frank and his friend Vyv took up the study 'of fonts in the neighbourhood. A very good point about this work was the map showing the places from which examples were taken,' wrote the official critic. They were awarded a school First Prize (Spring 1909). Vyv Trubshawe wrote later: 'we used to ramble round together at Bedales taking photographs of everyone and everything, developing together in the darkroom, or printing at high speeds by patent methods in the staircase cupboard in the Physics Lab—wherever we went the camera went with us.'

Many walks took place in the early hours of the morning. We called them 'midnight marauding' but Peter Eckersley and I rationalised them as 'scientific research' because some of the night would be spent at Wavy Lodge, where we kept a supply of chocolates and cigarettes. One night, the authorities woke up to the fact that a large number of Bedalians were roaming about the countryside between midnight and four o'clock in the morning. The practice was then stopped—at any rate for a time. Frank avoided these exploits. He was not lacking in courage but, in spite of his boisterousness, was highly sensitive to ethical values, and this tended to widen the distance between us as we passed through adolescence.

It was also widened by the 'class structure', common to most public schools, so that some prefects, dormitory captains and older boys fancied themselves as a cut above the younger ones. At this pioneer school we were not entirely free from this form of snobbishness; furthermore. Peter Eckersley and I developed an exclusive line of our own—a closed circle of esoteric jokes and allusions, together with an undercurrent of jeering at authority and Bedalian high-mindedness. Peter's jokes were salty and often uproariously funny.

One of the most colourful days I can ever remember was that of the Winchester Pageant in July 1908. The whole school had been given a holiday 'to commemorate Laurence Collier's success in winning the Brackenbury History Scholarship at Balliol'. On that day Peter and I were carried away by the massed costumes and armoured ranks and the magic of the whole spectacle. For years afterwards we were haunted by the songs and incidental music.

187

That term Frank was absent but the following year the three of us started off to bicycle the 20 miles to Winchester. We hoped to recapture some of the enchantment of the pageant but things went wrong and the account of the day, written in the third person by myself and published nine years later, is included for the light it throws on our relationships at that time.

From the start the expedition was doomed to failure, owing to the younger brother's firm resolve to be cheerful at all costs. The other two did not want to be cheerful—the day was too hot and sultry for that sort of thing. At that age the friends had an absolute horror of forced cheerfulness, which they called 'jollity'.

Another term of disapproval was 'typical'. Their attitude towards the world was cynical, in a young sort of way ... Consequently the younger brother's efforts at small talk were met with a stony reserve.

However, his optimistic nature rendered him fairly snub-proof, so he continued in the same garrulous vein until they all reached Winchester and staggered into the 'George' for lunch. Here the friends felt that the gardening suit [a nondescript ancient garment scheduled in the official school clothes list] was out of place among the well dressed people in the hotel; in fact they almost wanted to disown Minor; and so even the luncheon part was not a success.

After lunch Minor proposed a bathe in the Itchen but the two friends were put off by a bank of storm clouds that threatened to bring further disaster to the expedition. They felt that they had better be getting back whereas Minor thought they were being over-cautious, as indeed they were.

Shortly afterwards the party started on the homeward trek. The rain kept off, but no sooner had they reached the top of the first hill than a tyre burst; and that being mended, another tyre punctured—and so on until the ride became a perfect epidemic of tyre trouble. At last it was evident that they could only just get home in time for 'call over'; and although Minor insisted that all this tyre trouble had only occurred to put him in the wrong, Major and his friend took it in turns to lecture him on the wisdom of foresight. Poor little Minor!

188

On Sunday afternoons the juniors were sent out for walks with a senior in charge. On one of these walks (Spring 1911) Frank had his first experience of being air-borne; he wrote home:

> I had a fine time last Sunday afternoon. I took two kids out for the walk and coming down the 'Shoulder of Mutton' [a hill on the North Downs] we saw a host of Bedalians at the bottom in the field just to the right, gazing at something which we soon found to be a glider. We raced down and found that they were mending one of the bracing wires. I could take pages describing the machine. I never realised, however, what a beautiful sight these machines are, tho' I've seen hundreds of pictures.
>
> All the struts were made of polished wood and what I liked about it, on further examination, was that where the strength was needed they 'fairly laid it on'.
>
> The whole thing was controlled with a single lever, ([the] cradle on wheels [being] left behind).

> We did not have to wait long before we saw a 'flight'. It ran down a steep gradient and then flew about five or ten yards and skidded along.
>
> We got quite conversational with the owner, an awfully decent young chap. He said that it was really a hopeless day for doing anything as there was no wind to support it, but he had just got it out to show his friends.
>
> Then his three friends had a turn each. Then he asked if I should like a go, so as I had seen three or four flights and everything seemed pretty safe I had a shot. It was a wonderful sensation. I did not get very far as one of the chaps pulled the wing down a bit one side just as I shoved off. Nobody rose more than six feet the whole afternoon, but still it was a wonderful sensation ...
>
> Afterwards I helped to take it to pieces and pack it in the shed. I thanked the chap immensely. He seemed very pleased.

Frank was tall, slightly built, even skinny, but wiry and well coordinated. When he left school in Autumn 1911 he weighed just nine stone and nine pounds and his height was 5 ft 10 inches. In 1908 he captained a Junior League Soccer XI and later played for the 2nd XI against Churcher's College, Petersfield, In his school reports we read: 'Rather dainty and not quite robust enough. Has played frequently in the 1st XI (Autumn 1909). 'A good left-half. Apt to balloon the ball too much and run alongside his opponent rather than tackle at once' (Spring 1910). In his final report the Games Master wrote: 'A splendid half-back—displays great judgement in passing and always seems to be in the right places—has thoroughly deserved his 1st XI colours' (Autumn 1911).

We have seen how, as a small boy, Frank enjoyed a game of cricket. In May 1909 he first played for the second XI against Petersfield, and scored two runs. In a return match a few weeks later, he made eight runs. On this occasion the Chief was playing for the 2nd XI and Frank took a catch off his bowling.

Frank's cricketing career can be said to have started when he got into the 1st XI in 1910. Evidently he was a moderate performer for his batting average was 8.4. In his last year he played regularly for the 1st XI scoring an aggregate of 206 runs with an average of 14.7. He was spoken of as being a keen and good fielder, but seems to have had little aptitude as a bowler.

Due partly, no doubt, to Joe Hubbard's instruction, Frank won a school boxing competition in 1909, but tended to be inhibited by his own amiable disposition. In his last year, he set up a long-jump record in the School Sports (18 ft 10 ins) and won the high jump (4 ft 11¼ ins). He was a graceful high diver and keen on swimming. During the summer of 1909, in a severe test (usually taken in an enclosed swimming bath, but at Bedales that year in the open air), he tried to qualify for the medal awarded by the Royal Life Saving Society.

The prolonged coldness of the weather was, however, a very real hindrance [to practice], since it was never advisable to stay in long enough to go through all the tests at once. The day fixed for the examination, July 27, proved the climax in this respect. Never before had the rain come down in such a relentless deluge, never before had winter clothing seemed more needful. Frank and three others did not come up to the standard required for the medal, through hesitation, difficulty in getting the weight, or general weakness, but were judged deserving of the proficiency certificate.

I was present at this test and well remember my state of mind on seeing what seemed to me senseless and unnecessary suffering. Frank stood at the side of the water, calm but shivering. Later, while jumping over a corner, he slipped and fell across the iron top of the steps leading into the water, bruising himself badly. (Throughout these tests the girls manifested reserves of heat-retaining flesh and were apparently unmoved by the cold.)

Twelve months later Frank prepared to take the tests again, but his time, supplies depending on rain, there was no water in the large swimming bath. 'The small bath had been filled from the well, and the greatest possible use was made of it. The weather, however, was so persistently cold that the practices were necessarily short, and early in July enthusiasm began to flag. Later it became necessary to empty the small bath for cleaning purposes, so that no more practice was possible.' There were other difficulties 'and it was not surprising that at a certain staff meeting the question was raised whether the whole thing should not be given up. Put to the candidates themselves, this was answered by a unanimous "No". Though baffled in all directions, the little band of volunteers steadily stuck to its purpose, giving up precious free time whenever it was asked for, and when on the very last day of their term they emerged from the turmoil of packing and the like, to take the examination at the Marylebone Baths, London, we could but feel that, even if unsuccessful, it would at any rate be an honourable failure. Great indeed was our surprise and rejoicing when the news came that all had passed, some very creditably.'

Frank seized on every opportunity for skating, trying to put into practice what he had learnt on the rink at home. Father would carefully study his reports of progress and in reply offer the thoughtful advice of a skilful skater with an analytical mind. One of Frank's letters, written during the winter of 1906 or '07, tells how he borrowed a pair of skates. 'Mr Powell casually said he had (or thought he had) a rusty old pair which were too small for him.' Frank goes on to tell how he had 'ripping skating': 'I wish Father had been there to show them how to skate. Everybody did seem to skate rottenly after seeing Father.'

Frank's letters, even in 1907, show the same discursive quality as his Prize Work notes—'Earth Thermometers: The Procuring of Them'. He liked reporting, and his correspondence … show a leisurely style and regard for picturesque detail.

In February 1911 he had another day's skating, this time on Woolmer Ponds, between Liss and Farnham, about six miles from the school. He reported that his skates and boots were 'simply topping'. He 'finally succeeded in accomplishing the outside edge backward on both feet, after the 3.' He also did the spread eagle. Next day, although the frost held, 'Miss Thorp as usual put her foot in it and told the Chief that the kids would get cold so he did not give leave to anyone. They were all dreadfully disappointed.'

Golfing enthusiasts made a rough-and-ready nine-hole course in the school grounds. The Chief enjoyed a game and thought 'a round of golf the best of breaks in a working week'. Frank did not play much on the school course but remained keen and talked golf at meal times with the Chief when his turn came to sit at the top table. In November 1910, after I had left school, he wrote to Father: 'I am up at the top this week. The Chief was very funny this morning during breakfast. He said he would love to see you and Bob playing golf; he imagined you both having lengthy scientific discussions between each stroke. I made him roar with laughter by telling him that you came home with implements for playing with sites and adjusting screws, etc.'

During his last year he must have been loosening up and acquiring skill at lawn tennis, for when he returned from his Summer Term in 1911 I was surprised and impressed to find him in the final of the men's doubles at the Handsworth Wood Tennis Club. He and his partners won.

Frank joined the *Chronicle* Committee in June 1911 and for the Christmas Number introduced illustrations for the first time. In October he became sub-editor under Vyv Trubshawe. Among several joint contributions, in which their initials were intertwined ('F.V.B.W.B.T.') was the following parody of Rudyard Kipling's 'If':

> If you can't keep your feet when others clout you,
> And throwing chairs, are aiming them at you:
> If you can't keep your face, when all about you
> Are dropping bricks, and jolly bad bricks too;
> If you can pun, yet not be tired by punning,
> Repeat the stalest of the stale by far,
> And tell the same joke five or six times running,
> And when rebuked say, 'Yes, I know you are' ...

And so forth, ending with:

> Then, will the School, and everyone that's in it,
> Unanimously hail you 'Fool of Fools'.

In December the partners produced a gem, the point being a striking contrast between a loving mother's (Mumsydoo's) idea of a suitable little play for Christmas and the would-be dramatist's précis of his 'dramatical sketch', Xantithibus Unwound. This was not the only anticipation at that time of Max Beerbohm's Savanarola Brown.

For some years after they had both left they continued to make joint contributions over their combined initials. Two, which appeared in 1913, deserve mention.

The first purports to be 'A Letter from O.B.s in South-East Mongrolian Caliban, Swab Island'. The friends had noticed certain published letters from emigrants to 'backward' territories, describing their experiences amongst the natives. F.V.B.W.B.T. could not resist accepting the challenge. The description of their life 'out there—ever fresh and full of new and wonderful interest' contains some excellent guying of the Bedalian colonials. An account of their visit to the 'Wodgpondras', accompanied by their 'boopher' named 'Googles', gave them scope for some good simple fooling—topical allusions, bogus place names and 'local colour'.

The other was supposed to have been written by some Old Bedalians who had gone abroad 'in order to pursue a course of 'Harmogymnamics' under the celebrated Madame Cweitow Erdotzky. This distinguished Russian lady, they wrote, 'has already done much to propagate "the science of the accrelevation existing between Harmony and Muscular Corpuscles".' The address given was KrQSYL[45] Hall, Little Russia.

Bedales was a target for all sorts of new ideas, especially in the sphere of music, dancing, 'Free Expression' Eurythmics, and, after the Bargent's time, Swedish gymnastics. The friends must have heard vaguely about Jacques Dalcroze and Madame Bergman-Oesterberg's Physical Training College. There was, furthermore, a group of Russians at the school, some living in the neighbourhood, who might have stepped out of a Chekhov play. In their article Frank and Vyv combined all this experimental and exotic climate with characteristic allusions to Bedalian routine.

At KrQSYL Hall, it seemed, physical drill and cross country runs were united with orchestral rehearsal. 'Harmogymnamics' also took other forms. For instance: 'After the lectures we generally go on to the Swimming Hall, a wonderfully constructed building. We take it in turns to play in the orchestra under a cold spray, while the others sing their Wagner or whatever has been selected for the day. In this way Rhine Maidens can sing under the water and the Gods can descend to earth with a swallow dive without hurting themselves.' The article was illustrated by Frank.

In his autobiography Badley says of himself that he 'could never sing (or even whistle) a tune' and that 'in boyhood found in any kind of music nothing but boredom'; and yet music played a

---

[45] Spelt with the K, S, Y and L upside down, in cod-Russian.

most important part in the school life. Mrs Badley had been a student at Frankfurt: on Sunday evenings she played Bach and Beethoven, reverentially, and sometimes gave piano lessons. Oswald Powell, the Second Master, 'in addition to teaching modern languages took the whole of the school singing, making of it a great and living influence'. He had learnt most of his music from his wife, who was a fine pianist and accompanied him as he sang Brahms and Schumann. Jean de Reszke held that the voice should be placed well to the front—dans la masque. This was not Oswald Powell's idea of voice production; instead, he contrived somehow to bring into play his cheeks, beard and moustache as a sort of sounding board. But whatever the means the result was always pleasing and musicianly. Through him we became familiar with English Folk Songs and actually heard lectures by Cecil Sharp and recitals sponsored by him.

Badley was only stating the truth when he wrote: 'Simple, large-hearted and loving, Powell's was a sincere and transparent nature, like a lamp kept bright for the inner light to shine through. In all he did, and did so well, was revealed a rich personality, always unassuming and always helpful, that won the affection of all with whom he came in contact.'

It was unfortunate that the Bedalian predisposition towards new ideas, on one occasion, led to a change in musical leadership. According to the *Record* (1906–7, p.26) 'The Winter term of 1906 will be remembered by the choir as the term of Mr Tomlins' visits. We had heard of his doings in Chicago, in the training of choirs of children for the World's Fair and in the slum schools of that and other American cities. Mr Badley invited him to give a course of lectures and lessons here. In the Easter term we spent some time, at Mr Tomlins' suggestion and under his conducting, in learning a cantata, "Vogelweid" by George Rathbone.'

This was the official view. There must have been, however, few visitors capable of generating so much burlesque and parody as Mr Tomlins. It is impossible to forget or adequately describe his loud nasal voice or the striking quality of his teaching methods. At times comments from the basses and tenors would be so outspoken that he would turn his back on us, saying that he would refuse to face us again until we had quietened down. This form of non-resistance was not, as far as I remember, very successful. He left after one term.

Whether or not as a result of these influences Frank's singing voice was a little odd. It was rather breathy, as if the vocal chords were not connecting properly. Even before his voice broke a report stated that 'He often sings very harshly and not well in tune—keen' (Autumn 1906). Then, after it had broken: 'He is rather inclined to force his voice; wants more resonance' (Spring 1910). He nevertheless won two points out of five for his singing in a Prize Work competition in 1911.

Prior to his term's absence Frank had not been conspicuous in the school's musical life, but I see from programmes that in some concerts he had played the piano, had accompanied a violin solo and had taken part in a piano quartette. Around 1904 he and I, with two girls, had played in an eight-handed setting of Mozart's *Jupiter* Symphony.

Our piano teacher, Miss Smith, was gentle and charming. She would delight us with a performance of Schumann's *Papillons, Faschingschwank aus Wien* and other works which she played in school concerts, but sometimes, alas, broke down through nervousness. Under her instruction Frank made good progress at the piano. She reported him as 'very promising; ought to play well when his hands get stronger' (Spring 1909). 'He is not a quick worker and reads slowly' (Autumn 1909). His touch was musical but somewhat lacking in power. He seemed unable to bring out a theme above its accompaniment.

Frank's return in the Autumn term of 1908 marked the beginning of what was for him a creative period. From then on up to the time he left he produced ten out of a total of 27 compositions (he may well have been the first Bedalian composer), many of them being comic songs and light music. He began taking lessons in harmony from Miss Smith during Autumn term 1910, but by that time he had already written, or was working on, three piano pieces and five songs. For the most part he worked at the key-board and could play the compositions before writing them out. Some of his piano pieces were reminiscent of Grieg and Macdowell. Most of them still please me greatly. I first woke up to the charm of his work on hearing the wistful sixths of his *Pavanne* played over the phone connecting our house with that of our Aunts at Christmas 1910. Frank had been in contact with suspected scarlet fever and was in quarantine for a week or so.

As he acquired facility in improvisation Frank was never at a loss when called upon to play in school concerts. He seemed quite free from stage-fright and if he felt like drying up, with great presence of mind, he would extemporise something which he felt to be appropriate, Once, when he went on to the platform to play, he eased the rather solemn and tense atmosphere associated with these functions by removing the front of the piano and making a few minor adjustments to the hammers.

We became steeped in music but narrow and prejudiced in our tastes. Gustav Holst divides musical Philistines into two classes: those for whom music begins with, say, Beethoven or Wagner, and those for whom it ends with, say, the death of Handel. In this sense we were both imbued with the Philistine spirit. For us music began with Schumann, Chopin and Brahms. Like debutantes at their first dance we were swept off our feet at the Queen's Hall Schumann Centenary Concert on June 8, 1910. A report in the *Chronicle* said: 'Fanny Davies [a friend of our two Aunts] rendered the beautiful piano concerto with all her characteristic grace of manner and velvety softness of touch, and afterwards she and Mme. Desauer-Grün played together the well-known variations for two pianos.'

Frank became an active member and eventually Secretary of the school's Musical Society to which he sometimes gave lectures. One was on 'The Piano and its Evolution' (Spring 1911). He used a blackboard and explained the action of the dulcimer monochord, clavichord 'and those that were plucked—the psaltery, spinetta, harpsichord, etc.' According to The *Chronicle*, 'Best went well into the details of the actions and showed careful sections of the "Jack" action. He showed also the tangent method. Messrs, Broadwood had kindly lent models of their actions used in modern pianos which proved very useful in demonstrating. The lecturer concluded by playing his latest composition.

Not all Frank's lectures were serious. In spite of the 'little Bach' duets, he resisted what he considered the over-devout attitude of the Bach and Mozart enthusiasts, and in this mood he gave a lecture to the Musical Society—'The Lesser Instruments' was, I believe, the title. His subject had been accepted in all seriousness by the committee, but as the lecture developed it became clear to members that they were being entertained by an elaborate piece of clowning. Examples were played on all sorts of instruments, such as an occarina, a mouth organ, a penny whistle, and a curious box-like affair, with stops, that made a noise like a concertina.

At another lecture to the Musical Society, this time by a visitor, a Mr Harry Farjeon who taught harmony and composition at the Royal Academy of Music 'told of a Russian composer who on visiting some nephews and nieces heard the immortal chopsticks and played a gallop with the chopsticks continuing in the upper register of the instrument. The lecturer asked for an assistant to play chopsticks which Best ii. performed very wittily. Mr Farjeon then played the variations by several composers who had rivalled each other in the matter of compositions on chopsticks.'

Frank made no hard-and-fast distinction between serious or classical music and light music. For instance, he would discuss and analyse Pelissier's compositions with the same zest as he would the works of Wagner and Debussy. Throughout these last years at Bedales the influence of The Follies made itself continually felt. Peter Eckersley knew most of the songs by heart and entertained us with imitations of Lewis Sydney reciting 'Kissing Cup Race' or with some of that comedian's funny stories. There was probably a close parallel between the Bedalian tendency to make fun of everything and the new type of humour created by Pelissier's genius. Max Beerbohm, in the *Saturday Review* wrote: 'Now that I have seen The Follies I am not surprised at their vogue; nor do I think it will soon pass. Their fun has a savour of its own, a savour of high spirits running riot in the sheer silliness of invention, with yet an undercurrent of solid sober satire.'

At last, after thorough preparation by Peter Eckersley, we went for the first time to the Apollo Theatre. Here we heard in their original form the tunes he had sketched out for us fluently, though not, as we found, always accurately. Backed by the specially designed Double Grand Piano and charmingly harmonised they had a powerful appeal.

At some point Peter and Frank found themselves in the same dormitory and seized on the contemporary phonograph recording as more material for travesty. By modern standards the voices then sounded unbelievably harsh and nasal. Portentously, an announcer always gave the title and singer, ending his introduction with the words 'Edison Bell Rrrrecorrrd'. Here was an opportunity not to be missed. Together they bought the cheapest apparatus they could lay their hands on—one that could be relied upon to give the maximum distortion—and then recorded a song, composed for the occasion by Frank. The chorus, sung by the other inmates of the dormitory, went: 'Are we all very happy?—Yes, we are.'

In a Merry Evening (Autumn 1910), Frank's 'Overture in One Sharp and One Flat' was performed. Studying 'Sound' in the Physics Lab he had learnt, experimentally, that a perforated disc rotating in front of an air-jet produced a note. Using a series of concentric rings of holes, Frank and his friends designed a large instrument to play the first five notes of the C minor scale. They called it the 'KLANGENOHEILISSOCYCLO-STRIGOTONITON'. It was accompanied by the school orchestra. Unfortunately when the foot-lights were switched on, the speed of the motor-driven disc was reduced and this affected the pitch.

The musical critic wrote that the performance 'seemed to suffer from excess of percussion instruments' but 'that the theme was musically very pleasing indeed. It had at bottom the germ of a sound harmonic structure, which the composer seems to have realised, though it was entirely lost owing to what seemed to be a furious row in the kitchen …'

As Frank's last term drew to a close he came more and more into his own and acknowledged as a leader in entertainment. In October, in one evening, he produced three numbers. Firstly, his Opening Overture—The Yaboo [sic] Symphony: 'The great success of the above was not entirely due to the fact that it started off with a bottle of champagne, for, if the truth be told, this latter provided the only discordant note of the evening, produced by Master Infanto Prodigio Hughes [another friendly master, of Science and Maths] to the merciful unaccompaniment of an otherwise alarming orchestra. For which relief much thanks. We, the audience, admit that we were badly had, though it was chiefly the sight of Horsley armed with the gong that made us produce our cotton wool. The piece itself I can only describe as a Siesta in Best minor, consisting as it did of nineteen bars conducted in common time by Herr Vanderbest, and in uncommon time by a monster metronome.'

Second was Frank's 'Animated Pictures'. According to the report it was 'the event of the evening [and] the cleverest thing we have ever had … and Best has set up a record of laughter which will be hard to beat. And after all, the device is so simple that one wonders it has never appeared before. But that is the way with all great inventions! A cardboard disc with a single perforation rotating at some speed in front of the lens of the lantern—that was all, and the effect was a real cinematograph show.'

In the same programme was a 'Farcette—Changing the Guard, at the Imperial Palace, Berlin, suggested by our experiences in that city. This number was so popular that it was revived, along with some others, at the last O.B. meeting before the outbreak of War in 1914.

Frank's final appearance in this innocent form of variety entertainment took place shortly before leaving. Mother happened to be present and wrote: 'After tea at Mr Badley's table we got ready for the Merry Evening. First an imitation of reciting by Frank (I must tell you, an elocution class is now started at the school), with lip exercises like Uncle Arthur. Then followed a small farce by Harry Proctor, grossly over-acted by the author. It was great fun, ending in a smash up of plates in a restaurant. Great delight of the small fry sitting in front! After this two Morris dances arranged by Frank called 'Floor Spogging'. Four boys and four girls came in with tin pails and scrubbing brushes. They banged the pails together and went through various antics. Then we had to tear ourselves away to catch our train back to London, and missed the Opera to be sung in four foreign languages; but we saw Frank in his dress— pink satin and yellow wig.

Everyone agreed it was the best Merry Evening the school had ever seen. Frank, as the Spanish Prima Donna (Signora Optimo) and his whole opera were remembered long afterwards.

A week later he and his friends organised a variety show for the children at the preparatory school. Here they sang their own adaptation of a song from *The Arcadians*, with the theme: 'I've gotter motter—always merry and bright', seeking to create an impression of all that was clumsy, destructive and unruly. In the first verse they admitted their imperfections, singing, 'We are such rotters,' etc. The second verse, however, turned the tables:

> They are such rotters,
> We can't have our bit of fun
> We smash the windows and bust the doors,
> Cut the desks and ink the floors,
> The stick still hurts,
> We still get cursed and pye-jawed,
> We've often said to ourselves—we've said—
> The days of good jokes and bad puns are dead,
> So we're jolly glad we've been out-lawed.

Frank began to exploit the 'Till Ready'—that short phrase in the accompaniment repeated again and again while the comedian was gagging before starting each verse. For this song he hit on a distinctly catchy 'Till Ready'. The original tune is Tempo di Valse:

Instead, he took the first four notes of the verse, continuing them thus:

For the encore verse he played it high in the treble and worked down the key-board, as his team came galumphing in from the wings—young oafs, up against authority—to deafening squeals from the children.

During this closing Bedalian phase of abundance and blossoming Frank appeared three times on the stage in classical drama. His first (Autumn 1910) was as Bardolph in Henry IV. 'The actors were ready with their parts when, just at the end of the term, half-a-dozen cases occurred which, though the doctors could not affirm positively that it was scarlet fever, we had to treat as though it were beyond doubt.' The performance was cancelled. The second (Spring 1911), in Aristophanes' *The Frogs*, brought the comment 'Best 2 was excellent as Dyonysus, and his inane voice brought the house down.' In this play Mooner Wills's 'performance of Cerberus was considered the best thing in the play.' 'At first thought it seems indeed a hard task to undertake the manipulation of three heads, but the great Mooner managed it with all the dexterity in the world and his by-play and general movement must have been the outcome of real study of dogs' movements.'

Bedales' new hall, designed by the architect Ernest Gimson and built by Geoffrey Lupton, an OB, was completed just in time for the staging of *A Midsummer Night's Dream* in December 1911. In this, his third production, Frank had two parts allotted to him. The *Chronicle* wrote: 'Peter Quince made an admirable foil to the noisy weaver. Best kept up the old man's shrill piping voice very cleverly, and seemed to enjoy thoroughly the congenial part of stage manager to the Athenian rustics. In the character of Egeus he was not so successful, but this is a thankless part.'

Our parents made a special visit to see this play—and Frank's last performance before leaving. Mother wrote to me—then in Düsseldorf—as follows:

My darling Bobbitts,

We came home last night with Frank; the play went off very well and it was performed in the new hall. The dresses were very pretty, and the band played delightfully in spite of Mr Scott (A sort of flute Johny Ridley).[46]

The new hall reminded me so much of a country church that from force of habit I nearly dropped down to whisper a little prayer. The pews are very firm and of oak: [one] got rather stiff after 2 hours' sitting. Father got wriggling about, and then said he found them very hard, and inclined to be on the cold side. To make a Shakespearean pun (but I won't) they were really on "another" side! Frank made a microbe and peniciosity of himself. [Among Mother's pet names for Frank were 'pernicious microbe' and 'nauseating phenomenon'. When he was clowning she would look at him affectionately and pretend to shudder.]

[Oswald Horsley] was awfully good as Bully Bottom, and shouted out with a tremendous voice. Mr Badley came before the curtain and thanked us all very nicely for coming; he now beams round in gold framed specs, like Father.

Well, we had a splendid evening at Bedales, although it poured

---

[46] Poor Johny Ridley was one of the scholars at Nelson Street Adult School. He was liable to make inappropriate gestures and remarks during the proceedings.

with rain all the time and there was such a run on carriages [that] we had to go there and back in a motor with a cape hood (rather chilly round the corners). Next day we joined the surging crowd at the station, and after filling up all the regular carriages more were put on ...

We drank your health at Frascati's and also at the Euston over oysters and sparkling! Hope you will work well in 1912 and make it a good Leap Year in progress.

I forgot to say that Peter Eckersley came down in a waistcoat which was like Joseph's, of pit fame—long ago.

Dearest love,
from Mothery

In the evening they were joined by Oswald Horsley at The Follies. Frank continued Mother's letter with an enthusiastic and detailed report of the whole programme item by item: '... the marvellous opening chorus, giving samples of all the typical songs ... (coon song, warbling soprano, etc)'. Lewis Sydney's anecdotes, their burlesque version of *The Chocolate Soldier*, with three heroines, 'whenever any doubts arose as to what they were to do someone always suggested the waltz. Also, as the hero was supposed to be an old Gilbert and Sullivan opera man, during the course of the performance they introduced all the well known choruses from Pinafore, etc.

Then they potted Tree's *Macbeth*; but Pelissier again in the prologue said that he was sure it would appeal more if all the lines rhymed and they had a few songs and dances—and they did!

The scene opened with the witches throwing all the plays for potting into a magic trunk with red lights coming up inside. On the front was written 'Masculine and Feminine' [a reference to Maskelyne and Devant, the magic and conjuring people].

Instead of Malcolm's ghost, *The Englishman's Home* came up and said he refused to be potted. Lady Macbeth sang the sleep-walking scene with 'One—Two—buckle my shoe', etc. Pelissier came out of his room and, finding Banquo's boots outside, chalked the number on the soles and threw them down to be cleaned.

The fight began with a beautiful contrapuntal chorus, 'Lay on Macduff', etc, but they finished up with a sort of Pierrot circle, chasing each other in a ring and finally Meyer (the man who stopped the Johnston-Wells fight in Britain) came in and stopped them. They also introduced a fool who did the typical, 'wisdom shall folly, and folly shall quip and crank, etc' just like Ma's version.

They concluded with the Music Hall burlesque, with plenty of fresh turns. The climax of the evening was Pelissier as an Australian lady swimmer (very fat) doing a dive from 2,000 ft high into a tank containing three inches of water. Of course she climbed up a ladder and disappeared in the curtain and then they started the kettledrum noise (like dog jumping in a circus), but she refused to attempt it as she had not got a safety pin. Finally they flung down a dummy which, splashed the water out of the tank below the stage, and Pelissier, with flowing hair all wet, appeared from below the stage amid thunders of applause.

I never shouted so much in all my life. I wish you had seen it.

Dearest love from

Frank

Chapter 8
What Germany taught me

I missed Frank's performance because by then I was living with a German family in Düsseldorf and studying design at the Düsseldorf School of Arts and Crafts, the Kunstgewerbeschule. Looking in my archives I find numerous evocative letters of the period and the following amusing report, written for the *Chronicle*.

INITIAL EXPERIENCES OF AN EXILE.
Bedales Chronicle, November 1911

> Lately I have noticed several letters in the *Chronicle* from old boys and girls who are stopping abroad in order to learn German. I am also doing 12 months in the Fatherland for the same reason, and am living in a family with whom I am having a very enjoyable time.
>
> Before setting off for Düsseldorf, a notice was put in the local newspaper to the effect that a young Englishman, who intended stopping in Germany for a year, required a home to live in. Small family preferred, and no English spoken. Applicants should please state terms. Two days after the above had appeared we arrived in the Düssel village, weary and depressed from the journey. Two or three hours' sleep somewhat revived us, but—well, every traveller knows that peculiar 'be-anything-except-jolly' feeling that comes after a long journey. Strange town, nothing particularly interesting to do except look around, after-effects of journey, all combine to damp the spirits and inflame the temper.

206

It was while in this mood that Providence, or rather, the local newspaper, sent us the wherewithal to occupy ourselves, in the shape of a formidable pile of letters, which nearly took our breath away. They were, of course, the answers to our advert, but the number exceeded our wildest dreams. Strange to say, the prospect of reading these letters did not improve matters, and perhaps it's as well that we did not know to the full extent what was in store for us.

However, we soon started the work of translation on a systematic plan, classifying the letters into four classes: A, B, C and D, according to their merits. At first there was certainly some satisfaction in condemning an unworthy epistle with a vicious D, but that soon wore off. Later, when all the letters were classified, we visited the As, to make our final choice; but the best was so below what be expected, that we abandoned the lot, and taking the advice of the English parson, we found a family which is now giving every satisfaction.

But much toil had to be undergone before that happy day was reached, and as we broke open the first letter the lines of the poet came to my mind:

> The streets of Brum behind us,
> The dreary waste before
> Of thrice three hundred letters—
> Enough to make you swore.

The letters had a sort of monotonous variety; in other words, certain offerings were constantly recurring with desperate regularity. For instance, they had either a tastefully furnished room in a peaceful neighbourhood to offer, or else the pension (i.e., food) was good, or else they moved in the most refined and elevated circles. After the first hundred or so, sleep put an end to our sorrows for the day, but next morning brought fresh labour and another pile of letters, somewhat larger than the first.

Evasion was impossible, as the weather forbade us to go for a walk or see anything we wanted to see, so once more we plunged into the mass of clamouring ex-schoolmasters, ex-state officials, architects, artists, civil engineers, and, in short, just that miscellaneous assortment of curiosities as would delight the heart of O.G. These letters were mostly written by their wives, and, of course, each one felt sure that she could offer us just the home we wanted. They took great pains to convince us that they did not depend upon the pension price for their living, and therefore it would be exceptionally low.

And then their relations. One might be led to imagine the whole of the Düsseldorfian nobility was clamouring for my company, judging by the titles to whom we were referred: Baroness von Hochwohlgeborener Oberst von und zu—Senats Präsident am Königlichen Verwaltungs Gericht, etc, etc. At last, we got so bored with nobility that the mere mention of blood in the family booked the letter for a $D/2$.

Midday came and went, but still the stream of letters was unabated.

> Letters, letters all around
> And not a drop …

No, no, on second thoughts, I don't think that quotation is applicable in Germany. Notwithstanding the general monotony of appeals, there were one or two that were conspicuous for originality. Perhaps the coolest card we received was from one good lady, who was kind enough to put the public park and picture gallery at our disposal! Time does not permit me to describe the other 'shining lights', the sort, for instance, that specializes in the fact that the room at my disposal would be papered, or that the family dwell in a 'lustige étage'.

Time also brought my labour to an end, and somewhere about midnight judgment was dealt out to the last letter, and I surveyed the littered table, as a victorious general the field of battle. I felt tired and was half asleep, with my head on the table, when suddenly I noticed an unvanquished enemy poking its nose out from under the heaps of slain. It was curious that I had not noticed it before, as it was rather an unusual sort of envelope, bristling with seals and red tape. I tore it open as quickly as the aforesaid tape would allow, and the following remarkable epistle met my gaze:

Kaiserliches Schloss,
P.P. Berlin.

With backsight on your verhonoured announcement, believe I that for a young Englander containment seeking, in proper form offer can.

I bed well a Lordshiply residing (central heating, electric light and bath) of which one side on the Spree looks, and from where the middle of the town in few minutes to reach is.

Our small cultured family of seven parts consists; my man is often from home away but in our youngest son would the young Herr ample opportunity for conversation find.

Though I, as Frau of Gesellschaft outlandish speech understand, would, in my dwelling still only German spoken be.

The young Herr would receive good Pension, each dish being well cooked and cleanly served up. The pension price if not verbally arranged carries itself as three thousand marks monthly, which, in such conditions the usual price is.

Last year had we several distinguished visitors by us, who away, very much delighted went.

Mit Hochachtung
Augustina Victoria
Kaiserin Deutschlands Königin Preussens.

As references, allow I myself, the afterstanding Addresses in to give:

Herr Baron von Straussgates,
c/o Fräulein Thorp,
Dr Bebabes School,
Nr. Southampton.

Herr Hermann Voigt,
Hauptmann von Koepenick,
Brandenberg.

Baldwyn Tarash Graf von Schlobitten,
Wirklicher Geheimer Oberkonfusionsrath,
Berlin.

Letter, 14 October 1911

Dear Pa and Ma,

What is turning out a most wonderful place, on the outside seemed most doleful. The gathering gloom—afterglow of sunset—dark street—hushed stillness except for the tolling of that wretched Roman Catholic bell—the high forbidding-looking house and the flight of steps up to the door: it was all so like a scene out of *The Only Way* that one was forced to see the doleful sight and forget the happy.

After I'd gone in I went up to my room, got my music and had a little practice on the piano. Mrs Vits came in and we chatted for a bit, then went down to supper. I got quite chatty with my German on the first night and after supper they have a hymn and Vits reads a passage from the Bible. A few days of the good-wholesome-plenty-of-it style, but what is lacking in luxury is made up for in company and humour, for Vits—not Vitz—is quite a wag.

The whole family are very humorous. They appear very demure and well-behaved but don't make any mistake: the youngest at any rate has his 'off' moments. They are however ripping kids and I get on very well with them.

I have finished the drawing of the pots. On Wednesday, Herr Hochreiter was away and in his place a Mr Wagner. He seemed very satisfied with it, now that it is shaded etc. and it seemed to give satisfaction amongst the pupils. In your next letter you might enclose a copy of my Xmas card and with the help of the two I might get into a more decorative branch of the school. Herr Peyerimhoff with whom I began modelling is a very decent old chap. I've only modelled two simple sort of leaves with him.

I have decided, as you suggested, to have singing lessons. This morning I had my first singing lesson with Herr Senf. He is quite a nice little man but he speaks German very indistinctly and the little English that he knows, still worse. When he said 'good-bye', he said 'good-bicycle' by way of a joke. Rotten, isn't it. I brought my songs to him and he selected the 'Old Superb'. He had as much as he could handle with the accompaniment but he was pleased with the song. He has a ripping voice. Mine sounds muffled by the side of it.

On Thursday I went to a beautiful concert in the Tonhalle with Mrs Vits. We met there a friend of hers, a Baronness von Massenbach or something. You will probably hear about her later.

Yesterday, having been only warned of its arrival, and

hearing the sound of propellers, we went to the window and suddenly over the roof there appeared the nose of the Zeppelin Air Ship. Wonderful. Steady as a liner and going about 30 mph. It made an awful row. One could see the passengers inside the middle cabin and all.

There is nothing wrong with the way you addressed the letter except R.D. Best ought to be lower. I can now write German characters. Am very busy. Love to all.

Bob

———————

Letter, 18 November 1911

The *Walküre* was WONDERFUL and I can't possibly write it big enough. In the first place, I could remember the fire music and Siegmund's song before I went in (from pianola). And when they got into full swing I found I knew most of it. But the orchestration, the way these ravishing airs seethe up and down and mix together in wonderful harmony till I had green shivers down my back and in my cheeks. The voices were all tip-top. Hunding's voice was better than Wotan's. Sieglinde's and Frieka's were lovely. Brünnhilde was one of the tip-top Wagner singers. She looked the part absolutely, just buxom enough to be a warrior maiden, but only just. Sieglinde looked ideal, 'reizend' [charming] in fact. Siegmund looked a typical young God and had a wonderful voice. The dresses were all wonderfully artistic, these ripping dark red cloaks, Viking helmets with wings, chain mail and all. Wotan had a pair of gigantic wings to his helmet, dark red hair and a great lock over his blind eye—fine he looked.

The last scene was like a dream. It was all arranged so naturally, Wotan's farewell to Brünnhilde, the first bits of the fire music worked in, pine forest on the left, no palpable couch for Brünnhilde. He just laid her among the rocks on the edge of the pine forest. Then when he struck the rock with his spear, real flames proceeded to rim about all over the rocks and then just in

front of Wotan, and the perfectly whopping flame kept on appearing, and this exquisite fire music—I could scarcely sit still. As for Frau Pastor, she hasn't left off talking about it yet. It's the first time she's been to the theatre in Düusseldorf and being extremely musical I think she enjoyed it as much as I did. We met the Dalmeiers at the theatre and they sent kind regards.

Last week I was at Herr Blochum for St. Martin's Day. All the children turn out with lanterns in line in the streets at night. Looked very pretty. Paul [Funke] was awfully excited.

I have learnt 'Du bist die Ruh' and 'Who is Sylvia?' At present I am learning 'Von ewiger Liebe' by Brahms, which is wonderful.

So far I have not found the least trace of hostility towards England. In the Kunst School everyone is very amiable.

Letter, 2nd December 1911

At the Kunstgewerbe Schule with Hochreiter the Philistine I am doing some highly enlarged studies of poppy heads in three or four colours; later, following his system, I'm going to turn them

212

into lamps and lanterns. This though apparently useless for business purposes will probably prove interesting, as it will afford new lines and forms. With Peyerimhoff I have just finished my third model to Peyerimhoff's satisfaction I think. I am now going to do a rosette which is going to be very difficult. I am then going to do some acanthus leaves from different styles; it took a long time to get his consent to the latter because there is a general aversion to styles in the school, particularly French styles: Louis XIV-XVI. They simply repeat Cat Smith and say 'spoils originality' etc. etc. but notwithstanding, Peyerimhoff is a dear old man and always most friendly. He teaches the ground points of modelling well and when I've finished the rosette he has promised to let me do styles. This morning I have bought six shillings' worth of modelling tools under Peyerimhoff's supervision from the traveller who comes round every few months to the school. Even in the Stilgeschichte Zeichnen I find it very hard to get onto Louis. Hermann keeps on giving me plain sort of Gothic, Byzantine and Classical candlesticks when I want to be able to draw quickly that profundity of decoration *à la* Boisselier. Probably with repeated effort I shall come onto that later, but so far it is more Art than Trade drawing that I am learning. Kreis has not been around again.

Last night I went to see *Der Freischütz*[47] with Lena. Herr Dallmeier was kind enough to give us his two places that night and Sunday we are going to lunch there on our invitation. It is astonishingly kind of him and I enjoy the opera awfully, although the thing they did was a mixture of Macbeth, Mendelssohn's *A Midsummer Night's Dream*, the Xmas pantomime and other celebrated pieces. The voices and scenery were nevertheless very good.

I have now got a fairly definite idea as to why the Germans are so angry with us. If it interests you it is as follows. Some time ago a certain treaty was made over Morocco which was that England should have a free hand in Egypt and France in

---

[47] *Der Freischütz* (The Marksman): regarded as the first romantic opera, music by Weber, first produced in Berlin in 1821. Immensely popular.

Morocco. It is pretty cool, by the way, to leave Germany out. Another treaty was made later that France should keep an open door in Morocco, but lately, so say the Germans, France has been 'doing it across' German merchants in Morocco with the result that the Germans naturally want to come to an agreement with France. Again, France has brought troops etc. into Morocco which is against the treaty that Morocco should be kept neutral. For a long time past, Germany has tried to come to terms with France but France has always shuffled it off. So in order to come to terms they do the most peaceful thing they can, i.e. sending the Panther. Many advocated mobilising troops on the frontier; something had to be done to protect national honour and so they sent a small boat, a thing that we've done times out of number. But just because it's Germany we say 'hands off'. It is obviously a matter between France and Germany which was going forward in perfectly peaceable fashion when we stepped in and wantonly rubbed Germany up the wrong way.

It is quite a mistake to think that they have a natural animus against us. We are nearly related in race and they would prefer us to be friendly. The idea of invasion as painted in *An Englishman's Home* or *Invasion* of 1910 is to a German a shrieking farce. The military service in that way serviceable purpose, for a more naturally peaceful people could scarcely be found.

How is it that a peaceful man like Lloyd George could make such a speech, I don't know. Before, they'd always looked on us as at any rate a neutral if not friendly. France they'd always looked on as their natural enemy but now they say they see how the land lies and they can only expect enmity from us.

This I have got from Herr Pastor. Outside that, I have not heard a word against England or the English, and have been treated as a friend everywhere.

Professor Von Gephard (a well-known painter) was here the other night for a few minutes. Wonderful man. He proceeded to describe Englishmen he had met. Very interesting and amusing.

Letter, 9 Dec 1911

Dear Cheebles,

Thanks very much for copious letters, also newspaper cuttings. I have read them all, but I am not clear as to

1) How it was that we got a free hand in Egypt, France in Morocco and Germany nothing?

2) The terms of the Algeciras Act.

3) What was Lloyd George's speech.

When I get these points clear I may be able to form an opinion, but so far I've done more listening than disputing. I have only had the subject mentioned to me by two people—one Herr Pastor, the other Herr Dallmeier. Their chief thought was one of regret that two nations who are nearly racially related should be such enemies. This I can't help feeling is most lamentable but whether they've started the quarrel or we is a question about which I don't know sufficient facts to come to a conclusion.

We went to lunch with dear old Dallmeier and his wife and were treated in the most wonderful way. Mrs D said that the dinner was only going to be quite homely (bürgerlich) but when we teed off with champagne and caviar I said 'Yes I don't think'. We are very friendly. They told us how fortunate we were to have such '*reizende Eltern*' (lovely parents) which wasn't always the case in England. I proposed the toast of their sons and remembered you kindly to them. Between ourselves, Lena was what Hans would call 'champion taktlos'—an expression I have taught him. She arrived before me and as I came in I found her telling the Dallmeiers that the Freischutz was like a pantomime. I had to hurriedly put it right. She can put her foot into things socially as she could through skirt trimming.

On Monday I took Baronesse von Massenbach to the Brahms evening in the Bach-Saal of the Johanneskirche. Her taste in music resembles mine—starting with Brahms and working up through Wagner to Strauss. We both thoroughly enjoyed the performance which was wonderful. I treated her to the best seats (4.40) so we saw and heard magnificently.

215

Senf is quite on his feet again—I had a very interesting lesson this morning in which he went into the pronunciation of the words in a new song I have learnt 'The Last Greeting' by Levi. He was pleased with my rendering the first time I sang it. Tomorrow I am singing in an Unterhaltungs Abend for the Kränzchen [Ladies' circle]. I am giving them 'The Pipes of Pan' because compared to my other songs I find it extremely singable.

I am struck by the absence of style brass fittings here. Patterson S says the Germans are only copiers. That they give scope to originality much more than we in their buildings etc, there is no doubt. Whether they have much sense of the beautiful is another matter. I was at the judging of the Kunstgewerbe Competition when Kreis gave a speech over the merits of each prize-winning work. It didn't matter if a man had not the ghost of an idea of anatomy: so long as it was original it was booked for a prize. This judgement took place just after the news arrived that Kreis had won the National Bismarck Denkmal Preis which lent his decisions additional weight. In the evening he was paraded with a torchlight procession. I have seen some original lamps in shops made from basketwork.

***

Letter, 24 December 1911

Dear Doodles and Dankitz (*prolonged babydom*),

On Friday I sent off some charming little pots of flowers to Frau Dollmeier, Balg and old Mr Blochius, together with my cards on the back of which were 'Best Wishes' etc. in German, penned with laborious care under Frau Pastor's supervision. I haven't had a meal to lick the efforts of Edward's the whole time I've been here—but I must be beware of prejudice. Saw *Lohengrin*. Wonderful. Lohengrin a bit fat. Now singing Herr Senf's own songs.

***

Letter, 30 December 1911

Taking things all round I have had a very happy Christmas. The German Christmas being famous I will do my best to describe it but it is impossible to compare it with a 146 Christmas because here in Düsseldorf it is designed almost entirely for the junior part of the family, who are taught to anticipate it for months ahead. I got up at about 10, (I have never got up before 9.30 since the Kunst Schule holidays started) and wrote letters til lunch, the weather making a walk quite out of the question.

The lunch I will pass over as they don't make anything of it here. After lunch I went to the Post to get a ripping tie pin from Auntie Lucy Ward but the Zoll Amt being closed I had to wait till next day. From there I went on to a Children's Service where I found all the family. There they had the usual Christmas tree with candles etc. and the children sang carols and recited from the Bible. They have some very fine carols in Germany, especially one by Luther, but what seems to be their favourite carol, i.e. 'Stille Nacht', acts on me something like Figaro's wedding ('Come Sir Page') on the admiral. It seems to be the prey for all would-be composers to 'work up' in variations. During the last few days I've heard that pitiful tune twisted and tortured in a hundred different forms. I heard about five so-called 'Fantasies on Stille Nacht' for piano, harmonium and violin. I've heard it times out of number on the family musical box, where it really seems in its proper setting. I've heard a cantata written on the same theme which lasted about an hour, not to mention the fact that it's sung by the family nearly every day.

We left the Children's Service laden with boxes of biscuits ('Speculations'), came home and had tea. After tea there was a pause while the tree was lit and the children were given ample time for anticipation. The Grossmutter sat in one corner endeavouring to check undue frivolity on the part of the kids and generally swearing at them in fact. Herr Pastor has often remarked that when the dear old lady ceases to swear at the children, she is ill. At last all preparations were made, a carol

217

was sung by the children and a prayer said by Vits. Then we all trooped into the Weinachtszimmer, the procession being headed by Paul and myself. There the tree and general scene looked very beautiful and you must remember that they had a very different Christmas last year to contrast with, Vits being ill with double pneumonia and as a friend of ours would say 'at death's door'. Round the room were tables and each person had a place on a table. My place bristled with presents from the family. Dumbbells, a complete set of Goethe's works, several other fine poetry books, a book of Gephard's pictures (who paid

a personal visit here the other day) and numerous other things. In front of every place was a plate of Speculations, apples, oranges and sweets etc. Paul was wonderful—a relation had made him a complete Ulan uniform, the Ulans being the Lancers and one of the crack regiments. He looked exactly like a swagger little officer with his Tschakow just a little bit on one side, all absolutely accurate according to Hans who specialises in these matters. When he went to the girls and said 'Ah! famos' [from Offenbach's *Pariser Leben*], I'm sure you'd all have howled at him.

I made up my mind that my first object with my presents would be to revolutionise the system of lighting in this house, so I fitted them all up with Feuerzeug apparatuses including the Grossmutter who is perpetually in want of matches and always borrowing my apparatus (she finds her own now awfully useful), also one of the servants who always does the same and who I thought, if she had one of her own, might be trained to fill ours (the others) with petrol etc. I find these things awfully useful here, where matches are scarce and beastly. The two you bought me have worked beautifully ever since. I also bought them various electric lamps etc, gas lighters, and above all a candle bracket for a certain 'Geheimer Ort' which completely lacked lighting appliance. The bracket is now screwed in position much to the amusement but satisfaction of the family and altogether I got the name of a practical chandelier maker. After everyone had looked over the presents a bit, Hans and I played our aqua fortis for harmonium and piano and we were generally made merry; a general feeling of thankfulness pervaded, especially that old Vits was once more with them to celebrate Xmas. I could not help thinking of that ripping carol by Elgar

> In snow and rain
> In rain in sun
> Love is but one

or words to that effect; and so I finished up my first German Xmas which wasn't Xmas at all, by the way, as they always celebrate Christmas Eve.

During the last week I've been doing a few visits. On Monday I went round with Hans and Walter Vits (the student) to tea at a very nice house kept by these 'sisters' (*Diakonissens*) where they did us a wonderful tea, with about 15 sorts of cakes as sold at our favourite tea shop, almonds and raisins, apples, oranges and pears. On Thursday I went to supper with Herr Jaker at the Orphanage. Herr Jaker is a really decent man of the Dalmeier type. He keeps this Orphanage, which would interest Pa very much, and after supper conducted his choir of orphans who sang remarkably well, absolutely in tune and time, once more 'Stille Nacht'. They sing in a sort of scene made to represent the stable. In the middle was a manger with straw, in which was a lifesize but *palpable* wax doll. I must say I don't like the free and easy way they treat Christkindchen here. After the orphans had made their exit they called upon me for a song. So I gave 'em one or two in German which went down well. Afterwards Herr Pastor said he felt proud of his son.

(Dear Panks, I will continue this description of the performance at the Orphanage as I think you may find something humorous therein. They handed round programmes but seeing no mention of 'Stille Nacht' I thought I was in for an evening's enjoyment. On seeing a harmonium and piano, however, I began to have suspicions; sure enough, the Overture was a 'Fantasie', 81 certainly but on an old theme. Next came an

Xmas carol in which Miss Jaker sang a beautiful verse, but sure enough again, the chorus was our old friend. Lastly came a long recitation called 'The Bells of Innisfree' which is about Scotland. The two girls who recited were accompanied in the real Auntie Lucy fashion by harmonium, piano, a choir in another room to give distance effect, a choir in the same room, wonderful effects on two sets of cracked bells, clock striking twelve etc, and into the bargain that priceless theme 'Stille Nacht'.)

Yesterday we went round to Baron Von Massenbach's, who is an old Ulan Colonel. We took Paul with us in uniform, much to their amusement. After tea I again sung a bit and we had a very happy afternoon. Please send more coin and my ordinary pair of cufflinks. I will give and get presents when I come back ... I had supper with Herr Balg. He said he would like to know what a man has to go through to be an officer in the English Army. He had often read that 'So and So had bought a commission' and so he wanted to know exactly what that meant. Would Father get to know for him? The son of Herr Balg, who is doing his military service, was also there. A more perfect swank you couldn't imagine. He reminds me of Bullit—awfully decent chap. On Sunday evening with your permission I'm going to see the *Meistersinger*.

———

Letter, 12 January 1912

I went to the theatre in great excitement last Sunday evening having studied up to the last minute. I nearly wept when they struck up the overture. The Meistersinger motif appeals to me so awfully; and then that wonderful conclusion on the horns to the motif all combined to give me *Gänsehaut* in my cheeks and down my back. The first scene was beautiful. Walther had a beautiful voice but he was rather stiff and lumpy and was not made up well. Eva looked a bit too smiling the whole time and Magdalene was much too fat (she has to change clothes with Eva in the second act; this would have been quite impossible).

Hans Sachs looked and sang wonderfully and Beckmesser was ideal. I must say Wagner has got a sense of humour: I howled over the last scene; Beckmesser made himself a champion fool. I don't think the humour is anywhere far-fetched especially when you remember it all probably typical of the time. I am also awfully taken with Zunftberatung's motif which goes on all the time during the first entry of the Masters, while Beckmesser is talking to Pogner. Doesn't Wagner make conversation wonderfully natural? The way they seem to be talking, not singing, and the orchestra seemed to be playing quite on its own. You can divine every thought that passes from the orchestra. Well, I enjoyed it hugely.

You remember I said I might go and see the *Rosenkavalier*?[48] Well, I bought the words and analysis and started reading it when Mr Dallmeier telephoned me and said that owing to a previous engagement he and his wife could not go, so would Lena and I like to go? As I had not bought tickets I accepted gladly, went, and had one of the most interesting evenings I've ever had. The plot is farcical and of the light Viennese character, something between Fledermaus and Figaro's wedding. In the analysis, in fact, appear the following words: 'Mozart—zu ihm strebt Strauss empor ... manchmal für ihn und für uns ... ihm das gelänge'. Underneath I wrote 'hoffentlich nicht' and on seeing the thing through I don't think there's the least danger that it will 'ihm gelänge'. Why Strauss should first write a thing like *Elektra* or *Salome* and then such a story as this I can't imagine. I very much doubt whether the last scene would pass the censor, translated literally. The music for the first two scenes is wonderfully clever. The conversation flows in the most original manner and the whole time the orchestra is firing off motifs at an immense speed. I could see the analyses where we sat and followed most of them. I've heard it is much

---

[48] *Der Rosenkavalier*, Richard Strauss's musical comedy in Mozartian style with a libretto by Hugo von Hofmannsthal, had received its first performance at the Dresden Court Opera one year earlier on 26th January, 1911.

easier to understand than the other operas; the motifs are simple but are worked out rather complicatedly. Some of them are very beautiful. In the third scene, the Rosenkavalier dresses up as the chambermaid and takes the fancy of a certain Baron Ochs, who is a prize fool. The Baron invites him out to dinner thinking it is a 'her' and then begins a motif which hits off the Baron's frame of mind to a T. It is a thoroughly common waltz. During the last scene the waltz comes so often that one can scarcely believe it is an opera by Strauss; it sounds more like a scene out of the Quaker Girl or something like that. Though the waltz is, of course, only satirical and not meant to be beautiful, the people like it so much that the opera will probably be awfully popular for a time.

I haven't forgotten the works. I often wish I was once more back in it, though lately my yearning in that direction has not been so intense as at first. Papita will be fine, I'm sure, with enlarged cylinders. I'd love to have the wheel once more in my hands, on the road to Bedales or Llandudno. I hope Panks will get on all right with Cowell. I roared over 'Swank potting'; it's so typical. I found casting one of the interestingest jobs, though a trifle charcoaly. Now I must shut up.

Letter, 13 January, 1912. To Frank.

I have taken advantage of the fact that the German criterion of humour is a trifle broader than ours and during the last few days have performed in public, several times, a really typical example of music-hall humour. It is simple—makes no pretence at being funny—but nevertheless always meets with applause in German society and at the same time gratifies my sense of the typical. The scene to be imagined is the inevitable Zoological Gardens in the Harlequinade or any such scene, as long as there's a ticket office to one side. A man (me) comes in dressed in frock-coat and stoops down to the ticket office to get a ticket; at the same time a clown (Hans) appears and quietly and carefully parts the two tails of the man's frock coat. He then casually retires and returns with either a 12ft plank or else a small scaffolding pole; he then rolls up his sleeves for a colossal attack on the conspicuous portion of the man. On impact there is a deafening explosion; in the halls it would be made by a field gun in the wings accompanied by fireworks but in our production, I let off a pistol of Hans's which makes a row rather more than a real revolver. This last coup d'humour is always accompanied by roars and cheers from the company, who nearly cry with laughter. I've got a whole programme of such 'Variety' humour but unfortunately we haven't yet had time to bring it on the boards.

Last Friday night I think I had one of the biggest rags I've ever had in my life. It licks our little balloon escapade or any April fool I can remember. Hans had been ragging Frau Shäfer, the Grossmutter, who rather lays herself open for it, til the whole family including Frau Pastor were dead with laughter. Then Hans, Walter and I repaired to my room to think up something further. The idea came to us to fasten a little nut to a string, let it out of the window and swing it up against Frau Shäfer's window. After about five minutes the old lady asked us to stop fooling, which we did. But now began unforeseen developments. The maid came running up to ask if any of us were out in the garden, because she said she had heard someone in the garden! and had heard Frau Shäfer yell to Hans to come in! The presence of all three of us showed the impossibility of this—so the maid went down again. Immediately after, we had the string out again, but this time down to the kitchen and after one or two swings we heard Herr Pastor's voice: 'Who's there?' Quickly we pulled it up again and waited. Now you must remember that it was a beastly night, rain and much wind. On such a night last year the house was broken into and pillaged: of course we didn't think of that then. The next event was that the maid, very excited, came once more and said someone was trying to break in from the garden! and implored Hans and me to come down. Hans was already half in bed so I had to go down alone, expecting a good cursing from Herr Pastor—but no! When I got down I found him laughing in rather a sheepish way so I naturally thought he had twigged the jest and was greening the maids as well, for he began telling me how he had distinctly heard footsteps in the garden. I roared at this; so did he. I thought we were getting on splendidly. He then went upstairs to inspect the garden from an upper window. I prepared to follow him but the two maids begged me to stay and clung round my neck, so to speak. I asked them whether it wasn't rather curious that the thieves should try and break in at half-past nine. But it didn't strike them in that light, so I did a bit of melodramatic acting for them, pretending to see thieves all over the place. Herr Pastor then returned and, noticing he looked rather pale, I resolved to disclose the thing as artistically as possible. I rolled up my sleeves, selected a stick and went to the shuttered window—did the Martin Harvey business— opened the shutters and leapt into the garden. Then began a chase after imaginary thieves, behind all the bushes, beating my stick against the trees, rummaging among chairs and tables on the veranda, and all the time accompanied by peals of laughter from Frau Pastor above. As I returned through the open window, a deafening explosion from above made everyone's heart stand still. The whole thing reminded me so of 'When Uncle told the story of the ghost' that I lay on the kitchen table and roared. At the same time, the explanation dawned on Herr Pastor, while Walter and Hans appeared at the door to participate in the dénouement. Of course we all apologised very humbly but it was the most wonderful farce I've ever known.

Letter, 27 January, 1912

Dear Doodles,

To-day is Kaisergeburtstag,[49] which they run for all it is worth. Last night at about 7.30 the Zapfenstreich or military

---

[49] The Kaiser's birthday.

tattoo began; we heard the band on a neighbouring street and all ran out to see them. They had two bands and the inevitable flute-and-drum band *à la* Botanical Gardens last August. Hans was in seventh heaven as anything to do with the military he enjoys thoroughly; so we marched by the side the whole way. Along the Alleestraße, Königs Allee, Graf Adolphstraße, Bismarckstraße and finally ended up on the Alleestraße where the three bands settled down and played an ancient Zapfenstreich in three spasms, composed by Frederick the Great.

One of the features of a German military band is the Schellenbaum.[50] Though you'd think that such a fine looking instrument would make wondrous sounds, as a matter of fact the poor peacock is quite dumb and any schelling to be done is performed on a quite a modest-looking thing which follows after. They've completely purloined God Save the King and turned it into a march, but distorted by bangs and poms and syncopations required to fill in the gaps caused by the change of rhythm.

---

[50] A jingling military standard, popular with German, French and Turkish marching bands. Typically about two metres long, and not as shown (*right*).

225

'On Saturday I went to a Kaiser's Geburtstag Feier by a Boy Scouts' club ...'

This morning it has turned colder and I shouldn't be surprised if we don't get a bit of skating soon. After hearing the service in the garrison church, we repaired to the Kaiser Wilhelm Park where a parade of all the soldiers in Düsseldorf took place. Our friend Mr Southall would have revelled in it. The three bands were there and drum-majors galore. The soldiers were pretty thick on the ground and made a fine sight: Ulans, Artillery, Infantry, all in these big heavy overcoats and top boots. And then the officers. SWANK is not the word for them. It really makes me writhe to see some of these men, so fat that they can scarcely get into their uniforms.

After a bit of preliminary, the General gave a speech. Then they all gave three cheers for the Kaiser, guns were fired off and the parade began. It is a point of honour amongst the Ulans to march as badly as possible in order to show that they aren't used to it. Against this fine army we had the election last Thursday, where Social Democrats were elected all over the place. I roar to hear the way Hans cursed them and the general mediaeval ideas of political freedom, the way the SDS hate the clergy and everybody in general like poison, the way the Katholics (Zentrum) loathe the Protestants and vice versa.

226

Kreis came round the other day and congratulated me on my designs.

On Saturday I went to a Kaiser's Geburtstag Feier [party] by a Boy Scouts club. We walked through a wood and had a jolly afternoon in a Wirthaus. Funny to see kids of twelve etc. drinking beer and smoking. I think I shall get some skating this evening.

Letter, 17 February, 1912

Dear Ma, Pa and Panks,

I am delighted to hear about 'Tonka Superba'. I should love to be at home to drive it again. A run up to Llandudno and back would suit me to a T just now. The experiment on burner efficiency must also be awfully interesting. I think I shall come and look you up some time in April, if it's only to get some more clothes and things. Thanks awfully for Pa's letter. I quite agree with you over the old subject of historical styles and feel the want of exact knowledge in working out the detail for a bit of decoration. This morning I've been filling a page with little rough sketches and on Monday I shall start working them out.

On Tuesday I went to see *Tristan und Isolde*. If there's any doubt over Goethe's statement that 'Art makes a good companion but a bad leader', one has only got to study *Tristan und Isolde* for a bit. It was the embodiment of Wagner's outlook on life. Most beautiful it certainly is. I'm particularly taken with one of the love motifs which starts in the second scene and is completed in Isolde's 'Death Song' at the end. It starts simply but gets worked up into a wonderful tune at the end. Victor Haupt plays most of these things off by heart. Yes it's wonderful, but as a Lebensanschauung you couldn't find a more rotten, pessimistic, morbid piece. I mean to say, taken seriously as Wagner's outlook, he wrote the piece because he could marry a certain Mathilda Wesendonc. It shows the truth of the above. It was quite well done but Isolde was abominably fat and blobby. On Friday I am taking Mrs V to see *Carmen*. Victor's explaining everything carefully.

227

Letter, 16 March 1912

Dear Ma, Pa and Panks,

Last Sunday afternoon I went to see *Glaube und Heimat*[51] at the Schauspielhaus and I think it's one of the finest plays at the age. It has met with all-round approval here and the author has received the Schiller Prize. The story takes place in Austria at the time of the anti-Reformation and tells of an old peasant family who have lived in the same house for centuries. The grandfather, 'Old Rott', and the father, 'Christopher Rott', are both outwardly Catholics but really Lutheran. Their relations and friends are mostly Lutheran and are all being marched out of the land by the 'Wild Rider' of the Kaiser, but Old Rott, who has only got two weeks to live, can't bear the thought of being buried in a strange land and his son Christopher doesn't want to fall out with his wife. Christopher, who is wavering, is encouraged to declare his belief by the Bible and by the fact that his neighbour is chased into his house by the Wild Rider and killed. The wife decides to accompany Christopher on his enforced wondering, because of the son 'Spatz' (Sparrow), but the tragedy begins to deepen when at the end of the second act the drummer or crier proclaims that all children not of age must stop behind and be educated as Catholics. It's all the more pathetic because Spatz doesn't know that he's got to stop behind and is looking forward to the pilgrimage most awfully. The crisis is reached when the Rider comes to drive them out and Spatz refuses to leave his parents, so in order to evade the Rider he jumps into the stream that runs by the house; he gets under a water wheel and is brought up and drowned. Then comes a fight between Christopher and the Wild Rider in which Christopher gets the man on the ground and is just going to hit him with an axe when he comes to his senses and says 'Nicht so! Christi gebot geht mit auf Blut'. And then 'Ich gehe … nach Gottes Wort; das heißt … Verzeih … deinem Feind' (looks at the Rider) 'ist hart … ist eisenhart'. (Tries to give the Rider his hand but makes a fist instead. At last,

---

[51] *Belief and Homeland*, by Karl Schönherr.

with great will-power, he opens his hand and reaches it to the Rider.) 'Da ... mein Handt. Wer will, der ... kann ... Sie nehmen.' The Rider takes his hand and the Rotts shove their waggon away over the bridge and follow Old Rott who has also turned Lutheran. The Rider, who like all the characters is extraordinarily human, being led on solely by religious mania, watches the couple out of sight. Then with a vicious stamp, snaps his sword in two. WONDERFUL it is—simple, absolutely natural in every detail—written in this dialect, the most beautiful homely words you could imagine. I can't possibly describe all the little subtleties which go to make it so natural and pathetic, you must be sure and read it and then I think you'll agree with me.

Letter, 21 March 1912

Dear Pa and Ma,

Last Thursday I went to get a new Legitimations Karte from Kreis and asked his advice as to my future career in the school. He said he advised a certain Benirschke who teaches Innere Architektur [interior design]. I had previously had him, advised by one or two men who also attended the Saturday class for historical styles, so I shall try Benirschke for next term. I have done another sheet of sketches, very rough and impression-istic—Hochreiter was delighted. I am bringing all my drawings home so you will be able to see. They tell me that Benirschke is much more of a pro in our trade than Hochreiter and requires a lamp to be finally exactly drawn and worked out.

Whatever good points the German education system has, I am fed up stiff with the school that Hans goes to. Firstly they do a lot more work than is healthy for a youth of his age. In spite of that, for the last three months, at breakfast, dinner and tea, there is a perpetual complaining goes on. Because Hans had a bad report at Xmas, Herr Pastor seems to imagine that his son is idle. Hans is 15–16 and works up till 11 o'clock every night—he looks like a washed-out rag. To these complaints of Vits are added the complaints of Hans, over the school, the amount of work they demand, and the Masters who, to a man, they HATE LIKE POISON. Would you believe me, here's a class, second from the top, and not a single man likes going to school—it's scandalous! Whenever Vits starts swearing at Hans, I simply let go at him (i.e. Vits). I got so sick of hearing of Hans's faults that I pointed out to Herr Pastor the rottenness of the esprit de corps—of the masters and of the whole miserable institution; for a school that can make such a blot on the happiness of youth is nothing more than a miserable fiasco.

At Easter comes the moving-up time. They look upon it as a matter of life and death. If the chap doesn't get moved up then he has to wait another year. Oh! the breathless excitement at every time of the day as to whether Frans would be moved up or not. At Xmas everything was against him but later the odds changed and last Tuesday we heard he'd been moved up. But the man whom I have gym with (Oscar Schulter)—by far the most conscientious worker in the class, who you've only got to know to realise his thoroughness—was not moved up, to the surprise and righteous anger of the class, Pastor V and wife, in fact anyone who knew the man personally. That's just the point. The teachers don't know the children personally. You've no idea how tragic it is for a German child who doesn't get moved up. It's a remarkable thing how many schoolboy suicides there are towards the Easter time.

Trudi is coming over tomorrow. Have finished *Jungfrau von Orleans* and *Das Lied von der Glocke*.

Letter, 30 March, 1912.

Dear Pa, Ma and Microbe,

Less than two weeks and I shall be in good old dirty Brum. I'm keeping away boredom with theatres, concerts etc. Yesterday I heard Gounod's *Faust*—though the scenery was a trifle scratch at times I enjoyed it very much. I find the music more interesting and rich in harmony than Carmen, although Victor runs it down. It is certainly rather a parody on Goethe's *Faust*. Mephistopheles strolls around as the gallant cavalier, relieved with a thundering trick now and again and generally doing the 'funny-man'. On Thursday I went to the last of my Musikverein concerts. They are rather too ancient for my taste. *Also Sprach Zarathustra* was about the only really interesting thing they did. On Tuesday I went to hear Götterdämmerung again. It is really wonderful but I'm getting hardened to Wagner. By that I mean, the beautiful bits still gave me that wonderful creepy feeling that they did at first; but that's the same with all Romantic music—the beauty is still there but it doesn't bowl one over as at first (see Wordsworth).

On Monday, Hans and I went to dinner at Victor's and spent a very enjoyable evening in which Victor played and his sister also, and I sang a bit. This sister also tried to teach me the Boston but es ging nicht, chiefly because one has to disregard all rhythm therein. His sister's topping form.

On Sunday, having been 'proved' the previous Sunday, Hanna was confirmed in the Johannes Kirche. I went to the service which was beautiful. Afterwards we had a few friends in. Hanna received a lot of presents and flowers.

Letter, 27 April, 1912

Dear Pa, Ma and Panks,

I have now absolutely settled down and am starting having a jolly good time. My week at home has faded into the realms of dream and the effect in my mind is one continuous stay at Düsseldorf. But it was jolly good sport, the journey there—black and unpleasant—merging out into wonderful clear weather— and England. To hear the people talking English, after having become entwined in another nation's habits and thoughts, was extraordinary. When I got into the neighbourhood of Oxford and Leamington, the train seemed to be going appallingly slowly that through the last tunnel it went and then die Familie Best once more with Tonka Superba and the whole show. Then

my uncle[52] muling and pewking in the nurse's arms—and lastly
that dance with the dark place for sitting out, with little red
lights. I knew at the time it would all fade away and here I am
back in Düsseldorf and preparing for the time of my life. I have
joined the tennis club in the Zoological Gardens. They rook you
30 marks, on top of which comes 7 marks sub to the Gardens, as
the only entrance lies through them, and then there are sundries
for the balls and kids and things. I'm always afraid of getting
messed up with the tigers etc—they roar just as one's serving. At
any rate, the people look upon one as part of the attractions of
the garden, judging by the way they grin at you through the
netting. Being so near, one only meets the sports nuts and there
is a very decent set there.

I had a talk with Balg who sends regards and he's advised me
of a man called Brecht who charges from 14–15 marks per week
(four hours). I shall start with him next Tuesday afternoon for
two hours unless I hear to the contrary. The lessons will of
course be private and he will really teach me summat, unless I
much mistaken.

The Kunstgewerbe Schule holidays start August 1st and the
name of the sculptor is Prof. Netzer.[53]

How much does one give porters? The chap who saw me in
at Holborn (looked after my luggage while I was having supper
and got me a second-class) expected a shilling. When they say
'It's worth a shilling' after you've given them sixpence, do you
generally comply with demands?

I am doing a ripping lamp with Benirschke, of the refined,
constructional, vornehm [elegant] type.

———————

[52] Peter Eckersley.
[53] Hubert Netzer (1865–1939). German sculptor. In his earlier works—
Triton fountain in Munich (1893); *Promethues* group at Würzburg University
(1896)—he worked in a Neo-Baroque style but took on exotic Jugendstil
influences in his works of the 1900s—*Fountain of the Norns*, Munich (1907).
He taught at Düsseldorf Kunstakademie from 1910–30, i.e. from two years
before R.B. arrived.

Letter, 22 May, 1912

Dear Daddy, Ma and Panks,

During the absence of correspondence I have been pegging into my lecture all the time. I gave it last night to a well-filled meeting of Vits's Kränzchen of former Confirmantees—if I may use such an expression and in it. It lasted nearly an hour and in it I gave them a full description of Bedales, together with all my ideas on what an education should be, which have formulated a good deal since I've been in Germany. They listened very attentively and it aroused considerable interest and applause. As there wasn't time to discuss it then, they are going to discuss next time the problem of how to get more interest and pleasure in the work than there is at the present time in the German schools. While Pa in England is putting German education before the people, Bob is doing vice-versa in Germany—that's how it should be—and that's the only way to get the good points of both. As Vits said, one wants the German conscientious thoroughness together with the English, or rather Bedales, practical style and recognition of character training.

The other night I heard the *Troubadour* and nearly had a fit. I was getting rather bored with the Leo Fall type of music when suddenly there was a soldiers' chorus. What you think it was? The same tune as 'We are the King' and 'The Queen of Hankey-Pankey Land' of P.S. fame. Apart from this brief interest, a more rotten thing I don't think I've ever heard.

———————

Letter, 26 May, 1912

Dear Father, Ma and Panks,

I am getting on to interesting stuff with Brecht: double book-keeping etc. He's a personally decent chap and treats it as a favour if I stop and have coffee with him, as he says he's a lonely man and sick of bachelor diggings (he's going to get married in July and coming to England on his honeymoon). He's interesting

233

for me as a type of German schoolteacher. At the Kunstgewerbe Schule I was getting rather despondent because every new idea I got, Benirschke crushed with criticism and told me to run it out, thus making things go rather slowly. However his criterion of the artistic is absolutely sound and when I found out what he wanted I soon went ahead: 'Simplicity, Harmony of all parts—and if possible Originality' are what he aims at. My latest finished lamp is for a hall etc. I have also started on a little Empire-style candle of my own idea and as encouragement Benirschke lent me a book containing some samples of Empire lamps which I immediately made sketches of and shall later bearbeiten [develop]. Benirschke seems on the whole pleased. It struck me it would be rather nice if used up all my photos in a separate book, and also you're keeping my letters, aren't you, *à la* Pa's in Bonn?

I'm awfully glad to hear that you and Frank are coming. Frau Pastor wants you to come to lunch on Sunday. We shall then be back from wandering. I've bought a topping rucksack and water bottle and yesterday Hans and I made a training march to Neuss and back with full equipment. Hans is poorly in bed today with a sore throat, but I have applied some of my numerous remedies and I think he'll be all right for Wednesday.

Letter, 29 June, 1912.

Dear Pa, Ma and Panks,

The 'Parseval' airship has been here this week. On Friday she left and the 'Schwaben' came. I saw the two in the air together. The Zeppelin looked gigantic in comparison, sauntered along at a terrific speed, majestic

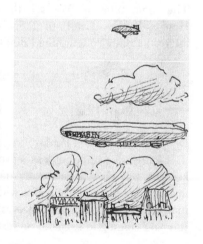

and wonderful. At midday, we heard that it had been broken in two places by the shed and blown up. I must try and get some photos.

Last Sunday evening I went to the first of my Goethe-Fest-Spiel evenings. They have got all the very best talent together so I had a splendid evening. *Wallensteins Tod*[54] was performed and although when you read it, it's a trifle transparent and illogical at times, it also acts extraordinarily well; there are no end of dramatic situations, great opportunities for armour and dresses, and sounds behind the scene afford great dramatic 'backing'. The acting was fine, quite the best I've seen—not a bit overdone. I saw the aforementioned English girl again in the theatre and said Good-Bye. She went away on Monday to a place near Hannover.

On Monday also I got a bit of a temperature again (the incidents have no connection) so I tried to shake it off with a hot bath and sweating. Next morning it was normal but towards dinner time rose again (99°–100°F) and did the same every day till yesterday. I went to the doctor again twice, but he only said 'It must take its time, as you've got chronic[55] catarrh'. It certainly seemed like it; always this stuff in my nose and sore throat, so I took things easy, gargled etc, and on Friday went again to school; there I got a rotten headache again, so went home, a rather depressed Bobbitz—Neuralgie (nerves)—chronic catarrh—it sounded as if I was an old man. The doctor told me to go to a specialist, which I did. I learnt afterwards that I've had a gathering in the left cheek bone, which he cleaned up by first cokaining the nostril, then punching a hole through with the nozzle[56] of a tube, when turning the water on—you've no idea the amount of bad-smelling matter which came out. I went again this morning, he went through the same operation—he's

---

[54] The third part of the *Wallenstein* trilogy by Friedrich Schiller, about the ambitious Bohemian general Albrecht Wallenstein, who loaned troops to the Holy Roman Empire during the Thirty Years War but was eventually assassinated by Irish mercenaries on the orders of the Emperor.

[55] Spelled 'cronic' in R.B.'s letter.

[56] Spelled 'nossil' in R.B.'s letter.

an awfully casual chap, rather like Brownfield[57]—takes my head under one arm and shoves things up my nostrils in the same sort of style. He said I must have had this gathering for some time past. It may have been at the root of the famous 'String Manufactures'. The same business will go on every day next week but I feel a lot better now.

Letter, 12th July, 1912.

Dear Father,

I remember last year the Admiral's wonderful description of the Band of Hope outing and how the reality corresponded to the description exactly. Last Sunday I saw the German equivalent and it was even funnier than Hans's previous account. It was the famous Düsseldorf Schützen Fest, held by a large rifle club. We went to the scene of the parade and after waiting about half an hour heard the sounds of the band—or rather, bands—because although the procession was not long, there were about five bands all within easy earshot and all playing different tunes. An attempt was made to conduct the parade with military discipline but as most of them had never served and, being Liberals, objected to anything military (the club is largely composed of smaller tradesmen), and as they had also poured courage into themselves beforehand (and plenty of it), the effect was wonderful. The way any proper soldiers who were there looked on and criticised made me howl. The procession was headed by the Schutzenmajor on horseback. The general uniform was black frockcoat, top-hat decorated with a wreath, white trousers, coloured scarf and belt. The Major came round the corner giving numerous absolutely false commands. He was one of the fattest men I've seen for a long time, moist with perspiration and generally trying to make an effect. The belt round his frockcoat showed off his figure perfectly. The effect

---

[57] Dr Brownfield, a teacher at Bedales Shool.

was improved by the fact that just as he came round the corner, his horse waltzed five times quickly round and round. The Major endeavoured to restore order by hitting its head with his toy sword. In the end the Major had his way.

By this time, the Schützen Brüders were lined up, decorated with flowers and a fabulous number of medals, orders etc. I noticed that at least 80 percent carried toy rifles so I asked Hans why a rifle club should only have toys. He said that only one company really practised shooting; the others shoot once a year and that's on this occasion, so they don't need to have rifles. I wondered what the object of the shooting club was if they didn't shoot, but I soon discovered it. On the command, the men made pyramids of their weapons and dispersed, so I turned my attention to the three chief officers on horseback. I say 'chief' because the number of officers was enormous in proportion to the men. The horsemanship of the three was remarkable—I gasped at their use of their spurs as a means of keeping on board. After a few minutes they stood in a row and proceeded to drink hock out of beer glasses. But the quantity! The Major was a regular dog and did the record. In ten minutes, the Lord Mayor was due to review the troops so the Major commanded 'St. Sebastian Company. Fall in!' As the heaps of weapons remained untouched, he repeated the command several times and at last, in exasperation, yelled to another officer 'Where is the St. Sebastian Company?' He soon had the answer to his question and at the same time I had the answer to my question 'What is the object of a shooting club if it doesn't shoot?' The answer came from the door of the inn Zum Hirschchen where a stream of the Schützen brothers filtered slowly out, wiping their mouths. And then a heated argument between the officers and men, the hurried scuffle to present arms, and the latecomers, made me roar. I hear they parade over to the meadow on the other side of the Rhine and then indulge in the good old German style.

I hear also that the parade home is even funnier and unsteadier than the parade there. But all that I missed. It's hard to find anything funnier than a band of middle-aged and elderly men playing soldiers.

Letter, 13th July, 1912. In Marien Hospital, Düsseldorf.

Dear Pa, Ma, Panks,

I am lying in bed, though am quite normal in temp. I have just had lunch—the food is good and plentiful. The nuns are letting me spoil them and haven't started trying to turn me Catholick yet. The Hospital is quite close to Mozartstr., so I walked over at about 5 last night. I am going 2nd Class (7 Mark per day) but they let me select a room where I get as little sun as possible, so I took my things out of my bag, and read till Zumbroich turned up. At about 6.30 he appeared and I went up to the operating room. I waited there about 10 minutes, while he was teeing off a little girl in the next room. The screen nearly brought the house down. I must say I do like Zumbroich—he's famed in D'dorf for his bluntness, he generally says nothing, but yesterday the whole time he was at work, he and the nurse were ragging each other, chiefly because he's Protestant and she was a nun.

I love the quiet businesslike way he goes about everything—took off his coat, rolled up his sleeves, laid all his tools out on the bench, and started cleaning up the inside of my nose and cockaining it. As far as I could gather he first took away the little bone ridge near the front of the nostril. It's a peculiar sensation hearing the crunching of bone and seeing it pulled out and feeling practically nothing. To enlarge the hole he used a sort of jaws on the tree trimming principle. I certainly felt a bit more then, but it really wasn't as much as I expected. He then told me he'd only got to trim up a bit—put the finishing touches on. For this he took a chisel and the nun 'tabbered' thereon with a hammer. The last process consists of ramming about ¾ yard of fine bandage up the nostril in order to stop bleeding. The blood soaks through but with the aid of hankerchiefs no mess is made. It will be taken out next Wed.

It wasn't at all terrible. The swellings every day have been getting me used to this particular form of occupation. For the first

3 times it didn't take much to lay me out on the sofa, but in the mean time I've got well i.e. physically fit, normal temperature … There is every likelihood of my being permanently cured.

Chapter 9
What Germany taught Frank

In his first 12 months after leaving school Frank was to live at home, surrounded by domestic comfort and parental love. Yet during the daytime his environment tended to be dirty, dusty and, especially during the winter, cold, for a syllabus of training in the factory had been arranged—'going through the shops, starting at the bottom'—according to a plan prescribed by many a manufacturer for a son who was later to take his place in the family business. There were about nine main processes, all demanding manual skills—some of quite a high order. He acquired a degree of proficiency in them all. He found that the whole trade gave him interest and satisfaction.

The cosy domestic atmosphere comes through in his letters, especially when he has a bout of mild illness. Within a few weeks of starting at the works he was in bed, nursed by Mother, he having been upset by the zinc-oxide fumes, the gas stove and the temperature of the Casting Shop. For his course, carefully prepared by Father, began in a specially constructed cubicle adjoining the main foundry. It was just large enough to contain a 'tub' (a wooden trough in which the sand is moulded), a primitive gas radiator and himself.

He had in him the makings of an imaginative designer. If the catch phrase 'a feeling for tools and materials' has any meaning at all, he was certainly given opportunities to acquire it. He was encouraged to experiment with the sand and the temperature of the molten metal and quickly came to realise what could, or could not, be done with moulds and castings, and to appreciate the interaction of techniques and costs. He also learned how one process will suggest something else as a by-product. He saw the beautiful patinas on the cast metal, and how impossible it was to preserve them. He quickly grasped that to find new colours and finishes was part of the designer's job.

In his search for new colours he was piloted by the foreman of the Plating Shop, William Passey. This erratic enthusiast could re-produce on brass by empirical methods the colour of almost any other metal. Though resourceful in practice, his theoretical outlook was medieval; an artist in atmosphere, his manipulations of reagents suggested the control of powerful forces not recognised in the text-books of Newth and Roscoe. Of Passey, Father used to say, "When his time comes to leave this world, he'll go off in a flash of flame!"[58]

As most of the formulae and techniques existed only in William Passey's head, Father thought that it would be a good idea if Frank, during his time in that department, were to take notes as to what precisely went on. Accordingly, in an atmosphere of RESEARCH, he set about applying THE SCIENTIFIC METHOD, as he had been taught it at school.

Frank's relationship with William Passey, always friendly, was partly that of apprenti sorcier (without, however, any disconcerting quantity of H_2O) and partly that of scientific expert commanding the respect of one whose schooling had been limited. To some extent, however, the foreman seems to have imposed his views on his colleague, for among Frank's copious notes occurs the following observation: 'As the acid begins to eat out the nature of the metal below the surface (my italics). One can almost hear the magician speaking the lines. These notes also show, once again, the influence of the 'Prize Work spirit'; from time to time we are even reminded of 'Earth

---

[58] See R.B.'s *Brass Chandelier*.

Thermometers—The Procuring of Them'.

Father's approach to business was not that of an administrator as we find them to-day. He would bury himself in some specialised technical or artistic problem to the total exclusion of everything else. He treated his business as an absorbing hobby and addressed himself to whatever aspect of it interested him at the time. As a policy for business management, nothing could have suited Frank better.

The year of 1912 was one of prosperity. The climate within the factory was enterprising and optimistic. Owing largely to Father's invention of the 'Surprise' gas pendant, the company had expanded steadily since 1893 and in 1908 the Sales chart began to climb even more steeply. The capstan lathes, first installed to produce gas-cocks and swivels, were being applied to making petrol taps and filters for the motorcycle trade. The department had developed and more workshops had been added in 1911. A patented pump for lubrication of engines was becoming extremely popular. But the proposal that a separate department would be formed to manufacture motor-cycle fittings had not been readily accepted. To quote one of the directors: 'There was considerable hesitation about selling machine-made technical products on the grounds of aesthetic inconsistency. We had won our reputation on beauty of design and ornament and to come out into the open market with mass-produced and utilitarian small parts seemed incongruous to Mr Best.'

In spite of these feelings about the 'Automatic Products Department', Frank seems to have spent some time in the Tool-room picking up very valuable experience.

There was something characteristic about the way Frank canalised Father's mystical attitude to quality into the operations of the 'A.P. Department' itself, using the company's trade mark, designed by the proprietor to indicate surprise, as a point d'appui. Together they visited the Motor Cycle show, where a transparency, lit by electric lamps was conspicuously displayed on the company's stand. Father wrote to me that above the trade mark Frank had put the question 'Seen Clarence?' and we've been getting up a bit of a gag in reply to possible questions as to who Clarence might be.

I still have the typescript of this gag and it would be difficult to imagine a more fanciful document. It begins with references to the directors and other leading spirits of the place and then continues: 'Although Clarence doesn't often show himself, as he is usually in spiritual form, or Geist as the Germans call it, he is quite as real as any of the directors or staff. "His eyes?" you say—well, they're pretty good in our Trade Mark, but nothing to what they are in reality. They are eyes that, even when invisible, can be felt, and the funny thing about Clarence's eyes is that he makes a point of keeping them on the quality of the workmanship right through the place.'

Then follow some 900 words of fantasy describing the attempts which had been made to snare Clarence. It seems that 'Whenever there was anything "extra special" about, he would be rustling somewhere in the neighbourhood, though generally invisible … to lure him on we set up our latest machine … to produce, what had previously been regarded as an impossibility—THE PERFECT TAP.' Clarence materialised, was lost, but finally, with the help of Sir Oliver Lodge and 'a camera with lens of a special capacity directed at the lathe' they noted:

> Again the rustling footsteps, the shadowy form … the blinding magnesium light, and the click of the shutter. Eager examination of the plate followed, and there the outline of Clarence's startled features could be distinguished. From that impression have been made all the blocks and punches which guarantee the quality of the firm. AND AFTER ALL WHAT CAN BE BETTER THAN THE "BEST"?

One wonders how the 'bit of a gag' was received by our prospective customers at the Motor Cycle Show. That Frank must have been keenly interested in the AP Department is clear from his report of the Paris Motor Cycle Show the following year.

After Frank and I had convinced Father that we meant business and were prepared to work, we found him willing to allow us time off, especially if the weather was propitious, for golf, tennis and other outdoor activities. Frank, naturally, took every opportunity for sport and played in at least one football match—'Staff v. Works'. He also had one delightful morning on the ice which, however, ended unfortunately, for within two weeks of his recovering from the toxic effects of the foundry he was once again confined to the house, this time for three weeks.

The frost had been hard and Frank rode the six miles to Bracebridge Pool in Sutton Park on his bicycle. He described it all to me with gusto:

> The roads were like marble. The sun was shining and quite hot. A friend of Father's overtook me on his Delage and towed me as far as Sutton. It pulled beautifully up the hills. Then I rode to the park and got to the pool.
>
> I have never been on such beautifully surfaced pool-ice. I could see my own reflection in it wie ein Spiegel (like a mirror). I got to work and practised edges hard. I was very 'out' at first but got into the swing later on. It was very warm and beautiful. I got chummy with several skating club people, under the guise of being son of the great R.H.B.
>
> At about 1.30, I and one other were left alone. I skated simple edges round an orange with him, then he went away and I practised more tricky things, which I was just getting into when I fell over.

Frank badly twisted his ankle. One of the pool men helped him up and took him off. He then had to ride home, after negotiating a stile with his bicycle and getting across the common. The path was so obliterated with snow,' he wrote, 'that I had to steer by the sun, chiefly. I found the 3-speed gear an absolute boon, as I could only use the left foot.' Father commented that 'It was all the fault of short skates and boots not well laced up' and immediately ordered up longer blades for him; he also had the boots strengthened up with patches round the ankles.

In games and sport Frank would try to help me with advice—or, more accurately, with conceptual descriptions and analyses of co-ordinated movements as he had experienced them. He must have had a well-developed kinaesthetic imagination, which even invaded his sleeping hours, for he wrote to me (an ineffectual skater), then in Germany:

> You are lucky to get a bit of skating. With regard to the outside edge, I managed to get the hang of it at Woolmer. The great feature of it, I found, was to get the necessary unstable equilibrium feeling about the whole action, i.e. leaning back and inwards at an absurd angle and travelling slightly on the back of the skate. I dreamt about it several years ago one night, and when I came to put it into practice it worked admirably. I venture to give you a couple of caricatures which may or may not help you.

He did, and added that 'The art of changing edges is like running the front wheel of a bicycle into a brick wall in order to avoid it. I have marked the extra little curl round at the end with X.' (22 January 1912)

When my brother and I first became aware of that sensational and rare object the horseless carriage, motoring was looked on as either a form of sport or material simply for jokes and comic songs about breakdowns, loud explosions and evil smells. This form of humour persisted right up to the 1914 war, when a song with the chorus 'He'd have to get under, Get out and get under' became popular. But between 1900 and the war, the trickle of power-driven vehicles passing up and down the Hamstead Road had become a brooklet—though not yet a stream.

As boys we looked upon the arrival of any motor car as an exciting event; no sooner did we hear the noise of one approaching than we would run to the window. We soon came to recognise the different makes and, in many cases, knew the name of the owner, discussing amongst ourselves the design developments shown in any new models.

A prominent local entrepreneur and motoring enthusiast, Mr Charles Palmer, by 1910 possessed several cars, amongst them an 8 hp Renault, and it was on his recommendation that Father ordered a similar model. The design and colour of the bodywork involved further decisions, for it was necessary to send the chassis, on arrival, to a coach builder. The vestigial carriage-like shapes and fittings were, by that time, gradually being replaced by more functional forms. Doors were higher. One heard the expression 'flush-sided'. We were approaching the Torpedo body, though the term 'streamlining' had not yet become common.

The body-work of Tonka, so called on account of the metallic yet musical note of its exhaust, was a compromise. The power source was two vertical cylinders and the maximum speed 28 miles per hour. The essential parts must have been exceedingly strong and reliable for in the twelve years that 'Tonka' served us, during which time it earned the family's affectionate regard, I do not believe that it ever let us down. Inside, three people could be comfortably seated abreast and two more on the 'dickey-seat' at the back. This load did not seem to affect its performance materially.

As for driving, we soon got the hang of it. When changing down, double de-clutching was absolutely essential to get into gear at all. It was impossible to choke the engine, even when cold, and if maximum power was required—as was the case most of the time—one trod firmly on the accelerator pedal until the foot touched the floor. There were then, of course, no driving tests, and within a month or two of starting our driving lessons from the dealer who had sold us the car, we were taking our parents for long runs.

In 1912, exercising his customary skill at adaptation. Father began to extend the garage he had designed and placed in an excavated portion of the small back-yard. An ingenious sort of pent-house was then added to accommodate a second and larger car. At the same time preliminary steps were being taken to acquire the Wolseley car which became known as The Cardinal. Mother's report reached me in Düsseldorf: 'On Friday [June 28, 1912], the twenty-second anniversary of our wedding day, we went on a Wolseley car for a run, to see how I liked it. We took the Aunties, much to their delight, and called among other places at the works of the Wolseley people, where we decided on the colour of the new car, and also the style of cabriolet covering. You will like it, I am sure. The driver took us round the little racing track, which is like a baby Brooklands[59] and has a bit on it like the Scenic Railway—a sheer drop down. I felt as if most of my inside had been left at the top. Then we took a run by Sutton, Castle Bromwich and along the Chester Road, where we did about 45 to 50 mph for a short stretch.

The Cardinal was powered by a 16 hp 4-cylinder engine. By modern standards the coach-work was immensely heavy—large enough to take seven passengers—but the design of the hood (or cabriolet covering) was advanced; an anticipation, in fact, of the so-called drop-head coupé.

Both Tonka and The Cardinal are associated in my mind with faithful service. They were treated as machines should be treated: that is to say, with the same sort of consideration as is due to animals. Frank had the driver's touch and a sympathetic attitude towards mechanical things; so, too, had our most excellent chauffeur, Mr 'Bob' Ewels, who entered Father's employment in November 1914, nursed him in his last illness and remained in the employment of the company until 1955, sharing our troubles during two wars.

I have now reached a point in the story when I find myself counting the separate occasions—the spells of a week, a month, a quarter—which remained for Frank and me to be together. From the time he left school up to the outbreak of war it was to be six or seven times. In 1912, the year under review, we had three opportunities, including a few days at Christmas, to meet, talk, play games and make music. The first was in April during my week's leave, home from Düsseldorf, when our enjoyment of dances and motoring was marred by news of the Titanic disaster. In my subsequent letter home, after going back to Germany, I'd talked about the strange effect of 'hearing people

---

[59] The world's first purpose-built motor racetrack, built near Weybridge, Surrey. It opened in 1907, doubled as an aerodrome, and was used for racing until 1939. It now hosts a vintage car museum.

talking English after having become entwined in another nation's habits and thoughts'. The key word here is 'entwined', for however woolly and obscure it may be at times, German is for many English people (though not for the French) an infectious, if not compulsive, language; so that on returning to England we would unconsciously drop into German, answering 'Herein' if someone knocked the door, or 'Bitte' if we did not hear, or even in longer phrases. Owing to family relationships Frank and I were quite especially entwined in that other nation's habits and thoughts, though, as we shall see, he and I reacted to the German environment in somewhat different ways.

Our second reunion that year took place during the summer holiday months, for by early August I had finished my German interlude. When I arrived home Frank was away in Wales at a camp for Old Bedalians sponsored by the Chief, who entertained them round the camp fire by reading *The History of Mr Polly* which had recently been published. During this camping holiday Frank had his first experience of climbing Welsh mountains, including, of course, Snowdon.

Frank joined the family later at Pwllheli and in due course acted as guide for my first ascent of Snowdon; we had been taken on The Cardinal to the foot of the Watkin Wynn pass. The day was gloriously fine and the visibility from the summit was, for me, breathtaking. Frank took several photographs and entertained me during the day with gossip from the O.B. camp—accounts of incidents from their climbing expeditions, encounters with Welsh bulls, and how they had floundered about in marsh land. The week had been rainy, and when distances were reckoned 'as the crow flies', the Chief had commented that the Welsh crow appeared to be a web-footed bird. I cannot remember whether we came down by the same way, or by the Miners' track. I know, however, that The Cardinal was awaiting us and I recall, too, the glow of satisfaction as I turned over in my mind's eye and ear all that I had seen and heard that day.

During the first week of October that year the Triennial Musical Festival was being held at the Town Hall. On the second day

Frank and I went to an evening concert where we heard the first performance of Elgar's *We are the Music Makers*, together with Sibelius' *Fourth Symphony*, in A Minor, then performed for the first time in Birmingham and commissioned for the Festival. Both works were conducted by the composers. Our account of this concert, published later in the *Bedales Chronicle*, constituted our first and only attempt at musical criticism. I am struck by its airy impertinence and superficial judgement. After a description of Elgar's work, mostly copied from the programme notes, we continued:

Henry J. Wood listened from the side gallery, and his behaviour, method of standing up, clapping and generally drawing attention to himself, could only be equalled by Wilkie Bard. Wilkie Bard was a gifted music-hall and pantomime comedian, whom we greatly admired. We were much attracted by his songs 'I want to sing in Opera' with its musical quotations, and 'You've got to sing in ragtime'.

The Symphony of Sibelius, conducted by the composer, was ultra-modern, but lacked that crash and exhilarating interest which we expect from such work. The discords were all there, but a more depressing piece could scarcely be imagined. The effect of the piece on the composer was also noticeable, judging by the shaky and doddering way he handled his baton he was suffering from a fit of the blues.

In subsequent conversation, Frank and I would compare this experience with a visit to the dentist. To be fair, we were not alone in finding this masterpiece depressing. In Gothenburg 'at the first performance the Symphony was actually received with hoots'. A Finnish critic called it the 'Bark-bread Symphony', recalling days of famine when the poor were forced to adulterate flour with ground bark. It was also described as 'doleful mutterings generally leading nowhere, a mixture of musical quassia and wormwood which suggests that the composer is dissatisfied with something and so, probably, is the general public'. In short it occupies an important place in the Lexicon of Musical Invective. In the *Birmingham Daily Post*, Ernest Newman wrote that although it was generously received, 'there is no doubt that the audience was sorely puzzled by it'. Newman added, however, that Sibelius's symphonies

> all speak to us of a civilisation and landscape different from our own, so that only familiarity with them can enable us to find our way therein ... The process may be made more intelligible to the ordinary reader by reminding him of drawings in which outline and texture and distances are suggested rather than actually drawn; the artist leaves out almost more than he puts in, but the spectator's imagination fills in the blanks ... His scores seem strangely bare.

As for the composer's fit of the blues, his portraits show 'a stern granite-like face frozen in what appears to be a perpetual scowl. Behind this aristocratic facade, however, there was another Sibelius—highly imaginative, nervous and emotionally insecure.'

Shortly after the Birmingham Musical Festival I left for a six months' stay at Neuilly-Sur-Seine, Paris. Frank followed me about a year later.

I have always felt that Father's warm and admiring attitude to Germans and Germany must have been partly the result of his enjoyable year in Bonn during 1862. I have tried to conjure up the charm of that period in my book *Brass Chandelier* through quotations from his letters. We share his delights in the pleasant sights and sounds:

> The place is truly a Paradise; everything is in leaf and full bloom. The place where I am living is an avenue of chestnut trees, as long as Livery Street. I cannot describe it except by drawing, but the trees are in full blossom, and the bees on them keep up a continual buzzing.

He seems to have hoped that, somehow, through his sons, he would be able to re-live vicariously that joyful period. He studied our letters even more eagerly than usual and occasionally, in my case, administered a mild reproof because they were not full enough. Due to sinus trouble and nervous apprehension, my stay at Düsseldorf had not been altogether unclouded, but he hoped that Frank's reports would reflect the amenities of the Rhineland City. He was not disappointed.

The two of them left Birmingham together on January 6, 1913. Outside Flushing their ship, the Mecklenburg, ran ashore. Frank's report of the incident was published in the *Chronicle*.

At 3.30, roused by the steward's bell, we packed up our belongings, and after coffee, lounged along to the dining room to wait for sounds of the harbour. In a short time we felt the usual lurch and went on deck to land, but found no harbour alongside. On questioning one of the stewards, he told us that we had run on to a sandbank in the fog, following it up quickly with rumours of how they had only once before had such a thing occur, and then they got off late in the afternoon; and judging from the explanation of the man's hand, their boat must have been nearly upside down, (this time it was rather different, one could not detect the slightest tilt on the boat). By this time the engines were reversing furiously, and all that one could see through the darkness, was a seething current of water flowing past from the stern. The wind was very damp and cold, but the fog did not strike me as being very dense, one could easily distinguish the electric lights from stern to bow.

Our hopes were raised as we saw the faint lights of the expected tug-boat nearing through the mist, but even when quite close we could not discern the outline of a boat. The three lights seemed to pass each other and fool about in a ridiculous way. They finally halted and to our astonishment we found they were lanterns resting high and dry on a steep shelving beach.

The passengers all flocked to the edge of our vessel to view the proceedings. The conversation was very humorous, as it slowly dawned on them that 50 feet below, the little breakers were lapping a stony shore. A row boat was then lowered, amidst directions shouted from every officer on board, and propelled along the side of our vessel with a rope, until it grounded. Three men were then picked up, and the row boat hauled back containing the harbour master and two other worthy officials, who all joined in the conversation with loud voices. The little boat then proceeded to carry out a series of orders which to the "unenlightened" brain equalled a pantomime; after landing the despatches, it was hauled backwards and forwards for fully an hour.

There being no symptoms of immediate help, we retired to our cabin, after a small breakfast, to snatch what rest we might.

Once more the steward's bell, once more on deck; everything is changed. It is quite light, and the mails and luggage are being transferred into the tug-boat alongside. We can now see how our vessel—fortunately travelling slowly—had run square into the dyke, which looked like a big sloping embankment, and rising about eighty feet out of the water it faded into the mist on both sides.

It appeared that it had been quite clear until we reached the river mouth, when it suddenly went foggy, and although the vessel made her way very successfully up the 'Scheldt' as far as the harbour, it could not see the lights, so overshot the mark and turned in too far up the river. A wireless message was sent to the nearest station to be telegraphed to the harbour, but the despatch conveyed along the dyke arrived first.

The passengers filed aboard, 150 or so, from the lower deck, on to the little tug-boat which was only just big enough to hold us all standing shoulder to shoulder. And so we backed away from the stranded mail boat which disappeared in the mist.

Throughout the whole incident, the passengers showed not the slightest trace of alarm. Fortunately we missed no connection as our through carriage was waiting for our arrival, but we were very thankful to get into Flushing Station safe and sound,, even though we were five and a half hours late.

The fact that Düsseldorf was a wunderschöne Stadt had been impressed upon us to such an extent that we had been inclined to dismiss the whole idea as part of Father's pro-German propaganda. But Frank soon found that this description was no exaggeration, for, indeed, he received the impression of a veritable garden city. The broad Königsallee, with its centre strip of ornamental water crossed by low bridges of delicate design and flanked by trees, was over half a mile long and formed a north-south axis. Gardens and parks were placed centrally and alongside the River Rhine. There was a fine waterfront and harbour for the large barges and tugs continually to be seen passing up and down the river. Steam pleasure boats of distinctive design also attracted the attention, and as Spring advanced Frank noticed rowing skiffs and fast motor boats. Displayed prominently on each side of the river were large numbered boards, thus: $\boxed{246}$ indicating the kilometers from the Prussian border. These were found to be useful for measuring distances when sculling.

Across the river Frank observed sandy beaches and above them grassy slopes topped by the ragged skyline of Oberkassel— a collection of tall gable-ends in a mixture of Jugendstil and High Gothic. He was also soon introduced to the Stadttheater, (the Municipal theatre and opera house) overlooking the Königsallee, where he was to enjoy many an inspiring evening. Further South was the Schauspielhaus (a 'Little Theatre'), one of the theatres visited by Mr Sam Cooke before he designed the Birmingham Repertory Theatre.

Frank was to spend two mornings a week at the Kunstgewerbeschule, where I had been, in its oldish building near the river. He also received private instruction in commercial correspondence and book-keeping by double entry from Herr Brecht who lived to the North of the city. This young man had india-rubber lips and a curiously slow and emphatic manner of speaking, possibly for the benefit of foreigners. Frank and he soon became friendly, going on walks and taking Fruhschoppen (early pints or 'elevenses') together.

The rest of Frank's time was to be occupied in studying German, the piano, singing in a choir, sport, and in pursuing an altogether pleasant social life. He took things easily and did not hesitate to retire for an hour or two's sleep in the afternoon if he felt like it. Gemütlich (or 'comfy-like') might be taken as the key-word for himself and the family with which he stayed.

It was a period of adventurous architectural design. Frank noticed the long stone mullions running from the first, almost to the top floors of some new department stores and office buildings. These impressive vertical lines were sometimes marred by Germanic exuberance, in the form of carved capitals shaped like human faces with serious expressions. The Steel-

Trust building, in sand-stone and marked by these gloomy facial carvings, stood at a corner of the Bastionstrasse, which crossed the Königsallee towards its southern end. Number 26 was the home of Frank's hosts.

Pastor Funke, the head of the family, was bearded, with his thick grey hear en brosse. He wore powerful glasses and, in the manner of those days, a black frock coat—even when on holiday in the country or on the river, He enjoyed the company of officers, attended regimental re-unions of veterans and liked to preach at the garrison chapel. Frank described him as 'an awfully decent old chap—very lovable and hard working'.

As for the family, shortly after arriving Frank summed them up in a letter to me:

> Frau Funke has brought up all the girls very sensibly. I think they are all three awfully nice—so let us pass on to Helene the eldest (24). She is small, rather plump and teaches at a school. Toni (21) is very decent and easy to talk with—plays toppingly and teaches kids on the drawing-room piano. Gertrude (17) awfully pretty little thing, slightly affected, but sings in a pet way—typically German. Certain points are common to all three, viz, always laughing at everything and having terrific jokes between themselves. Last night they showed me all their photographs of the family, which afforded endless mirth.

Paul, their only son, was a school teacher and away from home when Frank arrived. He was a cheerful soul, good company, given to gentle fooling, and, like his sisters, to dressing up for songs and turns.

Within their wide circle of friends was Kurt Brausen, the son of a maltster. Along with several others he was attracted by Gertrude, whom he eventually married. He and Frank became very friendly. The others of that gay company included Hermann Telle, engaged to Toni, the Budde brothers, Hugo and Otto, Rolf Kaiser, young Lysegang, the son of an artist whose studio Frank visited, Lisi Luyken and her brother, the children of Herr Baurath Luyken, an Inland Waterways official. From time to time Herr Luyken would invite his friends to excursions on his steamer. Together these young people moved around, taking refreshments at Schiffschen, the Rheingold, Bittners, or on the Annanasberg (a small hill in one of the gardens, and a favourite rendezvous), or going to the cinema ('saw a marvellous Italian film *Der Vater*' or 'saw *Quo Vadis*', Frank mentioned in his diary). They would meet at dances or at Sunday morning service at the Johannes Kirche, where Pastor Funke sometimes preached, or at each other's houses for coffee, Bowle (wine cup) and games. It was a time of romance and gentle courting. Some of the young men had been together in the same student Korps (fraternity) and would act as confidential intermediaries on behalf of a sister or sister's friend. There was much gossip and speculation as to who would marry whom.

Frank's attitude to the girls was affectionate but platonic. 'Ich könnte ein deutsches Mädchen lieben, aber nicht verheiraten,'[60] he was heard to explain, just to make his position quite clear. Sometimes, when he came in late and they had gone to bed, he would push a little note under the door to keep them informed as to the evening's happenings. 'He was like a brother to us,' they said, many years later.

When they were not out at some concert, opera or dance, they would spend the evenings at home playing games. Frank introduced them to Up Jenkins, Old Maid, Donkey, and his diary mentions a number of other games such as Halma, Wolf and Sheep, Skaat, 66, spelling games, writing games and, on one occasion, Mesmerising Kurt Brausen.

The family were extremely kind to him. Here, for instance, is the entry in his diary relating to his birthday on July 15th:

> A great day of feasting. After breakfast received Tisch of presents. Very practical and good. Practised and finished essay. Birthday tea and cakes, etc. Kino with Paul till 6.00—then music and songs. Kurt Brausen to supper—fine evening—speeches, Bowle, etc.

That evening there were also some preliminary celebrations of

---

[60] 'I could love a German girl, but never marry one.'

Toni's birthday (which actually came next day) when after
supper he had a 'long talk with her in the bedroom on school
life'.

Before Frank left I had warned him of the high-pressure
hospitality he might expect and the looks of pained surprise if a
second helping was refused. Challenged by the question, 'Und
schmeckt es Ihnen nicht, Herr Best?'[61] I had often found myself
with no option but to accept meekly what was offered. Soon
after arriving he wrote to me:

> I am sticking to it that I always have a small appetite. Frau Funke is
> never offended at my small helpings, though she pressed me a good
> deal.

My warning was really quite unnecessary. The German food
and drink suited him and he enjoyed them. The first evening at
the Funke's was marked by what in his diary he called 'a feast',
then:

> While Father was here we had some really good feasts, which
> showed that Frau Funke knew how to do it. Today we had the first
> everyday dinner. It was not bad really, though we had shape and
> syrup after soup and fish.

In Frank's diaries there are several references to food and drink.
Like Father, he drank only moderately but it was while in
Germany that he really began to enjoy a glass of wine or beer,
including those Früschoppen with friends. Before leaving for
home he copied out some 'recipes for tasty things to eat' (7 July)
and, on reading his diaries, I am sometimes reminded of the one
kept by our grandfather Robert Best and of an expedition to
Blenheim Park on June 10, 1834.

The warlike preparations, about which we had heard so much
at home, were, Frank found, only too evident through military
parades and displays of air-power and through civilian

---

[61] 'Doesn't it appeal to you?'

conversation, our liberal background and the screen provided
by the British Navy having to some extent obscured the fact that
our own government was playing a similar deadly game. His
reactions to Anglo-German tension were somewhat different to
mine, which had been partly conditioned by my arrival three
months after the Agadir incident in 1911, when war had
actually been imminent. I had been shocked by the intense
feeling even in the family of the Protestant pastor where I had
stayed—all the more disturbing seeing the kindness and
tolerance shown to me personally. The student duelling, the
disfigured faces, the school-boy suicides all added to my Angst,
which was only partly Freudian and due to family background.
By 1913 the Morocco question had calmed down and Frank
was not as susceptible as I was to these disturbing phenomena.
He must, nevertheless, have given some thought to the martial
climate, for in an article to the *Bedales Chronicle* he had the
following comments:

> I doubt whether there is another land containing such an
> outwardly patriotic people as the Germany of today, and indeed up
> to a certain point it could not enjoy anything more advantageous,
> but if it begins to work itself into a swollen head through talking all
> day about its army (which I grant is a magnificent masterpiece of
> organisation), it will probably bring about its downfall. Throughout
> history circumstances have proved that a nation becomes the
> toughest when oppressed.
>
> The young German, for example, makes a point of learning up
> the number of every regiment, its uniform and permanent quarters;
> perhaps it is equivalent to the Englishman who specialises on his
> county cricketers and their averages, or better, the various makes of
> motors and motor-bicycles. At any rate every nation has its
> speciality, and as they haven't yet developed the golf, cricket, or
> motor bore, they might do a great deal worse.

In the same article Frank also commented on a number of
Feiertage (official occasions) that were celebrated during his stay
in Düsseldorf and of the many centenaries that had played an
important part in Germany's history and that were then being
commemorated, such as the founding of the Iron Cross and the

victory of Leipzig. Furthermore, the Kaiser's Silver Jubilee was celebrated on June 16, following the royal wedding of Princess Louise and the Duke of Cumberland. Frank's article ended on an unconsciously ironic note:

> In conclusion, I may say, even if the Balkan disturbance has slightly affected trade here in general, the flag and decoration section must have beaten all records, as on all the above Feiertage the streets were swarming with black, white, red and other patriotic colours. It will be interesting to see what will happen in 1915; the feeling here will undoubtedly be intense; I can only hope our relations with France will remain as good as they are today.

Sport claimed much of Frank's time and attention. He was good at finding his feet and within four days of arriving was on the skating rink, accompanied by Kurt Brausen. According to his diary he had a 'grand time and was introduced to many', and during the next five weeks he skated regularly.

By the end of the first month Frank had walked up to the hockey ground to make enquiries and observe the form. A week later he was being tried out for the second eleven (centre half) and thereafter continued to play weekly until April when he turned his attention to tennis, playing regularly in the Kaiser Wilhelm Park with the three girls, Kurt Brausen and other friends.

He swam frequently, and on June 5th walked down to the floating boat-house at 246 to join the rowing club (founded in 1880) as a temporary member. There, for the first time, he was coached in sculling. The trainer, Wingate, was English and had been engaged six years previously. The names of the skiffs and boats in which he rowed weekly appear in the official history of the club, as well as in his diary: 'Schwanenspiegel, Hedwig, Backfisch, Forelle, and Moewe.' Once, he rowed Paul Funke in Hedwig the eight kilometers upstream to Hamm 238, a group of small houses and warehouses just outside Düsseldorf which somehow suggested a fishing village. A bend in the river forms a small bay, with a sand and shingle beach, below the high grassy bank of the river. Here they rested and 'after playing about with an oil barge' returned in 35 minutes.

Frau Funke was most reluctant to allow any of the girls to go with Frank on these rowing expeditions, but eventually her objections were overcome: 'Took Toni for a row! Permission from Frau Pastor staggers all.' (3 July)

Shortly after arriving Frank 'fixed up with Herr Hubert Flohr for piano lessons'. A pupil of Clara Schumann, this fine musician was well known locally and frequently heard in recitals of chamber music. He encouraged Frank to 'loosen up' and to get rid of the last traces of that over-conscientious attitude that he had picked up at home. The two seem to have got on well together. Frank noted his second lesson as being 'very comical' and a little later Herr Flohr was 'very bucked and played for 26 minutes after lesson (Brahms)'. Frank decided against singing lessons but, in the early days of his stay, joined the Johannes-kirche choir and attended practice regularly singing with it in concerts and church. The choirmaster was a certain Herr H Guillaume who was often to be heard in song recitals. On account of his beautiful bass voice and engaging presence he had many feminine admirers, including Toni Funke, who admitted that she schwärmte für ihn (had a crush on him).

Frank went to symphony concerts and to all Wagner's operas except *Parsifal* which was not to be 'released' until the following year;[62] the Düsseldorf repertory included that—for English people—operatic rarity, *Rienzi*. In Cologne he saw Meyerbeer's *l'Africaine* and Puccini's *La Bohème*, the musical idiom of which seemed to him somewhat modern.[63] He would keenly study the librettos and scores, trying over passages with the girls on the piano.

Helped by Herr Flohr, Frank worked away at his compositions: a fantasy for the piano, 'At Sunrise', as well as two songs, 'The Cuckoo' and 'The Island in the Year'. For some time I had been urging him to write out his works, which

---

[62] The production of *Parsifal* was limited to Bayreuth until 30 years after the composer's death. The copyright ran out on 31 December 1913.

[63] Owing to the time lag in musical understanding. It was actually written about twenty years earlier.

generally existed chiefly in his head and hands, and allow me to make fair copies of them. The thought that these charming pieces pieces might, for any reason, become lost filled me with misgivings. Such manuscripts as existed were sketchy and I was sometimes hard put to it to decipher them.

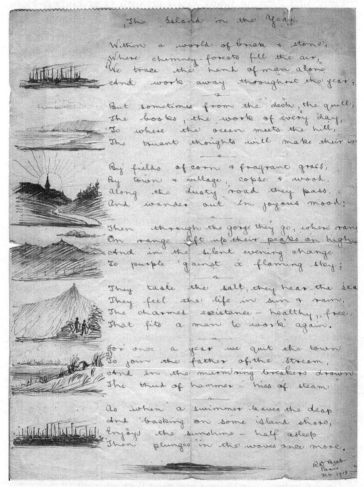

R.B.'s manuscript of 'The Island in the Year': 'Within a world of brick and stone, Where chimney-forests fill the air, We trace the hand of man alone, And work away throughout the year ...' Paris, February 1913.

260

On February 13, in reply to an enquiry, Frank wrote:

> Re: 'Fragment' [a short piano piece], it is rather hard to explain. The part before the half-way is exactly like the part after half-way except for broadened harmonies.

Then came several lines of staveless musical notation followed by an enlightening account of how he was beginning to work:

MUSIC IN GENERAL

> I have got through the dirty work in copying out the Pavane, but it is the limit for rhythm, on analysing. I am fairly full of Stamford's book Musical Composition and he says no one in their right mind would write manuscript at the piano. I have done quite a bit of the Pavane in my room. It is a bit of a swot, and quite impossible to concentrate if any other music is being played in the neighbourhood. Also, I have played the piece so often that it has become almost mechanical; and when I tested the veracity of the M.S. I found several howlers. I am so glad that I have broken the back of it, though, as it is quite the trickiest of the lot.
>
> I lash away at scales and studies daily, and though I am conscious of progress, if you asked me to play anything decently just at present it would be a case of 'Well, there you have me.'[64]

My words for the 'Cuckoo Song' were on a simple theme. It contrasted the conventional or poetical attitude towards the first signs of Summer with a cynical and even exasperated reaction to inappropriate and untimely 'cucking', associated with unsuccessful golfing, rain and bunkers—occasions when one felt like wringing the bird's neck. Frank wasted no time:

> I have got practically all the ideas for the Cuckoo song, and now that Sumer Is Icumen In has been sent from home, I can go ahead with the last verses. I fancy that it will be a triumph of combined burlesque when completed. The chief difficulty is in not making the music too good [ie keeping up the burlesque].
>
> The first half begins with a suggested growl of discontent and

---

[64] One of Aunt Lucy's sayings, when cornered.

working through pastoral motives (which include falsetto and 'Two Sticks Across'[65]) thrown in. Stephen Adams is embodied in the third verse. The growl sets in again allowing scope for eyebrows and breathing.

I shall turn to the second half later, but I am convinced that the rag-time [version] of Sumer Is Icumen In, which accentuates just the last two words of each stanza (giving the key note), combined with a Till Ready and Cecil Sharp accompaniment will bring the house down. (27 February)

Frank's setting was in fact most effective and comical. The change of mood from the romantic to the discontented and the cynical was marked by a discordant version of the bass ostinato figure of 'Sumer Is Icumen In'. As we shall see, this song was performed during the last Old Bedalian concert before the 1914 War.[66]

At that time we were also working together on 'The Island in the Year', inspired by our summer holiday in Wales. Frank wrote to compliment me on the words and modestly expressed doubt as to whether he could 'bring the music up to standard'. I could not help trying over in my mind's ear some ideas for the musical treatment, and suggested something on the lines of the opening dialogue between Pogner and Beckmesser from The Master-Singers, with its reiterated 3/4 figure interweaving with the voice parts. I even went further and sent him the manuscript of one verse for comment[67] but after receiving this reply went no further with the matter:

And now we come to a really tricky subject. I got one of the nymphs to play your song and sang it myself until quite flott [fluent]; it is

---

[65] From 'Liza' Lehman's Bird Songs.

[66] 'To my great regret the manuscript of this song disappeared in about 1944. If anyone reading these words can throw light on its whereabouts I shall be extremely grateful.' R.B.

[67] A poor executant, I had never fully realised the implications of getting other people to play what one had written. I did not actually try my hand at composition until some 30 years later. Frank completed his setting in October 1916.

really quite good, and that is the difficulty. I feel I can't work on it without doing so much that the original would be unrecognisable. It is not so much the ideas as the way they are worked out that becomes the first consideration in this sort of music. The other alternative is to leave it just as it is, in which case I think you ought to try your hand at the other verses and do the thing right out.

I have not seen the *Meistersinger* yet, but I hope to do so soon, and then take note of the part you refer to.

My opinion with regard to writing is that where part-writing is concerned, it is impossible to do it at the piano. I have put a third voice in the Holy City for the voice against the bass and proper air, and did it in my room after supper one evening; I got the harmonies and tune of the original well in my mind before putting them on paper. At present I have to find the best harmonies at the piano (as they are, as yet, too complicated to invent) and then write straight away without, playing first. Melody, however, is easy to hear, also simple harmonies. (15 March)

Frank worked about two mornings a week at the Kunstgewerbeschule, then under the directorship of Dr Wilhelm Kreis who, besides being a distinguished architect, had designed and supervised the production of furniture, textiles, silverware, and even cabinet work for pianos. His outlook was modern in the sense that students were encouraged to break away from traditional shapes and decorations.

The Deutscher Werkbund, which corresponded to the yet unfounded English Design and Industries Association, was at that time influential. The Director was a member, as were several of the staff, among them being Max Benirschke, an architect, in his early thirties. Although a follower of Rudolph Steiner, he never put forward the anthroposophical viewpoint in a dogmatic way. His instruction in Interior and what we should now call Product Design was years in advance of the corresponding course at the Birmingham School of Art. Frank started in his class and, in a letter, entertained me with an admirable caricature of this excellent teacher:

B is very decent. I am designing a hall lamp and he is giving me a fair amount of his time. None of the students works very vigorously

263

and the only girl in the class receives an extremely reasonable quantity of attention from them all. (30 January 1916)

Later, however, according to his diary, Frank 'got on badly with "B" at K.G.S.' (6 March). This is surprising, bearing in mind Benirschke's gentle nature. Did he, perhaps, go too far in some Bedalian, uninhibited sally? It could not have been serious, as subsequent entries show.

Father was continually looking round for new designs for the company and during Frank's flying visit home for my twenty-first birthday in April they must have discussed a suggestion that Benirschke be asked to do some light fittings. On his return to the Kunstgewerberschule, Frank 'spoke to Benirschke about private work'. It seems that 'he was very decent about it and would consider the question' (25 April). Evidently no time was lost, because in less than two weeks Frank 'received letter from Pa approving sketches by Benirschke'. Frank was to enlarge them and put in the structural details, and this he started to do two days later, having finished one of his own designs. What was Benirschke's lighting fixture like? From a minute sketch in Frank's diary (26 May) I guess that it was a ceiling fitting, consisting of a top spinning, vertical rods or a cylinder, with a convex glass at the bottom.

Prior to this exercise, Frank had been doing a full-size drawing of a hall lamp, a 'suspension'[68] and a bracket or wall light. These full-size constructional drawings must have been somewhat exceptional. During the previous year I noted that in this class the students were working almost entirely on coloured scale drawings. There were certainly no workshops where prototypes of the students' work might be made by hand. It was a pre-Gropius age.

The students tended to use geometrical forms for their designs, and the furnishings, fixtures and interior decoration

---

[68] A counterweighted rise-and-fall shade pendant, with three or four additional lights close to the ceiling.

which we saw in Düsseldorf at that time were, from the modernist viewpoint, years in advance of anything to be seen in British shops, although, paradoxically, the influence of British designers, such as William Morris, had made itself felt abroad.

In my book *Brass Chandelier* I have described the visionary attitude of the then head of the Birmingham School of Art, Mr Catterson Smith, and Father's impatience with some of the students' work, which he dismissed as 'an ethereal smudge'. Frank was on his guard and recorded his disapproval of the free and impressionistic style favoured by the Direction and Staff of the Kunstgewerbeschule: 'Judging of School Competition—prizes awarded to the shoddiest' (11 June). A picture exhibition which he visited was 'for the most part too modern and careless' (24 June).

Industrial Design is by definition design to sell, and on two occasions Frank had an opportunity of entering into the customer-producer relationship which is part of the designer's material. In spite of the modern tendencies in interior decoration—still under the influence of the Jugendstil but simplified—there was a market for die schönen einfachen englischen Formen (beautiful, simple English forms). At the end of January, Bernard Blackburn, a director of Father's firm, came out from England to sell the company's products. Frank joined him in Cologne, went to the Opera and next day visited customers with him, finding the 'Rheingegend rather steinige Boden' (the Rhine area rather stony ground). In June, another director, George Vale, visited Düsseldorf. Frank noted in his diary:

> June 25. All firms selling badly, partly through Easter disturbances—usual lies about being verreist (out of town).

> June 26. Train to Elberfeld, visited Tietz. Last lot sold well, but stock still too big. At next shop chap had no interest, had not even opened photos sent previously! Took Schwebebahn [overhead railway] to Barmen, there found two possible shops to approach through correspondence. No orders! Evening with Mr and Mrs G.V. at Blochius.

June 27. Train to Essen. There made appointment with West Deutsch for 3.00. Had lunch at Ratskeller after finding another badly copied fitting in Altdorf's. At 3.00 man of course verreist (really just above)—usual lies. No orders, day wasted.

June 28. Visited Köln with GV—first called on Bosch, then Farbach (without success)—Hagg and Bohl after lunch. Collected first orders, about £50 in all.

Frank's time at Düsseldorf was drawing to an end and our parents thought that it would be gracious personally to thank the Funke family for their kindness. Father was unable to leave the country at that time, so to me fell the honour of taking his place as well as the responsibility for conducting Mother to Düsseldorf. She was not a good sailor and was prone to train-sickness. I was therefore relieved to find ourselves at our destination, where Frank met us. He lost no time in taking us to the rowing club, and in the evening, his diary records we 'crossed threshold of No. 26 Bastion Strasse and distributed presents—after dinner music with Gertrude—English folk songs.' (24 July)

Next day Frank had a long talk with Max Benirschke and said goodbye to all at the Kunstgewerbeschule, after which the three of us went to the rowing club again, and while Mother was reading he took me for a row in Backfisch. We had lunch at the Schauspielhaus restaurant and I left Frank to finish an essay. This was followed by farewell visits to Herr Flohr and to various friends, dinner at the Zoological Gardens and a concert. During the next few days we enjoyed ourselves playing tennis with the girls, walking about the town and visiting friends.

Among them was the Blochius family—customers of the firm and lifelong friends of Father. On several occasions they had kindly invited me to their house, but I had not found their company particularly stimulating. With Frank in the circle I noticed a big difference. His entertainment gifts manifested themselves. With a little preparation he translated several English humorous anecdotes into German and soon had the company laughing uproariously. The somewhat heavy atmosphere, for which I now realise I was partly responsible, rapidly lifted. The fruit-cup circulated. He brought them out of themselves and soon they were capping his story with others. Frank had a way with him.

The following evening (Sunday) Frank's diary records—after tennis and a rest in the afternoon:

> Great feast at the Breidenbacher Hof for farewell official dinner. Kurt invited—wine great success—lasted till 11.30—toasts, etc. (27 July)

I remember that farewell party chiefly for its feeling of warmth and Gemütlichkeit. Frank had obviously made a deep impression on the Funke family and was accepted, not only as a brother, but as of a certain stature in conversation, music and entertainment. Mother proved a witty and beautiful hostess, following the conversation chiefly by intuition and somehow contriving to make herself understood, often with the help of Frank and myself as interpreters. The menu was lengthy, healths were drunk in an excellent hock and after coffee and liqueurs, the company switched on to lager beer, 'weil es so bekömmlich ist'.[69] Pastor Funke beamed from left to right through his powerful glasses, Frau Funke radiated an understanding benevolence. The girls showed a certain emotion at the thought of Frank's parting and the evening ended in a harmonious glow.

Our last day was described in his diary as 'Trude's Treat', for on that day we were the guests of Trude Lauten, an attractive diminutive brunette who, after a year or so in Handsworth Wood, had left a trail of disturbed emotions amongst the men folk. She met us at Cologne, where we took the fast electric train to Bonn and then went on by steamer to Königswinter. After lunch we made our way up to the Drachenfels, where the accompanying photograph was taken. Frank's diary concludes with:

---

[69] Because it's so good for one.

4.30 tea at Hotel, 5.30 late boat to Cologne. Food at Frischers (abschied)[70]—train to Düsseldorf.

We arrived home at the end of July and must have left Birmingham for the Old Bedalian Summer Meeting within a few days, travelling down by train. As we approached Petersfield we began to peer through the carriage windows in order to catch a first glimpse of the familiar landscape—Wheatham Woods, like a giant caterpillar crawling over the end of the downs, the bare triangle of the Shoulder of Mutton, the luxuriant wooded slopes of Stoner Hill, then the school itself, appearing above the trees, and finally the drab buildings of Petersfield station.

Once within the spacious grounds of the school, we looked around for somewhere to pitch a tent which we had brought with us. We chose a spot where, formerly, the wireless telegraphy experiments described earlier had been carried out. It was on the edge of the cricket field and beneath a belt of seminal-odorous chestnut trees. As we worked, we heard the familiar sounds, the striking of the hours, the crack of bat on ball, and the tolling of the bell marking the term-time routine. The sun blazed down over the pitch and thatched pavilion, designed and constructed in his spare time by one of the boys; from time to time we would pause and refresh our memory; through the summer haze we took in the two whale-backed shapes on the horizon, Butser and War Down, and the line of the South Downs tapering off by Harting and North Marden, scenes of many an expedition.

The events of the weekend followed a well-established pattern. Frank was not playing in the customary cricket match 'Past v. Present', but on Sunday morning took part in the swimming sports; his graceful diving was greeted with applause and was remembered years afterwards by at least one of the girls. In the evening we found ourselves singing the old hymns and psalms in the new hall. We listened respectfully to the

---

[70] Departing.

Chief's address but we could not prevent our attention from occasionally wandering to the light-fittings, designed by Ernest Gimson. They did not commend themselves to our trade judgement, for they seemed crude and unsuitable. We felt that Best & Lloyd could have furnished something more elegant than those irregular shaped bowls surmounted by octagonal sheets of iron. How wrong we were!

The evening service (known as The Jaw) was followed by a short concert, after which, under a starry sky, Frank and I strolled up the hill to our tent, humming some of the tunes we had heard. We discussed certain organisational matters, such as undressing without getting in each other's way, and disposal of clothes and shoes, and eventually fell asleep listening to the night noises.

Next day we divided our attention between a tennis tournament and rehearsing for the evening's entertainment. The *Record* reported:

> A Merry Evening of the good old kind was got up, consisting of songs, recitations, parodies and a charade, in which Montague and the Best brothers were as indefatigable and as amusing as ever. (JHB)

Frank's camping experiences of the previous year had kindled his enthusiasm for this form of holiday and, as was customary, he sought to transfer this enthusiasm to me. Any leadership I may have had, derived from elder-brotherdom, was now passing. If we had our own equipment, he felt, it would give us a certain independence in our movements and, accordingly, whilst still in Germany, he must have put me in touch with some English suppliers of lightweight tents for I remember fettling our camping gear and, in what seemed to me a totally inadequate tentlet, fortunately replaced later by a larger one, rehearsing for the Old Bedalian camp among the stray cats on our lawn.

Shortly after returning from Bedales we travelled up to Ravenglass in Cumberland and thence made our way up to the camp. There we found the Chief and about two dozen Old Bedalians. The site they had chosen was at the foot of Hard

Knott Pass on the bank of the Esk. The rocks and uneven ground had levelled themselves out into a flat meadow sheltered by trees, through which we could see the mountains of the Lake District. Here they had erected two large ridged tents, one for each sex, and a few yards away Frank and I started to pitch our own, which we had tried out at Bedales. We busied ourselves collecting bracken to spread below our ground sheet, digging a trench around to drain off floods, fixing our candle lamp to the bamboo poles, arranging our sleeping bags and assembling our fishing rods.

At this point the Esk varied greatly in depth and width. Alongside the camp it was shallow but by dams of rock they had constructed two bathing pools—The Big Wallow and The Little Wallow. About a mile from the camp was a natural bathing place which Frank called The Rhinemaidens' Haunt. There, the water was at least fifteen feet deep and on each side the rocks, some twenty-five feet high, made crude diving platforms from which Frank and others could show their skill. To me, it all seemed extremely dangerous and the Chief confessed later that he had been anxious lest one of them should break his head open on a submerged rock.

Our many expeditions have left me with vague impressions of scenic beauty, physical fitness and good company. Frank was in excellent form. The general conversation was uninhibited and lively. Interpersonal relationships were freeing themselves from that distortion which seemed peculiar to groups of school children—arising, inevitably, from being herded together and either wielding or being subject to naked power. Even the immature and sometimes insulting nicknames were fading out, though, to be sure, Frank and I were still addressed as Bug Minor and Bug Major, owing to our supposed resemblance to large long-legged insects. But Pauley Montague protested when I addressed him as Pig Eyes. 'Nobody calls me that nowadays,' he said. For the first time we were getting to know each other as adults and fellow human-beings.

Beyond the tents we played innumerable cricket matches (Oxford v. Cambridge, Age v. Youth, etc.). The fielders were scattered around and encouraged to use what in golf would be called natural hazards. A gap in the wall between camp and stream was known as The Stratagem, the fielder concealing himself behind and to one side of it, ready to pounce out if a batsman attempted to snatch a run. No such devices, however, could prevent the Chief from scoring thirty off one mighty swipe into the river.

Pauley Montague had brought a beautiful lute that he had made himself; to its soft sonorous twanging he sang to us, in his attractive husky voice, the unexpurgated originals of some English Folk Songs which we had practised with the school choir—but then only in polite versions!

On the 'one wet day' (I quote the *Chronicle*), 'three daring sportsmen [Frank, me and another] faced the elements with fishing rods and after a hard day's fishing brought back half-a-dozen sardinian-looking objects which they called trout.' These 'sardinian-looking objects', and indeed all the meals, were cooked by Michael Pease, the son of Edward Pease, the first general secretary of the Fabian Society. In 1907 Michael had helped to found what was probably the first school Local Fabian Society. He had been devoted to the science master, Dr Fred Hodson, and at some point had perfected a convincing imitation of this master's voice and mannerisms, making his voice crack and soar from a rich bass to a falsetto. Somehow this vocal trick became a habit and years later, when we met, I could hear the beloved science master speaking.

Oswald Horsley and Vyv Trubshawe published the following account of one unforgettable climb:

The last night that we, of the first week, spent there was exceptionally fine, and an expedition was raised to ascend Scaw Fell peak to see the sunrise. The start was made under a bright moon at midnight, and though once we were a little hazy as to our direction, we soon struck the right path again. If only for the true beauty of the night walk, we were amply repaid for our exertions, and although the sunrise on top was a minus quantity owing to the large banks of cloud, the mist effects were wonderful. About 5.30 a.m. we were all feeling rather weary but we descended to a small spring, had the primus out, and black coffee, bread and chocolate pulled us together wonderfully. We then descended to the bathing pool where a swim gave us a healthy appetite for breakfast which we got on reaching camp. Thus ended the pleasantest week of the vac. There remains but one thing more to say, and that is that Best minor brought his camera; we feel sure that no more need be said about this painful subject, and we feel equally sure we have your entire sympathy.

A few days later Frank and I left the camp together. It rained hard the whole day. Having sent on our equipment in advance we did the ten miles to Ravenglass on foot. It was our first opportunity to compare our German musical experiences at length and without interruption. By way of illustrations to our analyses and criticisms, we sang practically the whole way— extraordinary representations in which each took different departments of the orchestra, as when we were children. We would start with 'Didn't you like that bit when ... ' and one of us would lead off, leaving the other to take up the theme contrapuntally or to develop it. Frank's rendering of the neighing effects in 'The Ride of the Valkyries', I remember, was most effective. After some hours of this musical dialogue we arrived at the small hotel in Ravenglass with water streaming from our clothes. We changed and ate large quantities of rum-butter before retiring.

The next day we went on by train to join the family at Pwllheli. Once again we found ourselves involved in the world of entertainment, not only as performers but as students of style and form. We admired two engaging society entertainers who came to the resort year after year. We would ask them to listen to our turns and give us advice. We even had the impertinence to offer them tips of our own. They treated us with kindness and tolerance. Edward Towle, slightly built, fair complexioned, and of concave profile, was a light baritone, and his wife, comely and more generously proportioned, had a pleasant contralto voice. Punning was still accepted as 'funny', though it would often be received by the audience with groans, and their dialogue was full of puns. They sang drawing-room ballads ('Thora', 'The Rosary', 'I'll Sing Thee Songs of Araby' and others), folk songs ('Oh, No John', 'I Will Give You the Keys of Heaven', etc) and extracts from musical comedies (*The Quaker Girl* (also known as *Tony from America*), *The Chocolate Soldier* and *Our Miss Gibbs*. They also encouraged the visitors to join in choruses of 'The Village Pump' and contribute to the visitors' concerts. They were helped by an M.C. who had been endowed with a perfect comedian's nose. He would go round looking for talent among the visitors and rehearse volunteers in amateur sketches. In one of these he himself took a part—of a young man. There was a gasp when the audience realised that the usual order of things had been reversed—with much grease paint his nose had been given a natural tint!

Frank and I appeared on the programme in a number called Two Subtleties—the title having been found by the M.C. One of the Subtleties was a musical disquisition on the Till Ready. In our patter we introduced what must have been an astonishing line of pedantic punning and far-fetched bogus musicology, offering a fantastic pseudo-analysis of the origins and development of the Till Ready ('Ethelred the Till Ready' came in somewhere) with examples by Frank on the piano. I have often wondered since what the audience, mostly business people from the Midlands, made of this dissertation.

This was to be our last Summer holiday together. During the two or three weeks in Birmingham that remained before Frank left for a stay in Paris, we borrowed Tonka and snatched a visit to Tennal House, Harborne, for tennis and music with Helen and Mary Aston. After a set or two, tea was served in their drawing room, fragrant with freshly cut flowers and the sharp smell of the polished wood-work of their grand piano. Later, Mrs Aston and Helen played the Overture to the *Meistersinger*, arranged as a duet and Mary entertained us with extracts from the *New World Symphony*, played on a penny whistle.

That year the British Association met in Birmingham during September. At one of the soirées we had our last glimpse of Pauley Montague before he sailed for New Caledonia. He had

273

met Frank Aston at Cambridge and was a guest at Tennal House. Pauley was correctly turned out (white waistcoat and tie) but as we passed him on the stairs Frank Aston whispered, 'Don't look at his boots'. They were of a heavy shooting type, hob nailed and well greased.

Professor Auguste Hollard of the Paris École de Chimie, where Frank studied for six months, was a good-looking man in his middle forties. He was quick to notice and appreciate the incongruous and, when amused, his bearded face would break up into a network of merry wrinkles. He specialised in the electro-deposition of metals and made periodic visits to Spain, where he was retained as a consultant by a copper mining concern.[71] A friend of Bergson and interested in philosophy, he later wrote several exegetical works on the New Testament. He and his wife Pauline were both French Protestants and related to many pastors of that small church.

Madame Hollard was a devout and active Christian but her outlook, unlike that of her husband, tended to be narrow and evangelical. His exceedingly broad interpretations of the scriptures may, indeed, have been a half-conscious compensation for his wife's piety.

Frank lived with the family, which consisted of two sons and five daughters. The eldest child, Vincent, then about 16, was a thoughtful lad, with his father's sense of humour. He was killed during the last month of the First World War. Michel, about a year younger, impressed us with his daredevil tricks. One of them took place at Présle, about 30 kilometers north of Paris, where the Hollards had a small country house situated at the foot of a steep grassy slope some 80 feet high. Michel set himself the objective of coasting down from top to bottom in a small wooden go-cart, holding the single shaft between his ankles and attempting to steer with it. Within a few yards the go-cart would apparently be travelling at 20 to 30 miles an hour, and it would be a matter of seconds before he was tipped out, the vehicle

---

[71] La Société Minières et Métalurgique de Pinaroya.

often striking him violently on the back of the head, or following him down the slope, both somersaulting rapidly. Time and again he would make the attempt, coming in to tea bruised and bleeding. At last, one afternoon, the bearings of the go-cart almost red-hot, he successfully made the descent, and, encouraged, repeated the feat on a bicycle.

In George Martelli's book *Agent Extraordinary* there is an account of Michel's resourcefulness, during the 1914 war, in getting into the French forces while still under age, of his decoration for valour at 19, of how at 20 he led his platoon, and of his desperate exploits during the Second World War, spying for the Allies, locating the V1 launching sites, and providing British Intelligence with information. Sir Brian Horrocks has described him as 'the man who literally saved London.'

The girls' ages ranged from eight to 15. The behaviour of the eldest, Jenny, at that time seemed somewhat headstrong but was accepted with great forbearance by her parents. The others were well behaved, dear little things, pinafored and demure. Frank would be vaguely aware, however, of times when they were not so demure (especially if the other adults were out of the way), and of times for discreet jokes, surreptitious dressing up and circus acrobatics. Madame Hollard treated the girls, except perhaps Jenny, with Protestant rigour and simplicity. In no wise harsh, her relations with them were sometimes lacking in sympathy. They all married husbands living in parts of the world other than France. One, Mireille, became my second wife.

The Hollards' town house was at 201 Avenue du Roule, Neuilly-sur-Seine. Probably built during the Napoleonic era, it was not a terrace house as we know them, but was nevertheless attached at each end to other houses, all of the same period. On entering, one was aware of that indescribable atmosphere—a combination of wax polish, solid fuel stoves and skilled cookery—peculiar to the Paris dwellings that we visited at that time. In the hall a flush door below the winding stairs led to le watère. A second door therefrom opened direct onto the garden. Above, the polished wooden floors of the bedrooms

275

sloped and twisted. Frank's room was spacious, but the others were small and numerous.

Immediately opposite was a block of relatively modern flats in which Madam de la Fontinelle dwelt. To her, Frank went for his singing lessons. 'We shall try every other day for a fortnight,' he wrote. 'She is very anxious to get my voice right in the short time before I leave.' The widow of an artist, Madame de la Fontinelle had formerly been a professional singer and a pupil of Jean de Reszke, whose teaching methods she followed. She was, however, handicapped through having lost her own voice following some illness.[72]

Among the many houses open to Frank was that of Monsieur Hollard's handsome sister, Madame Lauth. At her pension for young ladies he was introduced to other youthful musicians. Her son, Henri, later became Chef du Choeur at the Paris Opera. Frank would often find him seated at the piano,

---

[72] A photograph of the period shows her seated at a piano. Behind her in the photograph is Reginald Morley-Pegge, who was then studying the French Horn and playing in some of the Paris orchestras. He had already started his fine collection of old horns and has since become an authority on brass instruments. The two good looking young women between Frank and Reg, are Anne Taylor, whom Reg later married, and her sister Edith. Both were enthusiastic Wagnerians. Anne was a competent pianist and would play the Good Friday music from *Parsifal* with the lights lowered. Their mother was a French widow of an English clergyman and had a small pension in the Avenue de Neuilly, where Frank would go for informal dances and musical evenings. Morley-Pegge is the author of numerous articles, including the section on the French Horn in *Grove's Musical Dictionary*, and a standard work on the history and development of that instrument, *The French Horn*, Ernest Benn, London. 1960. He had gone to Audley End, Saffron Walden, in 1908 as a pupil of Lord Howard de Walden's estate agent. He met some interesting people including Josef Holbrook, the composer whose works were sometimes performed on the noble lord's magnificent organ, one that could be played with rolls—most of them specially cut—like a pianola. Frank was stationed at Saffron Walden in 1915 and made frequent visits to Audley End and Wendens Ambo where he met the Acklands, who were distant relatives of the Morley-Pegges.

the centre of an admiring group of girls, to whom he would be discoursing on some work. Berlioz's Symphony Fantastique was one of his favourites.

Frank was enthusiastic about the concerts he attended, at the Salle Gaveau, the Châtelet, the Lamoureux Concerts, and others. His visits to the Opéra were not as frequent as at Düsseldorf but there was one outstanding musical event, the performance, in February 1914, of Wagner's opera *Parsifal*. He was impressed: 'Went to see *Parsifal* during the week and enjoyed it immensely, though we could not get good places. The scenery was quite the best I have seen and gave the effect of a beautiful pastel picture. The two rolling panorama scenes were just as good from end to end. The music, of course, is wonderful. Franz took the part of Parsifal. In the Grail scene and at the round table they had a choir of about 60 knights and pages sitting about. I should like to see it several times before criticising thoroughly.'

Evidently he studied the vocal score, for many years later I found that, among other marginal notes, he had written my initials and a question mark against Gurnemanz's song in the third act, as something I might possibly study. We never had a chance of trying it over together.

During the same month he was singing folk-songs ('Henry Martin', 'I'm Seventeen Come Sunday', 'Lord Rendal', 'The Two Magicians', and 'High Germany') at a concert in aid of the Girls' Friendly Society, and there is reason to suppose that he had a small part in *The Merchant of Venice*, performed that month at Le Petit Theatre Anglais under the direction of Philip Carr.

With Anatole France, Albert Besnard, Auguste Rodin and other distinguished people, our cousin, or 'Aunt', Alice Ward (Alys Hallard) was on the committee of this little theatre, and it was she who had introduced us to the Hollard family. She was very fond of Frank who became a frequent visitor to her little flat overlooking the Place Saint-Sulpice. They were also often seen together amongst the gilt chairs and Louis XVIth panelling of the International Lyceum Club for women writers, artists and musicians—a beautiful house in the Rue Penthièvre. There he attended concerts, lectures and theatrical presentations, and was introduced to many striking looking and intelligent French women with rich experience of life, dancing with them at tango teas, this dance craze having just become fashionable.

The Paris Lyceum Club owed much to Alice Ward and her friend Constance Smedley, another Birmingham woman. In a letter to me, at the time of Alice Ward's death in 1939, she wrote: 'Alys Hallard knew everyone in Paris and there was no literary salon where she was not a welcome and honoured guest. She penetrated literary fastnesses where no other English author had gained entrée and was received not only as a brilliant litérateur and colleague but as a woman whose charm and esprit ensured appreciation in a society where conversation and beauty of speech are the hall marks of success. Her very pen name was a proof of *le mot juste*.'

In Paris, Frank's interest in the cinema received a fresh impetus. He was given a permit to visit the Pathé studios through Monsieur Hollard, who was consultant to the company. There he saw several scenes being shot, the actors gesticulating, mouthing, and sometimes, indeed, speaking sentences aloud. Later, he submitted a short film script for some competition organised by Pathé Frères. It was called *Quelle heure est-il?* and from the style of the French it seems probable that Vincent Hollard helped him. In this typical product of his Merry Evening mentality, he contrived to get a number of people in a *jardin public très frequenté* running round in circles, enquiring the exact time, because everyone, by a curious coincidence, had left his watch at home. Two urchins alter the time of a clock overlooking a large square at the end of an avenue where the procession eventually debouches itself. Instead of 11.10 the time appears to be 11.56. Coming down, they mix with the milling crowd. The clock strikes 12 and the last stroke has the same effect on the multitude as a cannon-ball bursting amongst female rabbits (boulet de canon éclatant parmi des lapines). The film ends with the two kids celebrating their triumph by dancing a jig on a park bench. For this gallant effort he was awarded a prize of five francs.

I have referred earlier to the Best & Lloyd capstan lathe department for the production of motor-cycle fittings. Frank's interest in this development can be seen from a letter he sent to me dated 22 October, 1913. He spent a good time at the Paris Motor Show, and saw, on arriving,

> at the top of the stairs a chap pointing out the advantages of our standard pump fitted to the Triumph machines exhibited (England supplies 25 bikes out of 36 with pumps). All the French ones with perhaps two exceptions reminded me of cycle cars at Olympia that firms have obviously scraped together for the show, the only difference being that this time they were obviously push-bicycle firms.
>
> In some cases a desk behind an array of push-bikes was doing its best to hide an odd cylinder jammed in the middle of a tankless, driveless and tyreless frame.
>
> The general effect was as though the French motor-bikes, with their polished nickel deep tanks, their penny-syringe lubricators, messy little smooth pro-skid tyres, tiny saddles, long handle-bars, etc, had taken a fit and retired when the English bikes turned up. [Ours] did look well and no mistake.

We both deplored the changing fashions in motor car design and the replacement of the classic parallel lines by tapering bonnets, which we compared with the snout of a pig. Frank's report continued:

> I am sorry to say that the Humber, Rolls Royce and Wolseley have all got tapering bonnets and look proportionately foolish. There are a great many bodies which are simply luxurious padded boats, quite open for touring, and upholstered like a club arm chair.

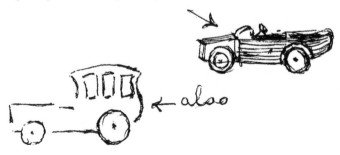

Frank was taken to a charity bazaar, in aid of one of Madame Hollard's worthy causes, where there was an auction sale of miscellaneous wares brought by supporters. Somehow or other he found himself, at short notice, in the role of auctioneer. His clowning in French—a language he found more difficult than German—made a deep impression. Never at a loss, he impersonated a French version of Uncle Arthur Short with much lip work and mouthing. 'Qui veut acheter ce loli petit louet?' he enquired, holding up some doll and appraising its balance as we had seen our uncle do when handling a tennis racquet. The performance was an immense success and is remembered to this day.

Frank came home from Paris on March 25, 1914. Our Wanderjahre over, we were now prepared to settle down for an indefinite period among those places and occupations we preferred to all others—home and the works, holidays in Wales, the Old Bedalian camp, music, amateur entertaining, grafting apple trees, working with Mother on her stamp collection, and sport, thus continuing the many-sided life we had led at school.

Frank made straight for the works but I cannot remember him being given any special assignment. Father would say, 'Look around, keep your eyes open and get to know the people.' In the evening Frank started by showing me the score of his Goblins' Festival, a one-step that he had orchestrated in Paris with the help of Reginald Morley-Pegge; at some point I actually heard it played, probably at a dance given by our parents. We then tried over one or two songs, among them being that curious composition Mental Disestablishment which, as we have seen, was originally suggested by our Aunt Lucy's delightfully inconsequential flow of talk.

Our Aunts expected from us a steady stream of affectionate teasing and we tried not to disappoint them. Our jokes, often immature and far fetched, were nevertheless generously appreciated. The 'Mental Disestablishment' song had come into focus one day on returning from a visit to their house Ivydene. The occasion may have been a birthday when, before they entered the room, we would remove some pieces of bric-a-brac from the mantelpiece, wrap them up, label them, and present them along with our own gifts. (Although perfectly aware of what to expect, they always feigned surprise.) Whatever the occasion of our visit, we had been impressed by Aunt Lucy's attempts to explain her latest system of memory training. She had found it helpful, she said. Be this as it may, we thought that the situation had been complicated by two further courses which she had taken up. One was a new method of psycho-physical relaxation, and another a series of exercises designed to improve the eye-sight. By way of demonstration she would hold up her index finger in front of her eyes and move it rapidly from side to side blinking the while.

We soon roughed in the main points of our song which were, briefly, that although memory training was to be deprecated in principle, it might still serve a useful purpose by de-tensing the very confusion it engendered. This happy state might be raised to a still higher level by practising methods of visual education.

> There are too many books of a dangerous kind,
> If the authors aren't careful they'll cop it,
> For one of my friends has been sent off his mind,
> So I really think some-one should stop it.
> It's this memory training and such tommy- rot,
> I've not got the patience to listen to 'em,
> But I've got a plan
> That's a lot better than
> All the memory training in Christendom.

> *Chorus*
> It's you've got—got—got to forget,
> Everything you ever knew,
> For the medical faculty all must agree,
> It's most beneficial for me and for you.
> So relax the cerebral tissues,
> I say man—don't look amazed,
> You must just whirl a digit,
> Till your eyes start to fidget,

Then your mind will be perfectly dazed—,
Then your mind will be perfectly dazed.

There were three more verses in a similar vein describing the benefits and disadvantages of amnesia. These words, for which I was largely responsible, rather appal me now but they were redeemed by a tune that I still find somewhat haunting. Among Frank's immediate circle in Paris it had caught on, and Reg Morley-Pegge, the Taylor girls and others had found themselves continually humming or whistling his 'Till Ready'.

During the month of May we drove Father over to Pwllheli in Tonka for a long weekend. There we met Albert Wood. It was on his strong recommendation that we had come to fish the Welsh streams during the springtime, our previous visits having taken place in August and September. On Saturday the sky was blue with light clouds and bright sunshine. A gentle breeze and a ripple on the water seemed propitious. We got to work with gusto. Albert Wood applied himself to giving us a good day's sport, pointing out the most likely pools and runs, and entertaining us the while with his own Welsh-gipsy idiom, interspersed with Anglo-Indian army expressions. After we had fished some hours with the fly he disappeared up-stream to throw into the water a quantity of earth to give it colour. We changed from fly to worm tackle. By tea-time several more brook trout had been laid to rest amongst the moist bracken which lined Father's well-weathered creel. Blood sports and the ethics of a civilised community had not then received the wide attention that Schweitzer has since generated. We gloated over that beautiful 'still life' in silver, brown and green. It was a day of unforgettable happiness.

As Spring turned to Summer our lives became more and more rich in texture. Frank was finding his feet at the works, developing some of his designs, analysing brass and other alloys by electrolytic methods in our laboratory, and helping with the foreign correspondence. In his spare time he was taking piano lessons and writing out some of his compositions. On Sunday mornings he would drive Father down to Nelson Street Adult

School and sometimes give a short discourse, which would be well prepared, lucid, humorous, and illustrated with blackboard sketches. On Musical Sundays, when the simple service would be combined with a concert, he was invited to play and sing. At the weekends we would drive about in 'Tonka', visiting the Astons or two former Bedales masters, both outstanding teachers and engaging characters who had accepted headships, Dr Fred Hodson having gone to Bablake School, Coventry, and Ernest Wells to Alcester Grammar School.

One motoring expedition nearly ended in disaster. Two representatives of the German AEG (which corresponded roughly with our English GEC) visited the factory and placed a substantial order for expensive lighting fittings. Having been asked to entertain them, Frank and I took them down to Broadway in The Cardinal for lunch, prior to a drive round some of the Cotswold villages. On the way home we chose what appeared on the map to be an attractive short cut through Condicote by Bourton Downs, intending to join the Five Mile Drive near Bourton Hill House. As we worked our way along the lane we found it had been extensively used for the transport of timber by traction engines. The ruts became deeper and deeper until The Cardinal's bottom scraped the surface of the lane and finally stuck. Our German customers were most cooperative. Coats came off, sleeves were rolled up, and with the floorboards of the car we dug ourselves out yard by yard.

That year Father had been elected captain of Handsworth Golf Club and on June 27 he carried out his duties, which were to provide the annual strawberry tea and distribute the prizes after the customary eclectic four-ball competition. On the next day our parents quietly celebrated their twenty-fourth wedding anniversary. The following morning when we came down to breakfast we noticed a certain seriousness in the atmosphere. Father pointed to the headlines of the *Birmingham Daily Post*:

ASSASINATION OF AUSTRIAN ARCHDUKE
HEIR APPARENT AND HIS CONSORT SHOT
DASTARDLY CRIME IN BOSNIAN PORT

The leader writer suggested that, although the murder had no serious political motive, it would have a serious political influence. Frank and I were not impressed.

During the next month events moved with a fatal acceleration right up to the final shock of August 4. The carefree attitude of the public calls to mind the unsuspecting mood of the Titanic passengers. To be sure, notable and even disturbing events were given prominence in the press but these only seemed to distract attention from the real threat. The death of Father's hero, Joseph Chamberlain, was announced on July 4. On July 13 the papers ran an exciting account of how Brock won the air race of five hundred miles from Hendon to Buc in seven hours. On the 14th Carson delivered an ultimatum in Ireland, and a few days later Lloyd George saw 'storm clouds in the sky', but this expression of apprehension did not refer to the risk of war but the Federation of Miners and Transport Workers.

On July 15, the employees at Best & Lloyd presented Frank with a gold watch to mark his twenty-first birthday. Once again, as for my own coming of age, a platform was erected in the yard between the bays recently built to accommodate the expanding capstan lathe department. In a short speech Frank said:

> It is extremely good of you to show your kindness in this way on this occasion, and I do value, and shall value, this present of yours; but it is not for the pecuniary value of the watch, for which I want to thank you most heartily, but for the kindness and goodwill which prompts the giving of it.
>
> Although I am 21 today and suppose I am a legitimate man I don't suppose you notice much difference in the way I walk round the place, and I don't want to change my resolutions and ideals I have always had. Although everything won't go smoothly for us, I feel sure that if we follow out the old motto 'Work of each for Weal of all' and everybody does his best for the community, when the hard time comes we shall pull through.

The typescript of his speech ends with the words: 'Here follows story of fish and sausages, better left to the imagination.'

In the evening our aunts, together with some other relatives and friends, joined us to drink Frank's health. After supper the guests took part in an informal concert. Frank and I had prepared a 'Topical Song' for the occasion, each verse beginning with the words 'Now we've written a verse for ... ' followed by the name of one of the party. For this song Frank had composed another attractive little tune and Till Ready:

Throughout these weeks Frank and I refused to allow our attention to be directed towards the real storm clouds in the sky. We were tired of the threat of war. It was a case of 'Wolf! Wolf!' We had heard too much of Britain's unpreparedness, Lord Roberts's call for conscription, *An Englishman's Home*, and all the rest. Why could they not leave us alone to get on with our fascinating projects? Besides, had the popular newspaper columnist Normal Angell not proved that 'Germany's success in conquest would be a demonstration of the complete economic futility of conquest'? The preparedness on which we concentrated was for the Old Bedalian camp (planned that summer to take place at Blair Atholl) and for our usual summer holiday at Pwllheli where rooms had been booked. This involved adding to our fishing tackle and camping gear, and perhaps exerting some extra pressure to finish off any special jobs at the works before we left.

Our mood could not have been exceptional, for even after the Austrian ultimatum to Serbia, reported on July 24, there was no suggestion in the press that Great Britain would become involved in a European War; and indeed, on the following day the *Birmingham Daily Post* reported 'continued firmness on the bourse in Vienna'. But on July 27, when mobilisation in Europe had already started, we learnt from the same newspaper:

> Today's news from the continent has had a stupefying effect on the man in the street, who finds it extremely difficult to realise that the great war which has so often been foretold may already have begun.

About a week later we travelled down to what was to be the last pre-war Old Bedalian meeting. The occasion was notable for another reason. The school had come of age. Over a hundred attended and amongst them were a dozen who had been at the first Bedales. These went over to Haywards Heath to revisit the old scenes.

On Saturday evening some of Frank's most amusing numbers were revived in a Merry Evening. These included 'the immortal and indescribable "Changing of the Guard"'. According to the *Record*:

> Kaiser Horsley, huge, red-faced, swelling out of his radiant uniform, formidable in moustaches, that tickled his eyes, and a voice that reminded us of the Sergeant at his finest; F. Best, Messrs. Warwick, Murray and Trubshawe marching pompously in couples, their legs stiff from hip to toe and describing quadrants of a circle at every stride, all to the strains of 'Die Wacht am Rhein', the inspection of hands, handkerchiefs and pop-guns snapping into Horsley's ferocious visage; and weird unearthly German orders: the fantastically waving line that fell in—all these are but details that feebly hint at the spirit underlying the whole.
>
> The last item, 'The Movies', wound up a delightful evening. We saw 'The News of the Week' and were also treated to an educational film, 'The Life History of a Tintack'.
>
> With commendable thoroughness this film began at the beginning, and showed the audience a line of slowly trudging figures—'Workmen going to the factory'. The next scene was but a vivid flash and startling clatter; the title 'Workmen going home for lunch'.
>
> Third in the eventful life history of the tintack came 'Workmen going back to work', a repetition of the first scene, varied by a certain beeriness in the demeanour of some of the actors … Then,

of course, the film ended with an even livelier edition of the first scene, entitled 'Workmen knocking off work and going home'.

'The Movies' must in the nature of things end in a typical burglar-chasing and free-for-all scramble effect, in which P.P. Eckersley distinguished himself through a series of flops and tumbles, grotesque and violent enough to break any professional.

There were also some songs by Frank and me, including 'Mental Disestablishment'. The reporter was kind enough to say that we were in our 'best' vein and that the Bedalians 'roared with laughter'.

The Sunday evening service was marked by a wise and far-seeing address by the Chief. He took as his theme 'What the School Stands For'. This, as he explained, was Health, Freedom, Comradeship, Service and Religion. There were, he said,

> two great problems, the solving of which must be the work of this century—the one dealing mainly with the outward and material side of life, the other with its inward spiritual aspect. The one is economic, social, political—the bringing of greater justice into the relations of man and man, and greater freedom into the individual life, fairer distribution of wealth, a living wage, more equality of opportunity to all, the right to develop all their powers, and use them for the common good, without any bar of class or sex.
>
> The other problem is an intellectual and moral problem: to re-shape our beliefs and motives, the very ideas of right and wrong on which our knowledge is based, on a surer foundation of truth and a wider conception of love. While rejecting none of the claims of reason, or the scientific method and outlook that the past age has won for us, the new age must reconcile with these intuitions of a faith that goes deeper still.

The climate of the Sunday evening music which, as was customary, followed the service, tended to be serious if not reverential. Only classical music generally found a place on the programme. Frank played one of Chopin's *Preludes*, and then followed it up with his own composition 'At Sunrise'. To the best of my knowledge this was the first original composition by a Bedalian to be performed at a Sunday evening concert.

Near the end of the programme we tried out on an unsuspecting audience our song 'The Cuckoo—Ideal and Real', the first part of which was reasonably in accordance with the Sunday-Evening-Music spirit. When, however, the mood changed from the romantic to the discontented and Frank's clanging version of 'Sumer Is Icumen In' appeared in the bass, titters of amusement began to spread round the hall, and as the voice part (myself) turned from the lyrical and poetic to golfing disasters, the bird 'cucking' at inappropriate times, and Frank's accompaniment becoming more and more frenzied, the titters changed to discreet laughter.

On the last evening of the meeting (Monday) we danced and finally sang 'Auld Lang Syne'. Then, to quote the *Record*, 'round after round of stentorian cheering brought to an end what all agreed was the best of all O.B. meetings.' In a foreword to my own war diary I wrote:

In spite of the threatening war-clouds as background, the O.B. Meeting was perfect—the brightest that has ever taken place. Even the newspaper reports pinned up in the quad seemed to make no difference to everyone's enjoyment. The Merry Evening, with all F.B.B.'s historic turns, the tennis, the Sunday Evening concert, the dancing, were all jollier than they had ever been before—and yet on the day the meeting broke up war broke out.

Sylvia Mundy said, 'The last happy days for a long time to come.' As it turned out, her brother was one of the first to fall in the retreat from Mons, with the L Battery of the Royal Horse Artillery.

Chapter 10
Taking to the skies

Frank arrived at the Royal Flying Corps's No. 2 School of Military Aeronautics in Oxford on 28 December 1916. By then the school had been in existence about eight months. No. 1 School at Reading, our rival in sports and games, was about six months older. The two schools constituted something of an innovation. Instead of officers picking up what they could of engine design, rigging and equipment at their training squadrons, all candidates for the Royal Flying Corps were now sent to one of these two 'ground schools' before actually learning to fly.

The R.F.C., which in August 1914 had consisted of only five squadrons, had been steadily expanding but not nearly quickly enough to satisfy Field Marshall Sir Douglas Haig. In June 1916 Haig 'had requested that the number of squadrons in France should be increased to 56 by the Spring of 1917.'[73] Four months later his proposal was accepted. As a result, 'the end of the Somme struggle in November 1916 saw 35 British air squadrons on the Western Front with 550 aeroplanes and 585 pilots'. On the other hand, the number of flying men killed, wounded and

---

[73] From H.A. Jones, *The War in the Air*, Vol. III, Oxford and Clarendon Press, p.297.

missing stood at 308, with 268 struck off the strength for other causes.[74] In addition, 'the early winter of 1916 saw British air supremacy challenged by German Jagdstaffeln (combat formations) equipped with superior aeroplanes. The Germans led in the technical race for the second and last time in the War.'[75]

Frank and I were thus helping to fill a big gap occasioned by rapid expansion and the casualties arising from a temporary German technical superiority. Though the training was more thorough than previously, the standards were perhaps not very exacting, so great was the demand for pilots.

Frank's training took two months. This was followed by five weeks of Elementary Flying at Thetford. We were then separated for four weeks while he trained at Dover on B.E.2cs and Martinsydes for Scouts, which were the Fighters of the First War. On May 7 we came together for an aerial gunnery course at Turnberry in Ayrshire which lasted a fortnight. Frank then underwent a period of further training on Spads (French fighter planes produced by the Société Pour L'Aviation et ses Dérivés) at London Colney before crossing to France for the second time on June 23.

As I write these lines I am impressed by the great good fortune which brought us closely together for eight consecutive weeks during the early months of 1917. It was an exhilarating experience. Frank's mood in a letter he had written in September 1916 was intensified: 'The world has assumed a different aspect. We are both full of hope and confidence.' The possibility of dangers was unimaginable.

Shortly after arriving at Oxford, Frank and I were taking a glass of gin and vermouth together while discussing our plans for the future, songs to be written, sporting activities, the rich field of technical material now being made available to us, and how much of it might be applied in the factory after the war. Suddenly

---

[74] From R.H. Kiernan, *The First War in the Air*, Peter Davies, 1934, pp 84–86.
[75] Ibid.

Pages from Robert's Higher Training Log. Wireless artillery and signalling made up seven categories of training. Ground gunnery included the use of Lewis and Vickers' guns. Photography and bomb dropping were also tested.

I began to realise that, until then, we had never really known each other as adults. I was no longer talking to a younger brother, but to a man—and one after my own heart. Any childish jealousies or irritation on my part gave way to a flowering of understanding and affection.

This sudden insight must have taken place at the R.F.C. club or at some bar, for at Brasenose College there was no room available as an ante-room. After our aperitif we strolled together across the quadrangle to the dining hall and took our seats on one of the benches at the side of the fireplace. This was our first experience of dining in hall, though in February 1915 Frank had spent an evening with George Murray at Trinity College, Cambridge. The dining hall seemed gloomy, even in daytime, being panelled up to the barrel-vaulted ceiling and lit by small mullioned windows. Presently some dons came in through a doorway in the end wall and sat down at high table below sombre portraits of founders and benefactors and the nasal

291

knocker over the door from which the college took its name. After a simple meal and a tankard of small beer we went to our room, No. 4/1, which we shared with a 2nd Lieut. Hanmer. Keen on hunting, Hanmer introduced us to the works of Surtees and to the Heythrop and Bicester hunts. We were impressed by the fact that as an undergraduate, Douglas Haig had occupied a room on the next staircase.

On the morning after our arrival (Friday, December 29) Frank and I set out together and walked past the Radcliffe Camera and up Parks Road to the red-bricked Clarendon Physics Laboratories where most of the lectures were given. Here we soon found ourselves engaged in brushing up our Morse—that 'strange and insidious disease, the lamentable epidemic of signalling' which we had first caught at Bedales in 1907, but now, instead of waving flags, we were set to operate Morse keys which registered electrically dots and dashes on a tape. A week later we passed our first test (six words a minute with one fault). 'Only one other person beside R.D.B. and self succeeded,' Frank recorded.

Two days later, on the last day of 1916, I wrote an equally eager letter to Beryl, from the R.F.C. School of Instruction, Brasenose College, Oxford.

My darling Brillo, at last I've got a clear half hour to write to you (jeers of disbelief from reader). There are three of us in a smallish room of hoary antiquity and only one bâtman so I have had to straighten things up myself this morning. I've got far too much kit and am sorting out the surplus A.S.C. stuff which I shall shove on to any unfortunate member of the family who visits us.

This is a topping place and very historic; in short, of colossal archaeological interest. Frank is absurd: he has bought a guidebook and just as we are going to sleep reads out that in 1087 Archbishop Bollinger had the room next door to us and on returning from a feast one day bumped his nose against the bedstead—hence 'Brasenose College'. The room was known thereafter as 'Bubbly's Bedroom'.

Yesterday I managed to work in a day's hunting along with our other roommate. I was in the saddle from 9.30 till 6.30, as we had to hack out 9 miles and back. I'm just a bit stiff, though nothing to speak about and it has done me a world of good. I had a topping horse (hired of course) and the weather was lovely. It was rather a poor country, no nice fences, and we had very little sport—one spasmodic run. However I enjoyed myself no end.

Last night I went with Frank to the local pantomime which wasn't bad—the theatre here is quite good. Next week The Bing Boys are coming so if you buck up and come we might all go.

There is an abundance of girls here and the R.F.C. are in great demand so do come and look after your oldest as he could do well with your company just now. The only thing is I have to be at the school every day from nine till five with one and half hours off midday. I could have lunch with you and I think I could get a leave of the mess at times. They have stopped weekend leave on account of curtailment of trains.

I am just going to send off the photos to Lafayettes. I decided on the two you chose after all.

This R.F.C. touch is a great scheme and I am awfully thankful we have managed to get in.

To say we found the work absorbing would be an understatement. After more than two years with nothing more complicated mechanically to master than the swingle-tree of a G.S. wagon, the course came as a complete change. We gobbled up all that was put before us with avidity. Even now, looking through my notebook, I am struck by the richness and variety of the fare. Frank's enthusiasm bubbled over onto paper in his letters home:

As for the work, what would take 20 of these pages to outline you could better understand in the same number of minutes down here yourselves. It's all very wonderful and will play a very important part in our future careers, and to think that we might have missed it all—drudging along in the old groove. (3 January 17)

The components of four stationary and four rotary engines were set before us in detail, while in a neighbouring park, under a low roof, the engines mounted on frames and complete with propellers roared away boisterously. On certain days we were taken out to the Rigging Sheds in Osberton Road to feast our eyes on the skeletons of aircraft and absorb technical information regarding their construction. And there was other fascinating equipment. Frank felt quite at home with the aerial cameras, but the machine guns and flying instruments constituted a completely new field of study. As we contemplated the bomb sights, release gear and bombs (ludicrously small by modern standards), we were reminded of H.G. Wells's *War in the Air* and the bombing of New York.

On the floor of a large room in the University Museum was spread out before our astonished gaze a most realistic model of the Ypres Salient. Some ten feet above, from a nacelle (the body of a pusher aeroplane) mounted in the balcony, one looked down on the trenches, the ruined buildings, the roads and railways, and—kite balloons (made from contraceptives, silver painted and on wire) apparently floating above each side of the line. Under the earth-like surface were a large number of torch-lamp bulbs which could be lit, singly or in groups from a control board, to represent the flashes of artillery and shell fire. A student would take up his position in the nacelle and conduct a shoot, working with a battery and correcting the direction and range after each shell exploded. 'Bloody marvellous,' we commented.

When later we came to find ourselves actually above the line, the visual effect was much the same as from above the model map. At any rate, we felt ourselves detached from the horrors going on below. We were spared any contact with the miles and miles of utter desolation.

Frank and I found the staff sociable and friendly, joining in games and inviting us to their rooms for music and drinks. It was a bright crowd—enterprising, imaginative and adventurous. Many of them are now blurred images, but some stand out sharply. For instance, the chief instructor, Staff Captain Sydney Smith and his wife, Clare, Lieut. Darrell Seale, the Adjutant, 'Baby' Denne and, especially, Captain Stammers.

Tall, dark, and slightly aquiline, Victor Stammers was about a year younger than Frank. He had enlisted in August 1914 and had transferred to the R.F.C., just in time for the Battle of Loos (15 September 1915), from the Queen's Westminster Rifles, via the Motor Machine Gun Service. He had a pleasant baritone voice. Frank would accompany him when he was trying over songs at our musical parties or at smoking concerts. He used to chaff us about our musical enthusiasms. When asked his opinion of Elgar he pretended that we meant a contemporary music hall turn, Olga, Elga and Eli Hudson who sang, amongst other things, 'The Sunshine of Your Smile'. His zest was infectious. He impressed us with his lectures on the principles of flying; these, as we shall see, he supplemented by private coaching.

For us, the information that Stammers imparted was almost entirely new. Looking over my notes I now realise how much of it was related to the unreliability of engines and their small reserve of power. Inattention to air-speed would lead to stalling (i.e. loss of control), probably followed in its turn by a spin, which might prove fatal if near the ground. 'Never turn when you are climbing,' I noted, indicating my ignorance with a marginal comment: 'Why?' 'Try not to use your engine when coming into the aerodrome,' he advised, 'but come down in "S" turns.' 'If you get into a spinning nose-dive put your control-stick central and forward.' 'Always select a forced landing ground every six minutes; choose a field about 300 yards square.' 'If a crash is inevitable unbuckle your belt in a pusher, but keep it buckled in a tractor.' (We were both of us later involved in crashes and forced landings on pushers and tractors.) The soundness of this advice was then amply confirmed. By unbuckling the belt one was thrown clear from a pusher, otherwise there was a risk of receiving the engine in the back. Victor Stammers built up our confidence. It all made sense, and confirmed our faith in the efficacy of basic scientific principles applied to sports—a faith which had been inculcated by Father.

Portmeadow lies to the north of the City of Oxford and alongside the river. It had been taken over by the R.F.C. as an aerodrome. Some three weeks after our arrival Victor Stammers invited us to join him there for our first flight. We jumped at the opportunity.

It was a cold January day. The sun shone feebly and when we arrived we saw that the grass was covered with patches of snow. There were then virtually no runways or landing strips as we now know them,[76] though in front of the Bessoneau Hangars—made of wood-lattice frame-works covered with canvas—there was an expanse of asphalt called 'The Tarmac' on which some of the machines would generally be parked. Tingling with excitement, we examined the Maurice Farman Shorthorn, or 'Rumpetty', which had been brought out of the shed. This machine, 'judged upon present-day standards, was "all wrong". A mass of wires and struts, there was no apparent attempt to produce a streamline or near-streamline machine. The aeroplane was an example of a thing that flew in spite of, and not because of, aerodynamic theory.'[77] Nevertheless, in its time it had led the way. 'In 1910 it set up a distance record on a closed circuit of 350 miles and in 1911 the time in the air was 11 hours.'[78] It also did well in a number of other pre-1914 tests. Victor Stammers still pays tribute to its airworthy character, while to Frank and me on that January morning it seemed a triumph of aircraft design.

Victor Stammers took the front seat while we waited near the machine, observing attentively what followed. It suggested some pagan ceremony. How many times later were we to officiate in this solemn ritual of starting up an engine. First chocks or wooden wedges were inserted under the wheels by an air mechanic moving around, as a server or acolyte might. Next we became aware of portentous control-words and responses: 'Switch off'—'Switch Off', 'Suck in'—'Suck in'. The mechanic now

---

[76] Few hard runways existed during the 1914 War; one (a circular concrete platform) was constructed before the war.
[77] From Leonard Bridgman, *The Clouds Remember*, Gale and Polden, Aldershot, p.7.
[78] Ibid.

raised his arms to heaven and grasped a blade of the propeller, rotating it slowly until sufficient petrol-vapour had been inhaled. Then, after a slight pause, came the call and response 'Contact', whereupon the mechanic began to swing the propeller with vigour but caution, for without adequate muscular coordination he might easily find himself a sacrificial victim. An error of judgement or feet slipping on the damp grass could mean a serious wound or even decapitation by the revolving blades.

Once firing regularly, the engine was allowed a few minutes

Frank on his maiden flight. 'Eagerly, Frank clambered into the nacelle ...'

gently to warm up. Victor Stammers then gradually opened the throttle, but the 70 hp Renault engine—a remarkable one in its time—did not respond adequately. An attendant Flight Sergeant, who had been watching these operations closely, now stepped forward and made some adjustments to the carburettor. At last the performance was deemed to be satisfactory. Eagerly, Frank clambered into the nacelle, taking his seat behind our instructor, who signalled for the chocks to be removed.

The noise increased. With the help of the mechanic the machine swung round and began to taxi unsteadily over the rough turf. After a short time they were facing the wind. The sound of the engine became deafening. Frank wore no crash-helmet or flying-helmet though for one flight our pilot still retained his G.S. hat, secured by a chin strap. While taking off, one received an impression of great velocity although, even in flight, the cruising air-speed of the Maurice Farman was not more than 50 mph. The icy stream of air cut the cheeks and made one catch one's breath.

And so, apart from the short glide on the Shoulder of Mutton in 1911, Frank became air-borne for the first time. There may have been more thrilling episodes in his life but I doubt it. Here at last was the real thing. Today, flying has become so common that it is difficult to imagine a world in which all but a tiny minority had never had this experience, or to realise the effect of low flying-speeds on the pilot's job. For instance, when taking off, obstacles like trees or haystacks sometimes had to be negotiated by flying round them. Few now know how it feels to be in an open nacelle or cockpit. One was really in the air—like a bird.

At a height of 50–100 feet the air became somewhat bumpy. Frank noticed the quick movements of the dual control, which reproduced what was going on in front. 'The spectacles were mounted on the top of a stick with fore and aft movement, and they were rocked from side to side to give lateral control.' At a few hundred feet the impression of speed vanished. The wings seemed to become very still, as if frozen in space. Presently they came above a wood at the side of the aerodrome. It looked like a collection of those pieces of dyed loofah arranged around architectural models to represent trees. It was as if one could almost reach down and stroke them. At no time did either of us have the slightest vertigo—that sinking feeling at the pit of the stomach which we had always experienced on high buildings. Soon came the first bank—steeper than the feeling that most passengers know from modern airliners. It was an astonishing sensation to look straight down the sloping wing. Beyond the tip was a doll's land, with baby houses and gardens, toy trains and toy motor cars.

They circled round Portmeadow several times at a height of perhaps 1,000 feet. Victor Stammers then throttled down. The roar ceased and, instead, for the first time Frank became aware of that musical sound—seldom heard to-day—of the air singing through the cross-bracing wires as they glided down. Soon the trees and bushes came alongside. The speed appeared first to increase and then to lessen. The music ceased. Back came the control stick into Frank's groin. The tail went down. With a scarcely perceptible bump, wheels and tail-skid touched the ground together and he found himself trundling over the turf, now with the hangars before him.

We thanked Victor Stammers warmly and began to exchange excited comments on our experiences. Frank had to cut these short, however, in order to get back into Oxford where he was playing in a hockey match—a game he had not touched since his Düsseldorf days. I took the opportunity to write to Beryl.

R.F.C., Brasenose, 22 January, 1917

Hope you won't give it me in the neck for not writing sooner. Events seem to have moved faster this last week and we don't seem to get a minute to ourselves.

First: we've made our maiden flight. The Officer in charge of the College, with whom we get on rather well, took us up for about 10 minutes only. It is the most wonderful sensation and quite different from what I imagined it would be like. I always heard that the earth seemed to slide away from you but actually you get a tremendous sensation of lift, especially when you saw over the housetops. You get a sort of feeling of being lifted a few yards and then hovering perfectly still—this may have been owing to the rather strong wind and to the fact that the 'bus' we went up in was a very slow one. Banking is rather an *émotion*, as the French say; the ground seems absurdly close until you see some cows looking like pinheads. The whole thing is so novel and interesting and so much is going on at once that one hardly knows which way to turn. If you try and pick up a building in the town, the machine starts banking and your attention gets riveted by the action of the ailerons. I have an idea I shall enjoy flying.

Awfully glad you are frisking up a bit. I'm becoming far more serious minded I'm afraid, with the continuous strain of theoretical aeronautics, which I find more and more to my taste. I think aero-engines with a background of love would be an ideal combination; so … come up here to, your oldest, who loves you more than ever, Bob.

Meanwhile, Frank, within a short time of our arrival, had found himself elected captain of the R.F.C. 1st Eleven, a side which till then had never been beaten. The club secretary was an OTC cadet named D.A.J. Monro. Frank found him 'a splendid fellow'. The two of them, he wrote, 'ran the show'.

Frank welcomed a certain change in the atmosphere. It was 'delightful after Birmingham and A.S.C. "Sokker", where the language of team and spectators nearly withers up the grass.' What Frank called the 'Varsity element' seemed to influence the standards of play. He found it most satisfactory. Frank's side played seven matches and remained unbeaten. Even the Reading School, their most formidable opponent, was beaten 3-0 in the first match of the Reading–Oxford cup.

Early in February thick snow put an end to all hockey for the remainder of the course. This was followed by a spell of frost, when he turned to figure skating which, as we have seen, he enjoyed so intensely. But even then the sporting possibilities of the locality were not exhausted. On the second Saturday after our arrival we 'set off after lunch on Indian with Bob on carrier for Frilford Heath Golf Links. Played nine holes. Very sporting links' (7 January 1917). The experience was so delightful that most week-ends found us playing in friendly games or in matches for the R.F.C. on one of the neighbouring courses.

There was also fox-hunting to be exploited. On the recommendation of 2nd Lieut. Hanmer, I had been out once with the Heythrop on a hired horse. On our last Saturday before leaving Oxford we caught the 7.42 train (L&NWR) for Bicester and had breakfast at Harry Bonners's place, the King's Arms. 'Hired two hunters for the day and hacked to Aynho for meet. First run nearly an hour—did not kill but good sport. Returned about 4.15. Tea and train back' (24 February). This was the first time we had ridden cross country together. I soon found that Frank was a sound horseman, taking his fences with his customary self-confidence.

Sports and games, which were then almost an official part of most regimental life, seemed here to acquire a particularly carefree character. Could this be through our association with that most sporting service, the Royal Flying Corps? Reading the diaries and letters of the Flying Officers of that period, one notices the contrast between their cheerful tone and the grim nature of their work. Even after 'the shooting down of an opponent in the air passed from the nature of a sport to a matter of necessity and cold business,'[79] the chivalrous, sporting attitude persisted.

As we shall see, Frank's letters from the front five months later described these mortal combats as if they were some friendly contest involving skill and a good eye. 'Oh, the wind blows good out here,' commented our 'ace' Captain Ball, after a narrow escape from death; 'I had good sport and good luck, but only just.' The same spirit was to be found among many of the German pilots. There seemed to be a brotherhood of the air, a sense of sharing the same sport, though later, to be sure, it all became more impersonal.[80]

The social climate seemed even more cheerful than during the Boxmoor-Watford period. Concerts, formal and informal,

---

[79] From R.H. Kiernan, op.cit., p.31.

[80] Ibid., p.65 and p.81.

followed one after another, generally at the R.F.C. club. Once again our names appeared on a programme together. After each concert, and on many other occasions, we would drift round to a party in one of the instructors' rooms. These Frank recorded briefly in his diary, for instance: 'Musical evening in Aste's rooms. Plenty of "tawny and bubbly"—Capt. Stammers, 2 Lt. Denne, Capt. and Mrs Smith—good sport' (31 January 1917).

Such evenings could sometimes get out of hand. At the start of February, Frank had to write a rather grudging letter, defending himself against a misconduct charge:

Royal School of Instruction, Oxford.

With reference to the charge against me of, while being on guard a) Allowing prisoners under open arrest to enter the same room as prisoners under close arrest; b) Allowing alcoholic drinks to be consumed by the prisoners; I beg to report as follows:

On February 1st 1917 at about 7.00 p.m., I was informed by the Orderly Officer that I was to go on guard after Mess.

I may say that I had already guarded 2/Lt Parkinson the previous Saturday and accordingly went to his room at about 7.45 p.m. where I found 2/Lt. Parkinson and one of the old guard. Lt Lilly was also under close arrest—this I ascertained from the old guard. Two others of the new guard entered and one of them was relieved by Lieutenant Lightbourne, on account of pending exams. The others went out to await his turn for guard.

After about half an hour, Lieutenant Hawkins and ~~Lieutenant Lawson~~ entered. These I knew to be under open arrest but I did not know that they weren't allowed in the same room as prisoners under close arrest providing there was an escort present.

As regards b) I was not aware that stimulants in moderation were not allowed to prisoners under close arrest, in fact on the previous Saturday I allowed 2/Lt Parkinson to have a drink with his lunch and seeing no attempt to conceal a bottle of whisky and [soda] siphon on the mantelpiece I wrongly concluded that it was permitted. I ordered half a bottle of wine for myself and allowed others to do so as well. (Lieutenant Lightbourne did not take any.)

At this juncture 2/Lt. Daniel Seal came in and told me to take Lieutenant Lilly to get his kit, so I left the room with him.

I need scarcely add how very sorry I am and while realising now that I acted wrongly I must say I didn't think I was doing so at the time.

Capt. Smith, the chief instructor, in red tabs and smiling expansively, served directly under the commandant, Colonel 'Stuffy' Saunders. He seemed to have a large measure of control. His official position, however, did not prevent him from joining wholeheartedly in these parties. Both he and his wife ('Dinky' Smith) were small in stature. She was charming— intelligent and musical. She and Frank would play piano duets together, sharing our flippant under-estimation of J.S. Bach's 'precise and characteristic notes'. In her book *The Golden Reign* she tells how she once found herself listening to a fine pianist playing one of the Preludes and Fugues. She was in the company of her friend aircraftman Shaw (Lawrence of Arabia), then stationed at Mount Batten, Plymouth. Both of them were overcome by a fit of the giggles. This was rather characteristic of the times—those post-war years. At Oxford we were already on the threshold of the frivolous twenties, the decade of Bright Young Things and Fallen Angels, people being called by school-boy nicknames, generally ending in 'y' or 'ie'. Noel Coward set the pace during that period, but many of us were by then secretly licking our wounds and mourning.

In early February 1917 Frank was busy with preparations for a particularly ambitious concert, the first since the one at the Curragh in October. Once again he was 'back in his old jacket', looking around for talent to make up his programme and rehearsing some of the performers, including Victor Stammers in his duet. The day arrived. He 'settled five or six important affairs in town, spent the rest of the morning in assisting in decoration and arrangement of Hall. Mess 6.30. Evening concert 8.30. Dons and Co present. Very swagger affair. Good performance. Afterwards sat in Capt. Smith's room with Bob until 1.30' (9 February). (I have forgotten what Frank and I performed that evening and indeed everything about the concert except the background of exotic plants, what we now call Top Brass, and the fine emotional speaking voice of Esme Percy, then a cadet in some Highland Regiment. As an encore number he was invited by the C.O. to recite 'La Marseillaise' as he had remembered Sarah Bernhardt declaiming it.[81]

On arrival in Oxford we wasted no time in putting together some songs for which Frank had composed the music. A device, used by Offenbach and others, had been revived. It consisted in taking some classical theme and giving it an up-to-date twist (at that time the rag-time idiom was the thing) with the name of the classical composer introduced into the lyric. A popular example was 'Oh, Mr Rubinstein' (based on the hackneyed 'Melody in F'). Wishing to go one better, we had just finished a song called 'Rag Maninoff', using the first few bars of the 'Prelude in C Sharp Minor' and guying the whole genre.

'It's a daisy,
'Sends me crazy,
'Makes me go all goosey—well you'd
'Think that nothing could be so divine –
'It's fine –
'Stimulates the senses just like wine—
'Gee! Ain't it topping.'

In January 1917 we saw Douglas Furber in a musical show at the theatre. It must have been near the start of his career as a dramatic author. (He also played in a number of parts but retired from the stage after Chariot's Review in 1926 and concentrated on writing. He was to become the co-author of over 70 musical plays including many of Jack Buchanan's, Jack Hulbert's and Cicely Courtneidge's productions.) On this

---

[81] This impressive piece of acting was repeated in 1954 when Frank gave a lecture on the great tragediènne at the Birmingham Repertory Theatre.

occasion we liked the way he chatted informally with the audience from the stage. Something in his manner suggested that he might be able to help us. In my letter to Beryl of 22 January, I told her:

> There was rather a good show here during the last week called *Charivari*. It was a mixture of the Follies type of show and a revue, but very clever. Frank and self were rather taken with the songs and finding that the leading man, Douglas Furber,[82] had written some of the songs in *Samples*, *See-Saw* and other comedies, we sent our cards round. He was very genial and we were rather surprised to find that he's written the words to 'Oh! Mr Rubinstein!' We thereupon asked him round to Brasenose to hear 'Rag Maninoff'. He was very taken with it—he liked the whole idea, said it was quite professional and we ought most certainly to publish it. He warned us of certain difficulties we might have with Rachmaninoff's copyright but told us to stick to it for all we will work. He brought one of the other men in the company—Crawford (the cricketer)—round to tea a few days later and he quite agreed. Crawford is a tenor in his crush-lovely voice too. On Saturday I had Furber and his wife together with his friend and one of the ladies (the girl who did the Honolulu maid with Melville Gideon in *Samples*. Frank was well away, entre nous) in to lunch at the Randolph and we had a very merry time. I came to the conclusion that they are rather nice people and may come in useful as well.

Frank wrote our parents a similar letter about how we had taken the first steps in getting our songs published:

> At the show last week we were very taken with the standard of a travelling Folly Troup called *Charivari*, led by Douglas Furber who composed the lyrics of most of the songs. We sent our card round and were asked to see him after the show.
>
> This we did and soon got chatting, saying we had an original song which might be of use to him. He then broke in that he had only taken to writing funny lyrics recently and casually remarked that perhaps his biggest hit had been Oh! Mr Rubenstein, which he considered quite his worst technically.

---

[82] Furber worked on 'all' of Jack Buchanan's shows, according to R.D.B.

Wasn't that an extraordinary coincidence? We soon explained that ours was a modest emulation of this very song, tho' we had both forgotten to associate his name with it when sending our note round. (22 January)

We invited Furber and his co-composer George Ellis to tea next day, which happened to coincide with our first flight. We received them at Brasenose College, where we had found a piano. We tried over our song for them. Stimulated by the experience of flying, we felt that a brilliant theatrical future was somehow opening out: 'Both he and his composer pal were quite impressed by it, but before doing anything further with it we were recommended to find out whether the copyright of the original 'C Sharp Prelude' would be damaged in any way by the new version, as he himself had had to scrap a new song at the last minute on that account, viz 'Oh! Mr Offenbach!' We are waiting to hear from the publishers.'

Two days later they returned to give us a second audition. There was nothing amateurish about our song, they said. Another two days went by and they re-appeared in the afternoon. Frank and I then went on to the theatre for a second look at *Charivari*. After the show we were invited to supper at the Furbers' rooms. We became so interested in the professional world of song writing and publishing that we did not notice the time. The college was locked when we returned. Somewhat disconcerted we went round to the Clarendon and there booked a room.

On Saturday the production of *Charivari* at Oxford finished. That weekend Frank was at Reading playing the Middlesex cadets but I find from my diary that I arranged a farewell lunch for Douglas Furber and his wife and George Ellis. Some of Frank's piano compositions were privately printed after the war, but by then fashions in songs had changed, and so for that and other reasons the lead which Douglas Furber had given us was never followed up.

It must have been during our flying course at Oxford that we had our last glimpse of Bedalians. Returning to Brasenose from the hockey match after our first visit to Portmeadow, Frank was stopped in the street by a certain Madame Jarintzoff, 'always Mrs Jarry to her friends'. She had been at the centre of that côterie which had suggested the article on 'Harmogymnamics' in the *Bedales Chronicle*. According to Badley this lady possessed two typical Russian qualities: 'a child-like receptivity to all impressions, ideas, feelings and artistic impulses, and an equally childlike readiness of response, finding an outlet in a self-expression free from all self-consciousness'.

Mrs Jarry was running true to form when, following her invitation, we arrived at her rooms a week after this chance meeting. Petite, dark, pale complexioned, with high cheek bones and a finely shaped rather prominent nose, she emanated charm and femininity. A faint perfume filled the room. Her husband, a retired Russian Admiral, had recently died. Her only son Demitri ('Jarry') was an old Bedalian. He had gained a postmastership (a prize for academic excellence) at Merton College, Oxford, had taken a degree, and had then joined the Brunner Mond Company as a research chemist. Enlisting in 1914 he had become an infantry captain, after being awarded the M.C. in Gallipoli and being wounded in France. On the day of our visit he was at Oxford on leave and taking tea with his mother.

That morning Frank had been 'half perished with cold in the Rigging Sheds' and had 'got the shivers'. He had been sitting over the fire all the afternoon with an overcoat on. Later, he 'managed with tea, fire, and music to warm up'. It was difficult to do otherwise in that uninhibited Russian atmosphere, although Jarry, as I remember, had acquired a certain *phlegm brittanique* and appeared to be somewhat reserved. It was as if he were wondering what his mother would say or do next. His mood was not lightened by the music which followed tea. Asked to play and sing, we tried 'The Island in the Year', with its crude verses and lush Elgarian harmonies. Neither appealed to him. A choir exhibitioner, he would have preferred something more distinguished, Elizabethan madrigals perhaps, or folk songs as sung by Pauley Montague.

307

The time came to leave. That day we had moved from Brasenose to Queen's College. Frank had had a light supper with rum and hot milk and then 'got to bed in new room after the day's chaos of shifting. Fortunately the faithful Hullah[83] was good in getting new room warm, etc.' Wherever he went, Frank had a knack for getting the best out of batmen, college servants, railway porters, and others. They liked him. At mess the following evening he seemed to be on very good terms with one of the college servants who was waiting on us (probably 'the faithful Hullah' again). 'You see him,' Frank said, as the waiter turned his back, 'He's one of our agents!'

While Frank was sleeping off his chill, Jarry kindly led me round to Lincoln College. His reserve vanished over a glass of port with a friend, Mr Sidgewick. Jarry was short and thick-set. He had a full oval face, small mouth and his mother's nose. He also 'had all his mother's vigour and many-sided ability. Both at school and at Oxford he showed the utmost promise'. He was about three years older than Frank, and had a much better brain than either of us. In the school hierarchy he was far above us. That evening and the following afternoon, when we were once again invited to his mother's rooms for tea and music, my heart warmed to him. The difference in age seemed to disappear. He was killed in France on October 8th of that year.

On February 14 we met Oswald Horsley for a few minutes. He was one of the Three Graces [see page 181] who in 1910 had grouped themselves round the Atwood machine in the Physics Lab. A captain in the Gordon Highlanders, he had been wounded three times, mentioned in despatches, and awarded the Military Cross. He and Vyv Trubshawe had together decided to transfer to the R.F.C. when they had met in France. We ran into each other in a restaurant. He was leaving as we were coming in. We felt cheered at the sight of that bulky figure

---

[83] Mr H.J. Smith, the College Steward, writes: 'The Scout in question must have been Charles Keeler. I remember him as a slightly built man with a bald head and white mutton-chop whiskers.' (Letter to the author, 28 October 1963.)

and bland expanse of face, cut in two by a wide genial slit of a mouth. His jocular allusions to significant school phrases were generally made with deliberation in a rich bass voice, as if he were choosing his words carefully.

A week before we were to leave Oxford, Mother and Beryl arrived singly on a Friday afternoon (16 February). There were three more working days to go before the examinations and we were being urged to give as much time as possible to revision, so next morning we resisted any temptation to entertain our guests. Instead, we applied ourselves to brushing up our Gnome, Le Rhone, and Clerget engines, memorising such matters as the design of thrust blocks, arrangements for lubrication, carburation, and valve timing. After lunch, the hockey ground being under water, Frank retired to the drawing room for a siesta while I conducted Mother and Beryl to Queen's College. Refreshed by his rest, Frank joined us later for a walk through Magdalen and then 'fooled about with thawing ice pack'. Tea at Brasenose was followed by a memorable display of fortune telling tricks. 'Baby' Denne somehow conveyed cards up the chimney. Later, when they re-appeared, rather sooty, he studied their order carefully and seemed to find significance in this. The Queen of Spades, called 'Mossy Face', played an important part. He was at his best, putting up with a lot of amiable leg-pulling. Beryl giggled and Mother seemed much diverted.

Denne had fair hair and bottle green eyes. He was a young man of great charm, with a quiet disarming manner as if he were continually expecting to be ragged. He was a friend of Victor Stammers. During the previous year the two of them had met at Northolt, where the instructional procedure seems to have been free from red-tape or style-cramping formalities. Although he had not then got his wings he was a superb pilot and had taken Stammers up for a flap or two in a Maurice Farman. Stammers had then, almost immediately, done his first solo, and in due course had been awarded his wings.

Later that afternoon (Saturday, 17 February) Father arrived unexpectedly and asked whether we would like to invite a friend for dinner. It all reminded us of one of his visits to Bedales. We brought along Lieut. Darrel Seal, the adjutant. During the previous week there had been a gigantic rag in his rooms 'with chaps about to be posted after exams'. This had been followed by a 'snowball fight and much merrymaking'. The next day he had gone away on leave and Frank had served as acting-adjutant in his place. He had not found the duties easy. A round dozen or so of officers were usually under close arrest and awaiting courts martial for various misdemeanours. It fell to Frank to 'arrange new escorts—some bother' he wrote. 'After much running about had a refresher in Capt. Smith's room.'

At the dinner, arranged by Father, the conversation took an unfortunate turn. Talking of flying hazards, I must have mentioned my tendency to faint at the sight of blood. Darrel Seal tried to reassure us. He said that only occasionally had he seen what he called 'raspberry jam', and that only as a result of serious crashes. After dinner, poor Mother had to retire with a bad headache, but 'the rest of the party spent the evening at Hubbard's soirée, Christ Church—music, dancing, etc.' (17 February)

The following day (Sunday) Frank and I 'showed the party round the instruction rooms at the Museum', including the model map of the Ypres Salient with its kite balloons and multitude of flash lamp bulbs. 'R.H.B. very taken with it all and left by 6 p.m. train. Capt. and Mrs Smith in for dinner. Music in their rooms after. To bed earlier.' (18 February)

Although Mother and Beryl stayed on at the Randolph we felt impelled to do some more intensive revision on Monday. The examinations were now only two days ahead. According to Frank's diary 'Engines' must have merited the closest study, and judging by the complicated nature of our notes and drawings, I can understand why.

With a clear conscience, however, we returned to the Randolph for lunch, to be followed by what Frank called another 'great afternoon at the aerodrome'. 'Took M and Beryl down to witness the Best Brothers' first effort at dual control with Capt. Stammers.' (19 February)

'We returned to the Randolph for lunch, to be followed by what Frank called another "great afternoon at the aerodrome" … 'Took M and Beryl down to witness the Best Brothers' first effort at dual control with Capt. Stammers.' Seen here: in the rigging sheds, with Frank in front, the author behind.

311

Oxygenated, and all aglow from the icy air stream, we sat down later to a highly conversational tea at The George. We were *illuminés*. In turn, Frank and I would try to put into words the thrilling impressions we had been receiving. An hour or two later we were once again together, a party of six, for Victor Stammers and Baby Denne had joined us. Now, the talk at dinner was wholly enjoyable. There were no ill-judged allusions to flying casualties. Mother joined in the fun eagerly. As after a cricket match, when each stroke and wicket is discussed, so the events of that exceptional weekend came under review, with digressions about music and dancing. Beryl, looking radiant, turned first to one man and then another, chattering away with her engaging slight Scotch accent and entertaining us with theatrical and sporting gossip. We had bought seats for the theatre that night. I can remember nothing about the piece (called Toto), but Frank recorded that it was 'a jolly good show'. The curtain came down, but the evening was not yet over. Back we all went to Brasenose College for more High Jinks, Baby Denne entertaining us once again with the vagaries of Mossy Face.

Mother and Beryl left next day after a farewell lunch at the Randolph. This was the last time we were all four to be together. We spent the rest of the day looking over our notes, covering seven weeks work, in readiness for the examinations the following day. These started at 9 a.m. in the Corn Exchange and continued for two-and-a-half days. We were 'both pretty tired afterwards, having finished at 6 p.m.' As on other occasions, we took refuge in the hospitable rooms of Capt. Smith 'for relaxation'.

Next morning (Thursday) we were back at the Corn Exchange, committing to paper what we knew of rigging, general flying, stationary engines and instruments. We now felt the worst was over. We relaxed in the Queen's College ante-room where a Rag was in progress and then went on to the theatre. That evening we were delighted with the imaginative acting of that distinguished actress Christine Silver. She was a friend of Sylvia Mundy's. Her brother, Arthur Silver, was an infantry captain (Leicesters) in the 59th Division and had met us in Ireland. The piece, Door Steps, was a one-act sketch. A street arab collapses outside an author's house. He takes her in, gives her soup, and is entertained by her Cockney speech. She proves to be an actress to whom he had refused a part, thinking she was too refined.

We were to see Christine Silver next day for tea. By then the examinations, which we had taken so seriously, were behind us, having wound up with a Morse sending-test at the Museum.

Then came Saturday (24 February), our day with the Bicester Hunt and our last at Oxford. That evening we played in a farewell concert at the R.F.C. Club. 'To wind up we went on to Hubbard's rooms.' The same evening we learnt that we had been posted to Thetford in Norfolk. Few of those taking the course had failed, such was the great need for flying officers at that time.

Next day was packed with activity:

Sunday, 25 February: Breakfast 9 a.m. (about). Rushed round afterwards, learning of 9.30 parade. In charge of THETFORD party. Bob, Wheatly, Sutherland, Brian and Leishman. Just caught 12.43 for town after big scramble, much luggage and Indian. Rode across town with Bob, luggage being in four-wheelers. Missed Col. K.—phoned Thetford Adjt.—got rooms at hotel. Had tea with Shorts and proceeded thence to Wimbledon. Met Smith family and Joy.

Monday 26 February: Breakfast 5 a.m. Got luggage and bikes out for 6 a.m. train. Arrived Thetford 9.26.

The Orderly Room to which we reported in Thetford was one of a number of huts at the side of a large field. Opposite was a narrow strip of trees, and around us flat and open country, much of it ploughed and not suitable for forced landings. As we surveyed the scene we were once again reminded of Wells's scientific fiction. To us, then, it all seemed rather fantastic. The air was loud with the noise of Renault engines. Our nostrils were filled with the tang of pine woods in the sharp Norfolk air, and another smell—still evocative: that of burning oil.

The Maurice Farman Shorthorns were continually taking off and landing. A round dozen of them were circling in the air, one or two flying rather low over the wood facing us, while another, recently crashed, was being towed away for repairs. We found that we had been posted to A Flight of No12 Reserve Squadron under Major MW Noel. After lunch one of the instructors took us up for ten minutes dual control. We then made our way to a hut for an introductory lecture by the Adjutant, Lieut Adams.

Later in the afternoon we returned to our billet, there entering surroundings which contrasted strangely, not only with the exciting spectacles and experiences we had just left at the aerodrome, but with the gay social life at Oxford. In short, we found ourselves participating in the gentle and leisurely life of a small-town vicarage (St. Cuthberts). The address was 1 Norwich Road. The Rev. Sweeting and his wife were a kindly couple, sharing their rations with us—food was by then not plentiful—until our own came through. Living with them was a married sister, 'portly withal' as Frank put it. Both the ladies played the piano and could read at sight. Before long Frank was delighting us all with his compositions, and enjoying their fine grand piano. It was during our five weeks at Thetford that he composed a charming version of I Will Give You the Keys of Heaven with syncopated decorations that continued the idiom of Oh! Mister Rubinstein and Rag Maninoff.

The day after our arrival in Thetford, I wrote to Beryl:

R.F.C., Thetford, Norfolk, 27 Feb 1917

Got here all right and am distinctly charmed with the place. Imagine a low sort of flat hill from the top of which you get a view of sweeping, open and brush-covered country, with occasional pine woods and a few cottages now and then. In the middle of this lonely heath you get hangar after hangar, machines dotted about all over the ground and the air, and 'Huns' in leather coats and boots strolling in a very leisurely way from one shed to another or standing about a little groups.

The air comes sweeping across Norfolk and makes you feel

314

hungry and fit. We each had an hour's flying this morning and practised a lot of landings. Even now, the whole thing seems absurdly natural and our Flight Commander is fairly satisfied with us so far.

We are billetted in Thetford which is about two-and-a-half miles from the aerodrome. The billet is good—we are with the Padre and they are making us very comfy.

I hear we get four days' leave when we pass out, so be ready to come to Brum in three weeks' to a month's time. Good time on Sunday night on the sofa, what?

Lots of love from your prize him, Bob

Our life with the Sweetings followed a regular pattern. On most evenings we either made music or 'assisted with the family jigsaw puzzle representing, say, an Eskimo village'. Being all of drab greys and green it constituted an advanced level of jigsawmanship. The family were sophisticated in this field, and sucking boiled sweets contributed to the soothing atmosphere. 'Please send us a large tin of bulls-eyes if you can purchase same,' Frank wrote home; 'we live on them at the billet and they can get no more for us.' (14 March)

The vicarage was about a mile-and-a-half from the aerodrome which lay near the road to Euston. Each day we would walk to and fro or use our motor cycles if petrol allowed. We took most of our meals in the mess. In the ante-room one would often find a group of officers and cadets round the piano listening to Frank playing his compositions, or joining in song after song from the musical comedies.

The instructors looked upon themselves as a privileged elite. They referred to us pupils as 'Huns'. This class structure found expression in the allocation of margarine, the limited quantity of rationed butter being reserved for the 'master race'. Since we all paid the same messing accounts this did not seem fair to many of us, so Frank set about reorganising the distribution on more equitable lines. He had a way of throwing his weight about with such charm that the authorities took it all in good part.

315

With all its faults the mess was better than none at all. One 'beautiful early morning we walked up to the mess, wondering why no machines were visible, to find the whole mess and ante-room in charred bits, also Vigo, the Big Dane dog who had accompanied us when walking burned to death with the fire. Breakfast at The Bell.' (22 March)

Frank's diary contains a day-to-day account of our progress. We had our disappointments: 'Good day for flying. Bob unfortun-ately broke skid and rendered our machine hors-de-combat. Revised for machine-gun exam. Spent evening with jigsaw puzzle at billet. Finished reading *The Aeroplane Speaks*.' (13 March)

We have seen how the Wright Brothers 'firmly eschewed all ideas of inherent stability' and how 'their aeroplanes could only be kept flying by the pilot's skill'. The Wright Brothers believed that an aeroplane should be flown, not just steered like a ship. No doubt it was with this doctrine in mind that the War Office had adopted the Maurice Farman Shorthorn as the standard instructional machine for elementary flying. I suppose they were relatively cheap to produce and before the war had had a record of noteworthy achievements in competitions and races. Victor Stammers was only one of many who found that they flew well. But they were inherently unstable. If put into a steep dive an inexperienced pilot might find difficulty in levelling up again. Before we had been at the station a week there was a fatal crash.[84] On that day (1 March) flying was suspended until the evening when Frank went up for 45 minutes, dual control, circling the aerodrome 10 times at a height of 500 feet and practising landings.

Crashes were common. On some days the aerodrome was littered with wrecks. One Rumpetty would land on top of another while the squadron commander tore his hair at such

---

[84] The name of the victim was Perraton. I remember walking with Frank 'round outskirts of aerodrome' four days later to the scene of the accident. A hole in the ground was still visible. Some said it was made by the poor fellow's large padded crash helmet which all pupils were obliged to wear.

displays of ineptitude. Frank hastened to pass on his impressions to our parents:

> It is surprising what a big number of struts, spars, and undercarriage are broken every day without so much as a scratch to the pilot. The undercarriages are very frail really and the least bump sideways on landing usually 'does the trick'. (16 March)

Because of the somewhat unstable design of the Rumpetty it was risky for inexperienced pilots to use them unless the weather was relatively calm and visibility good. There was generally less wind in the early hours; we were therefore often called at four o'clock in the morning. An orderly would go round to the billets knocking us up without, we hoped, disturbing our hosts. When conditions did not permit flying during the morning or afternoon we were marched off to the fitting-sheds for machine-gun instruction, or sent to the top of a tower for practice in bomb sighting.

In order to pass out from the Elementary Flying Course we were required to do five hours' solo. This was preceded by four or more hours of dual control, according to the pupil's natural aptitude. Frank was given 4½ hours' instruction before taking his first solo. Eager to get this first stage behind him he wrote home:

> We are both getting a trifle fed up with the weather, as we have been waiting practically 10 days for a suitable opportunity to begin our first solos. It is a bit 'thick' that such a spell of persistent wind should prevail just when we least wanted it. Had we done a bit of solo before it began, we should have been away long ago. Those who have had a few hours to their credit are sufficiently experienced to carry on, while it is too risky for beginners to make their first attempt. (16 March)

During this period of dual control we never climbed to more than a few hundred feet. It was 'not until the end of 1917 that suitable telephones were devised to make conversation between pupil and instructor natural and easy'. Up to that time instructions were shouted, or indicated by simple hand signals, sometimes accompanied by a clout over the head if a pupil's clumsiness became dangerous. As long as he could take the machine off the ground and land without crashing, it was hoped that he would not make too many mistakes in the air.

In every respect our instructor showed himself to be over-optimistic. Unknown to us, he would be continually correcting our mistakes, giving us the impression that we were making splendid progress and were fully capable of going up alone. His teaching methods were perhaps influenced by some alarming flying experiences of his own some time prior to his taking up teaching. He may therefore be forgiven if, when he took us up, he had insufficient confidence in our skill to leave us really free to fly the machine ourselves.

Fortunately he went on weekend leave after giving us about seven lessons. On that Saturday we tried to persuade his colleague to allow us to show what we could do. He decided, however, to take us once round the circuit to find out whether we were actually as far advanced as we had imagined. Once in the air he gave us 'free control for the first time' (17 March). The result was most alarming. I still retain a vivid mental picture of Frank's switch-back progress above the pine trees on the far side of the aerodrome. At one moment the nose of the nacelle would be reaching for the clouds. At the next, up would go the tail as the machine began diving for the tree tops. My own performance was equally disastrous.

We left the station after lunch wiser, but certainly not sadder, men for we had made an important discovery. It was this. Supposing the nose was bumped up by a gust of wind, then one would instinctively try to correct matters by pushing forward the 'joy-stick'. It was unwise, however, to keep the stick in this position once the machine was flying level. The secret was to bring the stick back to neutral as soon as the fault had been corrected. Obviously the same principle applied to the lateral control and manipulation of The Spectacles.

All this we discussed together while playing golf that same afternoon. We came to the conclusion that flying felt as if one were driving a motor car with a steering column of thick flexible

318

india-rubber. From that point on our kinaesthetic imagination did the trick. Frank had no more serious difficulties in flying—except one, as we shall soon see.

While Frank was writing to our parents, I was writing to Beryl.

R.F.C., Thetford, Norfolk, 16 March 1917

The weather has been concentrated bump and they have put a minimum limit of four hours' dual before you can go on solo. The last decent date was Tuesday when I unfortunately smashed one of the undercarriage skids, but put another in with the help of a few A.M.s [air mechanics]. I smashed it with a dud landing but I know exactly what I did wrong and I don't think I shall make the same mistake again. I was up about 20 minutes yesterday with the Major and he said my flying was O.K. I was up over an hour the day before and made at least 11 decent landings. I've done over four hours dual now and so I'm still awaiting a fine day. Ours is by far the most contrary [??] flight in the two squadrons, you will be glad to hear, although it is rather sickening to see men in the other flights getting in front of you. Yesterday there were six crashes on the aerodrome which is a record. None were in our squadron and no one was killed—only one chap was hurt and he came an awful 'stinker' so that his machine was a heap of ruins; other machines collected round in a circle and kept flopping down like great beetles. One chap landed on top of another and then the fun became fast and furious. One after another sort of bounced up and pecked on to a wing until it became almost amusing, especially as none of them were our machines and the other squadron had been boasting of the number of pilots they turned out. This morning the engine of Ferguson's machine 'petered' out over the river as he was taking off so he had to 'pancake' on the water. The bus turned over and he and his passenger got a ducking but were not hurt.

So you see, though things are going slowly they are far from dull. I don't suppose we shall be through for another week now.

I miss you as much as you do me and I daresay more, that we will make up for it, my darling when I get my next leave. Have you read *The Harvester* by Gene Stratton-Porter because if you haven't, don't—it's the worst book I've ever read. All my love, yours to a camber rib, Bob.

Frank continued to record our joint progress in his diary: 'Up early for flying—beautiful solo morning wasted on account of doctor's absence through illness. [Pilots were examined by a doctor before making their first solo.] Windy during afternoon, but it turned out a lovely evening with a perfect calm. Made first solo flight of two rounds—10 minutes. Naturally bucked. Dinner at The Bell—invited Padre and family with Bob and myself, a new experience for Padre. Evening voted a big success.' (24 March)

We were required to keep our Pilot's Flying Log Book posted throughout our term of service. From Frank's, it appears that on this day he had been taken up for 20 minutes' dual control at 5.40 p.m. before doing his first solo at 6.00, reaching 800 feet, and making two landings.

That day I had a mishap with my machine, which was smashed into by another man, so my first solo did not take place for another three days. In the meantime, Frank had been grounded through mist, hail, and wind. This, however, did not prevent us from enjoying several rounds of golf together.

As pupils were granted leave when they had completed their Elementary Flying we set about organising our activities so that we could go off together. Frank was not able to take the air until five days after his first solo. Flying was stopped at noon that day when we had both a total of about two hours to our credit. He had climbed to a height of 2,600 feet, practising figures of eight, and venturing a few miles from the aerodrome to explore the countryside. He felt a thrill of independence and freedom, mingled with astonishment, as he recognised one after another of the landmarks and objects he had seen at ground level. 'Good Lord, is that what it's like?', he said to himself. Clustered round the town were irregular patches of dark green, just as on his ordnance map. These were the woods and coppices. Further afield were the fens, showing up as hundreds of oblongs and quadrilaterals. Cutting across them in a ten mile straight line he could just see the Great Eastern Railway, punctuated occasionally by thin trailing wisps of white from the passing trains, the line curving about as it approached the town and followed the winding Little Ouse and River Thet. Disappearing in a north-easterly direction the main road to Norwich was unmistakable. At the town end he even thought he could see the vicarage. The church spires and towers were not readily spotted, but he found that he could recognise them by the shadows cast on the ground. Then, suddenly, he noticed a number of queer looking sand coloured blobs interspersed with small patches of vivid green. He realised, with a start, that these marked the golf links where we had recently been playing. It was all so much like a large map that he wanted, there and then, to try a longer cross-country flight, and was confident that he would be able to find his way.

On the following day there was no early flying. We got off at noon and after early lunch played three ball with the Padre. We both got 'sat on' by the Padre's excellent short play.' (29 March)

That night we had, as it seemed, no sooner dropped off to sleep than we were made aware of 'a big wind at 4.00 a.m. so retired to bed again'. We were, however, 'surprised to be sent for at 5.00'. We dressed hurriedly, made our way to the aerodrome, and took the air.

About three hours later we were still sailing round and round the aerodrome at about 1,000 feet. We had been keeping an eye on each other, and on our watches, so as to finish at the same time. Frank had already been up twice that morning—once at 5.50 and again at 6.50. On the second occasion he had reached a height of 5,000 feet. He went up again at 8.10. His and mine were then the only machines off the ground as the weather had now become bumpy. I was not unduly alarmed, however, when, after a quarter of an hour, I searched the skies for him in vain. He had probably decided to stay down on account of the weather. I would do the same. Shortly after touching down an air mechanic came out to meet me and said, 'I'm sorry to say your brother s crashed, Sir,' and then after a pause, 'but I don't think he's hurt.' I taxied back to the tarmac, climbed down from the nacelle, and there he was, imperturbable as usual. The only sign of an accident was some blades of grass on his shoulder strap. In explaining to me what had happened he seemed somewhat puzzled. He said he had 'been caught in a downward current of air, and was expecting, any moment to be bumped up again!' The account in his diary is somewhat different:

> Did two hours' solo before brekker. Very bumpy to end up with. Without knowing it, descended 1,000 feet. Got caught by gust after flattening out and completely smashed machine in consequence (*see photograph opposite*). Made mistake of not shutting off engine. Did not get a single scratch, however. Instrument board and front of nacelle untouched, otherwise not a single wire or strut untouched. Some Crash![85] Got off morning on strength of it and played golf with Bob.' (30 March)

A letter to Beryl tells of my own experiences in this regard.

R.F.C., Thetford, Norfolk, 29 Mar 1917

I did my first solo last night by dint of much imploring and did one circuit of the aerodrome and a good landing. This morning we arose betimes (4.00 a.m.), walked up to the aerodrome and started to explore that world of air which we have been waiting to explore for so long. I climbed up to 5,000 ft (which is the highest I've been so far) by making large circles and then set off to have a look at the surrounding country. I've never seen anything more wonderful in all my life. The sun rising on one side and on the other, mists and darkness. Not a breath of wind in the air and the old bus sailing along smoothly and sedately. The whole toy country was most awfully interesting, especially the golf links with the fairway is laid out like a plan. I was up for one hour 15 minutes at a stretch and came down in big 'S' turns full of joy and appetite for brekker. After that the wind got up as usual and it became very bumpy. I went up for another 55 minutes and got my eye in as regards bumps. I had the experience of running into cloud but I took care to come out of it again jolly quickly!

---

[85] Some years after the war my next-door neighbour in the 'Gents' of a London restaurant addressed me by name and said: 'I'll never forget your brother at Thetford that day he crashed. His instructor knew nothing about it and asked him how he had got on. "Oh, I did quite all right in the air, Sir," he replied, "but I made rather a careless landing—however, I think the engine is still intact."'

The Major is quite satisfied with us and wants to push us through before the end of the week. It is quite possible we might get through by tomorrow in which case I would wire you the train I would meet you at. There is also just a possibility that as Mother is going to stay at Auntie Maralla's, she might like us to spend our leave in town, in which case I should come to Ardmore *avec ta permission*. The whole thing depends on the weather and is rather vague. I've finished *Happy Go Lucky* and *Pip* [both by Ian Hay]—the former is extraordinarily funny and doubled me up. The golfing bits in Pip remind me rather of certain doings on Handsworth golf links. [Hay] has quite ousted Locke, Wells and Bennett in my affections.

I am frightfully sleepy and can scarcely write coherent stuff to you, my love. I'm simply dying to see you again and we'll have a horrible orgy of love. I often dream of you but you're never in anyone else's arms except my own. I've been playing a good game of golf lately.

Heaps of love,
Thine only,
Bob

Next day, Saturday, the weather was calm. We sat out our time (70 minutes) together before breakfast, then managed to get away by 9.51. We met Beryl at Euston and 'travelled à trois. Slept most of the journey. Quiet evening and music at home.'

Sunday afternoon found the three of us ploughing round Handsworth Golf Links in a leisurely manner, after Frank and I had accompanied Father to Nelson Street Adult School in the morning. What was it about golf with Beryl that aroused memories of discomfort? Of course—Cassiobridge and the West Herts Club! That barber's rash. Those bouts of shivers alternating with hot spells. That childish complaint, German Measles. Now, however, it was I who felt healthy and ardent in the company of my fiancée and poor Beryl who was not herself. After twelve holes the game was abandoned. Once home she was put to bed.

Next day she was no better. History had repeated itself. Beryl had measles.

To be sure this was no reason why Frank should not carry out his usual leave-time programme: 'Spent the morning in town, shopping vigorously—dentist—haircut—tea at Wedgewood Lounge.' In the evening we dined with our uncle Sydney Short, now a Major in the R.A.M.C., at the Queen's Hotel. There we were joined by Captain Sydney Smith and his wife, Clare, recently transferred from Oxford to Castle Bromwich just outside Birmingham. We were delighted to meet this amiable couple once more. Our uncle quickly took to them. He was, Frank noted, 'in great form'. So engrossing was the conversation that the Smiths missed their last train back to Castle Bromwich and had to order a taxi, but before leaving they invited Frank and myself to visit them next day.

We wondered whether contact with measles might not be exploited for an extension of leave. Accordingly I phoned Thetford to make preliminary enquiries. Later, we 'both took tram to Washwood Heath and walked to the aerodrome (C.B.). Tea and dinner with Capt. and Mrs Smith after fixing things up with the C.O. 28th Squadron. Heavy snow, so trained back. Late wire to return to Thetford immediately.' (3 April)

Were we pulling strings so that, through the influence of Captain Smith, we would be posted to Castle Bromwich for our advanced flying, thereby remaining together and near home? If so, we were soon to be disappointed, as Frank recorded:

324

Wednesday, April 4th. Got kit packed for 8 a.m. brekker. Caught 8.40 to Euston. Arrived Thetford 3.30. Bob posted to Sedgeford [near Hunstanton, Norfolk] and self to Dover. Supper at billet and packed kit. Paid mess bills, etc.

The corresponding entry in my own diary was: 'Hear that we are to be separated.'

On the following day my train left an hour or two after Frank's. While I was hanging about the billet Mrs Sweeting looked at me appraisingly. 'You're going to miss him,' she said. And so I did, as my diary confirms: 'Goodbye to F.B.B.—Blank depression.'

It was in the train that I felt the first real premonition. As I looked out of the carriage window, the landscape swam before my eyes. I felt homesick—as if I were going back to school.

Presumably, our Squadron Commander, Major Noel, was the wise and understanding officer who had decided to send us to different squadrons. During our five weeks together at Thetford the close bond between us had not gone unnoticed. We had been teased about our habit of announcing joint decisions. 'WE' propose to do this or that—'OUR' machine—'WE' are going away together at a certain time, and so forth. Someone might also have observed our contrasting natures—Frank's dash and optimism, my tendency to caution and reflection. He was to train for Scouts, the single-seater fighters of the First War, whereas I was destined for Heavies, the two-seater aeroplanes used for bombing and artillery observation.

I can now see that the risks we had been running were not only physical but psychological. If one of us had been severely injured or killed at Thetford it would have been, as it were, under the eyes of the other. To part from each other was therefore relatively merciful.

While the tortoise-like Great Eastern trundled gloomily North, with me on board, Frank was threading his way through the London traffic on his motorcycle followed by a four-wheeler loaded with his luggage. 'Victoria Station was something like a mild burlesque of itself in peacetime,' he observed. 'By dint of wangling the slightly livery guard, I got my machine, with tank half full of petrol, and luggage safely lodged in the van.' (5 April)

At Dover Frank found the atmosphere suggested overseas conditions. He had 'to get various passes etc. to be allowed in the area at all.' He phoned for a tender to take his luggage and followed behind on his Indian. The sense of mechanical power filled him with pleasure, 'for the road climbs abruptly and winds its way inland up the cliff for a good mile'.

The aerodrome was situated north-east of Dover, towards St. Margaret's Bay, close to the cliffs, on the far side of 'a sort of valley amid numerous military huts and barracks'. It was 'quite flat on top for some distance inland'. Nearby was the Naval Aerodrome. Below lay the harbour with part of the fleet at anchor. The cliff edge was 'lined with big guns at intervals, searchlights, anti-aircraft guns and wireless stations'. On the opposite side of the valley towered up earth walls surmounted by the big fort. In fact, the coast 'bristled with concealed possibilities in case of emergency!' (8 April)

All around, exciting events were following one after another so that, as it seemed, unless alert he might find with regret that he had missed some memorable spectacle. It was rather like the three-ringed circus we had seen as children. As usual Frank's reporting and sketches were lively.

> Yesterday I was sitting on the cliff and saw a Hydroplane alight rather heavily in the harbour. It appeared to be listing and the engine was shut off. Then I saw the pilot climb on to the top plane and a motor-boat making for it at a good speed, across from the far side of the harbour. It drew alongside. A rope was thrown to the pilot, now on one of the floats, who secured it to the boat and then got taken on board. Meanwhile the one side had been sinking rapidly (probably due to a broken float) and by the time the towing began, the Hydroplane was already in position. There was a good wind blowing and whether it was eventually towed to safety I do not know, but it soon disappeared from sight completely, with the motor-boat still tugging it below the surface. (9 April)

As Frank walked across the springy turf, he was reminded of Bleriot's landing on the Castle Cliff nine years earlier and the thrill with which we had received the news while at Bedales. Dover: it was an important name amongst flying people. It was from Dover that the first R.F.C. pilot had ever flown to France during war time. This was Lieut. H.D. Harvey-Kelly who was killed while commanding No. 19 Squadron some months before Frank joined it; and whether or not he remembered it Dover had been the first target in this country to be bombed from the air.

All round him the proximity of the enemy and the possibility of attack made itself felt. One night he 'got up at 12.15 to look at bombardment from bedroom window' (20 April). This was an attempted raid on Dover by five German destroyers. The *Times* of 23 April reported that 'At least two of them, and probably three, were sunk in a fight lasting five minutes. They were tackled by two vessels of the Dover patrol.' On another evening 'the French coast was clearly visible' (8 April). Frank realised that he was one stage further towards the goal he was straining to reach.

Frank remained at Dover for exactly four weeks. During this time one of his brother officers was killed and another seriously injured in a bad crash.[86] He himself encountered nothing worse than a gentle somersault after landing, a broken wing tip, a snapped centre section wire, and a damaged landing wire fitting. In spite of this mishap, he seems to have been fully occupied with the training. In his diary one seldom finds the normal references to music. He played a few holes of golf at St. Margaret's and from time to time would walk down to Dover with his friends for a cinema show or a game of billiards followed, perhaps, by 'a little chicken and ham and ginger ale'. (24 April)

Posted to No.49 Squadron, Frank found his Flight Commander, Capt. Adams, was 'a splendid chap, not too young or stunty, but an excellent pilot and coach'. (8 April) Not all showed this restraint:

---

[86] 'Barnes killed, machine burnt to the ground' (24 April). 'Poor old Heath had bad crash on Avro; taken to hospital' (1 May).

One instructor goes in for stunting in a manner that would not appeal to me in the least. From the aerodrome he comes into view from apparently somewhere out of the ground, then travels down-wind with a ground speed of about 120 miles an hour, some fifteen feet above the aerodrome, finally zooming into the air and turning at the far end. In approaching the hangars from the valley he goes right down below the ground level then climbs up the other side. (14 April)

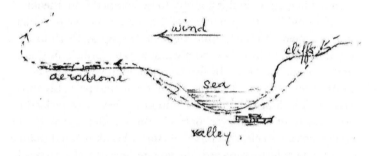

At first the weather was such that only experienced pilots could fly. 'For the time being the wind is going at 40 miles an hour. There are one or two "bird men" in the camp who go up and hover (air speed required to support machine being less than the wind velocity) over the same spot for as long as they feel inclined—gently rising or falling to break the monotony.' (14 April)

The stiff sea-breezes came shooting skywards over the cliff-tops to form turbulent eddy currents on the landward side. 'They say that if you have flown at Dover, you can generally fly anywhere,' (8 April), Frank wrote, adding that he had not experienced any bad bumps so far. For fear of engine failure, the pupil-pilots were not supposed to fly over the sea, where the air was generally smoother.

The day after Frank's arrival (Good Friday, 6 April) was 'a drencher' but on the Saturday he 'was taken up for the first two flights in a B.E.2c—quite a sensation, with the engine in front. Evening flight with McQuiston, who put the wind up me with some steep banks, suddenly.'

Easter Sunday showed a marked change, with 'scarcely a cloud overhead, just a sharp breeze off the sea, the first bit of respectable weather since Christmas'. Summer-time was introduced for the second time that year. Frank 'began to learn taking the machine off and practised landings'. They got into clouds but he was 'allowed full control'. During the next three days the weather was boisterous, 'with hail, heavy snow and lightning simultaneously'; but then the conditions changed and he was able to complete his course with only two more days of interruption.

The B.E. bi-planes,[87] 'born in one of the most stirring years of pre-War aviation, 1912, and the first British military aeroplane to land in France for the war,' were, Frank felt, real aeroplanes. Unlike the Farmans, they were to some extent streamlined, with the largest mass leading. They looked right. Thirty years later a spectator with no specialised knowledge of aircraft would have been astonished to see a First War pusher in the sky, but I doubt whether he would have bothered to look twice if he had seen a B.E., and still less a Martinsyde, at a height of a thousand feet or so amongst the small training bi-planes above one of our air fields. Although the pupil in front received the full blast of the propeller (making goggles essential), and sometimes became covered in oil from the breathers, Frank found flying a B.E. 'very fine after flying pusher machines' (9 April). There was something very definite in front to steer and land by, rather like a yacht. He sketched what he saw.

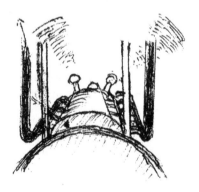

On Friday the 13th under a blue sky Capt. Adams took Frank round for a short run and then sent him up for his first solo on a

---

[87] B.E. from 'Bleriot Experimental'. The wing span of the B.E.2c was 35 feet.

B.E.2e, on which type he had by then done 3 hours 20 minutes' dual control. 'It was much bumpier later during the day' and while taking off over the valley he got into a spin—that nightmare of inexperienced pilots. With some justification he became alarmed, but had sufficient presence of mind to shut off the engine and extricate himself. 'Up to the autumn of 1916 not many pilots who had the misfortune to get into a spin in the air ever regained control.' How the nature of the spin and its cure were discovered is a fascinating story that we shall return to later.

In expounding his philosophy of self-control, Frank had an understanding correspondent in Father who, though subject to bouts of irritation, never lost his head. Frank wrote,

> Talking about getting the wind up before you're hurt you hit the nail on the head absolutely. If there is one thing that counts more than anything else in flying it is supreme confidence when in difficulty; fight the machine right to the end, always with the idea that something will turn it right in the end.
>
> I find *Lessons in Truth* more helpful in this respect than anything I know of; it is only the application of it that is hard, admittedly. All the old pilots say that the more you lose your head the more you involuntarily do the wrong things with the controls; and nothing is more correct. (19 April)

Two days later Frank had a more spectacular but less dangerous mishap.

> Just before lunch yesterday, I was landing on a B.E.2e and in taxying round from up-wind to down-wind to go across to the sheds, a sudden gust lifted one wing up and then raised the tail and skid off the ground as well. This jerked me forward, and pulling back the joystick (the natural remedy) the Bowden control caught against my coat and started up the engine. The action of the prop. settled what had been a 'moot point' and quietly turned the machine over on its back, breaking the prop off at the boss.
>
> There is nothing particularly dangerous about this sort of thing. It is one of the easiest things to do on a windy day, but it is annoying as it puts a machine out of action for a time.
>
> Bits of prop which somehow always manage to stick up in the ground like wickets thrown on to a cricket pitch. (16 April)

For the next ten days Frank was encouraged to take his B.E. further afield in cross-country flights. I find, however, no record of pupils being first conducted by an instructor to show them the lie of the land and the use of a map, nor is there any reference to formation flying. In these two respects the instruction at Dover differed from what I was receiving at Sedgeford.

The day after the accident just described he got into clouds. 'Flew for 50 minutes—missed aerodrome and carried on for 20 [more minutes] with not the least idea of whether N or S of sheds! Got over Ramsgate and followed coast down'. (16 April)

No one who has not been there can imagine the beauty of those cloud-scapes as seen from a First World War aeroplane— their dazzling whiteness, the unusual shapes, the peaks, mounds, rock-like crags, the caverns—or the thrill of flying slowly amongst the clouds, exploring the intricacies of a low mackerel-type sky,[88] banking steeply around and below an overhanging precipice or through the holes and tunnels, the blue sky beckoning at the other end. We felt free, with nothing between us and the beautiful clouds, towards which we would reach out as they flashed by, their proximity giving a smell of freshness to the stinging blast of air. All quite different from the brief glimpse of grey mist seen through the port-hole of an airliner, only to be followed in a short time by a somewhat monotonous panorama as the passenger looks down from thousands of feet on a vast white plain.

As for flying for any time totally surrounded by clouds, the exercise, to the inexperienced, could be disconcerting if not hazardous. Without the horizon as a check the pilot seemed to

[88] Strato cumulus. Vyv Trubshawe informs me that they used to play a form of 'hide and seek' amongst the clouds.

lose all sense of position and direction. He could therefore sometimes find himself coming out of a cloud in a steep bank, or spinning nose dive, or perhaps upside down. Even the compass would appear to be behaving in an eccentric manner. Unlike a marine compass the points were marked on the outside of a ring and seen through a small window. If the course became erratic, even though the pilot were unconscious of the fact, the compass would appear to be spinning wildly.

A few days later Frank had an opportunity to practise from the air his much-loved art of photography. 'Took first aerial photos—Sandwich neighbourhood given' (20 April) and 'Got above clouds on early flying. Took oblique photos with 5x4 naval air camera' (22 April).

That evening Frank did a 10 mile cross-country test, landing at Bekesbourne, near Canterbury. There he found that a landing-wire fitting had broken. A brother officer flew over to bring him back to Dover, where, later in the day, he passed his 'height test for graduation (8,500 ft)'. Next day he returned to Bekesbourne in a side-car with a spare and 'spent most of the day there while machine was being mended, then flew back'.

On the same day two occurrences are recorded in his diary which I have not been able to clarify: 'Pettigrew incident, landing in France' and 'Hun potted at in machine-gun practice on aerodrome.'

Although few of his colleagues seemed to relish the workshop training (reserved for bad weather) Frank addressed himself to it with his usual zest. All the time he was looking ahead, the idea being to acquire information which he could somehow use after the war. 'Talk about education,' he wrote, 'it is some.' His enthusiasm was echoed by Father to whom he submitted full reports. He worked in the sail shop (wing department, repairs, etc) sketching and describing how the special unbleached linen was stretched over the wooden frame, tacked and sewn at the back, strung on to the camber struts to keep it from bellying, then 'doped' which was much the same process as the Zapon lacquering at the works.

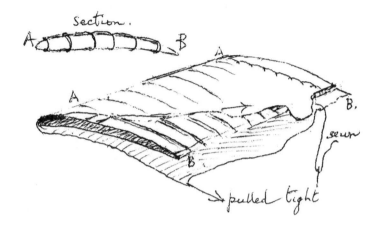

He also sent home a bit of his splicing and wire bending which everyone has to do when learning.

Frank was fascinated by the Constantinesco synchronising gear which, as he explained, 'enables the machine gun to fire through the prop, without hitting the blades though revolving at high speed.' It had been 'the subject of this morning's study and very interesting too' (17 April). He then went on to describe the pulsating pipe-line of oil which tripped the trigger when the blade was opposite the muzzle of the Vickers gun. It first came into use on a service aeroplane in the beginning of that month. The instruction at Dover must, therefore, have been kept right up to date.

On 25 April, I wrote to Beryl from the Royal Flying Corps, Sedgeford, Kings Lynn.

> I feel quite fagged out and not at all like writing to anybody. I've been doing three hours a day since Monday and yesterday I had a crash bringing a machine back from Thetford. The engine petered out just after taking off and I had to land in a ploughed field. I was thrown out and the thing landed on top of me, as it turned over [pictured]. I did not get a scratch and yokels and tommies soon got me out.

Have been up two hours today and have gained a lot of valuable experience.

What a priceless time we had, darling, didn't we? I don't know when I've enjoyed anything more. Monday night on the shore was a night I shall never forget—if ever there was poetry in the air, it was then. I hope you'll rub it into your people thoroughly how much I appreciated their scheme and thank them awfully for the guest touch, which was GOOD EE-NOUGH! If you see Auntie Sala [Lala?] again, tell her she was the last word in chaperones and give her my love.

I've decided the you're more beautiful than ever and every time we meet I get to love you more. Yours tired but very much in love,

Bob

The day before, 24 April, Frank had accomplished his '2nd cross-country landing (Lympne) which brought solo for graduating to 23¼ hrs.' Then, two days later, 'Made first solo on a Martinsyde—perfectly terrifying bumps for a new machine! Stayed up 40 mins, and don't know how I landed it as well.' As the Martinsyde was a single-seater, no preparatory dual control instruction could be given. It had started life some two years earlier. 'It ambled through the air with a rather gentle burbling sound' and had a top speed of 90 mph against the 70 mph of the BE2c.

During the remaining five days of the course he continued to get the feel of the Martinsyde controls—to acquire the sensitive hands which were to stand him in good stead a few weeks later when he came to fly those minute scout fighter planes.

One morning Frank was 'aroused at 4.45 a.m. for early flying', the C.O. having planned to establish a Squadron record.

First trip round Margate, Canterbury, Ashford, Folkstone, etc. Used compass and map a lot. Did two hrs 40 mins before breakfast. Fearfully bumpy just before lunch and even worse before tea. Sultry and thunder clouds. Did five-and-a-quarter hours during day. Squadron about 110 hours. Went to bed early and slept till 8.30 a.m. (28 April)

Sunday, 25 April, found him held up for three quarters of an hour while they 'tried to get Martinsyde started'. The sun was strong and to avoid the worst bumps he flew over the sea down the coast to Dungeness and back. The following day, at a height of 4,000 ft, he covered the 33 miles over Canterbury and the River Swale, the furthest point being Sheerness and the Isle of Sheppey.

On Tuesday, May 1 Frank made his last two flights on a Martinsyde, bringing his total solo flying time to 43 hours 45 minutes. His course at Dover was now nearly completed but, his appetite for work unsatisfied, he turned to copying out and amplifying his notes on the ingenious Constantinesco gear, while next day he 'spent large part of morning fitting up camera gun and polished off Ring Sight before lunch'. This consisted of a ring about two-and-a-quarter inches diameter which made allowances for the speed of the target machine. The gun was directed so that the enemy aircraft was flying towards the centre of the ring.

Two days later (3 May) he received orders to report for an aerial gunnery course at Turnberry in Ayrshire on the following Monday, the intervening time to be taken as leave. He took the 6 p.m. train for Victoria. I, meanwhile, had heard back from Beryl and replied at once.

Royal Flying Corps, Sedgeford, Kings Lynn, 29 Apr 1917

> Thanks awfully for your priceless letter. Things are taking rather an interesting turn. I've been detailed along with two other men (fairly promising pupils) to put in 20 hours' flying before the end of the week, bringing our grand total up to 40 hours. We shall then probably be sent as instructors to Brooklands of all places, where the work will probably consist of taking observers round to practise observing in FEs. However we mustn't rejoice too soon as you know what they are for chipping and changing about. I think the Major was rather pleased that I carried on as usual after that crash, however as I wasn't in the least hurt I could have scarcely had the face to put in the sick leave, could I? I put in five hours today and shall have to carry on like that for the next few days in case we have bad weather. I've really done more than my time to graduate, but they are not putting me through till May 1st as they have got enough this month.

Either way, please note if this stunt does come off, I've done absolutely nothing in the way of wangling for it, in fact it was an immense surprise.

I'm on early flying again on account of this new scheme and am simply flying all day—rather tiring. Sorry no more news. Give my love to Muriel and the baby—also your people.

Arriving in Birmingham early after some typical adventures with his motorcycle and luggage, he 'phoned home to learn joyful news that Bob was on leave as well'. He found Father and me busily fettling our tackle in preparation for a weekend's fishing at Bakewell. The moment he entered the house the atmosphere became charged with the warmth of his friendship, with his vitality and enthusiasm, as he exchanged notes with myself regarding our flying experiences. We had now both qualified as pilots. No time was lost in putting up our wings— persuading one of the domestic staff to sew the coveted badges on to our tunics.

Soon afterwards we rode off to the works on our motorcycles and had a look round and no doubt received the congratulations of the employees to which that gifted practical joker, Bernard Blackburn,[89] now virtually Managing Director, added his own brand of urbane and allusive gaiety. All three of us then 'called at the New Inns to toast the occasion after blinding up the Wattville Road' on our motorcycles.

Our Aunts, who had invited us for lunch, had a horror of intemperance. Of anyone who was suspected of over-indulgence they would say with a sigh, 'Why can't he be strong?' Frank and I were therefore especially careful to give an impression of strength—to restrain our high spirits lest it should be misinterpreted. But after the coffee Frank could not resist the temptation of some noisy 'foolery outside with the open exhaust of Indian (home for the first time)', ostensibly tuning it up. Two taxis then took us to the station to catch the very crowded 4.45 for Bakewell. At Ambergate we were joined by Mother who had been staying with her sister, Florence Brittain, in Sheffield.

---

[89] See Brass Chandelier, p.149.

Father had reserved rooms at the Rutland Arms hotel where he was by now well known. It is a plain grey stone building built in 1804 and originally owned by the seventh Duke of Rutland, whose arms outside made a welcoming splash of colour. In 1913 Mr Ernest Wood had been appointed as manager. At one time secretary of the High Peak hunt, he looked what he was, a landlord of the best type, used to field sports and a country life. His round face, healthy complexion and clear eyes gave an impression of sincerity. I can see him now as he stood talking to us on our arrival surrounded by mounted specimens of large trout, hunting horns, whips, trophies, masks, and a large turtle shell. He comes into this story later in a significant way.

After an excellent meal we wandered down to a bridge over the river and watched the evening rise. The sun was setting after 'a very hot day—almost oppressive'. Next morning we wasted no time before making our way down to the smooth flowing Derbyshire Wye. Few runs or rapids disturb its surface, but that day 'a strong East Wind' set up ripples and put our casting skill to the test.

Looking back at our family re-union I am glad that Father had an opportunity of giving rein to his passion for demonstration and practical instruction. He had not long graduated from wet-fly fishing, with its 'droppers' and 'tail fly' such as he had for years practised in Wales and in Scotland, where he and Mother had spent their honeymoon. By comparison with the beauty and skill of the dry-fly technique, 'flogging the water' may have seemed a little crude. Here, we were told, the fish were well educated and would turn up their noses at such tactics. The art of marking down your fish and casting over it was surely more sophisticated, more scientific than the methods of Albert Wood. Then, the accessories—the little bottle of oil attached with a safety pin to the coat lapel, the japanned tin boxes partitioned to take those fuzzy looking flies, the new reel and Hardy split-cane rod—were all objects of our admiration. For our benefit Father recapitulated the classic knot lore, passing on to a demonstration of casting, some slack held in the left hand and released at the last instant to avoid drag on the water. Casting a very pretty fly, he was really enjoying himself. In spite of those troubled eyes and sloping eyebrows, Mother's expression became less harassed as she also took a turn.

By teatime we found ourselves two miles upstream. Above us, on the left bank, stood the stone battlements and mullioned windows of Haddon Hall and the Peveril Tower. There we sat down to tea. Im Wunderschönen Monat Mai—the countryside was at its loveliest, we chatted quietly about fishing, about local people we had met on previous visits, and about the story of Dorothy Vernon's elopement with the Duke of Rutland. We were feeling relaxed and at peace with the world.

We returned to the hotel with our brace of trout. We were well satisfied with our day's sport. If a fish favoured us by rising to our fly now and again we were fully rewarded. The art and science was the thing. So strongly did Father eschew end-gaining that he gave an impression of indifference, if not displeasure, should a fish disarrange his beautiful cast by taking the fly—or such was Mother's comment.

If the sermon at the church the following morning, based on the theme of war economy, had any deep spiritual message I am afraid it passed us by. We felt even less inspired when we found that 'permission to fish in the afternoon was not granted'. As a poor substitute we played an 'absurd garden game', Frank noted. Then, after a farewell walk by the river and some music after supper, our leave came to an end. Next day (Monday 7 May) we travelled by train from Bakewell to Turnberry.

Arriving at Turnberry one entered the hotel direct from the railway station. We were struck at once by the opulent atmosphere with its aroma of good food, wine and cigars. The place had been taken over by the authorities just as it was—head-waiter, chefs, staff, cellars and all. The bedrooms, bathrooms and appointments were what one would expect in a first class golfing hotel. The bars were attractive and it was in one of them that we found ourselves on that first night. As we sipped our gin-and-italians I experienced, once again, that joyous feeling of companionship. After the second we began to get slightly hilarious, more with pleasure and high spirits than with the stimulant. On the way into the dining room we had to control an inclination to laugh uproariously. We sat down side by side and were once again hard at it, our heads together, comparing notes, making exciting plans for the future, discussing ideas for songs and dramatic sketches, and projects for the business.

Next morning we lit our pipes as we strolled about on the asphalt terrace in front of the hotel which, we discovered, stood on a low wooded ridge of hills. Below us we saw the Firth of Clyde, with Ailsa Craig on the left, the Isle of Arran to the right and, beyond, the Mull of Kintyre. We learnt that on a clear day the Irish coast was plainly visible. A drive to the hotel wound up the side of the hill from a narrow coast road. Between it and the sea we noticed sand-dunes and two golf courses. A wide flight of steps led direct from the terrace to some tennis courts at the bottom. A lighthouse near the ruins of Turnberry Castle completed the landscape. We looked at each other and nodded approval of the sporting and recreational prospects.

Immediately to the north, that is to say on our right as we faced the sea, aeroplanes could already be seen taking off and landing. The low wooded ridge on which the hotel stood continued north up the landward side of the aerodrome; it was surrounded by Bessoneaux Hangars. The flying speed of aeroplanes was then such that it was essential to land into the wind. But with a light breeze blowing off the sea, the pilot would be forced almost to touch the tree tops of the wooded ridge in order to avoid over-running the narrow aerodrome and crashing into the fences bordering the coast road. Further north, a large potato field provided what golfers call a 'natural hazard' for pilots with engine trouble trying to scrape home. Beyond, and a mile or so away, was a small fishing village called The Maidens. (It was here, on September 1 of that year, that I was to set up home for the first time.)

Founded earlier that year, the Turnberry School of Aerial Gunnery, like the Oxford and Reading schools, formed part of the general expansion initiated by Douglas Haig the previous

339

year. It was designed to give final gunnery instruction to pilots; another school for observers was situated at Hythe. As part of the training, we were taken up in a pusher, sitting out in front in a sort of balcony, and encouraged to loose off ammunition at a large flag towed behind an aeroplane at the end of some fifty yards of wire. Sometimes a careless pupil would mistake the towing machine for the target. A pilot who had just landed was seen to be pointing in anger to a number of bullet holes in his machine.

We would also dive at targets placed amongst the sand dunes, or at rafts floating out at sea. Tractor machines, with a machine-gun firing through the propeller, would be flown dual control. Once, as I remember, a misunderstanding arose. The instructor and the pupil each thought that the other was in control, until they ended in the sea! This was what befell Sir Robert Lorraine, 'the actor airman'. The consequences were not serious, except for a wigging from the C.O., Colonel Bell Irving.

We saw some sensational flying. I have a vivid recollection of Casey Callaghan, well known in those days as a stunt pilot, flying at about a thousand feet above the aerodrome. He would suddenly turn his machine so that the wings appeared to be almost perpendicular to the earth and then side-slip right down to within a few feet of the aerodrome, righting himself at the last moment.

The types of machines in use were limited to about four but from time to time, one or two German machines, with British markings of course, would appear in the sky in order to help the pupils recognise them in flight and as targets for the camera gun.

Much time was given to work on the machine-gun range and with the camera gun. We also attended a number of lectures. As I write these lines I have open before me my book of notes. Some of them recall the portentous and parrot-like accents of the sergeant instructor. They were most detailed and thorough:

The remainder of the gasses follow down the barrel and hit against the cone-shaped barrel mouth-piece, where they are spread out evenly and strike against the walls of the front radiator casing,

340

driving the air out and so causing a suction, which draws in air from the rear along the radiator pin.

But there was one aspect of the machine-gun lore on which our lives were to depend, for these lethal implements were inclined to jam, lock, and suddenly cease to function. Nothing could be more exasperating than to get the enemy machine nicely into the ring-sight, press the trigger—and then, after perhaps a short burst—silence. Or to be attacked by enemy machines and suddenly to find oneself deprived of effective defence. All this Frank was to experience in a matter of weeks, as we shall see.

We were shown, again and again, how to free these 'stoppages', but I cannot help wondering whether even more time spent in practising and rehearsing 'immediate action', i.e., 'crank handle onto roller'—'belt, left front', 'release crank handle', 're-lay, and carry on', together with the other three main stoppages might conceivably have altered the course of events described in the next chapter.

A comparison of my notes of the lectures on Fighting and Formation Flying with Frank's actual adventures shows that on the whole, the advice was sound and practical. Tactics of fighting were constantly changing, said the lecturer, a Captain Stookes of 60 Squadron, and this was confirmed later in one of Frank's letters home: 'Spinning is getting rather hackneyed now' (14 July). We were told that 'stalling, or flying slow, when the Hun was on your tail, had its uses.' Looping and the 'corkscrew or Immelmann turn' (a half loop followed by a vertical bank reversing the direction of flight) perplexed the German.

It was important to be able to identify machines in the air. The atmosphere and light made this deceptive. If you had a particular method that you fancied and felt strong on, you should work it up, as Capt. Ball had done. Success in fighting depended more on science and skill than on mere luck.

We were taught to take notice of the dead fields or angle through which the pilot was prevented, by the structure of his own machine, from firing. If you could manoeuvre yourself into one of them, you might approach unseen and take him unawares. Clouds should be used as a cover for ambushes and surprises. On seeing another machine a pilot should always approach it as if it were hostile until absolutely certain of its identity.[90]

Flying straight was dangerous. One should swing about to uncover blind spots. It was important to *keep one's height* and beware of decoy machines, to say nothing of 'Archie Traps', when the unsuspecting pilot might be lured into a barrage of anti-aircraft fire. If, in a formation flight, your engine went 'dud', you should not straggle but either go home or keep up your speed without losing height. All of which Frank carefully noted and, as we shall see, put into practice, although he was to find that the support from his formation was not always what he might have expected according to the lectures.

The procedure for getting the formation into position was explained to us in detail. The leader, having reached the required height, made wide circles round the aerodrome, other machines falling behind in position and cutting off corners if late. When the officer in charge on the ground below was satisfied that all were in correct positions he would put out a letter K in white strips on the ground and away they went.

While in some machines Morse messages could be sent to the ground by wireless, there was no telephony between the machines. Communication was made by certain signals, rocking the wings, and so forth. If your gun jammed, you were to catch up with the leader and rock the machine fore and aft. Coloured Verey's Lights (fireworks discharged from a pistol) were supposed to indicate that the pilot was going home, in cases of engine failure. A rendezvous was fixed to which the pilots should repair after a scrap.

Scouts escorting slow machines made S turns above them, always keeping in pairs. 'Although,' the lecturer concluded, 'there are so many things to think about in formation flying, you soon get used to it, and it becomes almost second nature to keep your position.'

---

[90] See Frank's letter of 28 July.

During what was to be the last fortnight of our partnership, the atmosphere suggested a holiday. The sun shone brightly. We played a round of golf nearly every day, using our own clubs, which had been sent on to us from home. On the first Saturday we 'got away to Ayr after lunch and met Jack Marshall at Hotel', Jack being my future brother-in-law, the husband of Beryl's sister.

Golf and work continued pleasantly enough during the second week. We were getting to know some of the other officers at golf, or at one of the bars over a game of billiards, or through Frank's playing of the piano. (One, Col. Philip Long, became a life-long friend of the author.) On the Friday we were asked to arrange a smoking concert. Frank recorded that he 'spent the evening routing around for material ... which eventually turned out a big success' (18 May). We were in high spirits, delighted to be doing some of our old numbers again— 'Rag Maninoff', our 'Rag-time Folk Song' and others. Frank's playing of the piano seemed exceptionally easy and effective. Our audience was responsive, joining in the choruses, and generous in its applause.

Time was running short. We felt that somehow we had still not fully exploited the sporting possibilities of this part of the Ayrshire county; so, thinking that the sea trout might be running, we got a lift to Girvan Water and fished with a wet fly for an hour or two. We had no spectacular success. But that night it rained hard. We were reminded of Albert Wood. There might be some colour on the water. But would the local fishing folk stand for a brandling fished upstream? We felt doubtful.

Sunday, 20 May. Exam 10–12. Work washed out at 4.30, so with rod borrowed from corporal set off for Girvan Water again. Funny incident—we thought we were being sleuthed by two figures, because we were fishing worm instead of fly. But the two figures turned out to be the President and Secretary of the local fishing club, and far from objecting they eventually supplied us with information and tackle for fishing worm. Dined at King's Arms and returned by car.

The next day saw our separation, though we were subsequently to speak to each other on the telephone. It was another wet day. The officers who had just taken the course were assembled in the lounge and first addressed by the instructors. Later, Col. Bell Irving gave us some final words of advice and encouragement. Frank and I left Turnberry at 5.10 and dined at Jack Marshall's house in Glasgow, then caught the North Western Express at 9.45. We changed at Crewe for the 3.40 for Birmingham, and I travelled on to Wimbledon.

This time there were no emotional twinges of the sort that I had experienced on leaving Thetford. My mood, like Frank's, was ebullient. Optimistic as ever, he was anticipating further pleasurable experiences on faster and more efficient flying machines, while I had in mind the girl I was to meet next day and whom I would marry within a little over two months, though marriage was not on my mind at the time, for I had been posted to Turnberry as a pilot instructor. What brought the wedding, as with many war-time unions, on was the prospect of my being settled for a few months at the same station, which encouraged our two families to agree that the marriage should take place without delay.

The final stages of Frank's training took place on much smaller and lighter aeroplanes than Frank had flown hitherto. By present-day standards, the First-War scouts were minute. The Spad, for instance, could have been put inside a room measuring 26 ft x 21 ft, with an 8 ft ceiling. They were also fragile. 'Everybody seems to crash machines during the day,' was a characteristic entry in Frank's diary. Above all, a sensitive touch was required to get the best out of the controls.

Frank's first flight on such a machine (a Bristol Scout) took place at Wyton, near Huntingdon, three days after leaving Turnberry. The following day his instructor, Capt. H.G. Corby, broke both legs and an arm. With his customary kindness, Frank went to visit him in hospital but was refused admittance so he ordered some grapes to be sent round. He then left by train for London Colney (about three miles south-east of St. Albans on the London Road) during the afternoon to complete the course before going overseas.

Next day (Sunday, 27 May) Frank took up a B.E.12 to survey the aerodrome and surroundings from the air. He went on to amuse himself by flying over 'Harpenden, Boxmoor, and all the old spots' where we had been together in 1916. On the 29th he flew a Sopwith Pup for 35 minutes, making two landings. This in its time was called the perfect flying machine. Frank made eleven flights on this aeroplane before turning his attention to the Spad (fitted with a 150 hp Hispano-Suiza engine)—the type that he was to fly in France. On June 1 he took part in a formation flight, the only one during the whole training course.

Unless a pilot was successful in approaching an enemy aircraft unseen, the expression 'dog-fight' aptly described much of the air-fighting in the First War. Two or more of these Scouts could sometimes be seen from the ground as specks in the sky, chasing each others' tails, banking steeply, looping, side-slipping, doing Immelmann turns, diving, and sometimes spinning. Although luck played its part, success in the main went to the pilot with the keenest judgement, coolest head and split second advantage in speed of reaction. The more experience of stunting a pilot could acquire, the better.

With memories of our asphalt rink, Frank wrote:

I have come to the conclusion that stunting, or advanced flying, is just like figure skating. You must start gradually and work it up. I like to begin and get my steep banks on each side quite right, like the edges in skating, before going on to stalling and side-slipping. A machine, like a human being, finds it easier to turn round to one side than the other, on account of propeller torque—the practice is the great thing.' (30 May)

On May 30 Frank was practising the spiral climb for the first time and had the satisfaction of shaking off the Major, who made two or three half-hearted attempts to get on his tail, but very soon got left below. Later he engineered his first spin. He explained:

There are flat spins and nose-dive spins, but in each case the path of the machine is the same as a piece of crumpled paper being towed rapidly on a piece of string ... At one time it was considered essentially fatal, but experience shows that like most things it can be both produced and remedied at will. (30 May)

Up to the autumn of 1916 not many pilots who had the misfortune to get into a spin in the air had ever gained control. Even nine months later it was still looked upon with misgivings by inexperienced pilots and as something to be avoided. That the evolution should only be tried with adequate height and knowledge of how to control it was soon made abundantly clear:

Yesterday, one silly chap put his machine into a spin at 1,200 ft and half righted it at 500, then disappeared into the trees. Most imagined that it was a case of Goodbye, and the ambulance was shot out, with us doubling in the rear, cross country. We could not find the machine at first, but later came across the pilot (a Canadian), a bit shaken, strolling about with a cigarette, having negotiated two trees and finished up in a hazel shrub.

There's a typical example of a chap who is not content to try things gradually and listen to every pupil's experiences before trying things himself. It will probably make a man of him now.

How it was discovered by accident that one stopped spinning by doing 'everything wrong' is a story with wide implications. The principle, in fact, applies to many new situations in which the habitual and instinctive response of the human being cannot be expected to give satisfactory results. Frank's approach to spinning was systematic and circumspect.

Having climbed to 6,000 ft, I stalled the machine (losing all flying speed) with engine cut off, joy-stick held back, and rudder bar hard right. The engine now swings over with dead weight and round to right. If the joystick is still held back and rudder kept on, a fast spin is produced. I did this and found myself looking perpendicularly at the ground over the bonnet. The ground becomes a blue with the speed of turning, and after the first 'vertical gust'[91] I retired 'into the office' and discovered myself contemplating the position of the controls and particularly the rudder. I placed this [i.e. the rudder bar] central— by kicking down left foot—content that I had got plenty of height to play with and still pulling the stick back to get the nose-up. However the bus did several more turns. Then I remembered to ease the stick forward, which sent the nose a bit more underneath me. With this, the machine immediately resumed its true flying speed and correct head resistance, and I quietly pulled her out, feeling rather funny inside and not a little bucked!' (30 May)

On Sunday, June 10th, Frank flew his first Spad, that French designed bi-plane. It was marked, said Frank, by 'a classic simplicity. The pilot was seated just behind and below the top plane. Part of the centre section was cut away so as to give him as good an outlook as possible upwards and forwards'. We have seen how lack of dihedral stability increased the manoevrability of an aeroplane. The Spad was noted for its absence of dihedral and it was easy to fly. (The distinguished French flying aces Guynemer, Fonck and Nungesser all used the Spad.)

On his first flight Frank's engine overheated and there was a flat tyre, the wheels having been damaged by another pilot when landing.

The aerodrome at London Colney, where so many scout pilots spent their last weeks in England, lay amongst park land and large meadows through which the River Colne gently flows. The neighbouring villages of London Colney, Shenley and Radlett each then consisted of only a few houses. Fifty years later, extensive development, which includes two large mental hospitals, has not obscured the charm of the scene.

The airfield itself must have covered nearly a square mile of level ground. At the north it was bounded by Harper Lane, and

---

[91] 'Wind-up' or fright.

on the east by Shenley Lane, which was lined on each side by hangars and huts. To the south the land rises gently, and in a clump of trees Frank found a 'picturesque little machine gun range' overlooking a wide plain, with St. Albans on the horizon.

Further south was Porter's Park, a fine wooded estate belonging to a wealthy stockbroker Mr Cecil Raphael. To the west came first the railway and then Watling Street. The four thoroughfares round the park and aerodrome formed an irregular quadrilateral.

During the three-and-a-half weeks of the training course the sun blazed. Frank found the heat at times stifling and oppressive, 'The very hard ground and lack of wind made good landings something above a fine art. The wing-tip, wheel or skid of the one serviceable practice machine got "done in" to a varying extent with each flight.' (16 June)

When flying was cancelled Frank still found plenty of scope for sporting activity. The Radlett golf course was only a mile or so away. His performance seems to have given him some satisfaction

Frank (on right) near the 'picturesque little machine gun range' near St. Albans.

for his diary records that on one occasion he 'played like a book with Clark and holed out some miraculous puts'.

Sometimes he would go off with his friends Barker (who was to join him at Estrée Blanche on June 31st) and Allen for 'a perfectly choice morning's tennis at the de la Rues'. This was Mr Stuart Andros de la Rue, the last of the family to be a member of the famous company of banknote manufacturers and printers. He and his wife lived at Shenley Hill, a large, well-proportioned house overlooking the south-eastern corner of the aerodrome and, beyond that, a wide plain. In the cool of the evening Frank would return for tennis and dinner in what he called this 'perfect house and garden'.

There is no mention of living quarters in Frank's diary or letters. This was unusual, for Frank took pleasure in a wealth of description. We know that some officers, including Albert Ball V.C., slept in billets, but the fact that Frank so willingly availed himself of the de la Rues' luxurious bath rooms at Shenley Hill suggests that he slept in a hut.

Once he went to the Shenley Village Hall for a dance and concert. 'A good programme', he noted; 'FUNN afterwards.'

He played cricket in various matches, notably on Mr Raphael's private ground, south-west of the aerodrome.[92] Said to be the same size as the Oval, it was as pretty a ground as one could wish to see. On the Radlett side was a small wood near the boundary and on the other, gardens and lawns with fine trees and rhododendron bushes rose to the large classical mansion where Mr Raphael lived. Tall and dark, Mr Raphael would not allow a match to start until he had come down to the spacious pavilion that he had built. When I visited the locality in June 1966 I found that the old man was still remembered. I also gathered that although he had done a lot for the village community, the local people were not entirely free from a certain racialism and he was not accepted as he should have been.

---

[92] He made 30 for the R.F.C., out of a total of 93, against the Irish Guards who made 75.

These outdoor pleasures were not the only bright spots in the 'good life' that Frank led during the course at London Colney, for his diary gives some final glimpses of those joyous visits to London, often for dinner and a show. No one who did not serve in the 1914 war has any idea of what these interludes meant. Even though neither of us had taken part in trench warfare, its contrast with the lights and gaiety of the West End was ever present in our imagination—the gasp of relief on those bespattered figures, just arrived on seven days' leave, as they got into their baths, then changed, and set out to do the town. Oh what a lovely war! It was all somehow infectious.

June 11 and 12 found Frank again staying with the Smiths at Ardmore, on short leave after being inoculated. He relished the civilised atmosphere of their house in the Marryat Road, near Wimbledon Common, as well as the music and the company of my fiancée, Beryl Smith, and of our cousin Joy Short, who lived further down the road. On arrival he 'slacked in the garden till eight' when dinner was served. Later, as he notes, 'Bob phoned from Glasgow re wedding.' Next morning, immersed deeper in home comforts, he took his 'breakfast in bed—arm rather stiff', and a 'long bath and dress', followed by a further slack in the garden before lunch. He then went on to the Shorts, where Mother was staying, for lunch, then another siesta and tea. That evening he returned to London Colney.

He enjoyed action, especially in sport, but above all he was happy in the simple pleasures of a comfortable home, music and company.

Six days later he completed the required flying time on Spads,[93] finishing up on a machine without a windscreen in which he got subjected to a spray of petrol. He had now accomplished 58 hours 11 minutes solo, of which five had been on Spads. On landing he took the first train to town, arriving at our Aunts' in time for an evening meal and a little music afterwards. Mother was still staying there.

---

[93] The wastage during the various pupil courses was about 28 per cent (Jones and Raleigh, Op. Cit. p,426).

On Tuesday, June 19th, both went by train to Birmingham for Frank's embarkation leave. Father met them at the station. Frank's programme followed the usual pattern. He tried on his new tunic at Allport's and then 'proceeded to the works in a taxi'. There he found that the company had become increasingly involved in the production of war material, including accessories and components for internal combustion engines. His contact with aeroplanes had suggested an idea for a winged lever or handle for a cock which he offered to the firm and this, as we shall see later, was taken up by the Bleriot Company.

Encouraged by Frank, our parents had taken to attending a music hall from time to time—those grim-gay popular entertainments in which one heard The Songs Which Won The War in different forms, the humour becoming more and more forced as the casualty lists lengthened. Frank thought that it would take our parents' minds off the war. Accordingly, that same evening, all three set off for the Grand Theatre (first house). The weather had broken. 'Steady rain already set in,' he noted and followed with a characteristic piece of information: 'Egg tea at A.B.C.' On their return, our two Aunts, overflowing with solicitous tenderness, came up through our garden from their little house in the Wyecliffe Road for some music and to say good-bye.

Next day, Frank and Father paid a visit to the Wolseley Car Factory, then producing the Hispano-Suiza engine which powered the Spad. Frank wanted thoroughly to understand the mechanism of this motor on which so much depended. 'The process of manufacture and testing were duly inspected,' he wrote in his diary. (20 June)

In the evening he was entertained to an early dinner at the Grand Hotel. Our uncle Doctor (and Major) Sydney Short made up the party. Then, after an affectionate leave taking, Frank left by the Great Western. Arriving at St. Albans shortly after midnight he found a 'motor lorry waiting for returning cricket team—useful'.

Frank kept notes of his last days in London before going on active service in France.

Thursday, 21 June. FOR OVERSEAS—ORDER, and so on the strength of it spent morning playing tennis at De la Rues with Clark. Got room at Euston and then met lads at Savoy, where we consumed useful dinner after 'shifting a few'. Maid of the Mountains—then supper at the Savoy after.

Friday, 22 June. Lunched at Carlton after phoning home and other calls. Reported at Masons Yard H.Q., receiving there instructions to leave by morning train. Dined at Troc, then went to Hanky Panky. Supper once more at Savoy, then to room at Grosvenor Hotel, Victoria. General rag with telephone, Clark and Barker.

Saturday, 23 June. Rose 6.30, feeling trifle muzzy and had cold bath. After terrific bustling of Barker, all three caught 7.50 train. Delightful crossing. Orders at Boulogne to proceed inland next morning. Quiet evening in the town. Place very dirty. Mild amusement at battalion of French Porters necessary. Share room with Clark, Barker and Brookes. Two ordinary and two camp beds.

With Frank's move to France, our lives were now heading in such different directions that I think I had better first explain my own situation with two letters of the period that I wrote to Beryl, and then step sharply into the wings.

R.F.C. Turnberry, 28 June 1917

I just had exact particulars of what the financial position is going to be. I'm going to get my Army pay made up to £700 a year by the Pater; I consider this ought to be ample to have a jolly good time at Maiden's or Girvan providing we are careful, but of course it would be a different style of thing to what you've been used to at Ardmore or at Jack and Muriel's. You probably heard all this before.

My people both think that we couldn't run a light car on that, but I'm sticking out for a sidecar as I think it would make a great difference.

The Mater asked me to mention that she is rather sorry that Stevens is coming as (I quote Mother): '—she will perhaps expect things like at Ardmore and although in many ways she would be a comfort to Beryl, personally I think she would be better to start away free from any home influence and also occupy herself in her new nest instead of having things done for her.' Take this for what it's worth.

With all this, I don't see anything to get the wind up about; Mother and Father will always back us up when it comes to it and I've absolute faith in you. You've got as good a head piece as I have and better. Muriel and Jack both think Maidens an ideal place to be at and if we keep careful accounts we shall be OK.

I've been round to Gawanbrae again and we should want our own linen (table and better) and cutlery—that's all. Mrs Girven would want to live in the kitchen for October—on, but there are three bedrooms, remember.

Whatever you do, bring good strong clothes and boots etc. Unless I am very much mistaken you'll get awfully fit here if you are properly clothed for it. Macintosh is essential.

I can't help a bit of awe and wonder at your love for me, her older love; in coming to live with me here. At the same time, though I don't want to disappoint you, I think he will enjoy the life here. My people are stuffing a gust up me about the seriousness of the step I'm taking but, like other great things, it looks awfully terrifying until you've taken the plunge.

We must live carefully, they're right about that, as things are awfully expensive—especially travelling.

Father is giving us £100 for a wedding present and £60 for our honeymoon, but advises us to bank the first for when we have our own house and not necessarily to spend all the second. (We shall run through it though, I know, or my computations are wrong.)

This care about money is quite a change in me, as since I started soldering I haven't worried my head much about it.

Suitcases and dressing gowns will be good. Send them home as I never taking dressing gown about with me.

Have read up the service. Remember me to Darnell Seale.

R.F.C. Turnberry, 30 June 1917

Perfect Love, you're quite right about the brooches, if Joy would like an R.F.C. one. To avoid wasting time, if Doris Tankard prefers the R.F.C. brooch, send all Edwards's brooches back and ask Uncle Percy to get you two R.F.C. brooches at about £5 each or get them yourself and send me the bill. If D.T. (that doesn't look nice, somehow) prefers a plain one, keep one of Edwards's, send the rest back and ask Uncle Percy to get one R.F.C. brooch only. I'm writing to Uncle P to get you a nicer one, subject to your approval, and giving him some places in Regent Street which advertised in the Tatler etc. I'm going to touch the Pater for these gifts if possible so have no qualms as to expense, dearest. Now, will you decide what show you'd like to go to on the great night and in due course ask Uncle P to get seats. Have a box if you prefer it, but there's no need to consult me as it only complicates things. If only I'd stuck to your orders about the brooches instead of being led astray by Muriel (don't tell her) I'd have saved myself a lot of trouble.

I think I have wangled an extra day on our honeymoon and if you would prefer to travel up to Scotland the same night that we come up from Cornwall, we can have six days there instead of four.

Sorry to hear about Darnel Seale. We had another tragedy yesterday—stunting as usual—awfully nice chap whom I wanted to introduce you to—crashed close to his wife's house. That makes six here and all avoidable. I've taken a solemn oath I'll never, never slump under 2,000 ft while I'm here.

I had a motorbike crash returning from fishing the night before last, riding on a chap's carrier. The silly ass ran straight into the front of a Ford that was coming towards us. We were both very lucky and apart from a few scrapes and shock (far more than with my F.E. crash) got off unhurt. The bike was a complete write-off. The M.O. made me go sick yesterday but I flew again today and am now OK.

Chapter 11
Closer to Heaven

> The estimated average effective service of a pilot or observer in France was four months in the two-seater corps and night-flying squadrons, and three-and-a-half months in the fighter-reconnaissance and day-bombing squadrons, while the effective service of a pilot in a single-seater [scout] squadron was no longer than two-and-a-half months.[94]

Frank survived a little over five weeks.

By the early winter of 1916 some of the finest British aeroplanes had been left behind in the technical race. It was a matter of months however, before the Germans began to lose a superiority which they were never to regain during the war. Among our aircraft, the Spad had led during 1916, but by the time Frank arrived overseas it was already on the way out.

The period now to be covered started about three weeks after the Battle of Messines Ridge (7–14 June 1917) had died down, and ended just before the Battle of Passchendaele (31 July–10 November 1917).

On June 24th Frank trained up to St. Omer and was told to report to No. 19 Squadron at Éstrée Blanche, near Aire. It was

---

[94] *The War in the Air*, op.cit. p. 426 (vol V, ch VIII).

'quite like old times being in France again'. He was obviously in exultant mood.

In the Field, Monday 25 June, 1917.

Dearest Father and Mother,

I have now got into the atmosphere again at last; it is funny to be once more 'at the Great War, Daddy'. Although in a way it seems the most natural thing in the world, yet to actually be in the R.F.C. and on the point of Hun Strafing has all the symptoms of a ridiculous dream, particularly after my castles in the air of over two years ago in an area not so far away—indeed included in the patrol area.

I can't describe it all right away so shall have to tackle it bit by bit. Yesterday afternoon I reported at the Pool. As a rule one is kept there messing about for a while but I was posted right away and only had to perch myself and kit in the tender already waiting there for me. I reported here at 7 p.m. and today am already feeling fairly well established in my tent. The mess is in a more or less permanent hut which contains a decent ante-room as well.

I have never received a better welcome anywhere than I did here last night. For one thing they had got a decent piano and no-one to play it; also the reports of our Turnberry concert had spread over here before me; consequently they greeted me, unquestioningly as you might say, with open arms! They are a very cheery lot of lads and 'rag' is usually the word every night, as far as I can gather.

Considering I have struck about the best, a) time of year, b) type of machine, and c) crew, it's what you might call 'PAS SI POUSSIÈRES' (not so dusty).

Fond love to all,

Frank

Although the atmosphere in the mess and on the tennis court was cheerful and welcoming there is reason to suppose that the offensive spirit of the squadron had been somewhat affected by the shattering losses of the previous months. This is suggested in a letter addressed to me from Frank's old school friend and partner in the model aeroplane competitions, Jack Gotch, whose squadron happened to be sharing the aerodrome with Frank's at that time.

No. 19 Squadron was having worse losses than we were. We lost seven machines in one day (14 men), and a few days later a whole flight of nine. Enough to get anyone down. Frank was one of the few who refused to be daunted by this sort of thing. Men of his stamp were still attacking superior numbers.[95]

Some notable pilots had served with No. 19 Squadron which could indeed be proud of its distinguished war record. A few months prior to Frank's arrival it had been commanded by H.D. Harvey-Kelly who, we may remember, was the first R.F.C. pilot to fly to France in war time. His personal leadership had kept the morale high. But on 26 April 26, leading three Spads, he had swooped down onto Richthofen's formation.

There was a short and vicious engagement, and all three British pilots were shot down. Badly wounded, Harvey-Kelly was taken a prisoner, but a few days later we learnt that he had died from his wounds.

It was during April and May of this year that Baron von Richthofen had developed his famous circus with deadly effect. He himself was wounded during July.

It is clear from Frank's letters and diary that his introduction to air-fighting was gradual. He may, therefore, have received a somewhat misleading impression of its dangers.

He nevertheless set about preparing himself, his aircraft and his equipment with great care. The day after his arrival he 'inspected camp, aerodrome, hangars, etc' and was then sent off to study from the air surrounding land-marks and towns behind our lines such as Hazebrouck, Bailleul, Poperinghe and Cassel.

Only the bare facts of his service at the front are recorded in his diary and Log Book.[96] But in his letters home we find a wealth of detail.

---

[95] 28 July 1958.

[96] The last entry in his diary is for July 4th, and in his log book July 24th.

357

Tuesday 26 June, 1917

Dearest Father and Mother,

I have now been posted to one of the flights and have been allotted my own machine.

The C.O. [Major WDS Sanday] is a topping chap with D.S.O. and M.C. I believe he soon sends you back again if you make a mess of things in general, so everyone has to look slippy if they wish to keep their jobs.

I am allowed to do as much as I like in the way of fitting up my own gadgets and accessories on my machine. No one else flies it, so we all have a chance to be specialists, in the highest sense, on our particular ones.

Primed with all the advice possible, [imparted] while the Flight Commander was having my engine tinkered up, I set off map in hand to survey the neighbourhood. I had heard so many stories of chaps going off and losing their way for the first time—frequently landing in Hunland—that I took jolly good care how I went about it. Having circled round the immediate neighbourhood and taken in the various land-marks pointing homewards, I wandered off for about 1 hour over all the old spots in turn where we shifted about in '15. All the towns, etc, look so different from the air, one really has to be careful. It is very laughable to take in at a breath, so to speak, points which we considered three and four days' trek distance. One travels at such a pace on these scouts.

Going back, I had to travel the last 10 miles at 800 ft and ran right into a good old summer rain shower. Though to my knowledge I have never flown in rain before, it is not half as bad as having castor oil sprayed at your face, which happened once or twice in England. I also noticed that the planes were absolutely dry all the time till I landed.

These are rather awkward machines for me to get 'right into the office' though for a small man excellent enough. Apart from my flying cap, however, I was quite dry.

After landing, I was told that it had rained hard at the aerodrome since about 10 minutes after I left, and they all thought I had got lost, probably over the lines, on account of strong wind— mild amusement and surprise.

There are so many things to learn that my comparison of a fighting pilot with the man who does the one-man band, with assistance of head, body, arms and legs, applies more than ever.

You might send me the three cock handles[97] to try, if they are ready for me at the works. My other requirements in clothing, etc. are on another sheet.

My tent is wonderfully waterproof for a bell tent and I am rigging myself up with all the advantages of previous experience.

I am reading *The Weather Map*[98] and find it very interesting.

I forgot to say that the two nights in London with the Lads in the same group as me were 'ones' and no mistake. We did the heavy at the Carlton and the Savoy, and even bought ourselves ices and cigarettes.

Dear love,

Frank

————

In the Field, 28 June, 1917.

Dearest Father and Mother,

I am beginning to feel my feet a bit now, not to say hands and wings.

Yesterday I was Orderly Officer, but did not have to hang about the telephone in quite the usual manner, as I had about one hour's beetle round towards the lines with a view to spotting aerodromes, which are always useful to know of; I returned for lunch. Even when you have got the position fixed well in your head—for we are not allowed to mark our maps to indicate anything our side of the line—it is very hard to locate a strange aerodrome as the hangars are so well disguised. We frequently find ourselves right over the place without knowing it.

During the afternoon the Major and Flight Commanders inaugurated the new tennis court with an opening set and afterwards all the officers played a four as well. They have been very busy with scythe, roller, hoe, brick dust, tape and netting for the last four days; the result is surprisingly good. [Here follows a

————

[97] This was the winged lever tap referred to elsewhere and taken up by Bleriot's.

[98] Very popular meteorological war guide by Sir Napier Shaw, published by the Meteorological Office of the Air Ministry. First issued in 1916.

request for tennis flannels, etc. to be sent out.]

In the evening I followed my first patrol, my orders—as is customary with beginners—being to accompany the others to the lines, tootle around behind for a little while when they cross over, get to recognise the land marks, then come back.

The late afternoon was distinctly DUD and the resulting sensation of following the patrol was far more theatrical than even I anticipated. The clouds were all over the place in varying layers and shapes; they appear to hurtle by you (just like the rolling scene in the Valkyrie Ride), while the machines in front, except for bobbing up and down, appear stationary, and frequently disappear headlong when the leader cannot find any gaps. It is very difficult to keep together under such conditions and if you get into the slip stream of the 'friend on ahead' you wonder whether your nether portion has slipped, as the machine acts like a stage horse jibbing.

The lines look absolutely red-brown from above and rather shapeless.

I fooled about at 12,000 for a bit, then stuffed my nose back home. After dropping through the main cloud belt I noticed it very black on ahead, and after a minute or two could distinguish a regular dusty coloured storm enveloping the whole of our home station area. I felt I could build up a wall along the screen in front and separate the sun from the shadow part in a yard or two's depth.

After marking time for a while in the clear, I saw it would be likely to continue for an hour or so, so I made back for the aerodrome I knew of bordering the town which used to boast of the famous Tina.[99] Here I landed (without smashing anything) and as usual ran into two or three chaps who were at one of the home stations with me. I phoned my own squadron, who were quite pleased with my course of action, and after a little champagne dinner (I regulated my consumption in inverse proportion to the instability of my machine to be flown home afterwards) I made my way back, landing at 9.30.

One experienced pilot found his way back through the hail, not being able to get out of it, with the result that the leading edges of his 'prop' were reduced to pulp. The ground was fearfully soggy also. He

---

[99] 'Tina of Bailleul', a legendary young French inn-keeper, favoured as much for her wit and beauty as for the beer she sold.

evidently dropped into it from above whereas I saw it loom up ahead.

They say that Tina was arrested about a month ago only, and the previous reports were false! One would imagine from hearsay that the young lady spends most of her time being arrested and shot.[100]

I will keep you posted as regularly as possible, but don't worry if you hear nothing as you know how irregular the posts are.

Fond love to all,

Frank

N.B. We brought down a Hun yesterday.

To see the patrols go off and return is rather picturesque, as with one type of machine they look more than ever like six bugs. They take off one behind the other like ducks off the water and land in much the same manner. (29 June)

Owing to low clouds and persistent rain, flying was suspended for the next four days. Frank turned this breathing space to very good account for, realising that success depended on attention to detail, he spent some time 'up at the hangars, busy getting small equipment "just right" which is as far removed from "almost right" as are black and white'. He had his flying cap 'unstitched and drawn in along the seams, also the front furry peak removed and the chin strap altered to take the stream further forward. With the upward huge rush of air from the windscreen it used persistently to be blown backwards'. It now fitted like a glove. Among his correspondence is a design, sent to the works, for a pair of goggles hinged so that the eye-pieces could be rapidly swung away and the vision unimpaired. He had constructed to his specification a folding cap case so designed as to reduce its size. He supervised modifications to the cushion on which he sat in his plane, for he had been 'jolly uncomfy and cramped sitting, on account of [his] height'. In his progress report to our parents he included an explanatory

---

[100] This rumour, as we have seen, was completely false.

sketch. He had the rigging of his machine altered to correct some fore-and-aft or lateral bias.

Lastly, he sent off the Mess Corporal to the town to buy furniture—'a tiny sturdy little kitchen table, cane chair, enamel basin, jug and "article" which,' he wrote, 'with a few petrol boxes furnish my half of the tent rather comfortably'. It was 'quite unlike previous bell tents ... inasmuch as it was literally waterproof'.

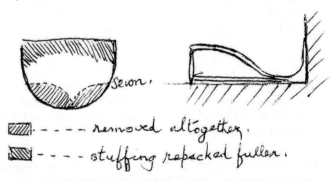

'Had the rigging of his machine altered to correct some fore-and-aft or lateral bias.'

Flying was resumed on Monday, 2 July, when Frank's diary records that he had his 'First real patrol, accompanying Sops as escort on photography. Archie very lively over Ypres. Returned with FEs and had vision of HUN at close range, lost him and patrols.'

The Sops probably referred to the Sopwith two-seaters of Jack Gotch's Squadron (No. 70) which had arrived on 27 June to share the aerodrome. On 1 July Jack Gotch himself returned from leave and the following day these two old Bedalians had a long conversation in No. 70 Orderly Room, where Jack was doing duty as Orderly Officer. No doubt they discussed the rigging of the 1909 model aeroplanes in the light of their subsequent experiences. Their two tents were within an approach-putt of each other and they kept in close touch until Jack went into hospital on July 20th with inflammation of the heart covering.

The record of No. 70 Squadron was as noteworthy as No. 19's. Its membership included several successful and much admired flying officers. For instance, Sholto Douglas,[101] then a Major, had served with it during the early Somme battles doing patrols over the line. Lt. Col. 'Stuffy' Dowding[102] had then been C.O. The work being done by the pilots and observers was in long-range reconnaissance, photography and offensive patrols, and they had already acquired a great and well-deserved reputation for gallantry in the face of the heaviest casualties suffered by any squadron on the front at that time. During the Battle of Arras (7 April) the Squadron had been commanded by Arthur Tedder[103] whom Sholto Douglas describes as a 'quietly observant man ... with a strong, but sometimes perverse, sense of humour,' something Jack himself confirmed.

Jack had come out towards the end of March and by now had had considerable experience. On 24 April he and his observer, Kibutz, had been officially credited with shooting down an Enemy Aircraft while on a reconnaissance flight over Cambrai. (No pilot was officially credited with an aerial victory unless it had been amply confirmed and verified.) On 12 July, according to his log book, his observer shot down another plane while on a photographic reconnaissance. They were attacked by four enemy aircraft and 'scrapped from near Menin to North of Ypres'.

Frank's 'first real patrol' referred to above almost certainly formed an escort to a formation from No. 70 Squadron then doing a photographic reconnaissance. From a comparison of the two Old Bedalians' log books, it seems probable that they were

---

[101] A senior figure in the Royal Air Force, eventually becoming commander-in-chief of Fighter Command in the Second World War and head of Coastal command during the Normandy Invasion.

[102] Became first commander of Fighter Command in 1936. Ennobled following his retirement in 1942.

[103] Went on to command the evacuation by air of Crete and Operation Crusader in North Africa during the Second World War, and organised the Berlin Airlift of 1948.

on the same formation flight. 'I was on escorting patrol today,' Frank wrote,

> for a large part of the time over 16,000 ft.[104] Archie was fairly lively. Altho' you see the little puffs of black suddenly appear all round, you do not hear it unless very close, when the machine does a quirk.
>
> I met my first Boche machine at fairly close range—he had the height of me. He was in a fast and furious hurry to get back home, however. In turning to get my height I lost both Boche and my own patrol. The others had all had a shot at him first! (2 July)

In a subsequent letter Frank returned to the subject of height and its effects. Evidently Father had been making enquiries.

> You were right about the meaning of 'having the height'. If you start a scrap with anyone below you, you have the advantage of being able to catch up at any time with the extra speed imparted through diving.
>
> The higher you get the less buoyancy there is—you are quite right there too. All machines have a height limit above which you can't climb them, and all machines get hopelessly sloppy about the controls and some machines flop and sideslip on a quick turn high up more than others. (23 July)

The day after the 'first real patrol' found Frank without a machine. His Flight Commander (Capt. Hagen), whose own machine had gone dud, had borrowed Frank's machine to take part in a royal escort over Calais, for the fourth visit by King George V and Queen Mary to the front. It was exceptionally hot. Excused duty, Frank took a tender to a cool bathing place provided by a mill dam and then, refreshed, returned to a game of tennis. This was followed by an excellent evening meal to which his friend, Jack Gotch, had been invited. Life in the Flying Corps provided intervals of the keenest enjoyment.

Frank's dedication to his work together with a compulsive

---

[104] It must be remembered that the First War pilots were equipped with neither oxygen apparatus nor parachutes.

urge to describe vividly these intense impressions come through in the following letter. Once again he confirms that Father had understood him correctly.

R.F.C. in Field, 5 July 1917.

Dearest Father and Mother,

You understand pretty well about the Flights. It is like being in the team straight away instead of reserve man waiting for someone to crock up! You will find about the composition of Flights and Squadrons in my early letter from Thetford.[105] I must not repeat it here. There is nothing confidential from the military point of view in any of my letters, so you can show them as you please.

I am giving myself about a week off drink and tobacco (only three more days to go)! I find it no effort and as yet makes no difference to me beyond a certain self-consciousness of 'aloofness' after dinner. However, short spells of ultra-temperance do no one any harm, though I disqualify the opinion of those who are permanently ultra-T.T.—if they have always been so—as I consider them no judge in the matter (so that's that).

Yesterday I was hauled out of bed at 3.15 for an early show and after a couple of eggs and tea the formation took the air, which at that time was very hazy and 'just not night', as you might say. (Everything is so stagey when, one after the other, the machines blind off and sail up in big circles on each others' tails.)

We climbed steadily all the way and yesterday it was very beautiful to see the sun rise at 10,000 ft above a layer of blue-brown haze which made a clear-cut line across the crimson ball of light gradually revealing the full shape as we climbed out of the haze, for above this level it is absolutely clear.

I soon found myself guiding the machine so that part of it, either wing tip or strut, shielded my eyes and allowed me to take stock, as advantageously as possible, of the Hunland Welkin (at last I have found a use for an old friend without it being made to ring).

We see the coast very soon after leaving the ground and when clear can sometimes see Blighty 'only a few minutes off'—doesn't it sound funny.

---

[105] A Squadron, commanded by a Major, consisted of three Flights, A, B and C, which were commanded by captains. There were four to six pilots per Flight.

Later, the mist gathered itself into clouds and obscured the ground completely over certain areas beneath us, whilst the distant west began to tinge with pink above the darkness of the night, which was still noticeable on that side. We had no encounters, though one requires an india-rubber neck at all times, to see whether anything is approaching your tail.

My engine was running very sweetly, which is always a great joy, and only ceased its hum to drop me down through clouds again over where I judged to be in a line for our aerodrome.

I was in bed again by 7 a.m. and slept till nearly 10. It started to rain just after I landed and continued for most of the day.[106]

Dearest love,

Frank

Patrolling, unmarked by clashes with the enemy, occupied his time during the next four days. But on 7 July 7 Frank saw two Boche machines. He at first mistook them for British ones. Presumably it was then too late to engage them or perhaps the patrol leader also failed to notice them. His patrol had been detailed to escort some D.H.4s over Courtrai and Lens. They failed, however, to turn up.

Later in the day he went up again and 'practised several spins and made one or two unsuccessful attempts to roll'.

Due probably to weather conditions, he made no flights on the 8th and 9th. At that time we read of the first of those heavy thunderstorms, the last in this story occurring on the day he was reported missing.

8 July. Last night we had one of the most complete thunderstorms I ever remember; it began soon after 1.30 a.m., opening with a huge bang just above us, and carried on with only one real break till about 5 a.m. I was very thankful our tent was waterproof as the noise of the rain on the canvas was almost as loud as the thunder itself.

---

[106] The last entry in his diary (Wednesday, 4 July) refers to this flight. He goes on to note, 'St. Omer, lunch, cashier, haircut, burberry, etc., violin evening in No. 70 Mess.'

On the 10th Frank went up for 18 minutes to try out 'a newer machine with more room for my legs, as a pilot in our flight has been posted back for rest in England after 10 months or so here—we all shift up in consequence'.

Then, on 12 July, he had a startling experience with very real danger. But before giving an account of this adventure, which for the most part will be in his own words, we will take a look at the sort of life he was leading on the ground. It seems to have been quite full and in its richness and variety had a certain Bedalian flavour.

Music continued to occupy him. Once again, as when he was serving in France during 1915, we find that curious juxtaposition of lethal technics alongside *Du holde Kunst*—not only light music, for he was often asked to play the piano in the mess, but serious study, as if he could look forward to a long period in which to reach higher levels as an executant.

> 16 July. I have received by post today the last four lessons in piano sight-reading which I wrote for a few days ago. You remember I started in Belgium in '15. I am beginning to appreciate their assistance and were it not for the fact that brother Bobby will soon have smaller and prettier hands (if less like the master craftsman) to do the dirty work for him [presumably an allusion to Beryl's playing of the piano accompaniments] I would strongly urge him to study the lessons in question.

From his letter of 14 July it appears that our collaboration in song writing continued. He was also busy polishing his manuscripts, for he liked his own compositions sufficiently to want them to be heard.

> 11 July. I have at last made an audited copy of my Terriers March and have sent it to Oxford [to be copied by hand]. In about four days from receipt of this you will probably get the first copy sent home. In case B.G. and Bob felt inclined to have it played at [their wedding] ceremony, I thought we would give the organist a chance to recover first, with a few days to try it over.

He set about arranging the sheet music, of which there was 'a large pile'. He had them bound together in 'the sail shop by doping strips of thin fabric up the back and then sewing them up the centre with machine. The best rough and ready job I've seen,' he added. His resourcefulness led to another assignment.

> 1 July. They have next put me on to assist in the direction of a rack for the gramophone records, of which there are some 200, also the numbering and classification of them! I might say that though many are badly worn we have some priceless ones of Wagner, Debussy and Co, as well as the usual complete revue list.

This rack, with its elaborate classification so characteristic of his zest for orderly arrangement, is fully described in the notes and references. It involved an ingenious system of coloured labels from which could be seen 'at a glance the style of record and how interpreted'.[107]

We have seen how Frank had designed a winged lever or handle for a cock which had been offered to the Bleriot Company. A copy of this company's formal acceptance was sent out to him. It enclosed an official sample order for '200 each, all to be completely finished and fitted with winged levers' (29 June). He commented,

> I feel distinctly flattered at Bleriot's accepting the cock-handle suggestion—but as a matter of fact one wonders they didn't apply it to start with, being so obvious. (29 June)

While occupied with the music racks in the mess, Frank also turned his attention to the walls, which were absolutely bare. He gave a hand, covering them with 'nymph' pictures (by Harrison Fisher), the pin-up girls of the period, 'whereof the subject matter', he wrote, 'verges towards the previous state of the walls, mais qu'importe?'

---

[107] The last entry in his diary (Wednesday, 4 July) refers to this flight. He goes on to note, 'St. Omer, lunch, cashier, haircut, burberry, etc., violin evening in No. 70 Mess.'

Although Frank was able to give up drink and tobacco he was very much alive to creature comforts. When not fighting, he tried to live a civilised life. He was particular about his tobacco (Carlisle). He appreciated a good night's rest (on a mattress especially filled with 'husks, or something similar'). His 'slumbering hours generally ceased between 9 and 10 a.m.' unless called out for dawn patrol. He enjoyed his 'fizz dinners' at Boulogne, Le Touquet and Paris Plage. He liked to be adequately turned out. His tailors had a tunic half-finished and he wrote enquiring whether it could be fitted in London if he were able to get a short leave for my wedding.

Frank's correspondence at the front must have been considerable. In addition to the long letters home and those to Nellie Simmendinger, he wrote replies, no doubt full and informative, to letters from relatives and friends and former schoolmaster at Bedales. He was bubbling over with ideas; indeed, his urge to describe and report was sometimes at odds with his desire to spare our parents anxiety, for their peace of mind and general welfare were continually in his thoughts. At this distance of time we may be glad that the urge to describe prevailed and we are left with these vivid accounts of his experiences.

With it all, his handwriting shows that he was keeping up his penmanship as taught by Father at Berrow. Like the calligrapher Edward Johnston, he believed in having the right tool for the job. Unfortunately, while in France he chipped off the iridium tip of his fountain pen trying to adjust it and asked for another nib 'as nearly like the old one as possible (soft and medium size)'. (18 July)

In the midst of all these varied activities it was difficult to practise his old love—photography, with its happy associations: those golden summer expeditions in the company of his friend Vyv Trubshawe, photographing fonts and facades, making snapshots of sports events, or carrying out studies of landscapes and portraits. He could make no snapshots while on active service because the regulations had been stiffened up, and it was therefore impossible to provide visual parallels to his love of reporting, but just before leaving home he photographed our parents who, as he put it, had been 'doing a bit of rotting'—fooling about. Developed and printed by our works photographer, Mr Dickenson, the results had followed him shortly after his arrival in France. 'Technically they are quite as good as I could have hoped for,' he wrote, and then went on to give detailed instructions as to the size, vignetting and the sort of paper (rough) to be used.

His flannels had been sent out to him and he threw himself into the men's singles on the new tennis court. Although beaten in the finals (4–8, 8–10), he seems to have given a fairly good account of himself.

> 11 July. Beautiful day today—not too hot. Have just put on whites for the first time and played my Flight Commander in the semi-final of the Squadron Tennis; just managed to win, 7–5, 6–1. The first set was very close—I am not sure whether I acted wisely in winning at all? (Ha! Ha!) I hope he won't fire at my tail [on our] next patrol.

(Although he did not fire at Frank's tail he actually cut it off five days later, as we shall see.)

If Frank interested himself in the broader social and political implications of the war, he showed no indication of it in his letters. His interests were many-sided, but in what concerned the prosecution of the war, like many another young man at that time, he was single-purposed, concentrating on the immediate tasks allotted to him. He nevertheless held strong views on what our general strategy should be in dealing with the increasing German air raids. Service overseas tended to make him critical of the civilian population. About air raids, he wrote that

> the R.F.C. out here are very sick with the protests and shouts that are going on at home, for although the air raids are admittedly serious, there is not a pilot who would dispute that home defence is comparatively cushy compared with strafing the Boche. We could stop the raids by leaving a lot of machines and trained pilots at home, but they would be saving a far greater number of lives by

preventing the artillery from ranging on our trenches. Even the job of instructing others to fly or shoot seems, in a way, more important—though I admit it is unfortunate for those who get bombed at home (about 0.001%?). (10 July)

Frank's concern for religious and philosophical matters continued. He re-read parts of *Lessons in Truth*.

It seems to me the only faith worth cultivating, under the present circumstances, is something of this nature, but it is singularly hard to discuss and can only be felt after all.

I shall have a better opportunity of putting it to the test now than ever before: and while on the subject I do hope that you are not all worrying about my personal safety; if there is one thing that affects me more than anything else it is the thought of that. I have never felt more contented or thoroughly satisfied than with my present job; after all it is the 'real thing'. Please try and persuade yourselves with infinite confidence that you will see me return later sound, both in body and spirit.' (29 June)

On re-reading his letters from France I am struck by his attitude to life, which seems characterised by a belief in 'Constructive Continuity', calling to mind Martin Luther's words:

If I knew the world was going to end tomorrow I must still plant new apple trees today.

By 11 July Frank had served with No. 19 Squadron for fifteen days. On ten of them he had flown, but during the remaining time he had been grounded by bad weather or because no machine was available. In spite of Archie he found it all interesting and enjoyable. He encountered nothing to cause undue alarm. On that day, however, came the first of those technical inadequacies that were to have serious consequences later. His log book indicates that the performance of his engine was unsatisfactory. He had 'difficulty in keeping up' with the others in the patrol. It was characteristic of him that on this and subsequent occasions he did not turn back but continued, although at a lower level than the others.

He was now to be brought face to face with the realities of air fighting, for on 12 July he 'Followed patrol escorting Martynsides'. His machine was climbing very badly and at a height of 14,500 ft he 'got into a scrap'. He described the incident in a letter to our parents.

> In the afternoon we had quite a set-to, but against six Boche scouts who had the height of us. Although there was a good deal of firing nothing definite resulted. I saw one Boche spin, but do not know how far he went down. I got a gun-jam and landed at another squadron [No. 23] with similar machines to ours, nearer the lines at Poperinghe, where I cleared the gun. There I met one or two old acquaintances.
>
> I am very much in the pink and there is a chance of a trip to the sea today in a car going on duty.
>
> The peculiar thing about this patrol work is that the beginner doesn't see one fiftieth part of what is going on all around, as there is such an immense zone to be scrutinised. I am getting a bit used to it now, but it sounds funny to hear the leader, when we are discussing it afterwards, say, 'Did you see that patrol of umpteen machines following us?' or 'I wanted to keep over our observations machines till they turned back'—when you never even knew they were there. To be able to distinguish quickly only comes with practice; it is a question of knowing what to look for. (13 July)[108]

The day after this set-to, Frank was involved in a second and much more dangerous adventure while on early morning patrol. The letter to our parents quoted above must have been written soon afterwards. His first impulse was evidently to say nothing about the second engagement for fear of alarming them. He changed his mind, however, and described both encounters in letters to me.

14 July 1917

My dear old boy,

    The Harrison Fisher pictures are more than a success in the

---

108 From his log book we learn that one of his co-pilots on this patrol failed to return.

anteroom—one might say the centre of attraction for the moment. The words of song also to hand—many thanks.

The day before yesterday we got into a proper scrap. I had been given a new machine which gave me more room for my legs. Although there was nothing actually faulty with the machine, it didn't climb as it should, so to keep my place in formation, I had to lose height.

There were about five or six Albatross scouts on top of us. In the split-arse turning we all got split up. I didn't get a chance to fire for a bit, and then my gun jammed right at the start—I must have done a false load previously. By side-slipping and zooming, their shots went very wide. The jam occurred after about five rounds. I looked round and couldn't see any of our little lot about (except one pursuing a spinning Boche below). I made off for the lines. I landed behind the line at an aerodrome nearer [to the line] than ours and then, after clearing the jam, had a chat with W.R. Brookes[109] and others I knew. (W.H. Clark[110] is missing from there.)

Here is a picture of a section of my Pitot tube [the air speed indicator]. Will you keep it safely for the present; there were also two other holes in the top and bottom planes, which caught the edge of a long burst of tracers that left a perfect cylinder of white smoke in the air.

Yesterday morning we were on early morning patrol. After an hour or so I found myself at 14,500 with the leader and two others over 1,000 ft above me (after trying all I knew to get my height); however, my engine was revving fairly well and not over-heating. I suppose I should have fired a white light and beetled off back.

All of a sudden I heard pooping behind me which was the first intimation that another Boche patrol were on my tail, but this time just a little below me. I had to decide pretty quickly what to do as they were still outclimbing me behind. I fired a few shots, with the hope of attracting the leader's attention, and then turned round, with the idea of having a flying smack as I passed. I am afraid my shots went wide, so I stuffed her nose down vertical, kept the engine half on, and rudder first one side then the other, and kept

---

[109] W.R. Brookes, with Clark and Barker, shared a room with Frank at Boulogne on the way up to the line.

[110] Clark, Barker and Allen played tennis together at the De la Rue house.

her there for 13,000 ft. Being absolutely sideways on, I could look over my upper shoulder at the Huns who were pooping at me all the way down. They left me at 4,000 where I had gained a good deal on them.

The description of my pal, who was not quite as high as our leader was, 'I saw four Boches below me; on turning they disappeared into nowhere in a streak single file.'

My engine was a bit giddy after that effort, however, I scraped her back spluttering a bit, with the help of the gravity tank, and crossed the trenches at about 500 ft. where I could see the occupants distinctly. The pressure was now picking up and after a short time I got my bearings and found the old landmarks to get back.

On examining my machine there were several holes through the wings, one through each of the bottom spars, also the prop, and one landing wire!

If I had spun down, by the way, the chances are they might have followed me and caught me flattening out while dizzy. Spinning is getting rather hackneyed now and not recommended so much for machines that will dive well, and whatever the shortcomings in other respects may be, this type is certainly a champion diver.

I felt I could have cried at the disappointment of the whole show and in reporting spoke fairly plainly concerning circumstances. To my surprise the powers were most sympathetic and very pleased to have both machine and me back again, the principal criticism being that I carried on too long under the circumstances. One of our squadron was being sent to Blighty for a rest after nine-and-a-half months out here, so the C.O. recommended me to get away for a bit with the friend whose description of the affair I have quoted.

As a result we all had a jolly good lunch at a coast port, then lolled about on the beach, had a strawberry tea—repaired to the pictures for an hour, then had a really good fizz dinner before driving back. I must say it did me a world of good. Although we have our rough moments in the R.F.C. we are certainly privileged in being able to get right away for a few hours, and also having a comfortable tent to sleep in every night. It is a thundering pity that the dear old infantry officers don't get £1 a day in France. They deserve it if anyone does.

I am being given a perfectly new machine now which should give decent results.

You probably know that all our work is done on the German side of the lines. The air is absolutely thick with machines in formations—black specks in the distance which approach and pass with incredible speed, or else lose themselves almost while you watch. You can understand how difficult it is to distinguish friend from foe nowadays—very different from the conditions at the beginning of the war when two machines scarcely ever patrolled together.

One attains a great deal of confidence after combats of this nature even if one doesn't bag any game.

The censor forbids any criticism of our methods but you can guess that had things been ever so slightly rearranged we should probably have given the Boches such a strafing, altogether, that they would have stuffed their noses down with even greater intention of approaching mother earth as fast as possible.

At first I thought of not writing home about it, but on second thoughts I think you might send this on, otherwise by the time the story has got round to Handsworth from indirect sources[111] they will all have heard that my machine was seen to crumple up at 20,000 or something equally ridiculous.

Cheeryoh and much love.

The conviction of a charmed existence goes a long way at times, doesn't it.

'Francisco'

The day following this adventure (July 15th) was Frank's birthday. He wrote to Mother:

I am sharing my tent with a funny lad who is known as 'The Bait'. This is an established policy in aerial work to attract the enemy's attention below you and while he is interested get him in the net from above. I think the idea of calling anyone 'The Bait' one of the funniest things I have heard for days; however, during the last two days I functioned in much the same manner for our own flight; unfortunately the second half of the scheme never commenced.

---

[111] He may have had in mind his old company of the A.S.C., stationed not far away, with which he was in touch.

So that you shan't get exaggerated stories from round about sources, I have told the story to Bob. I think you will feel a great deal more comfortable [that way] than if you thought I was hiding the facts from you. There is nothing to worry about really, as I am getting more and more confidence every day. The more you do the more formidable you become.

I do feel thoroughly contented and fit, and far from imagining that my job is a dirty one, for nine-tenths of the time it is 'cushy' compared to that of the infantry subaltern. It is a perfect delight to be able to change into cool whites and have a priceless game of tennis. The court is playing better every day—and so are we—with use.

We have two or three new officers with us now, one a 'rag-time specialist' and the other a Cambridge cricket blue.

We are all living for the happy days to come and doing our best in the meantime.

Fond love,
Frank

Frank's birthday was marked by a short test-flight on a fresh machine. His log book records 'Engine OK. Leak in top Water Tank.' Next day (16 July), 'Did not leave ground' but was 'written off by one behind, taxying onto my tail, cutting fuselage in two just behind the seat'. This accident occurred at about 6.00 p.m. but at 8.00 p.m. he 'brought new machine from St. Omer.'

We have got a new flight commander, Capt. C.R.J. Thompson,' he wrote home,

a splendid chap who has been with the squadron for months. The last one succeeded in writing off another machine allotted to me by taxying into my tail while I was waiting for an opportunity to take off. The fuselage was cut neatly in two just behind the seat and on looking round I found his 'prop' had stopped about a foot off my head. My machine looked just like a wasp severed in the act of guzzling jam i.e. 'Quite happy above the waist.' (23 July)

On the same day as this accident Frank wrote to our parents, who were at Bakewell:

376

Awfully glad to hear you did so well fishing after a dull beginning.

I am back again on drinks and baccy now—extremely moderate in both, however. As a squadron, ours is about as sober as any—probably more so. At lunch, very few have anything stronger than lime juice. One appreciates a little 'Beano' once in a way all the more. I thoroughly enjoyed my Boulogne outing.

We have been having it very quiet regarding work just recently, and are told that there is scarcely a Hun to be seen. Like everything else it goes in waves, I suppose, but brother Boche must be sorely tried for his personnel at the rate things are going.

Frank was trying to get special leave to attend my wedding which was to take place on Saturday, 28 July. 'All leave off for a time,' he informed me on a card.

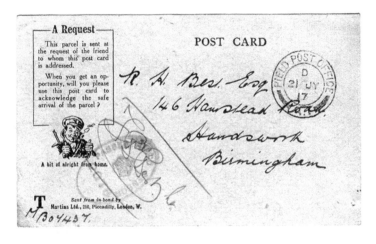

Intense preparations were being made for the Battle of Passchendaele, planned to open on 31 July. He was unsuccessful in his applications.

21 July

Dear Bob,

Had a priceless day yesterday at Le Touquet—Paris Plage. It is a pity all leave has been stopped for the moment. I am afraid that

that has just about knocked it on the head, for us.

Get yourself a wedding present from me. I've nothing to spend my money on out here, so you can tune up from £10 to £20, while the situation is so excellent.

Love to both,

Frank

Will send you a cheque when you unite.

According to his log book Frank took part in no patrols over the line between 15–20 July when he was in the air at 5.26 a.m. for 2 hours and 26 minutes, accompanying a formation of D.H.4s on a bombing raid. 'We gave the Boches a bit of stinko,' he wrote to me. The last six entries in his log book were:

21st	4.17 pm	Test	24 mins	Took machine over Lillers and Allouagne. Very misty.
22nd	10.04 am	Patrol	2 hrs 23 mins	Wonderfully clear. Saw 1 E.A. below & 7 E.A. which hurried off.
23rd	7.06 pm	Patrol	1 hr 55 mins	
24th	5.45 am	Test	17 mins	Very hot.
	4.15 pm	Patrol	1 hr 45 mins	Thick cloud.

The following day he wrote home describing the patrol which forms the last entry in his log book, as well as the reunion with his old friends in 46th Divisional Train.

R.F.C. in the Field, 25 July 1917

Dear All,

In spite of our oft irregular post, this may just catch you all at Wimbledon on the great day, as spectators for the great mixed-doubles event. It is sure to go off well and success is assured in such able hands—need I say more? As regards leave, far more important and urgent cases than mine have been refused; so we must make the best of it without grousing.

Yesterday we had another pukkah 'Valkyrie patrol'. I call it that when the clouds are the only surroundings. As you can judge, it is far harder to keep together under such conditions, but the flight formation was the best I have seen so far, for in spite of the 'dud' visibility which constantly obscured one or more of the machines from view, we stuck together from start to finish.

Archie appears from nowhere on these occasions, just the same, and, if anything, gives you an idea of where you are, as they have their pet areas for it.

The whole of yesterday was terribly sultry on the ground, so in a way the chill at 14,000 ft was quite pleasant.

It is hard to describe, but the light of the bright sun striking on what I should think must have been a fine form of sleet made it look like a beautiful white dress scintillating with those little white sparkly things all the time. (I don't know what you call them— perhaps E.G. will be radiating in the same manner on Saturday, but she will have a job to keep on swishing past at 90 miles an hour to make it all go streaky and complete the phenomenon.)

Yesterday evening was certainly one of the most pleasant yet, for I got leave to go in the side-car carrying the post to a town quite close to where Jack's old crew are stationed. I paraded up and down trying to find their billet (you can guess what it's like in these villages) and was met with many broad grins and gaping eyes from sundry drivers and N.C.O.s who recognised me in my altered capacity. At last I came across them and had a most priceless time reminiscing and exchanging news, etc.

Don and Capt. Court were away but 'Dad' Whittall and Jack

were in very good form and sent all sorts of messages to you all—particularly concerning the wedding—which may better be imagined. (They must all be the same since 1AD.)

My old batman Dickinson, also Wheeler, and Corporal Bishop of Best & Lloyd I came across together while reviewing the jolly old Wagon Park and Horse lines after supper.

They were moving today, which has ushered itself in with a good honest thunderstorm. It is bad luck for them all.

That was a day of days at Fermoy when Bob and I made our final decision to transfer. I wouldn't go back for worlds. It is only the first plunge that is difficult after all.

Tons of Love

'Francisco'

As entries in Frank's log book ceased on 24 Tuesday, we do not know what happened during the following three days but the absence of letters suggests that they were uneventful. His last letter said:[112]

R.F.C. in Field, 28 July 1917

My dear All,

Saturday—the great day. It does not see me at the ceremony. As a matter of fact I celebrated the occasion this end by a little scrap with a Boche 2 seater on my own. It is the first occasion that I have been able to pump stinko into them at close range and give the Hun a thoroughly rotten time of it by choosing my own time and place for the attack.

I saw this machine flying towards me at my own height (about 12,500) and thought it was one of ours returning after reconnaissance; however, taking no risks I steered off at right angles and after making a large circle which brought me back over the other machine (about 300 ft higher this time) and in a line between it and the sun, I prepared to escort him back safely over our lines when I discovered it was a Boche after all! He had got red-brown crosses on pale coloured discs which, with its dark upper surface, made him look very like a British machine with the usual red, white and blue bull's eye.

---

[112] From a copy in Father's handwriting.

By the way, the reason I was alone was that a minor defect on my own machine caused a delay at the beginning, so I set out later on another.

I now made quite sure that there were no scouts up in the sun also waiting to 'work the dirty across me' and after just looking round the gadgets inside the office to check temperature and pressure etc. I let her rip with the approved sights well on, at close range.

The observer did his best to retaliate and a stray shot caused a leak in my water tank which prevented me from seeing properly; unfortunately my gun jammed also after about 30 rounds so I was forced to break off.

I must have put the wind up him and given him something to go on with, for I saw the shots going straight into the fuselage. I last saw him nosing down but, I believe, under control. If only I hadn't got the gun jammed I might have finished him off properly. The C.O. was pleased with me which counts for more than a little.

In answer to your questions, zooming is a sudden climb—

—and the Pitot tube is the air-speed indicator tube and sticks out in front to catch the full blast. Will answer other points later—just off to see Jack again.

Imagining ceremonies have been great success. I thought of you all and felt very happy during the wedding ceremony hour.

Fond love,

Frank

PS: One gets ever so much more confidence after little shows of this kind.

That day (Saturday, 28 July) Beryl Smith and I were married at St. Mary's, Wimbledon and the organist played Frank's March of the Terriers while the congregation was assembling.

In the evening of the same day, Frank went over to Noeux-les-Mines, six kilometres south of Béthune. 'So,' to quote Jack

Best many years later, 'poor old Frank spent his last night with us and went through all the old records on the gramophone. It was a most remarkable thing that it should have happened thus and I have always felt that Frank would have chosen it so, if he could have foreseen the future.'[113]

The next day (29 July), Jack continues, 'there was a terrific thunderstorm when I was riding to Chocques to the dentist.' One flash, unpleasantly close, caused Jack's horse to shy. There is reason to suppose that Frank was in the air at about that time. He failed to return.

According to some notes left by Father, Frank's mechanic, Mr A. Cheshire, stated that the formation had consisted of Capt. C.R.J. Thompson (the Flight Commander), Lieut. C.D. Thompson, Lieut. McEntagert, Lieut. B.A. Powers and Capt. Gordon-Kidd. The tyres of both Frank's and Capt. Thompson's machines had come off as they were preparing to take the air. Frank walked back while the machines were re-tyred. They were the two last to take off, the others being out of sight. Frank had remarked, 'I must catch them up—now we'll go off warring!'

A few days later our parents received the following letter:

30 July 1917

Dear Mr Best,

I very much regret to tell you that your son Lieut. Best is reported missing since y'terday morning. He went out y'day morning at 8.00 on patrol with six others. At 9.30 in company with another officer he attacked some German aeroplanes just E of the lines. There was a storm coming up from the W and when they broke off the attack (during which there is reason to believe that they brought one German machine down) they were soon overtaken by the storm; the other machine turned up all right but says he did not see your son after the attack on the H/A,[114] but does not think that the German machines were able to shoot at

---

[113] 2 November, 1958.
[114] Hostile Aircraft.

him, so thinks he must have landed, after being lost in the storm, on the wrong side of the lines: and I sincerely hope that we shall hear that he is safe and a prisoner, and if we hear anything I shall let you know at once. I am most awfully sorry for you, as I know how terrible the anxiety and uncertainty is.

Yours sincerely,
W.D.S. Sanday, Major
No. 19 Squadron
9th Wing
R.F.C.

A second letter (6 August) from Major Sanday informed them that Frank's kit had been despatched and that all personal letters had been destroyed. He then went on to answer a request for further information:

What I meant to imply was that when your son was last seen he was in an advantageous position with regard to the Enemy machines, and that they were not in a position to be shooting at him; and from that, I gather your son turned West, or rather was turning West when last seen, so I think there is reason to hope that he has landed safely, but of course one can never know—it is not easy to always even land safely.

If I hear anything I will most certainly telegraph; meantime I should advise you to ask the Red X Association, Geneva, to try and obtain information for you.

I sympathise with you so much in your anxiety.

Yours sincerely,
W.D.S. Sanday
Major
I am doing all I can to obtain news.

On 24 September our parents received what was to be a final report:

Sir,

I beg to inform you that the following information has been received from the War Office concerning your son, Lieut. F.B. Best, North Mid. A.S.C.—

'In a list of English flying losses during the month of July 1917

383

published in the *Deutscher Allgemeiner Zeitung* (a German publication) the following report appears:

'B.3531. Occupant dead.

'This has been identified as referring to the above-named officer. However this report has not been accepted as official, so should be treated with reserve.'

Yours faithfully,

E.H. Hill, Lieut. Col.

Officer to the Territorial Forces Records

In a letter dated 15 May, 1919, C.D. Thompson, writing from Buenos Aires, described the patrol. His version does not altogether agree with that of Major Sanday, but this may have been due to the passage of time or to the fact that they were scattered and different individuals may therefore have seen things differently:

Dear Mr Best,

I have only just received your letter, which was forwarded to me here from England, written on 30 January.

I am afraid I cannot be of much use to you in the matter of finding your son's grave as no one knew how he came down. I remember the day of the storm very well which was 29 July 1917 because I had to come down at Bailleul. If that is the day your son was missing, we were working over the area YPRES—PASSCHENDAELE—WERVICQ—WARNETON. It was a miserable day with hardly a Hun in the sky, and thick clouds at 5,000 ft all along the lines. Owing to the bad weather and the absence of Huns we merely cruised around in the area indicated instead of going out further round to MENIN and ROULERS.

We were together for some time but eventually got scattered by their A.A.[115] fire which was remarkably good that day owing to the low height we were flying and the help the clouds gave the German gunners for ranging. Owing to the low visibility it was very hard to pick up formation again so most of us continued cruising around by ourselves till the rain got so bad that we went home or as near home as each could get.

Those are the facts as nearly as I can remember them on the

---

[115] Anti-aircraft.

day of the big storm but I cannot say for certain whether your son was reported missing on that day or not, as one rather loses count of dates when on service. I am most awfully sorry I cannot give you any more precise information, as I knew your son very well and he was a great favourite in the mess owing to his bright and genial nature and skill on the piano. The man who saw him last as far as I can remember was young Powers, but unfortunately he was also killed later. The only thing I could suggest, if you know the number of Frank's machine and you say that it was published in the *Flugsport* is to write to the Red Cross to make inquiries from the German Flying Corps records and find out where his number was found. Their records were very complete and if you could get access to them you would certainly find out where the machine fell, who found it, etc, etc.

Yours sincerely,
CD Thompson

Exhaustive enquiries in which, among others, our cousin Alice Ward threw herself wholeheartedly failed to provide any answers to our two outstanding questions: how exactly did Frank lose his life and where, if anywhere, was he buried?

Chapter 12
Is there anybody out there?

No answers were ever found to our questions. Frank died, in conditions unknown, leaving a great void. That void has lasted all my life and it is chiefly for that reason that I wrote this book: to provide a memorial where no other exists. No one could tell us where my brother's mortal remains were buried, or even whether they were buried. In the Arras Memorial, at the Faubourg-d'Amiens Cemetery, his name appears among those 'Officers and Men of the Air Services who fell on the Western Front, and have no known graves'. At the Birmingham War Memorial, once every eight months, a certain page is turned over and for two or three days his name is on view. In the Library at Bedales, some may notice the name of F.B. Best as they look up from their work. It appears over the second window from the left as they enter. But in a few decades the last of those who actually knew him will no longer be alive. Without some record such as this he would become just a name. This would be regrettable.

In some ways he was a remarkable young man. Developing rather late, he showed much zest for life and such a wide range of interests that at time he must have had difficulty in choosing between them. His sense of the burlesque and farcical was memorable. His musical and other gifts never went out of his head; and I have yet to find anyone who, meeting him, did not receive kind treatment at his hands. It is a paradox that such an amiable character should end his days in aerial warfare—an occupation that obviously gave him great satisfaction.

While mentally reviewing these last months of my brother's life I have tried to think back into his mood at that time, comparing it with my own and with that of many of his companions. How did he feel about the Germans, the war, about Life and Death? How far, if at all, was he out of touch with 'reality'? I have found myself pondering deeply over this apparent contradiction: that a young man, idealistic and gentle, could take part in such lethal activities with such relish. How could Frank, who showed affectionate understanding towards almost everyone he met, write about murderous attacks on his fellow mortals in this vein:

> I must have put the wind up him and given him something to go on with, for I saw the shots going straight into his fuselage! It's the first occasion that I have been able to pump stinko into them at close range and given the Hun a thoroughly rotten time of it by choosing my own time and place for the attack.

That he was living his life intensely and on a high level of self-fulfilment is clear from the note of exultation that creeps into some of his letters:

> That was a day of days at Fermoy when Bob and myself made our final decision to transfer. I wouldn't go back for worlds.

The fascination of flying those first war aeroplanes has already been fully described. Even the aerial fights constituted a challenge to individual skill and judgement that is never likely to be repeated in war. I was blessed with little of my brother's courage and *élan* but it is no exaggeration to say that my three months over the line on artillery observation in the winter and early spring of 1918 was one of the most exhilirating and enjoyable episodes of my life. The fact is that Frank's attitude to his job at the front and all it implied was in some ways shared by many flying officers.

Even so, reading his diaries and letters, one cannot help wondering whether he was somewhat unusual in his detachment, and in the intensity, variety and quality of the impressions he was registering—the 'Valkyrie' patrols, the scintillating cloud effects, the blue-brown haze across the crimson ball of light, and so forth.

His attitude to the war may have been affected by the fact that, unlike his friends Vyv Trubshawe and Oswald Horsley, and in spite of his service in France during 1915, he had never experienced the grisly horrors of trench warfare—'The earth turned to thick gummy mud, ghastly and evil smelling'.

We were, of course, being misled as to facts and issues by our own propaganda. To quote H.G. Wells:

All the great states of Europe before 1914 were in a condition of aggressive nationalism and drifting towards war; the government of Germany did but lead the general movement. She fell into the pit first, and she floundered deepest. She became the dreadful example at which all her fellow sinners could cry out.

But had Frank known what we know now, would he have acted differently? I doubt it.

Of special interest are Frank's attempts to understand the big events of the day, his views representing, to some extent, public opinion in the forces at that time and place. He approved 'the tone of old Woodrow Wilson's note' on the occasion of the sinking of the Lusitania.[116] (5 May 1915)

---

[116] The Lusitania was a British passenger liner that was en route from New York City to London on May 7, 1915 when it was apparently torpedoed by a German submarine. It sank in 15 minutes, drowning some 1,198 civilians, of whom 128 were American. The attack was immediately denounced by the American president, Woodrow Wilson, who demanded that Germany pledge to never attack citizens of neutral countries again. A propaganda battle then followed, in which Germany claimed that the ship had actually been sunk by the British in order to bring America into the war.

We never thought he'd have the face to write anything so politely, which when paraphrased amounts to ... 'Now we don't want any excuses—is the submarine game going to stop?'

I can't possibly imagine what will happen. It is all such a great game, but Italy looks like doing something at last. (18 May 1915)

Frank felt that the sinking of the Lusitania had its 'bright side', in that it gave England something to shriek about; this also applied to the gas attack. 'It will take a lot to bring neutrals to their senses,' he wrote, 'likewise many Englishmen'. (18 May 1915)

In May, Lloyd George was appointed Minister of Munitions and the *Daily Mail* was burnt by the London Stock Exchange for its attack on Kitchener.[117] Frank wrote,

... here we nearly all agree that what [the *Daily Mail*] said was correct, but that its *manner* of doing it was dirty, to say the least of it, and uncalled for. (5 June 1915)

In June of the same year Frank noted with approval that the papers were 'fairly ramming home the "Organise the Nation" theory.[118] It will be fine,' he thought, 'when anyone failing to carry out his duty at home will be liable to punishment by military law. All the military will welcome conscription, as far as I can see.' (2 June 1915)

Frank speculated on the course of events in Gallipoli.[119] 'Could we penetrate to the road artery which supplies the tip of the peninsular—no matter how far back? Then, if Germany can't get her supplies through Russia to Turkey, how far will she succeed in smashing her way through Servia [sic] without the adjacent States?' (17 August 1915)

---

[117] See Introduction.

[118] In 1915, British politics was split on the question of introducing forced conscription and state control of industry.

[119] Strategic peninsula in eastern Turkey, between the Aegean Sea and the Dardanelles straits. Subjected to a failed eight-month naval attack by British and French forces, successfully repelled by the Ottoman empire.

Towards the end of September Frank wrote: 'We are all in fairly high spirits now, not only on account of the marvellous way that the Russians have extricated themselves from behind Vilna, but also because of the expectations that are being talked about (which I cannot publish) referring to the whole of the Western Front.' (25 September 1915)

Frank's call for regimentation of the civilan population with 'punishment by military law' was symptomatic of the general witch-hunt for spies, slackers and *embusqués* which was being whipped up by the gutter press. Otherwise sensible people found themselves trying to establish a 'more-patriotic-than-thou' position, and to segregate human beings into 'We' and 'They'. I suppose that I was as prone as anyone else to this form of war-hysteria, which intensified as the casualty lists lengthened.

In this competitive situation, however, the roles were sometimes liable to be reversed, so that a fundamentally patriotic individual such as Frank would suddenly find himself the object of oblique criticism. One wonders what his feelings were on reading the following observations in the *Bedales Chronicle* from the pen of his friend Vyv Trubshawe:

> Bug minor and I write furious letters to each other arranging to meet each other if … and that is as far as it gets, because on that particular day I am in the firing trenches and he is showing off his spurs on his untamed cab horse somewhere between the two ends of the 46th Divisional Train A.S.C., which is moving North or South and as far away as possible. Still I am determined that we shall meet and that right early …

Vyv Trubshawe has since talked to me freely about what he calls his 'snootiness' (which he has subsequently regretted) towards us both at that time, on account of our serving in the A.S.C. As I have explained, it was symptomatic of the period; neither Frank nor I were free from it. But we need to remind ourselves that Frank and his colleagues had in no way sought a sheltered job. We have seen how four of them had volunteered for training before the war, the corps in which they served being settled largely by chance. If they ever thought it would be safer serving in the transport section, experience of the Boer War would not have been particulary reassuring.

Besides, it would have seemed ungrateful and disloyal to the friendly group of officers and men of No. 3 Company and above all to Jack Best, whose leadership so inspired Frank and those others with whom he served.

Having tried to recapture some of the often conflicting thoughts and emotions to which not just Frank but I and others were subjected while carrying out our duties, I still find myself somewhat perplexed. A hint, however, which may lead to better understanding, is given by the poet-philosopher Saint-Exupéry, who qualified as a civil air pilot in 1921 and lost his life while serving with the French forces in 1944 after a distinguished career in the French and Argentinian Air Mail services.

War is wrong, he tells us in *Terre des Hommes*, and we are right to hate it, but there are certain experiences that seem to satisfy some essential need. Life takes on a reality that it had not before. The secret of this reality is not to be proved or demonstrated by logical arguments. If a certain soil suits certain orange trees, that is *la vérité des oranges*, i.e. essential for orange trees. So, if certain religions, certain forms of culture *favorisent dans l'homme cette plénitude*, that is *la vérité de l'homme*—his reality. When wild ducks migrate, domestic ducks attempt a clumsy flight and change into migratory birds. They beat their wings, scorn the seeds, grain and worms, and wish to become wild ducks.

Clearly this is all a challenge to pacifism. How can one provide a soil in which the adventurous spirit can develop alongside the doctrine of Love Your Neighbour and Reverence for Life?

As for Frank's religious views, his unreserved acceptance of *Lessons in Truth*, it would be unwise to dismiss them as a form of escapism. I now realise how little I understood this side of his character. I cannot remember ever discussing 'ultimate realities' with him, as he and his brother officers had done in 1915.

During the war, however, there were certain beliefs that we both accepted unquestioningly. One was 'Survival after Death' (after all, had not Sir Oliver Lodge, a physicist, practically proved it?) and another was that death was preferable to defeat by the Germans.

It is true that his optimism was unshakeable and that he wished to spare our parents anxiety. He was constantly pre-occupied with our parents' welfare and happiness, sent them carnations from Engelman's at Saffron Walden, and was insistent that Father should not overwork. I am convinced, therefore, that he tended to exaggerate the comfort and safety of his life at the line in order to reassure them. But when he wrote about 'the conviction of a charmed existence', I cannot believe that he meant the words to be taken literally, or that he had any illusions as to the real dangers of his duties. As I have said, he was a late developer and not given to analysing his philosophical ideas or expressing them in a mature manner.

That he held strong views and tried to put them into practice is clear from the story of his life. Having heard him lecture and explain relatively difficult propositions I would guess that, had he lived, he would have taken up some form of teaching activity in which ethical or spiritual values played a part. This might, or might not, have been associated with our business. He had his own version of *The Perennial Philosophy*. Up to the end he held to the hypothesis that God is Love and in the words of Job 'Though he slay me, yet will I trust in him.'

News that Frank must be presumed to be dead came to our parents while taking a short fishing holiday at Bakewell. Some years later I heard from Mr Ernest Wood of the Rutland Arms how they received the news. He said that he would not easily forget Mr Best's stoical calm or the expression in Mrs Best's eyes.

Mother's behaviour (and for that matter mine) towards our nanny Emma Hopley left much to be desired in the time she was with us. Emma liked Father, who was grateful for anything she did for him; she was also much attracted to Frank. Mother and I were, however, a sore trial to her. When an opportunity eventually presented itself, she very wisely turned to another job and became a qualified hospital nurse. And yet it was to Emma that my mother first turned for help and consolation.

Emma had been with our family for sixteen years and had looked after Frank when he was still a small child. She had forgiven Mother and did what she could to lessen the strain. 'To me he was perfect,' she said, 'and I think his love for his father and mother the most beautiful thing I ever saw.'

Mother's struggle to readjust herself is apparent from the following letter to Mrs Simmendinger of Kingstown.

> ... altho' there was so much to do and answer, I felt quite unable to attend to my duties, so when Bob and his wife came to visit us, they made me return with them to their little furnished house in Ayrshire [i.e Gowanbrae, at the Maidens].
>
> The complete change did me good, and now we are trying to carry out Frank's expressed wish that we should not unduly grieve. But it is terribly difficult; he had so many interests: music, art, gardening, photos.—wherever I turn something talks of him and his bright future as we pictured it together! (28 October 1917)

Frank had made a number of bequests to his friends and relatives. Father wrote to each one:

> It is about Frank I am writing. He left his affairs in my hands before going to France in 1915 in the form of a sealed packet in which he outlined his wishes leaving me considerable liberty of discretion, but we could not bring ourselves to open it for nearly 12 months after his being reported missing, for his mother clung to the hope that he might still be alive. However, it is opened and I am now carrying out his wishes. They are characteristic of him and considerate towards his old friends and interests ...

During the summer of 1918 proposals for a Bedales Memorial Library[120] were initiated, and it was to this project that a proportion of his legacies found its way, with the consent of the

---

[120] Designed by Ernest Gimson, now Grade 1 listed. Furniture by Gimson and the Barnsleys: brothers Sidney and Ernest and Sidney's son Edward.

Bedalians, or their trustees,[121] named in Frank's memorandum. This sum was increased by an amount he had left for the purchase of a grand piano to be used for school concerts, the instrument having in the meantime come to the school from another source.

To Nellie Simmendinger went his tie pin made up into a ring. Other bequests were made to our cousin Sydney Anderton, who had since fallen, to Paul Funke and Vincent Hollard, sons in the two families with which he had stayed while abroad, to Nelson Street Early Morning Adult School, and to the Boys' Club in Mornington Road, adjoining the works.

Lastly, he 'desired a sum of money to be dovoted towards "the equipment of a room for the social interests of employees of Best & Lloyd" and to this was given the bulk of the money. For some years after the First War it formed the Works Canteen. It was later occupied by the 'B & L' Select Club.

———

I have tried to sum up my brother's character, attitudes and history, and to understand the paradoxes that these give rise to. Two things continue to preoccupy me and deserve recording. One is the flavour of my own life in the eighteen months or so after Frank's death, and what now seems a false, even desperate, lightness; the other is my impression of Germany in the 1920s in the light of what Frank and I had experienced a dozen years earlier. I offer both to the reader without comment.

———

Clifton Court, Rugby, 31 May 1918

My darling Beryl,

I understand about you going into the home and think it very wise. I don't know the address of the home so shall send this to

---

[121] The three Bedalians were Vyv Trubshawe, Sylvia Mundy and Oswald Horsley. It is doubtful, however, whether Horsley ever learnt of Frank's bequest.

Woodland Ice. The sooner it comes off now the better (providing medical requirements are fulfilled) as you will be well sooner and I shall be able to come up and be with you. There will be some happy days ahead, I hope, when it's all over.

The dance was a huge success, only marred by the fact that nearly all the men who weren't dancing got disgustingly drunk. Luckily they kept away from the visitors but I did feel ashamed.

You see, there was a Major Forbes at the neighbouring aerodrome who was invited and that same day I went to the aerodrome and found it was Leslie Forbes, with whom I went to a dame school and have known all my days—at the tennis club and gold club. He took me up to try my hand in an Auroc during the afternoon and I find that my nerve's all there. He did a few spins and side slipped to within a few feet of the ground.

He was absolutely bucked at meeting me again and so was I. I asked him to sell me a bottle of bubbly so that we could bring it to the dance and celebrate our meeting. He refused to accept payment and brought up a whole case of drinks!

Now, here's the tragedy—these non-dancing drunkards got hold of this stuff and became absolutely paralytic. Mrs Mulliner blamed Leslie and myself, though she was too nice to say so, and altogether I've been awfully ashamed of the whole thing, especially as everybody agreed that the actual dance was a great success.

Yesterday I took the Pater out fishing and had a lovely day. We got no trout but five bream with a fly, averaging about a pound each.

It is rather astounding about Unity More,[122] isn't it?

I think of you and long for you at least umteen times nightly—dar-ar-ar-ling.

Thine, Bob

———

Clifton Court, Rugby, 6 June 1918

Am awfully sorry you're suffering from the heat. It gives me beans when I get hot as well as a nerve down the left side of my 'bottine'

———

[122] A popular dancer who gave up her career to get married in 1918 after having appeared in Ship Ahoy! (1914), Peter Pan (1915) and Happy Days (1916).

has been slightly affected. Fortunately the weather has been quite cool here for the last few days.

Childbirth is wonderful—one seems to get a sort of glimpse of the workings of that mysterious affair called 'life'. It seems extraordinary that one marvels at it being possible at all. And as it is possible and quite frequently occurring, in point of fact, one begins to wonder if there's anything really impossible, when the great Spirit gives its mind to it. Peter Eckersley is of a very inquiring turn of mind and was awfully impressed with it all. He was in close touch at the time.

I am sending you a rotten book which Walter Schürhoff gave me. It may while away the midnight hours (I seldom stop reading till about 1.00 a.m. myself) but to my mind there's too much 'Gay Hazard' and 'little mare' along with 'the feud' and 'jesting'.

I'm also sending my own playlet which, with the exception of the appearance of the Brigade Major in the Mess, is a fairly faithful account of events as they occurred to our squadron when the Huns started this push on the St. Quentin front. Treat it as more or less confidential at present. Mulrony is Capt. White, Stanton is the old skipper Hanlon, and Guest is supposed to be me. Jones is a man called Knight, who did crash in exactly the manner described; even Mulroney's remark about the bridge debt is true.

The concert is to take place tonight. Last night we had a rehearsal with Latham (the Rugby master) who is getting quite a pal of mine. I am singing 'Piccadilly, London West' and Frank's song 'The Rag-Time Folk Song'.

I am going down to Derbyshire for tomorrow and Saturday to get a bit of fishing with Father but I will try and write you from there.

There is a new character to add to my synopsis of previous chapters—to wit, one Lt. Slack, a boy who shares the room with me now. He stammers and is not over endowed with brains, I think. For all that, he is good company and rather amusing. He has money and comes of quite a good family; he started his military career at Sandhurst but was turned down through inability to pass the exams.

I enclose some snaps of our huts at —— near St. Omer. The man in the middle of the one is Whitey and at the other is myself. Pickup is on the left and Severne on the right.

My suit—RAF blue—is jolly well cut and gives me great joy.

———

British Flying School, Vendôme, France, 6 September 1918

This morning I did my first bit of instructing. I have got three pupils who have never flown before and I am giving them dual control. The methods have changed an awful lot since I learned to fly and are now far more systematic. You have a speaking tube to the 'Quirks' (as they call pupils here) and having got your height you proceed to give them the entire control. You let him get the machine into any mess he likes without you touching the control and you talk to him the whole time—explaining what he's to do to straighten up the bus again. It is very interesting work although you do get some bloodsome young fools nowadays who take hours of patient work before you can send them are solo and even then they crash. I am quite in the swim of things now and am on drinking terms with nearly everyone in the two squadrons.

I am reading a French book all about Wimbledon called *L'île inconnu* (by Pierre de Coulerain, Aunt Alice's friend).

————

British Flying School, Vendôme, 30 September 1918

I don't know about the partridge's legs—they seem to be a neutral sort of tint. I enjoyed myself awfully shooting on the Chateau grounds yesterday (see letter to Lorna) that clean forgot to notice the colour of the partridge's legs.

Who is the Mrs Handley that you went to call on? She isn't the wife of Bertie Handley I suppose? I didn't seem to have heard of her before.

I am hugely thrilled and running a flight. It keeps me well occupied and gives me just that scope for managing things which I used to enjoy at the works and which I haven't been able to indulge in since I started soldiering.

I have just heard from the Hollards that my old friend Vincent (their son) has been killed. I was very shocked to receive the news, as I was hoping to see him again on my next leave. Mme Hollard expected him en permission in a week or two and I was so looking forward to meeting him.

————

397

British Flying School, Vendôme, 6 October 1918

Very little more news except flying—flying—flying. I'm getting my flight into something like ship-shape now and have got a great help in the unit commander who has two flights under him (three units go to a Training Depot Squadron), mine being one of them. He is a conscientious old stick and chews the fat rather a lot but is a good chap to work with. I've got off two more solos in the last two days and one complete pupil (my first). My flight has been top of the flying list in hours, so all goes well.

I had a good afternoon on the Château grounds yesterday and got a couple of brace, which was the most any of our party got. I'm getting the knack, dearest. You have to aim about umpteen yards in front of the beggars as they travel at such a lick. I brought off one very long shot. Cheerio ....

———

British Flying School, Vendôme, 23 October 1918

My dearest Darling,

By the way, I've never had an answer in re. Dress Allowance (as the lawyers say) and also in re. christening the baba. We ought to give Peacho his job.

I did over three hours flying yesterday and the flight did 18 hours thus making us top of the Caudrans.[123]

I had a cheery letter from old Sam [Sloan] yesterday which I will reply to in due course. I've got some topping 'Dope Boards' being made. These are sort of blackboards so that you can see data at a glance. Frinstance the hours flying that each pupil has done, the condition of each machine and engine etc.

I love giving my quirks advanced dual instruction and assuming the role of showman for their benefit. You keep up a patter down the telephone during a spinning nosedive and then turn round and watch the quirk's face when you come out of it. They do make me laugh at times.

This is the style of thing: Telephone (speaking very slowly and distinctly):   We—have—now—reached—3,000—feet.   No—

———

[123] A Caudran was a four-engined aeroplane.

standards—should—be—performed—below—this. To—do—a—spin—I—first—throttle—down—(Engine slows down)—gently—pull—the—stick—back—(the nose goes up)—at—the—same—time—pulling—on—full—left—rudder. (The nose drops sheer down at an alarming angle.) You—will—doubtless—notice—that—we—are—spinning. (The Quirk clutches the nacelle and stares at the ground rushing round.) To—come—out—of—the—spin, we—apply—opposite—rudder—and—gently—ease—the—machine—out—of—the—resulting—vertical—nose—dive (The bus dives like ————, the wires sing and the Quirk's eyes start out of his head) etc. etc.

Rather funny, n'est-ce pas.

Beaucoup kisses for the precious BaBa and thine own self,

Your old Hubby,

X Bob x

British Flying School, Vendôme, 2 November 1918

Darling Old Thing,

In re. Dress Allowance (as the lawyers say): one hundred powoo-oo-oo-nds [à la Harry Tate] be it and I wish I was with you to receive the ear-bite to seal the compact. It had better be work quarterly (the allowance) but I enclose £25 cheque on Megs[124] for this quarter; you can then draw on Lloyd's for £25 straight away and you will be capitalized up to end of March 1919, see? Fair doos, n'est-ce pas?

Para., umpteen, reference: Christening, Junelet, Baba, icky, for my information and necessary action, noted please.

I say, do you realize that this jolly old war's going to be over very soon now? I've been thinking a lot about what we're going to do and where we're going to live. I shall have to work hard until I'm 30, I think—after that I ought to be able to enjoy life in a quiet sort of way. I'm afraid the first year's going to be rather a stiff proposition. I can see your old hubby greatly changed from the 'full-out' skipper RAF to a harassed old manufacturer—far more preoccupied the old Jack—and the pall of work upon him with a vengeance. Then there's the great question of where we're going to

---

[124] Griggors Bank.

live. The perennial dispute of Handsworth versus Edgbaston will be brought to a head, believe me. I should dearly like to stop in Sutton, but for the tremendous time it would take me to get to Best & Lloyd's. It's a game, though, isn't it?

I was very interested to hear about the mutual friends of the Wilkinsons' and your jolly old self. There's no doubt but what we could have a full-out time in Staffordshire if we laid ourselves out for it.

The flu problem seems to be getting rather acute in Blighty. For God's sake be careful and go straight to bed accompanied by a hot water bottle if you feel wonky.

Today has been dud for flying, thank Heaven. I had far too much work to do lately. My flight has turned out as many pupils as the other two Caudron flights put together, during the last month. This morning I 'walked up' the 'drome with Percy Carter (the French N.C.O. liaison officer). We saw tons of stuff the birds are pretty wild and we only got one shot in. This afternoon I had some practice with clay pigeons.

Yes, four weeks to go for my next Blighty leave and I intend to make up for lost time when I get it.

Thine, as ever.

Bob XX

I still gaze the hours at that photo of you and the baba.

————

British Flying School, Vendôme, 14 November 1918

My darling Wifey,

It will not to the long now before we're united for good. I've just spoken to the Major and he says that owing to the special circumstances, he will let me come home end of next week. Once home they'll have a job to get me out here again. I don't suppose I shall have much difficulty in getting my release. And then I must work and I look too dear old Beryl to get hold of my old head and push it up against the grindstone, because I've been done nothing in the way of work for four years.

I haven't done any flying for at least a week and the last three days have been one protracted carouse. However I must say I don't feel any the worse for it.

Three things I've quite made up my mind about. 1) We'll have a young beano when I get home. 2) We'll push the Mater and Pater off on a prolonged holiday. 3) When I've got things going we'll go away for a second honeymoon.

Doesn't it seem like a dream though! My mind keeps on running over the events of the last four years and the wonder of it all makes me thrill in the same way that certain heroic music does.

Thine as always, longing to be back so that we can live happily ever after.

———

In April 1919 I wrote to Beryl's mother. Mrs Smith had been very ill—she would die the day after receiving the letter—and I commended her on her courage in her illness and took the opportunity to talk about my faith in Frank's survival beyond the grave.

27 April 1919

My dear Mrs Smith,

One of the things that has made us all so sorry lately has been the knowledge that we could do so little for you when we would like to do so much and I've thought that if in any way I could reassure you about certain things, I should always remember the fact with pleasure.

Firstly about Beryl—you know that we're even fonder lovers than ever. Every day I find fresh things to love her for and new reasons for blessing the day we met. We are always quite happy together at home and though I have to be away at the works a lot just now, this will not always be—in a little time we shall be able to go about together a lot more than now.

Then there's the baby who gets stronger and more of a pet day by day. She is a great comfort to Beryl at this trying time.

For my own part I want to make you feel sure that I will try to look after them both as well as you've looked after Beryl and do everything I can to make them happy in years to come.

There's just one more thing—I must say how much I admire the brave way you are looking things in the face. It's one thing to face the odd chance of a bullet and so forth but an infinitely more difficult matter to keep a stiff upper lip through an ordeal like yours. I shall always remember your courage with something of a thrill, because I'm sure that it's the right thing. You know my views on life hereafter; they have grown into more of a habit than anything else. I am absolutely sure that Frank's true self lives still and that we shall meet again—so that when the end comes please know that I for one shall not look upon it as the end but rather as the beginnng. The bodily end is made to appear fearful as a sort of bogey so that people shan't hold life too lightly.

I hope you will understand the feeling behind all this and feel at ease about dear old Brillo and June.

———————

Later that summer I received a letter from Sylvia Mundy, whose brother was one of the first to be killed in the retreat from Mons with the L. Battery of the Royal Horse Artillery. The letter includes the transcript of a spiritualist or ouija board séance, held to try and make contact with Frank. Spiritualism had become very popular in the years after the First World War.

29 Cheniston Gardens, Kensington W8, 6 August 1919

Dear Bob,

Enclosed are some of the writings I told you of. There was a lot more but I've cut out those I thought would be of most interest to you. I'm so awfully glad (and much relieved incidentally) to have had that talk with you and shall send the word whenever I get anything further of interest.

Sorry you had to go straight home on Tuesday but I hope we shall see something of you both during the winter when you have to come up. Do please give my love to your people: I wish we were going to Criccieth too.

All kind remembrances to your wife.

Sylvia

SÉANCE 24TH JULY 1919

Who are you? '*Frank Best bug minor.*'

Do you meet any Bedalians? '*Jarry often talks about you*'

And do you often meet my Frank too? '*Yes rather Iefussly systematic seol to Ines simes*'

Do you mean you have systematic times to meet? '*Yes yes*'

Have you tried to write before? '*No I could see so little chance of getting you alone*'

But it really was you yesterday? '*Yes but on[ly] a bit of what I said was true*'

She put in some then? '*Yes*'

But you remember me clearly? '*Yes*'

[Next question and answer have been cut out, presumably by Sylvia]

That was a priceless letter you wrote when I was engaged. '*Oh now!*'

You're quite cheery now? '*Yes I miss Bob awfully*'

Who shall I tell about this? '*Bob*'

Do you ever see Bryson? '*Yes he is here now*'

Won't he try and write? '*I don't know he is awfully shy about such things*'

Do tell him to try and send word to his people. '*Yes I'll tell him*'

Are you glad now that you tried? '*Well I should jolly well thin[k] so*'

Are you quite fit now? '*Yes! Thanks awfully I'm as fit as can be*'

And what are you doing? '*All sorts of stunts that would amuse you. Yes so Oswald*[125] *wants to see you awfully about something special I think so I'll say goodbye for the pres[ent] come again another tim[e] good night Sylvia*'

Just write your nickname once more. '*Bug Minor*'

—long pause—'*Oswald I want you to tell Seward [?] you don't believe in Yosne beowealrsn*'

What?

---

[125] Possibly Oswald Horsley, killed in a flying accident while testing a machine that his C.O. had taken out the day before and not been entirely satisfied with.

REVISITING GERMANY
(written 22 March 1923)

On returning from a ten days' visit to Germany, I was asked by some of my friends to write up my impressions, so in the hope that these would be of some interest, I hastily threw together a few notes and dictated them at odd times.

My journey took me to Leipzig for seven days, and then to Berlin, where I was fortunate in having friends. My object was primarily to inspect glassware at the Leipzig Fair, which is an exhibition of trade samples open to business people only. Nearly all German industries are represented. Foreign industry is also represented in the Austrian, Swiss, Czechoslovakian and Hungarian buildings.

My impressions of the Fair are recorded separately. As for travelling, it is not so comfortable as in pre-war days. First- and second-class carriages are distinguished only in name, as there is an interchangeable number outside each compartment, which can be altered to suit the demand.

Walking round, one is struck by the gloomy appearance of the people. The smaller children seem pretty well, but children of about four or five generally do look plump. A number of boys about 12 years of age looked very thin and pale, probably owing to the shortage of food during the war.

One gets very much the same impression that one had in England during the early part of 1918. Rationing, scarcity of butter, no green vegetables, people bringing bread and sugar to the restaurants in order to save the expense; people eating their sandwiches in the foyer at the opera, all help to strengthen this impression. At the same time there are the usual signs of wealth and extravagance which are associated with a rising market.

I saw a few soldiers and I noticed a great change from the pre-war smartness in their appearance. The uniforms of policemen, soldiers and officials look old and shabby. The policemen and soldiers are still wearing their field grey. The foreigners visiting Germany may be deceived by the small number of ragged people. This doesn't mean that the people aren't poor or in need of clothes. In pre-war days there were very few ragged untidy people, and this still holds good today. The reason for this is difficult to find, but it may be due to some instinct for respectable appearance or to the secondary schooling which is compulsory.

The people who are hit hardest by the inflation of the currency, are the professional classes—Lawyers, Doctors, School Teachers, Clergyman and also those who were dependent on investments in securities bearing interest at a fixed rate. The professional folk for some reason or other do not get adequate remuneration for their services, and the rentiers are reduced to extreme poverty. One hears stories, which I have no doubt are true, of a dangerously large number of suicides amongst these classes, and one wonders what effect the partial extinction of the professional classes will have on the future of the country. Possibly it may not be as serious as at first sight, owing to the better standard of education amongst the artisan class.

I had a very moving insight into the professional man's position. One of my friends in Berlin is a Lutheran Clergyman and as a Cathedral preacher (there are only three) can be looked upon as one of the principal Padres in the country. His stipend is 270,000 Marks a month, which, if we take the increase in the cost of living as 3,500 [times], gives us 77 Marks a month in pre-war purchasing power. His flat, which is a fairly large one, is provided rent free, but he can't afford books and must have great difficulty in educating his two sons. Needless to say his wife has to do all the cooking and housework. Rather an interesting sidelight is thrown on the present trend of affairs by the fact that the older son, whose natural bent is towards the Church, has been forced to take up industrial studies. He divides his time between the University and the factory, and his aim is to qualify as a professor of industrial matters (Kaufmännischer Lehrer). One might mention he seems to find the study of industry more interesting than he bargained for, and is throwing himself heart and soul into his work.

A good many students get jobs in the mines or factories

during their holidays and thereby earn enough to keep them going during the term time.

The dearness of books has led to such a run on the libraries that they are half empty.

The case of rentiers and pensioners is pretty hopeless. One hears of old people having to go to bed in the afternoon as they cannot afford coal or light.

The municipal theatres, at any rate in Leipzig and Berlin, are still going. At Leipzig a good seat costs a German about 10,000 Marks, but it costs a foreigner about 30,000. Furthermore, his passport can be demanded at any time in the theatre. Germans too are obliged to have a certificate of nationality.

The standard of the work produced seems to be as high as ever and the two nights that I went to the opera at Leipzig, the theatre was full.

My Padre friend spoke to me at length of the problem of the Jewish invasion. He said that a number of Jews had come in to Germany from the East on account of the exchange and also the ease with which money could be made. He compared them to vultures. He had stories to tell of people arriving in labourers' clothes and in a few weeks settling down in the best part of the town as gentlemen ('Vornehme Leute').

I heard that signs of demoralisation are not wanting. An eye-witness told me that in the racy restaurants all the best people have their silver-topped tubes of cocaine and this is emptied on the back of the hand and taken quite openly.

They seem to make far more of religious differences in Germany than in either France or England. They are afraid that the Rhine province will secede owing to the large number of Catholics there. They told me that the Pope is getting a great deal of influence through the Catholic or Zentrum party, and they expressed surprise that England did not side with Germany in 1914 because we were both Protestant countries (!)

Naturally the question as to who was responsible for the war formed the subject of many heated arguments. Everywhere I found the people looked upon the invasion of Belgium as an

406

error in diplomacy. Their attitude is briefly this: 'We were technically in the wrong, but had you been placed as we were, you would have done exactly the same thing'. This argument is repeated monotonously when one mentions such events as the Lusitania, the use of poison gas, Flammenwerfer, and so forth.

The so-called Belgium atrocities were indignantly denied and were attributed to French propaganda. The propaganda of the Allies was very much more efficient than their own, according to their point of view, although at the present time one sees a great number of posters and leaflets regarding the Ruhr question.

It is interesting to note at no time during the war was there any nickname for the English or the French, such as we had for the German (e.g. Hun or Boche).

Feeling runs very high against the French and the Belgians; Germans cannot understand why the Belgians, who they look upon as a hybrid and inferior race, should be allowed to worry them about so. Notices are put up in all the hotels and restaurants that the French and Belgians will not be served. One hears stories of atrocities committed in the occupied territory, which must have some foundation of fact, and they argue that whereas things which happened in Belgium (!) occurred in a war between two armed nations, the French are now victimising a defenceless people. They believe that the French have two aims, and these are the complete ruin of German industry, and the setting up of an independent Rhenish Republic, to which Germany is to acquiesce as the price of release from further reparations. In considering what has already been paid to the reparations account, they insist, with a certain justice, on capitalising the taxability of the territory which has been taken from them, allowing for the cost of governing such territory. They are firmly convinced that England's attitude to the French is one of fear for, as they point out, the French have enormous military and flying strength, and with their submarine power might give us an awkward time if it came to a war.

The feeling towards the English is not bad, especially if a little tact is exercised. First I found the notes rather difficult to deal with. I kept all notes of denominations corresponding to English silver in my trousers pocket, but when I pulled out a handful containing some 10,000 Mark notes to pay for a drink, the people were rather annoyed and seemed to think that I was a profiteer. One has to realise that apart from the discrepancy between the internal purchasing power and the exchange value of the Mark, there is a good deal in the psychological effect that big figures have on the people. They imagine that 10,000 Marks is still a large sum of money.

As the Padre said, in 1914 their attitude towards us was one of hate, which later changed to regard (Acht), but which has now changed to disdain (Veracht). One man expressed very much the same ideas as were published by Professor Wells in the *Manchester Guardian Commercial*:

> The effect of the Armistice and the Peace Treaty in Germany has never been quite realised in England. Whether the military situation was such as to compel surrender and, if so, why, are questions which it is beyond me to decide. The point is that before the surrender took place certain words were spoken by the Entente which led, and could only lead, the Germans to expect different treatment from what they got. Mr Wilson's Fourteen Points are vaguely worded, but their drift is unmistakable. It is equally unmistakable that they were not observed. The Englishman feels a certain discomfort when they are mentioned, but he does not take the matter very seriously, he prefers to pass on to German guilt, upon which he is very strong. For the moment, however, let us stick to his [our?] own.
>
> By its non-fulfilment of these Points, the Entente has placed itself morally in the position of a man who, having a dog he wants to punish nearly within his reach, says encouragingly: 'Come along, old fellow, it won' t be so very bad!' and then punishes it—well, as if the words had never been spoken.

These ideas are present in the minds of almost every German one speaks to.

The experience of war is a seductive topic of conversation and I was awfully interested to hear how their soldiers had fared. The private soldiers seem to have a poor opinion of their Officers and N.C.O.s, who infuriated the men in the latter stages of the war by sending home to their wives and families rations which they had robbed from the men.

You hear little about the Kaiser which is favourable, even from people who were formerly his most loyal supporters. His second marriage has done a lot to alienate public regard. All the people I spoke to thought he was keen on preserving the peace. They think that he was vain, and in the latter stages of the war, people were astonished when he insisted more and more on his personal responsibility to God rather than to the people. They have never really forgiven him for going off to Holland. As for the Crown Prince, my friends gave me the impression that the least said about him the better.

I am always rather amazed at the German's capacity for reading, studying, pondering over questions and thinking things over till his head must ache. One chance acquaintance brought up an amazing amount of knowledge concerning England's political and military history. At the mere mention of Belgium, he counter-attacked by telling me what Nelson did at Copenhagen. I thought to myself 'if they haven't forgiven Nelson, they'll remember the Ruhr for a very long time.' I don't think that the vast amount of thought and analysis necessarily leads them to the right conclusion, in fact I suspect that it often has the opposite result. It is a well-known fact that if you repeat a word over a sufficient number of times it ceases to have any meaning; in short, I believe that they often 'think themselves silly'.

My own opinion has always been that although they are coarser and in many ways more brutal than ourselves, the average German is as straightforward and honest as the average French or Englishman, were it not for this terrible vice of thinking things over till they imagine black is white and white is black. On the other hand, any of the political crimes which we commit are due almost entirely to complete and culpable ignorance amongst the majority of the people. You will certainly find strange misconceptions amongst even highly educated

Germans. I am sure the majority don't realise that Africa, Canada and Australia are self-governing colonies, and they have mistaken notions as to what the Prime Minister in England can and cannot do.

Goethe seems to hint at this habit of studying so hard that the inner kernel of a subject is missed, when he makes Faust say to Wagner [his assistant]:

> If feeling does not prompt, in vain you strive
> If from the soul the language does not come
> By its own impulse, to impel the hearts
> Of hearers with communicated power
> In vain you strive—in vain you study earnestly.

Although in this case the allusion is presumably to speaking, the principle applies to all human actions. One of my Berlin friends said that Bethman Hollweg was far too much of a theorist to make a good diplomatist or politician, and the results of his Heath Robinson subtlety are lamented on all hands.

During the whole time I lived in Germany before the war, I was more or less conscious of a feeling akin to fear. I don't think this was entirely due to a presentiment of war, although at times I felt overwhelmed by the military preparations and discipline. There was some other reason for this revulsion, and I found, during my last visit, that it was still with me. I believe it is something to do with the inherent animal coarseness which you can't help noticing in a lot of the people. English folk have a reputation in other lands for bovine coarseness, but the German coarseness is somehow different. I think I detect signs of brutality, or shall we say cruelty, in their nature, and it dawned upon me that this must be true when I saw their national monument, the Völkerschlacht Denkmal at Leipzig.

If this is really an expression of the national character, it is also a criticism of it, and if on the other hand, the monument is a caricature, one wonders why the people haven't laughed at it enough to make the authorities pull it down. It impressed me so much that I spoke to several of my friends and asked them whether

Germany's Völkerschlacht Denkmal at Leipzig: 'German coarseness is somehow different. I think I detect signs of brutality, or shall we say cruelty, in their nature.'

they found it coarse and brutal. At first they said that they had never noticed it in that light, but afterwards they generally agreed with me.

The Völkerschlacht Denkmal [the Monument to the Battle

411

of the Nations] was finished in 1913 to commemorate the battle of Leipzig. An impression of overwhelming ruthless power is conveyed by this mass of stone, about 300 feet high and broad in proportion. The architect evidently had in mind the slave-made work of older civilisations. In a ring round the rough blocks which form a sort of dome are 12 barbarous-looking knights leaning heavily on swords. Over the main door is a figure of St. Michael brandishing his sword, while on each side of him, in a wilderness of low relief, are the corpses and skeletons of the fallen. In colossal letters across the front are

carved the words GOTT MIT UNS, as if to reassure the gasping sightseer. Inside is a high domed circular hall, lit by four arched windows. There are two balconies; the lower is some twelve feet from the floor and supported by pillars carved to represent what the guide told us were masks of fate, their chins resting on the floor and their eyebrows touching the balcony. My own impression of these faces, was that they were depraved and bestial: eyes prominent and half closed, the tongues slightly protruding in a way which suggested nothing but approaching death.

Standing on either side of each pillar were giant warriors: bull-necked baboon men with low foreheads and protruding eyes as if swollen with sorrow. Above the lower balcony were four monstrous allegorical figures (each 30 feet high) depicting the German virtues. A mother suckling her twin children represented 'The Power of the German People', and a figure whose right hand was endeavouring to ignore what the left hand did, was said to represent the 'Will to Self-Sacrifice' (Opferwilligkeit).

Round the arched windows were figures of the maimed and disabled, and covering the inside of the dome, in a pattern of concentric bands, rode 365 more warriors.

There are many kind and delightful gentlefolk amongst the Germans, but I cannot help feeling that there is an underlying element of coarse cruelty which is rather admired by the nation as a virtue, otherwise how is it that such a monstrous work was ever put up. In any case they are a curious mixture and difficult to understand.

413